Managing Network Resource
Alliances, Affiliations and Other Relational Assets

Dear Atul,

All the best and looking forward to continued conversations

Best wishes

Managing Network Resources

Alliances, Affiliations and Other Relational Assets

Ranjay Gulati

OXFORD
UNIVERSITY PRESS

OXFORD
UNIVERSITY PRESS

Great Clarendon Street, Oxford ox2 6DP

Oxford University Press is a department of the University of Oxford.
It furthers the University's objective of excellence in research, scholarship,
and education by publishing worldwide in

Oxford New York

Auckland Cape Town Dar es Salaam Hong Kong Karachi
Kuala Lumpur Madrid Melbourne Mexico City Nairobi
New Delhi Shanghai Taipei Toronto

With offices in

Argentina Austria Brazil Chile Czech Republic France Greece
Guatemala Hungary Italy Japan Poland Portugal Singapore
South Korea Switzerland Thailand Turkey Ukraine Vietnam

Oxford is a registered trade mark of Oxford University Press
in the UK and in certain other countries

Published in the United States
by Oxford University Press Inc., New York

© Ranjay Gulati 2007

British Library Cataloguing in Publication Data
Data available

Library of Congress Cataloging in Publication Data
Data available

Typeset by SPI Publisher Services, Pondicherry, India
Printed in Great Britain
on acid-free paper by
Biddles Ltd., King's Lynn, Norfolk

ISBN 978-0-19-929935-5
ISBN 978-0-19-929985-0 (Pbk.)

1 3 5 7 9 10 8 6 4 2

To my parents who gave me the thirst to learn

To my teachers, colleagues, and students from whom I have learned so much

To my family who have supported me on this journey to learn

☐ PREFACE

My research over the last decade has shown that interorganizational networks not only influence the creation of new ties between organizations but also affect their design, evolutionary path, and success. I subsequently extended some of these ideas to other types of interorganizational ties in contexts ranging from large to entrepreneurial firms. This book brings together much of this research under one fold. Most of the chapters draw heavily from my published articles, many of which are coauthored. At the start of each chapter, I clearly indicate the published source from which the chapter has been drawn and also acknowledge my, coauthors, if any for that published work. While I have adapted the front end of these chapters to draw out the common thread of network resources that cuts across the book, the research reported is from the original articles mentioned at the outset of the chapter. Some details on the data and methods have been abbreviated for the book. While some of the chapters in this book are based on solo-authored articles, in the case of coauthored chapters it is important to note that the research reported is based on collaborative work with the listed authors.

This book is more than simply a retrospective collection of my published work. All the chapters have been adapted to cohere under a common unifying theme. In doing so, I have recrafted the conceptual underpinnings of the articles to allow them to be parts of a broader story. In some sense this was an exercise for me to try to draw out a common thread that ran across many of my prior works and to do some retrospective sense-making.

In drawing on the sociological paradigm of embeddedness to explain inter-firm behavior, I develop here the concept of 'network resources' as an important but overlooked factor to explain both firm behavior and outcomes in interorganizational collaboration. Network resources are valuable resources that accrue to a firm from its ties with key external constituents including—but not limited to—partners, suppliers, and customers, and thus exist outside a firm's boundaries and within its social networks. Networks thus become conduits that make available to firms valuable resources and information that may reside within their partners. The ties are thus sources of valuable resources and information that can influence strategic behavior by altering the opportunity set of actions available to a firm and also outcomes by making available resources. They may also be viewed by external constituents as signals of legitimacy inasmuch as they signal the availability of key resources to those firms. Consequently, the manner and extent to which a firm is embedded in a prior interorganizational network enable firms to obtain resources and information that significantly influence the behavior and also key outcomes for the participating firms.

While several chapters in the first two parts of this book focus on demonstrating the impact of network resources originating in a firm's network of prior alliances, I also reflect in several subsequent chapters on other possible networks from which such resources may be derived and how these influence firm behavior and outcomes. Further, I consider the likely dynamic of co-evolution of disparate networks in which the accumulation of one may facilitate the acquisition of the other, opening up multiple conduits for firms. This suggests a complex interplay across disparate networks that shape each other and through this coevolutionary process impact the cumulative network resources that become available for participating firms. For example, in some chapters I examine how accumulated prior alliances of firms shape the creation of new such ties. In others I consider the role of interpersonal ties such as board interlocks in influencing alliance formation. Finally, I also study the influence of prior employment and board ties of upper echelons of entrepreneurial firms on the likelihood of landing partnerships with higher prestige investment banks. The settings in which these ideas are explored range from large US and global corporations to start-ups in the biotechnology sector.

In looking back at some of my own published work that is included here, I discovered that I had not always referred to the core construct in those articles as network resources. The terms I used before range from 'embeddedness' to 'relational capital'. In bringing these disparate works together, I have tried to streamline the terms and bring everything under the single rubric of network resources. I hope that by doing so, I bring greater clarity to the reader and sharpen the message while also providing a consistent thread that runs across this work. As these articles were not written with this unifying theme in mind, they contain elements that were important in the original presentation of the research but are not given center stage here. In no way do I wish to detract from the contributions of the original research. My de-emphasizing of a particular point is simply to maintain my focus on the single theme around which this book is woven. Yet in bringing a range of published work under a common umbrella, I run the risk of making that umbrella too large. I acknowledge these concerns and in the final chapter reflect on the need for further sharpening of the concept of network resources. The field has already taken this message to heart, and many recent studies—my own and those of others—have sought to further delineate the concept of network resources.

This book has not been a solitary affair. It is the product of a joint effort I began fifteen years ago when I first embarked on a research career. Numerous colleagues have been very generous in guiding my thinking and without them this work would not have been possible. I would like to acknowledge the many people to whom I owe a debt of gratitude for helping me shape this research program. I must first thank my doctoral dissertation committee (the late Aage Sorensen, Nitin Nohria, and Paul Lawrence) who worked tirelessly with me to formulate these research questions. Upon graduation, I was fortunate to work with an excellent set of research collaborators who joined me in discovering new ideas and generously allowed me to use some of those collectively researched papers for this book. These researchers include: Martin Gargiulo, Monica Higgins, David Kletter, Harbir Singh, Lihua Olivia Wang, and Jim Westphal. I would also like to thank a number of friends and colleagues who generously agreed to read earlier drafts of the entire manuscript and provide detailed comments. These include: Bruce Carruthers, Glenn Hoetker, Dovev Lavie, Nitin Nohria, N. Venkatraman, and Jim Westphal. I also had a number of helpful conversations about the book with Ha Hoang, Tim Rowley, M. B. Sarkar, and Aks Zaheer. I would also like to thank the following individuals who helped me attend to the details of pulling this book together and carefully read the entire manuscript, made editorial suggestions, and cleaned up all references and text. These included: Lynn Childress, Alberto Gastelum, Kate Heinze, Linda Johanson, Lisa Khan-Kapadia, James Oldroyd, Andy Rich, Sharmi Surianarain, Maxim Sytch, Tom Truesdell, Bart Vanneste, Franz Wohlgezogen, and Sachin Waikar. A number of my colleagues have over the years been catalysts for many of the ideas that have appeared in my published works that were the basis for this book. They include: Gautam Ahuja, Bharat Anand, Ron Burt, Jerry Davis, Yves Doz, Bob Duncan, Jeff Dyer, Paul Hirsch, Tarun Khanna, David Krackhardt, Ravi Madhavan, Mark Mizruchi, Jack Nickerson, Willie Ocasio, Christine Oliver, Phanish Puranam, Hayagreeva Rao, Jitendra V. Singh, and Ed Zajac. Finally, I would like to acknowledge my family. My parents Satya Paul and Sushma Gulati nurtured in me the desire to learn that has sent me on this lifelong journey. My wife Anuradha has given me the encouragement and support so very essential for such a long-term effort, while my children Varoun and Shivani provide the joy of distraction that allows me to step away from it periodically.

☐ ACKNOWLEDGMENTS

Acknowledgment is made to the following for permission to adapt the following material:

Chapter 2 adapted with permission from 'Network Location and Learning: The Influence of Network Resources and Firm Capabilities on Alliance Formation' by Ranjay Gulati published in *Strategic Management Journal*, 1999, (20/5): 397–420, © John Wiley & Sons Limited.

Chapter 3 adapted from 'Social Structure and Alliance Formation Patterns: A Longitudinal Analysis' by Ranjay Gulati published in *Administrative Science Quarterly*, © 1995, (40/4): 619–52, by permission of Johnson Graduate School of Management, Cornell University.

Chapter 4 adapted from 'Cooperative or Controlling? The Effects of CEO–Board Relations and the Content of Interlocks on the Formation of Joint Ventures' by Ranjay Gulati and James D. Westphal published in *Administrative Science Quarterly*, © 1999, (44/3): 473–506, by permission of Johnson Graduate School of Management, Cornell University.

Chapter 5 adapted with permission from 'Does Familiarity Breed Trust? The Implications of Repeated Ties for Contractual Choice in Alliances' by Ranjay Gulati published in *Academy of Management Journal*, © 1995, (38/1): 85–112.

Chapter 6 adapted from 'The Architecture of Cooperation: Managing Coordination Costs and Appropriation Concerns in Strategic Alliances' by Ranjay Gulati and Harbir Singh published in *Administrative Science Quarterly*, © 1998, (43/4): 781–814, by permission of Johnson Graduate School of Management, Cornell University.

Chapter 7 adapted from 'Size of the Pie and Share of the Pie: Implications of Network Embeddedness and Business Relatedness for Value Creation and Value Appropriation in Joint Ventures' by Ranjay Gulati and Lihua Wang published in *Research in the Sociology of Organizations*, © 2003, (20): 209–42, with permission from Elsevier.

Chapter 8 adapted from 'Shrinking Core, Expanding Periphery: The Relational Architecture of High Performing Organizations' by Ranjay Gulati and David Kletter published in *California Management Review*, © 2005, (47/3): 77–104, by The Regents of the University of California. By permission of The Regents.

Chapter 9 adapted with permission from 'Getting Off to a Good Start: The Effects of Upper Echelon Affiliations on Underwriter Prestige' by Monica C. Higgins and Ranjay Gulati published in *Organization Science*, © 2003, (14/3): 244–63, the Institute for Operations Research and the Management Sciences, 7240 Parkway Drive, Suite 310, Hanover, MD 21076 USA.

Chapter 10 adapted with permission from 'Which Ties Matter When? The Contingent Effects of Interorganizational Partnerships on IPO Success' by Ranjay Gulati and Monica C. Higgins published in *Strategic Management Journal*, 2003, (24/2): 127–44, © John Wiley & Sons Limited.

☐ CONTENTS

☐ LIST OF FIGURES

☐ LIST OF TABLES

Introduction

Interorganizational networks: from alliances to a constellation of ties

Over the past two decades, researchers have become fascinated with the growing array of cooperative ties that firms are entering into with each other. While much of the previous research has focused on the dynamics of competition, scholars are increasingly redirecting their interest to aspects of cooperative behavior. One of the fastest growing sets of interorganizational ties has been strategic alliances that firms enter into to achieve a common goal. Strategic alliances can be defined as any voluntary and enduring arrangements between two or more firms involving the exchange, sharing, or codevelopment of products, technologies, or services. The rapid proliferation of alliances between firms in the past several decades has led to a growing stream of research by strategy and organizational scholars who have examined some of the causes and consequences of such partnerships, mostly at the dyadic level. Researchers in various disciplines, including economics, sociology, social psychology, organizational behavior, and strategic management, have sought answers to several basic questions regarding alliances: What motivates firms to enter into alliances? With whom are they likely to ally? What types of contracts and other governance structures do firms use to formalize their alliances? How do alliances themselves and firm participation patterns in alliances evolve over time? What factors influence the performance of alliances and the benefits partners derive from alliances?

In their quest to answer these questions, many researchers have examined alliances from economic perspectives. Within economics, there have been several approaches to the study of alliances, including industrial economics, game theory, and transaction cost economics (Kogut 1989). Management researchers have also begun to look at the formation of alliances, and common questions asked in this research have revolved around why alliances occur with such frequency and when firms are more likely to enter them (e.g. Barley, Freeman, and Hybels 1992; Powell and Brantley 1992; Hagedoorn 1993). The answers have varied. Transaction cost economists have argued that alliances are hybrid forms intermediate to the extremes of markets and hierarchy (Williamson 1985), and that they occur when transaction costs associated with a specific exchange are too high for an arm's length market exchange but not high enough to mandate vertical integration (Hennart 1988). Other scholars have suggested that many firms enter alliances to learn new skills or acquire tacit knowledge (Kogut 1988a, 1988b; Hamel, Doz, and Prahalad 1989; Hamel 1991; Gulati, Khanna, and Nohria 1994; Amburgey, Dacin, and Singh 1996; Powell, Koput, and Smith-Doerr 1996; Khanna, Gulati, and Nohria 1998). Institutional theorists have suggested a bandwagon effect in which firms succumb to isomorphic pressures and mimic other firms that have entered alliances (Venkatraman, Loh, and Koh 1994). Others have pointed out that alliances may result from firms' quests for legitimacy (Baum and Oliver 1991, 1992; Sharfman, Gray, and Yan 1991). Lastly, scholars of corporate strategy have suggested that firms enter alliances to improve their strategic positions (Porter and Fuller 1986; Contractor and Lorange 1988; Kogut 1988a, 1988b).

While these perspectives have been influential and helpful, they have failed to recognize some of the social factors that may shape the dynamics associated with alliance formation. Industrial economics and transaction cost economics, in particular, have focused on the influence of firm and industry structure, and the nature of goods and services being transacted, but have neglected the possible role that history and social relations between organizations may play in shaping the formation of new alliances. Economic sociologists, on the other hand, have suggested that economic action and exchange operate in the context of historical relationships constituting a network that informs the choices and decisions of individual actors (Laumann, Galaskiewicz, and Marsden 1978; Granovetter 1985; White 1992).

Economic sociologists define a network as a form of organized economic activity that involves a set of nodes (e.g. individuals or organizations) linked by a set of relationships (e.g. contractual obligations, trade association memberships, or family ties). This approach builds on the idea that economic actions are influenced by the context in which they occur and that one such source of social influence is the position actors occupy within a network of organizations. Thus, from this vantage point organizations are treated as fully engaged and interactive with the environment rather than as isolated atomistic entities impervious to contextual influences.

Firms can be interconnected with other firms through a wide array of social and economic relationships, each of which can constitute a social network. These include supplier relationships (e.g. Dyer 2000), resource flows, trade association memberships, interlocking directorates (e.g. Davis 1991), relationships among individual employees (e.g. Burt 2004), relationships with endorsing entities such as investment banks (e.g. Podolny 1994; Higgins and Gulati 2003), and prior strategic alliances (e.g. Gulati 1995a, 1995b). While firms may be connected through a multitude of connections, each of which could be a social network, some may be more or less significant than others and researchers have rarely focused on more than one network at a time (for a review of research on interorganizational relationships, see Galaskiewicz

1985*a*). Furthermore, to recognize the true importance of a social network, it is important to understand the nature and purpose of the network as well as the contents of information flowing through it (Stinchcombe 1990; Gulati 1999). In recent years, researchers have increasingly begun to explore the complex interplay that may occur among disparate networks in shaping each other and in simultaneously shaping firm behavior and outcomes (Gulati and Gargiulo 1999).

Toward a more socialized account of firm behavior

The purpose of this book is to provide a more socialized account of firm behavior and outcomes by introducing a network perspective to the study of interorganizational ties, while taking care to avoid what Granovetter (1985: 483–7) referred to as the pitfalls that arise from either an oversocialized account or an undersocialized account of behavior. The core construct I discuss is that of 'network resources', resources that accrue to a firm from its ties with key external constituents including—but not limited to—partners, suppliers, and customers, and thus exist outside a firm's boundaries. These ties become conduits for valuable information and resources that a firm can tap, and these in turn are likely to shape their behavior and outcomes. While the bulk of my book focuses on one type of interorganizational tie—strategic alliances—the book is not restricted only to those ties and both the empirical base and the conceptual underpinning here are relevant to a broader class of interorganizational ties.

An important theoretical basis of my research is that the network of interorganizational relations in which organizations are embedded influences their economic action and performance. Underlying the embeddedness perspective is the quest for information to reduce uncertainty, which is an important driver of organizational action and can influence outcomes as well. I first discovered the importance of interorganizational ties in shaping firm behavior and outcomes during the completion of my doctoral dissertation, which examined alliance formation. The following examples from my dissertation illustrate my findings:

1. Every year the Personal Computers Division at the former Digital Equipment Corporation (DEC) (since acquired by Compaq in 1998 and HP in 2002) invited all its alliance partners to a four-day conference. DEC's primary goal in organizing this event was to share information with their partners on their own strategic direction in the year ahead and to elaborate on the broad role of alliances within this strategy. The partners were encouraged to make similar presentations. Many DEC managers present at this event took this opportunity to initiate new partnerships with

other firms present. Perhaps of more interest, many of DEC's partner firms initiated new alliances among themselves at these conferences as well. The event thus provided a forum much like a 'bazaar', where many new deals took place.

2. Cadence Technologies, a leader in electronic design automation, has entered into a number of 'technology partnerships' over time with their leading customers such as Harris, Toshiba, National Semiconductor, Ericsson, Intel, Phillips, IBM, Mitsubishi, Kawasaki Steel, and SGS-Thompson. Within such partnerships, the customers share Cadence's development costs for new products that are especially useful for their own purposes. Customers provide Cadence with financial resources and maintain their own engineering staff on-site at Cadence to assist in the ongoing development efforts. These technology partnerships, many of which were initiated in the mid-1980s, have led to a number of subsequent alliances by Cadence with the same set of firms. Many of these relationships have been initiated and championed within Cadence by the partner's on-site engineering staff at Cadence.

3. Cadence Technologies had decided to incorporate some database features within their software products in the early 1990s. Rather than develop a database on their own, they sought an alliance with an existing database company. They were looking not only for quick access to leading-edge technology but also for ongoing support and development as the technology evolved. A number of promising companies were short-listed. The final choice was ODI technologies, a company based in Burlington, Massachusetts. The primary reason for this choice was that two Cadence partners—IBM and Harris—had ongoing relationships with ODI. A senior manager at Cadence Technologies commented:

> We had included ODI in our final list based on its technological competence. But then we were interested in knowing more about their business integrity and support structure. Once we realized that they had prior relationships with IBM and Harris, we called managers within those two and had extensive conversations about ODI. . . . These factors were very important in our decision to pick ODI.

4. Oracle, a leading database company, was seeking access to some software (an Ada compiler) for its customers in the early 1990s and sought an alliance with a software company that had expertise in this technology. Technological considerations enabled them to narrow their choice down to five companies. Ultimately they chose Alsis software because both Oracle and Alsis shared a common partner—Hewlett-Packard (HP). Oracle and HP have had a close working relationship that encompassed a number of alliances—HP had two full-time Oracle account managers while Oracle had an entire HP accounts division. When the HP account

managers for Oracle heard about Oracle's search for a partner, they provided a strong recommendation of Alsis.

As these examples suggest, many contemporary ties are initiated in the contexts of existing sets of relationships that are conduits for valuable information that in turn shape the behavior of firms. In some instances, these ties provide a direct impetus for new ties; in other instances, they guide the choice of new partners. In some of my subsequent research I found that in many instances a prior context of ties also has beneficial consequences for the performance of those ties as well which may come from the networks channeling information and/or other resources from a firm's partners. While some researchers have highlighted the constraints that networks create for actors, I have focused more on the opportunities networks offer. In this context, networks of contacts among organizations can serve as important sources of information and resources, and the pattern of ties among them may be as significant as the number of ties.

While social network research originally focused on how the embeddedness of individuals influences their behavior, I have adapted and extended this argument in new ways to interorganizational networks. My dissertation research focused on two distinct components of a firm's social network and their impact in shaping firm behavior by serving as conduits of valuable information. The first is the firm's comprehensive experience with interorganizational ties. The second derives from the overall structure of relationships in which a firm is embedded and encompasses both its direct and indirect relationships with other firms. DEC's partners' seeking out alliances with each other because of their ties with DEC illustrates the latter component. Not only does their shared tie create an opportunity for them to learn about each other but also it predisposes them to enter an alliance with each other. Thus, both the extent to which a firm is embedded in the social network and the specific manner in which it is embedded are influential.

My dissertation developed the ideas of economic sociologists of the importance of social networks in shaping the flow of information and opportunities (e.g. Granovetter 1985; Baker 1990; Mizruchi 1992), and provided evidence suggesting that firms, as well as individuals, develop embedded ties characterized by trust and rich information exchange across organizational boundaries (Eccles 1981; Useem 1982; Dore 1983; Powell 1990; Uzzi 1997; Zaheer, McEvily, and Perrone 1998; Dyer and Chu 2000). The notion that a firm's social connections channel information and in turn guide its interest in new ties and also provide it with opportunities to realize that interest is closely rooted in the processes that underlie a firm's entry into new ties. As some of the examples discussed above suggest, in instances where firms independently seek to initiate new ties, they often turn first to existing relationships for potential partners or seek referrals from current allies to potential partners.

Quotes from managers I interviewed at two organizations about their entry into one specific type of organizational tie—strategic alliances—illustrate these points:

On many occasions we are approached with new alliance opportunities by our prior partners. Sometimes it's about a project with them, and in other cases they refer other firms with whom they are acquainted. As a result, in recent years it has become increasingly rare for us to partner with somebody with whom we were not previously acquainted directly or indirectly.

Many of our new alliance opportunities are not discovered by us in vacuum. Rather, they emerge through our interactions with other firms and we collectively agree on new projects. I believe an important part of this process is timing. For a new project to be right for you and your partner, it is not only a question of content but also of timing.

In aiming this theoretical lens at this phenomenon, in this book I expect to both expand our understanding of the effects of interorganizational networks and extend and enrich the theoretical underpinnings of network resources. I examine the factors that influence the critical decisions firms face regarding interorganizational ties (e.g. the number of alliances they enter, their choice of partners, the governance structure they use to formalize alliances, and so on) and consider social and behavioral influences on the performance of such interorganizational ties. In short, I apply and extend a social network perspective to some of the key questions associated with the formation of new ties and discuss how this perspective provides new insights on important social and behavioral factors that may influence both interorganizational ties and firm performance. Introducing networks into the calculus of the interorganizational ties of firms allows an examination of both the innate propensities or inducements that lead firms into ties and also the opportunities and constraints that can influence their behavior. The network perspective also provides a unique context in which to observe the dynamics of network formation and development over time, allowing development of a richer theory that accounts for such dynamics (Gulati and Gargiulo 1999). By considering the interplay across different kinds of networks such as strategic alliances, board interlocks, investment bank ties, venture capital ties, and alliances, I can also consider the multilevel nature of interorganizational networks that can arise from the combination of different kinds of networks likely to reinforce or impede one another.

Some of the key facets of interorganizational behavior can be understood by looking at the sequence of tie-related events. These include the decision to enter a tie, the choice of an appropriate partner, the choice of structure for the tie, and the dynamic evolution of the tie over time. While all interorganizational ties may not necessarily progress through the same sequence of events, the decisions these events entail constitute some of the key behavioral issues that arise in ties. Mirroring this sequence are the following research questions examined here: (*a*) Which firms enter interorganizational ties and whom do they choose as partners? (*b*) What types of contracts do firms use to formalize the ties? (*c*) How do the ties and the partners' participation evolve over time? A second important issue for interorganizational ties is their consequences for performance, both in terms of the relationship itself and of the firms entering the tie, leading to these two research questions: (*a*) What factors influence the success of interorganizational ties? and (*b*) What is the effect of interorganizational ties on the performance of firms entering them?

While several chapters of this book focus on the antecedents and consequences of interorganizational alliances for firm behavior and outcomes, in select chapters I take a broader look at the role of other types of interorganizational connections. These include board interlocks, investment bank ties, venture capital ties, supplier partnerships, customer partnerships, and intraorganizational linkages. Furthermore, while the focus of the book is primarily on the role of this multiplicity of networks in channeling information, I acknowledge and discuss how network resources originate also from a firm's networks serving as conduits of material resources. I look at the effects of network resources for both the behavior and outcomes for firms.

While the socialized account provided here focuses primarily on a social network-based perspective, some chapters depart from this focus to consider other social factors that may also shape important behaviors and outcomes associated with the entry of firms into alliances. The accounts I provide also do not preclude economic theories that may be important in explaining the outcomes of alliances. A unifying theme, however, is the provision of a socially grounded account that highlights the importance of network resources in explaining firm behavior and outcomes associated with their interorganizational partnering activities.

Bringing in network resources

As highlighted above, an important focal point for prior research on interorganizational ties such as strategic alliances has been to understand the material imperatives that drive firms to enter into such partnerships. The emphasis on material resources and capabilities as catalysts for interorganizational ties resonates closely with the resource-based view of the firm, which highlights the importance of material resource endowments (Wernerfelt 1984; Dierickx and Cool 1989; Barney 1991; Mahoney and Pandian 1992; Peteraf 1993). While resource-based strategy research has typically focused on explaining sustained performance differences across firms, the role of resource heterogeneity in explaining strategic change and strategic actions is becoming more salient. Scholars developing the resource-based perspective have highlighted the importance of social factors and the role of unique firm history, but no attention has been given to the networks in which firms are situated (Barney 1991). Rather, the focus has remained on material resources that reside within a firm's boundaries. Only recently have researchers begun to probe the possibility that a firm's network resources may be instrumental in channeling information and resources to firms and in turn shaping their behavior and outcomes (e.g. Gulati 1999; Jensen 2003; Zaheer and Bell 2005; Lavie 2006).

In this book, I draw on the sociological paradigm of social embeddedness to explain interorganizational behavior. To do this I introduce the concept of 'network resources' as an important but overlooked factor in both firm behavior and outcomes. The networks in which firms are placed are conduits that allow firms to leverage valuable information and/or resources possessed by their partners. Such advantages bestowed by interorganizational networks may be conceptualized as a network resource that may both restrict and enlarge the opportunity set of actions available to firms by channeling valuable information but can also shape actions and outcomes by providing resources that their partners are willing to share with them. Distinct from the resources that reside *within a firm's boundaries*, network resources arise *outside a firm's boundaries and within its social networks*. Most broadly, such resources encompass resources that a firm's partners may possess and are available to a focal firm through its connections with those firms.

The focus of this book is admittedly narrow and focuses primarily on the informational advantages these same ties bestow on participating firms and less on the flow of material resources that may flow through these very same ties. I detail and discuss some of my research (solo-authored and in collaboration with others) over the last decade that has shown that preexisting interorganizational networks can cumulate into a valuable source of resources that are resident not within a firm's boundaries but accrue to it from its networks that are valuable conduits for information and resources. In the conclusion of this book I take a more forward-looking stance and detail how network resources result not only from networks serving as conduits of valuable information but also serving as conduits for valuable material resources that may be resident in the partners of a focal firm (see also Gulati, Lavie, and Madhavan 2006).

The notion that a firm's social connections and accompanying network resources guide its interest in new ties—and provide it with opportunities to realize that interest by providing valuable information—is closely rooted in the processes that underlie a firm's entry into new ties. I first observed this when I was conducting field interviews at a number of firms: I found that many new opportunities for alliances were presented to firms through their board members and existing sets of alliance partners. In the instances in which firms independently initiated new alliances, they turned first to their existing relationships for potential partners or sought referrals from them to potential partners. By making available more information about potential partners, interorganizational networks could help a firm move toward viable partnerships. Similarly, networks channel information to potential partners and thus alter the extent to which partners consider a focal firm to be viable. I concluded that these firms behaved this way because social networks are valuable conduits of information that have important implications for alliances. Consequently, the manner in and extent to which firms are embedded is likely to influence several key decisions, including the frequency with which they enter alliances, choice of partner, type of contracts used, and the alliances' development over time.

In my study of interorganizational alliances that I began with my dissertation and used as the basis of a number of the early chapters in this book, the benefits of network resources accrue in two distinct forms. First, social relationships are indicative of the extent of a firm's access to network resources. In the context of alliances, I argue that a firm's cumulative prior alliances serve as network resources in that they reflect the firm's experience with alliances. This experience in turn translates into specific skills related to the formation and management of alliances (Lyles 1988). In addition, experience gives firms visibility and external recognition, making them attractive partners to other firms. These factors in turn increase the likelihood that the firm will engage in additional future alliances. Take for instance the comments of a vice president at Cadence:

Through our vastly successful technology partnerships program we have built ourselves a reputation in the industry for being an effective and reliable alliance partner. Today, we are pursued by other firms to enter alliances much more frequently than we pursue potential partners.

A second benefit of network resources is the access to information they provide. A firm's experience with alliances allows it access to information on its prior partners—about both their specific capabilities and reliability. The role of accumulated network resources in the formation of new alliances becomes particularly relevant in the context of evidence that, despite their popularity and presumed strategic importance, alliances often fail. Indeed, some skeptics argue that interorganizational alliances are nothing more than a fad, or at best, a transitory stage toward other more permanent organizational forms (e.g. Porter 1990). In this context, network resources provide partners with information that mitigates some of the risks associated with such alliances. As the typical comments below indicate, firm managers rely extensively on their partners from past alliances for information:

We have ... close working relationships with most of our alliance partners. As a result, we are familiar with many of their own goals and capabilities. Since they also know about our specific skills and needs, many new deals are created interactively with them.

In some cases we realize that perhaps our skills don't really match for a project, and our partner may refer us to another firm about whom we were unaware. . . . An important aspect of this referral business is of course about vouching for the reliability of that firm. Thus, if one of our longstanding partners suggests one of their own partners as a good fit for our needs, we usually consider it very seriously.

We originally initiated technology partnerships with a number of key industry players in the mid-1980s. These in turn have led to numerous repeated alliances with the same set of firms. With each partner maintaining on-site staff at our facilities that was only to be expected. They are familiar with many of our projects from their very inception and if there is potential for an alliance we discuss it. Likewise, we learn about many of their product goals very early on and we actively explore alliance opportunities with them. . . . One thing that also makes it easier for us to enter new alliances is our extensive experience with doing alliances. Forming a new partnership is not a big deal any more—we have our own formula and we know it works!

These comments suggest that firms do indeed benefit from their past ties, especially as related to their ability to enter new partnerships. An experience with interorganizational ties provides firms the requisite skills to enter new ties, the visibility to attract new partners, and access to crucial information about new opportunities.

It is not only the magnitude of a firm's prior ties that matters but also (*a*) the distribution of those ties across partner firms and (*b*) the ties of past allies. A firm may thus have numerous ties but they may all be with a limited number of firms, or it may have widely dispersed ties but with isolated partners who have no other alliances. In yet a third scenario, a firm may have numerous partners who are well connected to other firms (Kogut, Shan, and Walker 1992). As highlighted above, an important component of network resources is the access to information a firm's networks provide. If information is exchanged across direct and indirect referrals, then the specific pattern of a firm's ties allows it access to different degrees of information. One manager at a larger computer software firm put it this way:

No matter how much effort you expend in market intelligence efforts, you can never know about all the firms there are out there. Furthermore, in many cases you don't know what you want until you see a particular product of a firm with certain skills that triggers a new idea. In many such cases we rely upon our existing alliance partners as well to point out new possibilities with other firms. Sometimes these firms have alliances of their own with our partners, in other cases, they may have in turn been referred to our partners, in other cases, they may have in turn been referred to our partner by someone else. . . . If you step back and look at the entire industry, it's becoming like a spider's web where we all learn something about each other through the network.

Clearly, the network of prior ties is a rich source of information for firms. Through their networks, firms may learn not only about new opportunities with existing partners but also about firms of which they were unaware. Firms regularly exchange information with their partners about themselves, as well as about other firms. Thus, a firm's specific location in the network can have important ramifications for its future alliance behavior.

In the context of strategic alliances, I also discuss the accumulation of a firm's network resources and how these influence some of the fundamental dynamics of subsequent alliances. That is, networks of prior ties and the resources resulting from them influence not only the creation of new ties but also their design, evolutionary path, and ultimate success. The concept of network resources provides valuable insights into strategic alliances and is an important contribution to the study of social networks. The creation of an alliance is in itself an important strategic action, but the cumulation of such alliances into a social network has major implications for future strategies. Given the limited understanding of the dynamics of networks, alliances provide a unique arena in which action and structure are closely interconnected and the dynamic coevolution of networks can be examined (e.g. Gulati and Gargiulo 1999). Furthermore, the study of interorganizational networks is now a burgeoning field of inquiry, and strategic alliances have proliferated, meriting further examination (for a collection of articles on interorganizational networks, see Mizruchi and Schwartz 1987). Synthesizing insights on alliance networks with those on interpersonal networks can provide an important cross-level perspective of interorganizational relationships (Galaskiewicz 1985b; Zaheer, McEvily, and Perrone 1998; Rosenkopf, Metiu, and George 2001; Gulati and Sytch 2006a).

In some of the later chapters I broaden my horizons beyond only looking at interorganizational alliances as the set of ties that enable a firm to accumulate network resources. Further, I discuss how networks and the resultant network resources can not only channel information and resources but also serve a symbolic purpose by signaling the quality of the firm to key endorsers of those firms. In some of the later chapters in this book, I discuss how network resources signal valuable information about the firms holding them to other key stakeholders. For example, the ties of entrepreneurial firms to venture capitalists, investment banks, and alliance partners serve as powerful signals to the investor community and thus may facilitate the success of their initial public offerings (IPOs) (Gulati and Higgins 2003). Similarly, I discuss how network resources based in the affiliations of the upper echelons of entrepreneurial firms are influential indicators of firm quality that enable these young companies to attract prestigious investment banks (Higgins and Gulati 2003, 2006).

My definition of interorganizational ties that may constitute the basis for the network resources a firm comes to possess is admittedly broad. While the bulk of the book focuses on one set of interorganizational ties—strategic alliances—several chapters look at additional ties that may also be crucial in shaping firm behavior and outcomes. Such connections range from ties with investment banks at the time a firm goes public to the connections forged through board interlocks. I further explore the interplay of these disparate connection types by assessing how the accumulation of one type may facilitate the creation of others.

An important goal of this book is to not only bring conceptual clarity to the study of interorganizational networks by introducing the concept of network resources but also to outline some important directions for further research in this important and fruitful arena of research. The empirical research reported here is intended to illustrate more the beginning than the end for research in this burgeoning arena of inquiry. It is my hope that by bringing some conceptual coherence that is grounded in empirical research, this book will provide directions for promising future research.

1 Overview of the book

In the Introduction, I stated that the purpose of this book is to provide a more socialized account of firm behavior. By applying a social network perspective to some of the key questions associated with interorganizational ties, I hope to provide new insights on important social factors that may influence both firm behavior and performance. An important goal of this book is to make salient the concept of network resources, which refers to valuable resources based in the multitude of ties a firm may have with key constituents outside its formal boundaries, including partners, suppliers, and customers. As I have suggested in the Introduction, network resources can benefit participating firms by serving as conduits of not only valuable material resources but also information. Such resources can benefit firms by reducing their search costs for new ties. They can also mitigate uncertainty by providing access to timely information and creating reputational circuits that limit moral hazards. In some instances, a firm's network resources also provide signals to critical third parties that offer potential benefits to those firms.

Introducing the concept of network resources expands the realm of the resource-based perspective from resources within a firm's boundaries to external resources based on network membership and location. Furthermore, the concept of network resources highlights the importance of unique historical conditions and suggests a path-dependent process by which firms accumulate network resources that are sticky and can become the basis of sustainable competitive advantage. The concept of network resources adds specificity to this understanding and suggests an important means by which history matters.

This book is organized into several sections, each with multiple chapters. I also provide details of some of the data-sets used across some of the chapters and the methods used in two appendices at the end of the book. A short description of each chapter follows.

Part I: Network resources and the formation of new ties

This section focuses on how network resources influence the behavior of firms in forming new interorganizational ties. The focus here is primarily on how networks are conduits of information that in turn shape the subsequent behavior of firms. In Part I of this book in particular, I consider the impact of such resources on the formation of one particular type of interorganizational tie—strategic alliances—and specifically how a firm's network provides it differential access to new partnership opportunities. Because new alliances further contribute to the network resources available to those firms, in many ways this is a situation where more begets more. In this part of the book, I also explore two main aspects of alliance formation and the degree of influence of firm network resources on each. I examine the factors that influence which firms enter alliances, and correspondingly, I explore how network resources may influence their choice of ally. I propose that firms derive valuable benefits from their network of past ties in the form of timely and valuable information, that in turn impacts and shapes their proclivities for entering into new alliances as well as their choice of partners. As a result, this network of past ties becomes an important channel for providing firms with network resources that play a key role in shaping the alliance opportunities available to them.

Although network resources can benefit firms in a variety of ways, they are important here for two prime reasons. First, they can reduce search costs by allowing firms to discover new opportunities for alliances with partners who are simultaneously willing to form an alliance with them. This requires a deep awareness of a firm's own needs and those of others in the market—specifically, what others want and when. Thus timing is a key element here (e.g. Gulati 1995*b*).

A second benefit of network resources arises from their ability to mitigate moral hazard concerns widespread in such alliances (Gulati 1995*a*). Despite the rapid growth of both domestic and international alliances in many industrial sectors, managers still consider alliances risky—firms entering alliances face considerable moral hazard concerns because of the unpredictability of partner behavior and the likely costs of possible opportunistic behavior by a partner. Consequently, for firms to build alliances that both address their needs and minimize the risks posed by moral hazards, they must first be aware of potential partners and their needs and, second, have information about the reliability of those partners (Balakrishnan and Koza 1993). Simultaneously, those potential partners must have requisite information on the focal firm. The network resources a firm possesses can facilitate its entry into new alliances by providing information that reduces uncertainties and alleviates some of the risks of opportunism inherent to strategic alliances. Firms that possess greater network resources by virtue of their embeddedness in interorganizational networks are more likely to enter into new alliances than more isolated players (Gulati 1998, 1999). Furthermore, firms with a positive reputation in these networks are more likely to be identified as reliable alliance partners. In short, networks are valuable sources of information that enable firms to learn about new alliance opportunities with reliable partners.

In this part of the book I also show that network resources can originate from (a) a firm's direct and proximate ties (relational embeddedness), (b) its more distant and indirect ties (structural embeddedness), and (c) its location in the overall network (positional embeddedness). I examine the role of each of these facets in reducing both search costs and moral hazard concerns. I also consider the effect of network resources on proclivity to enter into new alliances not only at the firm level, where I consider the frequency with which individual firms enter into new alliances, but also at the dyadic level, where I consider with whom firms ally.

In addition to determining which firms enter alliances and their choices of partner, network resources provide information that significantly influences how alliance networks originate and evolve. Alliances and the networks that result from their cumulation are clearly dynamic entities that can evolve well beyond their original designs and mandates, and the divergent evolutionary paths alliances follow can have significant consequences for their performance (Harrigan 1985, 1986). Network resources can thus be viewed as resulting from firms' specific relationships with prior partners, and the distribution and impact of such resources in an industry can be shaped in important ways by the cumulative networks of prior ties it contains.

Chapter 2 assesses the role of network resources in shaping which firms enter into alliances and which do not. The results of a longitudinal study demonstrate that the proclivity of a firm to enter new alliances is influenced by the extent of material and network resources available to it. In particular, network resources, accrued through a firm's embeddedness in prior alliance networks, significantly enhance the extent to which a firm enters into new alliances. Using the firm as the unit of analysis here, I examine not only the effect on alliance activity of the cumulative alliances it has entered but also consider the implications of its relative location in the network of past alliances. While exploring the relative importance of network resources, I also consider the material resources that reside within firms that have typically been theorized to explain the alliance behavior of firms.

In identifying the factors that influence alliance formation, this chapter introduces and discusses interfirm network resources in depth. I propose that firms accrue network resources from the interfirm networks in which they are located. These resources, in turn, influence the extent to which firms enter into new alliances by channeling valuable information to them. Thus, network resources are sources of valuable and timely information residing outside a firm's boundaries that can influence alliance formation by altering the available opportunity set. Consequently, the tendency of firms to enter new alliances is influenced by the magnitude of network resources they have.

While Chapter 2 explores how network resources obtained from prior alliance networks serve as a catalyst for firms to enter new alliances, Chapter 3 extends these findings by showing that network resources impact not only a firm's proclivity to enter new alliances but also its choice of partners. As in dating or marriage, a firm's decision to enter into an alliance is intertwined with the general availability of appropriate partners and a given partner's availability and willingness. Consequently, firms must be able to identify potential partners and have an idea of the candidates' needs and requirements. Firms also need information about the reliability of those partners, especially when success depends heavily on partner behavior. Specifically, this chapter demonstrates that the informational benefits of indirect ties between a focal firm and its possible partners, both one-level-removed ties and more distant ones, affect the likelihood of its entering a new alliance. A focal firm is more likely to enter into an alliance with a previously unconnected firm if they have common partners. Furthermore, the greater the distance between a focal firm and a potential partner in a social network of prior alliances, the less likely they are to ally. These findings suggest that the social network of indirect ties is an important constituent element of the network resources that a firm possesses and serves as an effective vehicle for bringing firms together. The findings also indicate that dense colocation in an alliance network between a focal firm and potential partners enhances mutual confidence by making firms more aware of the possible negative reputational consequences of their own or others' opportunistic behavior.

I conclude Chapter 3 with a brief discussion of a follow-up paper with Martin Gargiulo (Gulati and Gargiulo 1999) that shows how network resources provide essential information that influences not only the behavior of individual firms but also the evolution of strategic alliance networks themselves. Our research demonstrates that the entry of firms into alliances can lead to the growing structural differentiation of the industry network as a whole. This progressive differentiation enhances the magnitude of the resources available to all firms within the network, which in turn shapes their actions. As a result, the effect of proximate network resources on a firm's proclivity to enter alliances and its choice of partners is moderated by the extent of the overall network's differentiation. This follow-up study also highlights the iterative process by which alliance networks emerge: new ties modify the structure of the network of previous ties, which then shapes the formation of future cooperative ties. Interorganizational networks therefore evolve from embedded organizational action in which new alliances are increasingly embedded in the same network that has made them more likely in the first place. To empirically test these claims, this study specifies the mechanisms through which the existing alliance network shapes a firm's choice of allies.

In Chapter 4, I shift the focus from network resources based on interorganizational ties to those that arise from a firm's interpersonal connections, specifically board interlocks. Board interlock networks are unique formal mechanisms that create network resources by providing an opportunity for corporate leaders to exchange information, observe the leadership practices and styles of their peers, and witness the consequences of those practices. Because of these mechanisms, the board interlock network can be considered an important element of network resources for a firm. The study detailed in this chapter was conducted with Jim Westphal, and it shows how board interlock ties to other firms—specifically, relationships among CEOs and their outside directors—can increase or decrease the magnitude of network resources that accrue from those ties, in turn affecting the likelihood of alliance formation, depending on the quality of those relationships.

Exploring how board interlocks serve as network resources and affect alliance formation provides a more comprehensive account of the constituent elements of network resources because it not only allows an examination of an interpersonal network—board interlocks—as a constituent element of network resources but also because it allows an exploration of heterogeneous social processes that underlie interlock ties and their effects on the creation of strategic alliances. In other words, this chapter explores how board interlock ties may both promote and discourage the creation of new alliances, depending on the behavioral content of the tie. As a result, there may be both advantages and disadvantages to embeddedness in social networks and their contribution to a firm's accumulated network resources. Thus, in the light of this book's larger discussion of how network resources impact alliances, this study shows how network resources are affected not only by the presence of network ties but also by the specific nature (positive or negative) of those ties. Furthermore, it shows how a firm's network resources originating in one domain (i.e. board interlocks) enable it to accumulate additional network resources by entering into other kinds of ties (i.e. alliances) that in turn benefit the firm in other ways.

To summarize, Part I of the book addresses the formation of interfirm alliances and proposes that the development of such alliances and the networks that result from their accumulation is the result of a dynamic process involving both exogenous resource dependencies that prompt organizations to seek cooperation and an evolving embeddedness dynamic, in which the shifting network of prior alliances progressively influences the likelihood of alliance formation and partner choice in each period by providing firms with access to information through their partners. In the unique endogenous process by which network resources accumulate, the network of prior ties influences new ties, which in turn modify the network and lead to its further development over time. Using longitudinal analysis, I further demonstrate that the influence of interorganizational networks on the formation of new alliances may change with the network's development. To examine the interplay that occurs across different kinds of interorganizational networks I also study the role of board interlocks in shaping alliance creation. Part of the discussion of network resources centers on how they help firms obtain information about the reliability of potential partners, thus reducing both search costs and potential moral hazards.

Part II: Network resources and the governance structure of ties

Whereas Part I examines the role of network resources in the formation of new ties by firms, Part II assesses how network resources influence the formal structure used by firms in formalizing their ties. As highlighted above, an important source of uncertainty in such partnerships arises from moral hazard concerns regarding partner behavior. It is likely that network resources originating in sets of prior ties between firms not only provide information that allows them to enter into new partnerships but also impact the structure they may use to formalize the alliance. In this section, I continue to explore the role of network resources arising from networks serving as conduits of information that reduce uncertainty and also consider their effects on the governance structure of those ties.

In Chapter 5, I examine how the familiarity gained by firms through their prior alliances engenders network resources for them that in turn foster interorganizational trust and reduce the need for hierarchical controls in the partnership. The empirical research presented suggests that trust mitigates appropriation concerns and is in turn an influential determinant of the governance structure of alliances. Consequently, what emerges is an image of alliance formation in which cautious contracting gives way to looser practices as partners become increasingly embedded in a social network of prior ties. Although most research on this issue has focused on static situations, this study looks at contracting between firms over time and demonstrates the role of emergent network resources as a key factor in dynamically influencing the choice of governance structure in new alliances. This chapter supports this claim in two interrelated ways. First, it postulates that the familiarity gained through prior alliances engenders network resources that foster interorganizational trust. Both knowledge-based trust resulting from mutual awareness and equity norms and deterrence-based trust arising from reputational concerns can substitute for contractual safeguards. Second, it shows empirically how this trust reduces the need for strict controls in an alliance, thus making alliance partners more likely to adopt less hierarchical structures for their alliances. Consequently, cautious contracting and hierarchical controls lessen as firms accumulate network resources through increasing embeddedness in a social network of prior ties.

While the transaction cost logic traditionally used to study the governance of alliances recognizes that greater appropriation concerns result in more hierarchical governance structures in alliances, it focuses primarily on task attributes as a determinant of likely appropriation concerns and fails to consider the role of network resources in creating trust that reduces appropriation concerns. Chapter 5 corrects this oversight by acknowledging the role of network resources arising from past ties in shaping governance structure. In doing so, it also rectifies another omission: prior research has implicitly considered each transaction between organizations an independent event, ignoring the interconnection across them that emerges over time through a series of interactions. By introducing the role of network resources, this chapter opens the possibility that transactions may have history and this in turn may make them temporally interdependent. It also suggests that this history of prior interactions serves as a resource for firms, enabling them to enter into looser contractual arrangements for even more complex activities.

The remarks of a senior manager at a computer software firm where I conducted interviews for my dissertation illustrate some of this dynamic (Gulati 1993):

Our technology partnerships are organized as detailed equity-based contracts.... These in turn have led to numerous repeated alliances with the same set of firms.... In our subsequent alliances we don't bother to write detailed contracts. That would not only be tedious but also an insult to our relationship. Sometimes we give our lawyers only a few days to write up the contract, and that too after the project may already have begun.

This type of behavior could result because once the firm in question has an equity alliance in place, it is secure in the knowledge that it has a real hostage and is comfortable entering into loosely contracted alliances with the same firms in the future. However, informants later reported that the logic for their use of looser contracts was not driven by such thinking. Rather, the most important consideration for them was that they were now familiar with their partners and deemed them 'trustworthy'.

While appropriation concerns are clearly an important determinant of alliance governance structures, Chapter 6, based on joint research with Harbir Singh, highlights another influence. Just as network resources provide information that mitigates appropriation concerns, such information can also reduce the risks associated with the coordination of tasks between alliance partners. In line with this idea, this chapter focuses on the expected costs of coordinating tasks between alliance partners. Coordination costs are viewed as distinct from more narrowly defined transaction costs that focus primarily on moral hazard concerns. The notion of coordination costs is introduced here to capture the uncertainty arising from the anticipated organizational complexity of decomposing tasks among partners, along with the ongoing coordination of activities to be completed jointly or individually across organizational boundaries and the related magnitude of necessary communication and decisions. Because coordination in alliances is a significant challenge, the anticipated interdependence resulting from the logistics of coordinating tasks can create considerable uncertainty. These costs are very distinct from the appropriation concerns firms face in alliances. For instance, even if two allied firms face no appropriation concerns, they must still coordinate the division of labor and interface of activities and products. Whereas coordination costs arise from the coordination of tasks, appropriation involves cooperation issues among the actors. As for appropriation, this chapter suggests that coordination uncertainty can be managed with hierarchical controls—many researchers have noted that hierarchical controls facilitate superior task coordination, especially in situations involving high interdependence and coordination. Consequently, the alliance governance structure chosen at the outset reflects not only anticipated appropriation concerns but also anticipated coordination costs arising from the complexity of allocating and coordinating joint tasks.

The empirical study in this chapter suggests that the choice of alliance structure is influenced by concerns regarding both appropriation and coordination costs. Governance structures are thus a response not only to appropriation concerns but also to those emanating from the likely coordination challenges. By shaping both these anticipated concerns at the time of alliance formation, network resources affect the type of governance structure used.

From the standpoint of my investigation of network resources in this book, it is important to note that this study suggests that prior ties that engender network resources by serving as channels of information can mitigate both types of concerns. Thus, network resources can shape the contracts used to formalize alliances not only because they limit appropriation concerns but also due to their impact on the anticipated coordination costs in the alliance. This research has significant implications for the study of the alternative bases for hierarchical controls in alliances and is distinctive in three ways: (a) by specifying the concept of coordination costs, it highlights the influence of coordination uncertainty in determining the choice of governance structure in alliances; (b) it reveals the multiple logics used by alliance participants in determining governance structures by modeling the influence of anticipated coordination costs after appropriation concerns have been accounted for; (c) it demonstrates that trust engendered by network resources and the prior ties that create them can significantly reduce the coordination costs of alliances, in turn shaping the governance structure used to formalize them.

To summarize, the first two parts of this book explore how networks of prior interfirm ties such as alliances and board interlocks generate network resources for firms by providing them with valuable and timely information that influences their proclivity to enter into new alliances, their choice of partner, and the type of governance structure they use to formalize their alliances. I specifically demonstrate that the strong influence of network resources on a firm's behavior can be attributed to their role in providing timely information about the reliability of potential partners. Simply stated, network resources reduce search costs and provide information that helps firms minimize the unpredictability of partner behavior. Furthermore, by minimizing uncertainty and engendering trust between alliance partners, network resources also influence the governance structure of alliances.

Part III: Network resources and the performance of firms and their alliances

Because of their role in channeling valuable information and resources, the network resources firms possess can also be influential in determining the success of ties those firms make and, more broadly, the success of the firms themselves. In this part of the book, these insights are extended by examining how network resources influence the performance of firms that enter into interorganizational partnerships. In other words, in this part I consider whether firms with greater network resources extract greater value from their new ties than other firms with fewer such resources. Most prior researchers have struggled with methodological issues involved with studying the performance of interorganizational partnerships and that of the firms that enter into ties. While I do not provide detailed discussion or any empirical support for the role of network resources in shaping the performance of individual ties, I contend that such resources are likely to affect the outcomes of ties and that this is an important arena for future research. I also discuss how firms with a deep understanding of network resources discover the role of multifaceted sets of ties in accumulating them and in learning how to deepen the increasingly heterogeneous ties that they form.

Chapter 7, based on joint research with Lihua Olivia Wang, assesses whether firms benefit from new interorganizational ties and the network resources that these generate. The focus here remains on one particular type of interorganizational tie—strategic alliances. I examine the effects of network resources on the total value created and the relative value appropriated by each of the partners in an interfirm alliance. The results show that network resources based on the embeddedness of the partners' prior ties affect total value creation for all partners in the alliance but not the relative value appropriation between the partners. This finding departs from those of prior research that has used event study methodology to explore the likely benefits of new alliances for individual firms. This study took a dyadic approach in assessing both the total value created for all partners and the relative value appropriated by each partner in a joint venture (JV). The empirical research in this chapter shows that network resources resulting from the alliance networks affect the total value creation of all partners but not the relative value appropriation between the partners.

Chapter 8 is based on part of a larger research project I undertook with David Kletter and his colleagues at Booz Allen and Hamilton. I take a more expansive view of networks and the resources that ensue from them by going beyond a single set of ties as the basis for a firm's network resources. The chapter suggests that many firms are now adopting a relational view in their interactions with four key stakeholders: customers, suppliers, alliance partners, and internal subunits. Faced with pressures of commoditization in product markets many such firms are embracing a new architecture in which they are simultaneously shrinking their cores—doing less and less themselves—and also expanding their peripheries by addressing a larger portion of customers' needs. This necessitates a mutually reinforcing virtuous loop in which firms try to deflect market pressures for price competition by building closer connections to their customers and offering more solutions to their problems. This requires firms to expand their peripheries through alliances with others who may provide complementary products/services required by their customers. At the same time, these same firms shrink their core to benefit from other suppliers that are more narrowly specialized and have the advantages of focus, economies of scale, or a local cost advantage. Outsourcing of increasingly critical activities requires firms to collaborate with suppliers much more frequently and deeply than before. Similarly, to bring all these different pieces together seamlessly for the customer requires much greater and smoother collaboration among the internal business units.

Based on a comprehensive survey of senior executives at Fortune 1000 firms and field interviews at several top-performing firms, the research reported in this chapter indicates that this increasingly relational view of organizations is being adopted more quickly by high-performing firms than their lower performing counterparts. The findings suggest a more expansive view of network resources that encompasses significantly more than those arising from a firm's alliance ties, with those originating from connections including a firm's ties to customers and suppliers, along with ties among its internal subunits. Furthermore, firms can elevate the intensity of each of these relationships by working up a ladder detailed in the chapter. Thus, network resources originate from a heterogeneous array of ties and are in turn affected by the quality and intensity of those ties. This phenomenon, evident across an array of industries, is one of the hallmarks of a new operating model described in this chapter: *the network-resource-centered organization.*

Part IV: Network resources in entrepreneurial settings

The discussion so far has focused on how prior interorganizational relationships can channel information and resources that generate network resources for participating firms, which in turn shape the formation and governance structure of new ties, as well as the performance of focal firms. Network resources specifically help firms reduce search costs for new partners, limit the cost of coordination between partners, and minimize the unpredictability and risks of hazardous behavior by alliance partners, which in turn can shape behavior and outcomes for those firms. They can also be conduits of valuable material resources that are resident within the partners of a focal firm.

The role of network resources in shaping behavior and outcomes for firms is particularly evident in the entrepreneurial arena. Small companies represent considerable risks, especially for external investors and for endorsers who may assist those firms in obtaining capital. Such risks are particularly acute in science-based industries, such as biotechnology, where long development cycles often force firms to seek out capital markets and endorsers well before they have any products or revenue streams. In this context, among the first constituents seeking information on soon-to-be-public entrepreneurial firms are potential underwriters. Underwriting organizations need information on the reliability of start-up firms. Network resources available to entrepreneurial firms in this context can allay endorser concerns by providing important evidence of a start-up firm's legitimacy. Thus, in this instance network resources are beneficial to firms by signaling their quality to important intermediaries whose support they may require.

In this context, I assess not only network resources that originate in a firm's prior alliances but also those created through interpersonal connections of its upper echelon's affiliations through prior employment and board memberships, as considered for larger firms in Chapter 4. Specifically, I examine the network resources available to entrepreneurial firms through the interpersonal connections of their upper echelon, and how these affect the procurement of support from prestigious endorsers prior to the firm's going public. In this instance, endorsement ties with investment banks may be considered another avenue for building network resources, reinforcing the notion that one form of network ties often begets another through a system of complex interplay.

Part IV, based on a set of studies I conducted with Monica Higgins, shows how network resources provide information that influences both behavior and economic outcomes for smaller entrepreneurial firms. Our research began by assessing the role of network resources in helping start-up biotechnology firms overcome uncertainty by securing key endorsement ties from investment banks and investors. Chapter 9 suggests that important intermediaries such as investment banks look beyond objective signs (e.g. firm size, age, or product stage) to symbols of a firm's legitimacy, such as the career histories of its upper echelon, when deciding whether to endorse a young firm. Here, as in Chapter 4, the network resources available to firms originate from the interpersonal ties of their upper echelon. In particular, we consider how a firm's upper echelon's set of experience serves as a symbol of quality for others.

Our findings reported in Chapter 9 reveal that the proclivities of firms to enter partnerships with prestigious intermediaries and to garner financial resources are influenced by the specific kinds of career-based affiliations associated with the firm's upper echelon at the time of its IPO. Thus, the greater the perceived legitimacy of a young firm, as indicated by the career experiences of its upper echelon, the greater the prestige of the investment bank that firm is able to attract as the lead underwriter for its IPO. This chapter examines this effect across multiple facets of upper echelon affiliations and shows that young biotechnology firms that have upper echelon affiliations with prominent pharmaceutical and health care organizations are better positioned to garner the support of prestigious underwriters. Similarly, upper echelon affiliations with prominent biotechnology firms place new firms in a better position to secure such endorsement. Finally, the reported results demonstrate that the greater the range of upper echelon affiliations across the categories of upstream, horizontal, and downstream organizations, the greater the prestige of the firm's lead investment bank.

I conclude Chapter 9 with a brief discussion of a follow-up study with Monica Higgins (Higgins and Gulati 2006) that explores the effects of upper-echelon-based network resources on the performance of a firm's IPO. The study further assesses whether this is a direct effect or one mediated through the connections a firm builds with its chosen investment bank. The study proposes that network resources here may not only arise from the interpersonal connections of firms but also through the endorsement ties that firms may have created with their investment banks. The results suggest that network resources originating from both upper echelon experiences and ties to investment banks are beneficial to firms and help them obtain the support of investors at the time of their public offering. Further, the upper-echelon-based effects on performance occur both directly and indirectly by shaping a firm's choice of investment bank. This chapter illustrates the complex interplay among network resources from different sources and their effects on a firm's performance.

This chapter offers a broader view of network resources that originate in the prior employment experiences of the upper echelon of management, showing how such resources may benefit those firms in obtaining new ties with prestigious investment banks that in turn constitute yet another facet of network resources that can be valuable to firms at the time of their public offering. Both these avenues to network resources are theorized to be conduits of valuable information and resources for these entrepreneurial firms. Implicit in the findings reported here is a claim that network resources beget more network resources. In this chapter and elsewhere I also pose the question about the possible limits to the benefits of network resources if any.

In Chapter 10, we extend this research by investigating the contingent value of various types of interorganizational relationships at the time of a young firm's IPO. The focus here is on network resources that arise from the interorganizational ties a firm possesses at the time of its public offering. The research in this chapter focuses on the varying implications for firms of network resources originating from their ties with three key stakeholders identified in prior studies: venture capitalists, investment banks, and alliance partners. This chapter explores which network ties matter when for a start-up firm. It shows that the influence of network resources created from strategic alliances and endorsement relationships differs depending on the market environment. The findings suggest that different types of market uncertainty focus investor attention on different factors, and because network ties provide important signals of a firm's potential, they become more or less important depending on the nature of investor concerns in that specific market context. Building on Chapter 4, the results here affirm that the effect of network resources may be contingent on the type of the ties underlying those resources. Further, the results show that the contingency may arise not only from the varying nature of those ties but also from the overarching market context in which those ties occur.

I conclude the book with a forward-looking chapter that delineates some of the future trends and likely arenas for future research within the broad realm of network resources. I have outlined what I view as some key domains for fruitful inquiry and tried to provide some concrete research questions that future researchers may want to consider.

The importance of understanding network resources

When I began my research on interorganizational networks, much of the prior research on the causes and consequences of interorganizational ties was at the tie or firm level, and the external context in which they occur was considered only through measures of competitiveness in product or supplier markets. However, I have found that although interorganizational partnerships are essentially dyadic exchanges, key precursors, processes, and associated outcomes can be defined and shaped by the interorganizational networks within which most firms are embedded. Such networks engender resources in that they may provide a firm with access to information, resources, and technology, as well as efficiency advantages based on reduced governance and search costs. They may also serve as important symbols of focal firms' legitimacy for critical third parties. This, in turn, may allow those firms to enter into new ties more frequently, narrow their search for partners, and obtain additional benefits as a result of endorsements from critical third parties.

Consequently, a more systematic study of a firm's network resources can have both descriptive and normative outcomes that provide valuable insights for theories of strategic management, organizational theory, and sociology. Incorporating social network factors into our account of the interorganizational behavior of firms not only provides a more accurate picture of the key influences on the strategic actions of firms but also has important implications for managerial practice. For instance, an understanding of how network resources influence the formation of new ties can provide insights for managers on the path-dependent processes that may lock them into certain courses of action as a result of constraints from their current ties. They may choose to anticipate such concerns and proactively initiate selective network contacts that enhance their informational capabilities.

Furthermore, by examining the specific way in which network resources and the underlying networks may constrain their future actions and channel opportunities, firms can begin to take a more forward-looking stance in regard to the new ties they enter. They can be proactive in designing their networks and considering the ramifications of each new tie on their future choices. They may also selectively position themselves in networks to derive possible control benefits (Burt 1992). Similarly, numerous insights result from understanding the complexities associated with managing a portfolio of alliances and the relational capabilities required to do so successfully. Ultimately, managers want to know how to manage individual ties and portfolios of ties, and a recognition of some of the dynamics that influence the evolution and eventual performance of ties at both the dyadic and network levels can be extremely beneficial. The challenge for scholars studying networks and interorganizational ties is to bridge the chasm between theory and practice by translating some of their important insights into practical tactics for managers. I believe this book accomplishes this task.

This book looks at a range of interorganizational ties that generate network resources for participating firms. I began my research with an examination of the role of interorganizational strategic alliances as formative elements of network resources. In subsequent research, I discovered that the network resources that may shape a firm's behavior and outcomes need not necessarily emanate from its prior alliance networks alone. I have expanded this view bit by bit. First, I explored the antecedents of alliances entered by firms and found that the entry of firms into new alliances is shaped not only by the network of prior alliances but also by those arising from its board interlocks. I also found that while the outcomes associated with a firm's new alliances may be shaped by the effects of its prior alliance network on competitive and cooperative dynamics, outcomes for the firms themselves are likely to be impacted by the much broader set of ties that constitute its network resources. Such ties encompass connections with key constituents including customers, suppliers, alliance partners, and internal subunits. Each of these becomes respecified by managers as 'partners' with whom the firm must work seamlessly to obtain beneficial outcomes. Ultimately, in the context of start-up companies I looked at the role of network resources emanating from the experience of firms' upper echelons and from ties to prestigious endorsers.

Part I

Network Resources and the Formation of New Ties

2 Network resources and the proclivity of firms to enter into alliances

While there are numerous theoretical and empirical accounts of the formation of alliances, their primary focus is on understanding the *intra*-organizational resource-based considerations that promote alliance formation (e.g. Berg, Duncan, and Friedman 1982; Mariti and Smiley 1983; Hagedoorn 1993). By focusing on the existing material means and competence (or lack thereof) that may propel firms to enter into new alliances, scholars approaching alliance formation from a resource-based perspective have generally paid less attention to important social factors that could influence the availability of and access to alliance opportunities in the first place. That is to say, they have overlooked the role of network resources in determining the opportunity set firms may perceive.

As I discussed in Chapter 1, factors resulting from the embeddedness of firms in a rich social context can be influential in altering the network resources available to firms, which may in turn shape their behavior. By neglecting such factors, prior research that focused on competence-based drivers for alliance formation implies that firms are atomistic actors performing strategic actions in an asocial context (Baum and Dutton 1996). In such studies, the external context remains encapsulated within measures of competitiveness in product or supplier markets, with limited consideration of a firm's social structural context or how this can influence strategic actions and outcomes in important ways. Economic sociologists have demonstrated how the social structure of ties in which economic actors are embedded can influence their subsequent actions (Granovetter 1985) and that the distinct social structural patterns in exchange relations within markets shape the flow of information (Burt 1982; Baker 1984), which in

This chapter is adapted with permission from 'Network Location and Learning: The Influence of Network Resources and Firm Capabilities on Alliance Formation' by Ranjay Gulati published in *Strategic Management Journal*, 1999, (20/5): 397–420, © John Wiley & Sons Limited.

turn provides both opportunities and constraints for actors and can have implications for their behavior and performance. Such an embeddedness perspective, which highlights the salience of networks, is applicable to both individual and interorganizational networks (Baker 1990; Podolny 1993; Gulati 1995*b*; Powell, Koput, and Smith-Doerr 1996; Gulati and Gargiulo 1999).

To develop a more socialized account of firm behavior, this chapter *identifies the factors that determine which firms enter into alliances and which do not.* I focus here on the firm level and consider social factors related to a firm's network resource endowment that influence the extent to which it participates in alliances over time. My extensive fieldwork suggests that although strategic alliances are essentially dyadic exchanges, key precursors, processes, and outcomes associated with them can be defined and shaped by the networks within which most firms are embedded. Here I look at the extent to which firms' participation in alliance networks influences their proclivity to enter new alliances. Furthermore, I propose that firms accrue network resources from the interfirm networks in which they are located. These resources, in turn, influence the extent to which firms enter into new alliances.

This chapter makes two distinct contributions to the research on strategic alliances and social networks. First, it expands the realm of the resource-based perspective from resources within a firm's boundaries to network resources that result from network membership and location. I previously defined network resources as sources of valuable information residing outside a firm's boundaries that can influence strategic behavior by altering the opportunity set available. Second, by introducing the concept of network resources, I highlight the importance of unique historical conditions and path-dependent processes that can be a significant basis for 'sticky' firm resources.

The empirical study I conducted examined the influence of network resources on the alliance behavior of a panel of firms over a nine-year period. These network resources accrue from the participation of firms in the network of accumulated prior alliances among industry participants. For each period in this study, this network includes all alliances that have been formed up to and including the previous period. This network of cumulative prior alliances updates each year to incorporate the new alliances formed, and this new network influences alliance formation for subsequent periods. Thus, when observed over time, the formation of new ties in each period alters the very network that influenced the ties in the first place. The passage of time, then, results in an endogenous network dynamic between action among embedded firms and the network structure that guides and is transformed by that action. I explore this in further detail towards the end of Chapter 3.

Theory and hypotheses

NETWORK RESOURCES AND THE ENTRY OF FIRMS INTO ALLIANCES

To understand why network resources resulting from interfirm networks are important to firms and their alliances, we must consider the factors usually associated with the formation of alliances. One of these considerations is partner reliability. In Chapter 1, I discussed how network resources facilitate alliance formation by providing information that reduces uncertainties and alleviates some of the risks of opportunism. In short, ties accumulated over time can make available rich information regarding new alliance opportunities with reliable partners (Kogut, Shan, and Walker 1992; Gulati 1995*b*; Powell, Koput, and Smith-Doerr 1996).

However, networks may also constrain a firm's set of choices for alliances by (*a*) limiting the circle of potential partners about whom it has information and (*b*) providing no information about nonparticipants. Indeed, the network resources firms receive from their participation in interfirm networks are akin to the social capital of individuals that Coleman (1988: S98) discussed in his seminal essay on the topic:

[S]ocial capital inheres in the structure of relations between actors and among actors. It is not lodged either in the actors themselves or in physical implements of production. Because purposive organizations can be actors ('corporate actors') just as persons can, relations among corporate actors can constitute social capital for them as well.

Earlier, scholars have described social capital as a resource akin to financial and technological capital that exists within the social relationships in which an actor is embedded (Loury 1977, 1987; Bourdieu 1986). At higher levels of aggregation, social capital has generally been used to describe features of social organization that facilitate coordination and cooperation for mutual benefit (Putnam 1993: 35–6), while at the individual level, social capital accrues from the pattern of contact networks in which individuals are placed. Scholars within the resource-based perspective have also highlighted the role of organizational capital resources, which include a firm's contact network (Tomer 1987). In this context, I consider the implications of network resources not so much for the performance of firms but, rather, as important enabling conditions for future cooperation.

Most firms are embedded in a variety of interfirm networks, such as board interlocks, trade associations, and R&D cooperatives. To view any of these networks as a basis for network resources, it is important to consider the extent to which the network serves as a channel of information and the kind of information it transmits. As I suggest in Chapter 1, one increasingly important network that has become an influential channel of information is the network of prior alliances (Kogut, Shan, and Walker 1992; Gulati 1995*b*). This network encompasses the set of alliances that industry participants have entered until the previous year. With the rapid proliferation of alliances in the last several decades, most firms are now embedded in a wider network of prior and current alliances. Most alliances involve prolonged contact between partners, and firms actively rely on such networks as conduits of valuable information that can act as a catalyst for new alliances. Such networks are dynamic, however, and can include all past alliances, whether active or not, at any given time. With the formation of new alliances, the prior alliance network updates and becomes influential for subsequent firm behavior.

The information provided by network resources can enable the creation of new alliances by three distinct means: access, timing, and referrals (Burt 1992). Access refers to information regarding the capabilities and trustworthiness of current or potential partners. By providing such information, an existing network can influence a firm's available set of feasible partners and its attractiveness as a partner to other firms. The comments of an alliance manager I interviewed vividly illustrate this point:

> Our network of [prior alliance] partners is an active source of information for us about new deals [alliances]. We are in constant dialog with many of our partners, and this allows us to find many new opportunities with them and also with other firms out there.

Thus, it seems that firm managers actively seek information about new alliance opportunities from their prior alliance partners, and potential partnerships may be with previous allies or others.

Timing entails having informational benefits about potential partners at the right time. A firm seeking attractive alliance partners must approach them at the right time and pre-empt their seeking alliances elsewhere. For example, one alliance manager highlighted timing as a critical facet of the information provided by his firm's social networks:

> In our business timing is everything. And so, even for alliances to happen the confluence of circumstances have to be at the right time. We and our prospective partner must know about each other's needs and identify an opportunity for an alliance together in a timely manner. . . . Our partners from past alliances are one of our most important sources of timely information about alliance opportunities out there, both with them and with other firms with whom they are acquainted.

Thus, in addition to providing access to information about each other, the close contact resulting from prior alliances ensures that partners learn about joint opportunities for alliances in a timely manner.

The third benefit of the information firms receive through network resources stems from the indirect referrals firms provide to each other about their previous partners. Thus, the nature of information available to a firm is based not only on its immediate network ties but also on where it is situated in the broader network. For example, prior partners may refer their own allies to a focal firm for partnership. As a result, two firms may learn about each other via a shared alliance partner who introduces them and perhaps vouches for their reliability. As one manager pointed out:

In some cases we realize that perhaps our skills don't really match for a project, and our partner may refer us to another firm about whom we were unaware.... An important aspect of this referral business is, of course, about vouching for the reliability of that firm. Thus, if one of our long-standing partners suggests one of their own partners as a good fit for our needs, we usually consider it very seriously.

Such comments suggest that indirect ties in the network of past alliances influence a firm's ability to enter new partnerships, allowing it to more easily enter alliances with firms with whom it shares one or more partners. As networks channel information through both direct and indirect contacts, such resources accrue not only from the extent of a firm's participation in networks but also from a firm's location within them. As a result, the specific patterning of a firm's ties allows it access to different types and degrees of information.

Furthermore, the information exchange in alliance networks can go beyond indirect referrals to encompass the whole network.

The network of prior alliances is a rich source of information from which firms can also learn about new firms of which they were previously unaware, and these new firms join the focal firm's set of potential alliance targets, increasing the likelihood of partnership. Thus, I propose the following hypothesis:

Hypothesis 1: The greater the extent of a firm's network resources that originate from its network of prior alliances, the greater the likelihood that it will enter a new alliance in the subsequent year.

FIRM CAPABILITIES AND THE ENTRY OF FIRMS INTO ALLIANCES

In addition to providing informational advantages from prior alliances, network resources also help firms develop managerial capabilities associated with forming new alliances, which in turn enhance network resources. Membership in a network of prior alliances requires firms to have entered such ties in the past, and by participating in alliances, firms can develop alliance capabilities that accrue as a result of historical learning (Dierickx and Cool 1989; Barney 1991; Dyer and Singh 1998). While strategy scholars have primarily applied capabilities-based arguments to explain sustained performance differences across firms, variation in capabilities can also be the basis for strategic behavior (e.g. Kraatz and Zajac 2001). In this instance, my concern is not with technological or material resource-based capabilities but with organizational capabilities that enable firms to form alliances with greater ease.

Alliances are complex organizational arrangements that can require multiple levels of internal approval, significant research to identify partners, detailed assessments of contracts, and significant ongoing management attention to sustain the partnership (Gulati, Khanna, and Nohria 1994; Ring and Van de Ven 1994; Doz 1996). Due to the considerable managerial challenges associated with forming alliances, let alone managing them, the possession of alliance-formation capabilities can be a significant driver for firms considering new alliances. The comments of one of the managers I interviewed exemplify this:

Forming a new alliance is not as easy as you might think. There are considerable political, legal, and organizational hoops to be jumped.... In my experience, some firms are wonderfully adept with forming these things [alliances]. They have systems, procedures, and personnel, all of which click together to make new alliances happen.

An important basis for alliance formation capabilities is experience-based learning. Early evidence of organizational learning from experience, which was provided by the extensive empirical research on learning curves, suggests a lowering of production costs with experience (e.g. Fudenberg and Tirole 1983; Ghemawat and Spence 1985). There is also evidence from research on organizational learning that firms may build organizational capabilities from experience and then engage in repeat experiences that further refine their capabilities. Levinthal and March (1993) talked about how firms engage in exploitation of existing capabilities—as opposed to exploration of new prospects—due to their propensity for continued use and development of existing skills. Along similar lines, evolutionary economists and organizational theorists have suggested that firms are driven by routines, and once routines are in place, firms may engage in similar sets of activities repeatedly and improve on those routines (Nelson and Winter 1982; Amburgey, Kelly, and Barnett 1993). Some of the bases for such learning include building appropriate routines that result from a process of 'error detection and correction in theories in use' (Argyris and Schon 1978). With greater experience, firms can also enhance their absorptive capacity from alliances (Cohen and Levinthal 1990). Furthermore, top managers within the firm may acquire mindsets that focus their attention on forming new alliances as a primary strategic avenue for growth (Boeker 1997).

Evidence from previous research on strategic alliances suggests that the benefits of experience can translate into specific skills for the formation and management of alliances (Lyles 1988; Arregle, Amburgey, and Dacin

1996; Amburgey, Dacin, and Singh 1996; Dyer and Singh 1998; Anand and Khanna 2000*a*). Once firms begin to enter alliances, they can internalize and refine specific routines associated with forming such partnerships. One manager I interviewed commented on the importance of experience in alliance formation:

One thing that also makes it easier for us to enter new alliances is our extensive experience with doing alliances. Forming a new partnership is not a big deal any more—we have our own formula and we know it works!

Some of the firms that I interviewed enhanced their alliance capabilities by setting up separate organizational units to assist with the creation and management of their strategic partnerships (Dyer, Kale, and Singh 2001). These units provide valuable initial input to specific divisions considering alliances in the form of legal and managerial templates that cover relevant issues. They also help divisions interface with the legal department and provide guidelines to consider in selecting a partner. In several instances, such units also disseminated information about alliance formation as a strategy to their managers and scanned the market for new alliance opportunities. Other firms I interviewed had developed standardized procedures to facilitate the creation of new alliances. These procedures included clarifying decision-making authority, setting guidelines for projects considered appropriate for alliances, specifying companywide legal frameworks for alliances, and creating a checklist of *ex ante* issues to be considered for the future management of alliances.

   Because of these structures and systems, managers were more familiar with alliances and the tasks associated with alliance creation were simpler. I found consistent evidence that firms built these concrete alliance formation capabilities with experience, which in turn enable them to form new alliances more often and with greater ease, which leads to the following hypothesis:

Hypothesis 2: The greater a firm's alliance formation capabilities, the greater the likelihood that it will enter a new alliance in the subsequent year.

Empirical research

METHOD

I tested the impact of network resources and firm capabilities on strategic alliances using longitudinal data from a sample of American, European, and Japanese firms in three different industries from 1981 to 1989 (described in Appendix 1 as the 'Alliance Formation Database'). To compute network measures, I constructed adjacency matrices representing the relationships between firms, with separate matrices for each industry for each year (details in Appendix 1 under the section labeled 'Constructing the Social Networks'). For each matrix, I included all alliance activity among industry panel members up to the prior year.

Using these matrices, I examined the factors affecting the likelihood that a firm would enter into an alliance in any given period. Each firm-year record was given a dichotomous-dependent variable that indicated whether the firm entered any alliances in the given year. Variables for cliques and closeness were included to measure centrality, which indicates the magnitude of network resources available to a firm. The number of all prior alliances a focal firm had entered with any partners, new or old, captured the extent of the alliance formation capabilities a firm may have developed from its experience. I also assessed the alliance formation capabilities of focal firms by measuring the diversity of their alliance experiences, based on the assumption that greater diversity can lead to greater capabilities related to alliance formation (results not reported here). Diversity was defined as (a) the kinds of governance structures the firm used to formalize its prior alliances, and (b) the nationalities of its partners. Finally, I introduced an additional variable to assess possible temporal factors associated with alliance formation capabilities. Presumably, recent entry into an alliance would make alliance formation capabilities more salient than an experience further in the past. This could also be interpreted as the extent to which firms are likely to engage in activities similar to those they have recently done (Amburgey, Kelly, and Barnett 1993). Thus, I examined whether the length of time since a firm last entered an alliance influenced its current likelihood of entering a new alliance. To do this I introduced a variable measuring the length of time since the firm had previously entered an alliance. Both linear and quadratic terms for this variable were introduced (results not reported here).

In my analyses, I controlled for several factors that might also impact the alliance behavior of firms. Firm-level control variables included financial size, solvency, debt, and performance. I also included an industry-level control variable capturing the density of cumulative alliances in each industry up to the prior year.

I included a series of dummy variables for each year to capture any effects of temporal trends related to current technological and environmental conditions that may have influenced alliance formation. Dummy variables were also used to control for the nationality of firms and sectoral differences.

Table 2.1 describes variables included in the analysis and the predicted effects for each independent variable. All the independent variables are time-varying and were updated each year for the period of this study. Each variable was lagged by one year to predict firm behavior. Descriptive statistics and correlations for all the variables included are provided in Table 2.2.

Table 2.1. Definitions and predicted signs of variables

Variable name	Definition	Predicted sign[a]
Alliance	Whether the firm entered an alliance in a given year	Dep. variable
Cliques	The number of cliques to which a firm belongs. Normalized to industry maximum	+
Closeness	Freeman's measure of closeness indicating how closely linked the firm is to all other firms in the panel. Normalized to industry maximum	+
Experience	Cumulative total of alliances the firm has entered until the previous year	+
Debt	Long-term debt of the firm divided by current assets and normalized to the industry median	NP
Solvency	Quick ratio: current assets minus inventory, divided by current liabilities and normalized to the industry median	NP
Performance	Return on assets from previous year normalized to the industry median	NP
Size	Total assets of the firm in the previous year normalized to the industry median	NP
Density	Density of the network of alliances formed in the industry until the prior year	NP
Time	Variable ranges from one to nine for 1981 to 1989	NP
DUSA	Dummy variable set to one if the firm is American (default European)	NP
DJPN	Dummy variable set to one if the firm is Japanese (default European)	NP
New materials	Dummy variable set to one if firms are in the new materials sector (default automotive)	NP
Industrial automation	Dummy variable set to one if firms are in the industrial automation sector (default automotive)	NP
Rho	Indicator variable generated by the random effects model which displays the extent to which there were unobserved differences across firms that were accounted for by the random effects model	NP

[a]NP, no prediction.

ANALYSIS

I modeled alliance formation using the following dynamic panel model, in which a variable's positive coefficients indicate that it promotes alliance formation:

$$p_i(t) = F(a + bx_i + cy_i(t-1) + u_i)$$

where $p_i(t)$ = the probability at time (t) of the announcement of an alliance by firm i; x_i = a time-constant vector of covariates characterizing firm i; $y_i(t-1)$ = a time-varying vector of covariates characterizing firm i; u_i = unobserved time-constant effects not captured by the independent variables; and F = the normal cumulative distribution function. In running these estimations, I used a random effects model to control for unobserved heterogeneity. See Appendix 2 for details.

Table 2.2. Descriptive statistics and correlation matrix

Variable	Mean	SD	Lowest	Highest
1. Alliance	0.18	0.38	0	1
2. Cliques	0.31	0.25	0.05	1.00
3. Closeness	0.38	0.21	0.02	1.00
4. Experience	4.28	6.60	0	46
5. Debt	1.09	0.93	0.11	15.06
6. Solvency	1.37	1.15	0.31	7.66
7. Performance	1.16	0.95	0.34	8.33
8. Size	1.22	1.07	0.21	12.27
9. Density	0.09	0.02	0.04	0.15
10. Time	4.0	2.58	0	8
11. DUSA	0.33	0.47	0	1
12. DJPN	0.39	0.49	0	1
13. New materials	0.37	0.48	0	1
14. Industrial automation	0.31	0.46	0	1

Spearman correlation matrix

	(1)	(2)	(3)	(4)	(5)	(6)	(7)	(8)	(9)	(10)	(11)	(12)	(13)	(14)
(1)	1.00	—	—	—	—	—	—	—	—	—	—	—	—	—
(2)	0.37	1.00	—	—	—	—	—	—	—	—	—	—	—	—
(3)	0.42	0.66	1.00	—	—	—	—	—	—	—	—	—	—	—
(4)	0.34	0.39	0.40	1.00	—	—	—	—	—	—	—	—	—	—
(5)	0.21	0.03	0.18	0.06	1.00	—	—	—	—	—	—	—	—	—
(6)	−0.05	0.25	0.24	−0.13	0.24	1.00	—	—	—	—	—	—	—	—
(7)	0.00	0.35	0.11	0.42	0.15	−0.16	1.00	—	—	—	—	—	—	—
(8)	0.26	−0.05	−0.10	−0.04	0.05	0.23	0.11	1.00	—	—	—	—	—	—
(9)	0.29	0.18	0.03	0.13	0.00	0.05	0.01	0.12	1.00	—	—	—	—	—
(10)	0.18	0.20	0.23	0.29	0.09	0.05	0.05	0.10	0.49	1.00	—	—	—	—
(11)	0.02	−0.12	−0.16	−0.05	0.08	0.19	0.00	0.08	0.07	0.03	1.00	—	—	—
(12)	0.00	0.15	0.03	−0.01	−0.03	0.00	−0.06	−0.07	−0.06	0.07	−0.34	1.00	—	—
(13)	0.19	−0.13	−0.15	−0.06	0.02	0.00	−0.06	−0.03	0.33	0.00	0.08	0.09	1.00	—
(14)	−0.07	−0.14	−0.07	−0.10	−0.05	0.08	0.02	0.00	−0.12	0.00	0.03	−0.02	−0.37	1.00

RESULTS

I assessed the hypotheses sequentially in a series of panel probit models, presented in Table 2.3. Positive coefficients of variables indicate a higher propensity to ally with respect to that variable; negative coefficients show a lower propensity to enter an alliance. Asymptotic standard errors are in parentheses. The first model is the base model, which includes the control variables and examines the effects of the material-resource-based attributes of firms and systemic factors. Models 2 and 3 provide two alternative tests for hypothesis 1. Model 2 tests the additional effect of network resources, as measured by the number of cliques to which a firm belongs (Cliques), on its alliance behavior. Model 3 is identical to model 2 except that it uses an alternative measure of network resources—closeness centrality (Closeness). The two measures of

Table 2.3. Panel probit estimates (standard errors in parentheses)

Variable	I		II		III		IV		V	
Constant	−2.03*	(0.18)	−2.27*	(0.19)	−2.43*	(0.21)	−2.09*	(0.20)	−2.21*	(0.18)
Cliques	—		0.36*	(0.08)	—		0.22*	(0.06)	—	
Closeness	—		—		0.94*	(0.21)	—		0.77*	(0.24)
Experience	—		—		—		0.17*	(0.04)	0.22*	(0.05)
Debt	−0.31	(0.62)	−0.44	(0.32)	−0.40	(0.31)	−0.41	(0.30)	−0.34	(0.28)
Solvency	−0.02	(0.06)	−0.05	(0.07)	−0.04	(0.07)	−0.03	(0.07)	−0.03	(0.07)
Performance	0.00	(0.00)	0.00	(0.00)	−0.01	(0.01)	0.00	(0.00)	0.00	(0.01)
Size	0.01*	(0.00)	0.02*	(0.00)	0.02*	(0.00)	0.01*	(0.00)	0.02*	(0.00)
Density	0.17*	(0.05)	0.16*	(0.05)	0.17*	(0.04)	0.10*	(0.02)	0.13*	(0.02)
Time	0.08*	(0.02)	0.07	(0.05)	0.07	(0.04)	0.03	(0.05)	0.04	(0.05)
DUSA	0.11	(0.14)	0.12	(0.09)	0.12	(0.08)	0.10	(0.09)	0.10	(0.08)
DJPN	0.08	(0.11)	0.08	(0.12)	0.07	(0.11)	0.05	(0.10)	0.05	(0.11)
New materials	−0.66*	(0.19)	−0.15	(0.10)	−0.17	(0.12)	−0.10	(0.10)	−0.14	(0.10)
Industrial automation	−0.41*	(0.11)	−0.11	(0.08)	−0.13	(0.08)	−0.08	(0.07)	−0.11	(0.08)
Rho	0.27*	(0.06)	0.21*	(0.07)	0.18*	(0.05)	0.20*	(0.06)	0.18*	(0.06)
n	1,494		1,494		1,494		1,494		1,494	
Log L	−584.32		−551.17		−535.22		−527.56		−515.21	
χ^2	84.14*		91.15*		98.57*		102.49*		105.34*	

*p < .05.

centrality that serve as indicators of network resources are correlated and thus are introduced in separate models. Models 4 and 5 introduce the measure of firm capabilities (Experience) while retaining the two measures for centrality separately in each model.

All five models in Table 2.3 were significant overall, as indicated by the χ^2 test using their log-likelihood values. In models 2 and 3, I sequentially included the network-resource variables measuring the relative location of the firm in the alliance network. The results confirm hypothesis 1, which suggests that firms that are centrally located in the alliance network (based on Cliques and Closeness) are more likely to form new alliances. Furthermore, the significant improvement in the χ^2 statistic suggests a better fitting model once the measures of network resources are included.

The results for the influence of alliance formation capabilities on subsequent alliances are mixed. As Table 2.3 suggests, Experience, which measured the effects of a firm's cumulative history of alliances on its alliance behavior, was positive and significant in both models 4 and 5. This indicates that the more experience firms have with forming alliances, the more likely they are to enter new alliances. It is important to emphasize that the use of a statistical model accounting for unobserved heterogeneity ensures that estimates for this variable were both consistent and efficient. The improvement in the χ^2 statistic further indicates the value of including this variable in the estimations.

While past experience with alliances had a significant effect, no significant results were obtained for three additional measures of alliance capabilities that assessed the diversity of alliances each firm had previously entered and the length of time since it last entered an alliance (results not reported here). Measurements of diversity in terms of contracts used and nationalities of partners were nonsignificant. Furthermore, linear and quadratic specifications of duration effects for alliances were also not significant (results not reported here).

The results in Table 2.3 indicate no support for most of the material-resource attributes of firms introduced as controls—Debt, Solvency, and Performance were all nonsignificant at the .05 level, despite trends for all three variables toward negative effects on the likelihood to form alliances.

Size, Density, and Time control variables had significant and positive coefficients, suggesting a positive influence on a firm's likelihood to enter an alliance. The changes in significance of Time across models 1–5 point toward some interesting trends. In model 1, Time has a positive and significant coefficient ($p < .05$), suggesting that there may have been a broad temporal trend toward increased alliances by firms in the last decade. In models 2 and 3, which include the network resources variables, however, Time is nonsignificant, suggesting that these temporal effects are interpreted by the network-resource variables included in these models. In other words, Time was capturing differences in network resources over time. The inclusion of a quadratic term for time did not alter these results; its coefficient was also nonsignificant. Therefore, only results with a linear term for time are reported here. The main effects for the key variables did not change when I included dummy variables for each period.

The control variables for nationality and sector show mixed results. In some instances, they were marginally significant and in others nonsignificant, suggesting that these factors may be of limited relevance. The variables for nationality, DUSA and DJPN, were nonsignificant, suggesting that firms from the United States and Japan are no more likely to ally than firms from Europe.

Both sector dummies, New Materials and Industrial Automation, were significant in model 1 but not so in models 2–5 (the default sector was automotive), suggesting that intrinsic sectoral differences were interpreted by the network-resource variables included in those models. In other words, in model 1, New Materials and Industrial Automation were capturing sectoral differences in firm network resources, which was explained away when the firm network-resource variables were included.

While the relative significance levels of the sector dummies suggest intrinsic differences across the three industries on the likelihood of alliance formation, they do not tell us whether the main effects hypothesized in this chapter differ across the three industries. Rather, they simply indicate that the constant terms for each of the industries may differ. To assess the industry differences further, I estimated unrestricted models for each of the industries (results not presented here). By examining each of the industries independently, no restrictions were imposed on the slope coefficients. The signs of the coefficients indicated that the postulated directionality of the main effects observed in the pooled sample hold true in each of the sectors. I also conducted a similar test for firms of different nationalities. The results suggested that the main effects were consistent across firms of different nationalities when examined separately.

The random-effects model used generates a coefficient Rho, which indicates the extent to which unobserved heterogeneity was found and corrected for by the model. The positive and significant coefficient for Rho across all models suggests that unobserved factors that could influence the alliance behavior of firms were accounted for by the statistical model.

Conclusion

The results of the longitudinal analysis confirm that, over time, the proclivity of a firm to enter new alliances is influenced by the extent of network resources available to it. Results show that network resources, as indicated by a firm's location in the interfirm network of prior alliances in which it is embedded (and the positions of its partners), were a significant predictor of the frequency with which firms entered new alliances.

There is also some evidence that the capabilities firms amassed by forming past alliances positively affected the frequency with which they entered new ones. One capabilities measure was a significant predictor of new alliance activity by firms in all models, but other measures were nonsignificant. For example, I found no effect for the length of time since a firm's last alliance, suggesting that there may be limited or no depletion of alliance capabilities over time. In addition, neither of the two measures of the diversity of prior alliance experience of firms (in terms of governance structures used and nationalities of partners) was significant. This suggests that perhaps the capabilities associated with managing a diverse set of alliances and partners are not as important for firms as the partnership per se. This could occur because once firms have developed the administrative control procedures for creating new alliances, they are able to use that knowledge in any kind of alliance. Additional facets of diversity of alliance experience that could have been taken into account (e.g. diversity of objectives and scope of activities) were not part of this study.

To ensure the robustness of the findings, I included numerous control variables postulated in prior research as important material-resource considerations for firms entering alliances. Surprisingly, many material-resource attributes of firms, such as liquidity, solvency, and performance, were not significant predictors of alliance activity. Given the longitudinal context of this study and the time-varying nature of most of the variables included, I also ensured that I adequately accounted for any broad temporal trends that could influence the findings. I tested for such temporal trends with dummy variables for each year and a single linear term for time. The nonsignificance of the time variable, which usually captures residual factors, in the models in which network-resource factors were included is indicative of these variables' explanatory power.

Results for the regional origin of firms reveal some interesting trends. Contrary to my expectations, there were no significant differences between the propensities of American and Japanese firms to enter alliances and those of European firms. In separate analyses, I also found no significant differences between American and Japanese firms. Because these variables are nonsignificant even in the baseline model, I believe that this result indicates that many of the expected national differences are explained by some of the controls I have included. This was confirmed by a separate estimation in which I found that the dummy variables for nationality were significant when introduced on their own but failed to retain significance once the remaining controls were introduced. I also ensured the robustness of my findings by conducting subgroup analyses in which I looked at firms from each region separately. Results were consistent across the three subgroups, suggesting that network resources and firm capabilities exert influence across national contexts.

I also explored sectoral differences in greater depth to ensure that similar dynamics occurred across sectors. I conducted subgroup analyses in which I ran models separately for each industry and found very similar results across the three industries. This indicates the robustness of findings for the role of network resources in alliance formation. An assessment of the dummy variables for sector with the pooled sample reveals interesting trends. The significant and negative effect of these variables in the baseline model suggests that firms in both new materials and industrial automation sectors were less likely to form alliances than those in the default sector of automotive. These effects were no longer significant once I included measures for network resources. This indicates that important differences in propensities for alliances across sectors are explained by systematic differences in network resources available to firms across those sectors. There may be important institutional considerations underlying both sectoral and national differences in alliance propensities that have not been fully explored here but could be examined in future research.

EXPANDING THE RESEARCH DOMAIN

This chapter addresses several concerns with prior research on strategic alliances. First, as I discussed in Chapter 1, the primary focus of research on alliances has been to ask the 'why' question to understand some of the reasons that firms enter alliances. Part of the problem with why questions is that they may lead to a neglect of some of the conditions that make certain behaviors likely (Oliver 1990). A second, related concern is that many prior studies have considered the unit of analysis to be the alliance, as opposed to firm participation in alliances, rendering it difficult to undertake a firm-level analysis. Also, much of the empirical research on alliances has been cross-sectional or pooled cross-sectional in scope. Even the few efforts to introduce a network perspective to the formation of alliances have typically taken a pooled cross-sectional approach and thus have not been able to examine systematically how the evolving financial, economic, and social circumstances of a firm may moderate its alliance behavior over time. Finally, past consideration of firm and industry imperatives and the description of external context in competitive terms have typically taken an atomistic view of firms that does not account for the actions of other firms or the relationships in which focal firms are already embedded. Moreover, this perspective ignores the interactive nature of the market, whereby participants discover market information through their interactions in it (Hayek 1949; White 1981).

This chapter tackles some of the concerns above by assessing the alliance behavior of firms over a period. The longitudinal research design allowed me to examine the conditions under which the formation of alliances by specific firms becomes more or less likely. Using a network perspective to study strategic alliances also provides valuable insights into the broader domain of interfirm networks. The creation of an alliance is an important strategic action, and the accumulation of such alliances constitutes a network. Thus, alliances may be studied as both endogenous and exogenous factors. The former can be examined by looking at the influence of interfirm networks on the formation of alliances, while the latter can be studied by considering the effects of the network of accumulated alliances. In this study, both were examined simultaneously by assessing the influence of the interfirm alliance network on future alliances in a longitudinal study. Studying the development of an alliance network over time provides unique insights into the evolution of networks, where strategic action and social structure are closely intertwined (Gulati and Gargiulo 1999).

Above all, however, this study expands the scope of the resource-based perspective from resources residing securely within a firm's boundaries to external resources that result from network membership and location. The ongoing cycle between a firm's historical industry alliance network and the formation of future alliances suggests a path-dependent process by which firms accumulate network resources that are sticky and can become the basis of sustainable competitive advantage (Barney 1991). Many scholars have suggested the importance of unique historical conditions and path-dependent processes as significant bases for firm resources (David 1985; Arthur 1989). Thus, the notion of network resources adds specificity to this understanding and suggests an important means by which history can matter.

MANAGERIAL IMPLICATIONS

Incorporating network factors into an account of alliance behavior not only provides a more accurate representation of the key influences on the strategic actions of firms but also has important implications for managerial practice. For instance, the focus on the implications of network resources for enabling a specific strategic action by firms could easily be extended to the role of network resources for firm performance (see Part III for more on this). Network resources are usually heterogeneously dispersed within an industry and due to their unique historical basis can be difficult to imitate, making them a viable avenue for sustainable competitive advantage. Moreover, this study also suggests that the organizational search for alliances may result in a path-dependent process in which the gradual formation of a network structure increases the information available to select firms, albeit also limiting the effective range of potential partners a firm is likely to consider (Arthur 1989). Firms may thus become victims of their own history. Only firms with a rich history that endows them with network resources and rich capabilities for forming alliances are likely to consider entering new alliances, and some firms with more limited resources may find themselves unable to enter new alliances indefinitely.

Managers could choose to anticipate such concerns about their participation in networks and proactively initiate selective network contacts that enhance their informational capabilities. They can be proactive in designing their networks and in considering the ramifications of each new tie on their future choices because network resources are based in part on the locations of firms in the network. Furthermore, the informational advantages resulting from network resources must be factored into the calculus for partner choice. This choice must be influenced not only by the appeal of a potential partner for the project at hand but also by potential partners' locations in the network. A firm should consider building up network resources by seeking out strategic alliances with central firms that enable the further development of new alliances, especially if it is considering embarking on a major strategic initiative driven by alliances. Thus, once managers understand the dynamics of alliance networks, they may choose path-creation strategies rather than allowing their choices to become path-dependent. Specifically, they should take a forward-looking perspective to visualize their firm's desired alliance network of the future and then work backwards from it to shape their current alliance strategy.

3 Network resources and the choice of partners in alliances

In the previous chapter, I presented a dynamic, firm-level study of the role of network resources in determining the frequency with which individual firms enter into alliances. Extensive fieldwork along with detailed empirical analysis of longitudinal data on firm behavior showed that by providing firms with information about potential partners, network resources are an important catalyst for entry into new alliances, especially because such ties entail considerable uncertainty and hazards. Additionally, the study assessed the importance of a firm's material resources and alliance-formation capabilities as determinants of its proclivity to enter into new alliances. The results revealed that firms with greater network resources based on their positions in prior interorganizational networks are more likely to enter into new alliances. The results also suggested that firms' capabilities with alliance formation—as measured by their past alliance experience—can be significant predictors of new alliance activity.

But with whom do these firms form alliances? Although researchers have examined why and when firms enter alliances, they have left relatively unexplored the question of with whom firms are likely to ally. Transaction cost economics, for example, assumes exchange relations between two partners as a given and then seeks to explain how those relations will be formalized. This omission of factors that may guide alliance formation is particularly significant because 'the forces which bring an organization to interact are not the same as those which determine with whom the organization will interact' (Paulson 1976: 312).

In many ways, the factors that influence alliance formation are similar to those associated with marriage. Just as an individual's decision to marry is tied to the desired attributes, choice, and availability of specific partners, a firm's decision to enter an alliance is a function of the type of partner sought and the availability and willingness of a given partner to enter into a relationship. One research stream that views tie formation between organizations in this manner

This chapter is adapted from 'Social Structure and Alliance Formation Patterns: A Longitudinal Analysis' by Ranjay Gulati published in *Administrative Science Quarterly* © 1995, (40/4): 619–52, by permission of Johnson Graduate School of Management, Cornell University.

is resource dependence theory. Organizational sociologists who advocate this theory have typically viewed tie formation as driven by resource dependence among actors (Pfeffer and Salancik 1978; Burt 1983). In this view, organizations create ties to manage uncertain environments and to satisfy their resource needs. Consequently, they enter ties with other organizations that have resources and capabilities that can help them meet these goals.

While resource dependence theory provides a good explanation of the factors that influence the propensities of organizations to form ties with one another, it overlooks the difficulties such organizations may face in determining with whom to enter such relationships. In the context of interfirm alliances, this theory ignores specifically the mechanisms by which firms learn about new alliance opportunities and overcome the fears associated with such partnerships. Instead, a resource dependence perspective assumes that firms exist in an atomistic system in which information is freely available and equally accessible to all and opportunities for alliances are exogenously presented.

To understand why network resources are important for firms in shaping both their proclivity for entering into alliances and their choice of partners, we need to consider the circumstances usually associated with such ties. As I discussed in Chapter 2, firms entering alliances face considerable moral hazard concerns because of the unpredictability of partners' behavior and the likely costs of opportunistic behavior by a partner. Such concerns are further compounded by the inherently unpredictable nature of such relationships— rapid changes in the business environment may cause organizations to alter their needs and orientation, thus affecting their ongoing partnerships. Consequently, to build ties that effectively address their needs while minimizing the risks posed by such concerns, firms must be able to identify potential partners and have an idea of a given partner's needs and requirements. Firms also need information about the reliability of those partners, especially when success depends heavily on the partner's behavior (Bleeke and Ernst 1993).

As highlighted earlier, an important source of information that guides the interest of firms toward new alliances with specific partners is the social networks in which the focal firms are embedded. Faced with uncertainty, firms usually leverage existing network resources to acquire information that lowers search costs and mitigates the risk of opportunism in potential partnerships. Granovetter (1985) noted that 'the widespread preference for transacting with individuals of known reputation implies that few are actually content to rely on either generalized morality or institutional arrangements to guard against trouble' (490). Individuals rely on 'trusted informants' who have dealt with the potential partner and found him or her trustworthy, or, even better, on 'information from one's own past dealings with that person' (490). By providing firms with access to information about potential partners, network resources based on prior ties play a critical role in helping firms mitigate uncertainties regarding potential partners. At the same time, they influence the extent to which firms become aware of potential partners and thus have a large impact on the opportunity sets firms perceive for viable alliances.

While the previous chapter established the importance of network resources as a catalyst for firms to enter new alliances, it set aside the question of with whom those partnerships are formed. The study detailed in this chapter considers how network resources determine partner choice rather than when or why firms entered partnerships. This requires shifting the unit of analysis from the firm to the dyad. Thus, the study examines the factors explaining which of all possible dyads resulted in alliances during the observed period and the role of network resources in shaping those outcomes. In particular, I explore how network resources can drive the choice of partners for alliances. While my focus here shifts the unit of analysis from the firm to potential partner dyads, the overall perspective still very much involves how firms' network resources shape their proclivities to enter new alliances and their partner choices. Thus, network resources reside not only within the overall accumulation of ties a firm possesses but also within the pattern of dyadic ties a firm creates through its specific partnerships. While exploring the role of network resources in shaping which pairs of firms (of all possible pairs of firms) enter into alliances, I also consider the effects of resource dependence on these outcomes.

Theory and hypotheses

STRATEGIC INTERDEPENDENCE

Strategic interdependence describes a situation in which one organization has resources or capabilities beneficial to, but not possessed by, the other and vice versa. Aiken and Hage (1968) noted that organizations face such interdependence 'because of their need for resources—not only money, but also resources such as specialized skills, access to particular kinds of markets, and the like' (914–15). Though much of the early research on strategic alliances focused only on the firm or industry level, it was nonetheless influenced by this perspective, which suggested that firms would ally with those with whom they shared the greatest interdependence.

At the firm level, scholars have sought to show the role of resource contingencies as an important predictor of a firm's proclivity to enter alliances. Eisenhardt and Schoonhoven (1996), for instance, found that firms in vulnerable strategic positions were more likely to enter new alliances. Mitchell and Singh (1992) explored the role of incumbency in guiding alliance behavior in emerging technological subfields. Similarly, other scholars have looked at

firms' attributes such as size, age, and financial resources as important predictors of their propensities to enter strategic alliances with one other (Barley,
Freeman, and Hybels 1992; Kogut, Shan, and Walker 1992; Burgers, Hill, and
Kim 1993). A rich literature on the formation of relations among social service
agencies that developed in the 1960s and 1970s also supported this perspective
(for a review, see Galaskiewicz 1985*a*). This research built on the original open
systems model of resource procurement but added an exchange perspective
that suggested that organizations enter partnerships when they perceive critical strategic interdependence with other organizations in their environments
(e.g. Levine and White 1961; Aiken and Hage 1968; Schermerhorn 1975;
Whetten 1977). Richardson (1972), in a theoretical economic account, also
proposed that the necessity for complementary resources is a key driver of
interorganizational cooperation. Applied to the dyadic context, these arguments suggest that firms seek ties with partners who can help them manage
such strategic interdependencies (Litwak and Hylton 1962; Paulson 1976;
Schmidt and Kochan 1977).

Additional research efforts based on resource dependence perspectives have
been at the interindustry level: researchers have tested the role of strategic
interdependence empirically by predicting the number of alliances formed
across industries (Pfeffer and Nowak 1976; Duncan 1982). These studies have
revealed distinct patterns, such as densely linked cliques, and have tried to
explain these patterns using principles of strategic interdependence. Shan
and Hamilton (1991), for instance, described how country-specific resource
advantages within the biotechnology sector have guided Japanese firms'
choices of partners for specific kinds of alliances. Along the same lines, Nohria
and Garcia-Pont (1991) documented how the specific strategic capabilities of
automotive firms have moderated the pattern of alliances among them. This
research suggests a baseline hypothesis that firms are driven to enter alliances
by critical strategic interdependence.

Hypothesis 1: Two firms with high strategic interdependence are more likely to form
an alliance than are other, noninterdependent firms.

ALLIANCE FORMATION AND NETWORK RESOURCES

Although interdependence-based perspectives provide insights into tie formation between firms, they may not adequately account for alliance formation.
For example, not all possible opportunities for sharing interdependence across
firms actually materialize as alliances. An account of alliance formation that
focuses only on interdependence does not examine how firms learn about
new alliance opportunities and overcome the obstacles to such partnerships.
Implicit in such accounts is the assumption that firms exist in an atomistic

system in which information is freely available and equally accessible to all, and opportunities for alliances are exogenously presented.

As highlighted earlier, contrary to the view presented above, there is considerable perceived uncertainty surrounding the formation of new alliances by firms. This uncertainty stems from two main sources. First, organizations have difficulty obtaining information about the competencies and needs of potential partners. This knowledge is essential to assess the potential value of an alliance. An organization aware of the competencies and needs of a potential partner is in a better position to assess whether the alliance can simultaneously serve both its own needs and those of its partners. Yet organizational needs and capabilities are multifaceted and ambiguous. Accurate information on needs and capabilities of other organizations may be difficult to obtain before an alliance is initiated. In most cases, it may require access to confidential information that would not be revealed outside an established partnership. This paucity of information is even more marked between firms from different geographic regions.

The second source of uncertainty that affects strategic alliances is the scarcity of information about the reliability of the potential partners, whose behavior is a key factor in the success of an alliance (Gulati 1995a, 1995b). Such behavioral uncertainty is intrinsic to voluntary cooperation; indeed, it plays a central role in Coase's theory ([1937] 1952) of the firm and in the transaction cost perspective (Williamson 1985). Organizations entering alliances face considerable moral hazard concerns because of the unpredictability of the behavior of partners and the likely costs of opportunistic behavior by a partner (Kogut 1988a, 1988b; Hamel, Doz, and Prahalad 1989). A partner organization may either free ride by limiting its contributions to an alliance or may simply behave opportunistically, taking advantage of the close relationship to use resources or information in ways that may damage its partner's interests. In addition, rapid and unpredictable changes in the environment may lead to changes in an organization's needs and its orientation toward ongoing partnerships (MacIntyre 1981).

The paucity of reliable information about the capabilities, needs, and behavior of potential partners creates a significant informational hurdle for organizations considering strategic alliances. Yet the explosive growth of strategic alliances suggests that organizations are able to overcome such hurdles with frequency. How do they do it? Are there systematic patterns in the formation of alliances? Are these driven by the firm's social contexts? And what consequences does the behavior of partners have for the social context in which new strategic alliances take place?

I propose here that by channeling information about the availability of new opportunities and the reliability of potential partners, network resources resulting from a firm's network of prior alliances can be a powerful catalyst in shaping not only the proclivity of a firm to enter into new alliances—as I showed in the last chapter—but also with whom a focal firm partners. The information shared in such networks guides alliance formation in two main ways. First, networks make potential partners aware of each other's existence, needs, capabilities, and alliance requirements, and thus reduce search costs. Without such information, an alliance between two firms is less likely (Van de Ven 1976).

Second, network resources can mitigate moral hazards by providing information to firms about potential partners that can diminish the risks of alliances and significantly influence the formation of new alliances and the firm's choice of partners. As discussed in the previous chapters, interorganizational networks create valuable network resources that provide information about not only the availability of potential partners but also their reliability. This can happen through both proximate and more distant network ties. For instance, at the more proximate level, when two firms have common third partners, either party's damaging behavior will likely be reported to the common partner, and the reputational consequences of this information-sharing can serve as an effective deterrent (Kreps 1990; Raub and Weesie 1990; Portes and Sensenbrenner 1993; Burt and Knez 1995). Thus, because network resources not only provide information but also create reputational circuits, they are likely to promote greater awareness and confidence among potential partners, which in turn is likely to lead to more ties between them.

A broader view of the influence of network resources suggests that the reputation and visibility of an organization among its peers is strongly influenced by its status. The greater an organization's status, the more it has access to a variety of sources of knowledge, and the richer is its collaborative experience, both of which make it an attractive partner. In this instance, as in many others, the status of individual firms is intertwined with the network resources available to them (Podolny 1994). The signaling properties of status are particularly important network resources in uncertain environments, where the attractiveness of a potential partner can be gauged primarily from such indicators, which in turn depend on the organizations (or types of organizations) already tied to this partner (Podolny 1994). This phenomenon has important behavioral consequences: if the status of the partners firms choose enhances their own attractiveness, organizations will tend to seek high-status partners.

Figures 3.1 and 3.2 depict two different theoretical explanations for firm action: (a) the atomistic, strategic interdependence view and (b) a social structural view. In Figure 3.1, information is depicted as freely available and equally accessible to all actors. Firms in such a context are rational actors aware of the strategic interdependencies they face and thus systematically identify partners through whom they can resolve those interdependencies. By focusing exclusively on strategic interdependencies as drivers of alliances, however, this perspective ignores factors that may lead to the availability of alliance opportunities in the first place.

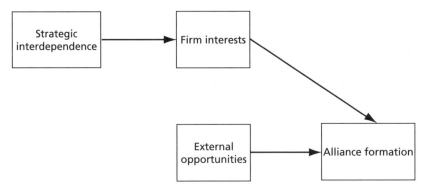

Figure 3.1. Strategic interdependence theory of alliance formation

In contrast, the social structural model (Figure 3.2) points to the important role of social networks in guiding firm action through the exchange of information about the availability, reliability, and specific capabilities of current and potential partners. That social networks are conduits of valuable information has been observed in a variety of contexts, ranging from interpersonal ties, which can relay employment information (Granovetter 1973), to interlocking directorates, which are channels of information on organizational practices (for a review of the literature on interlocks, see Mizruchi 1996). One theme throughout this body of research is that the social networks of ties in which actors are embedded shape the flow of information between them (e.g. Granovetter 1985, 1992; Emirbayer and Goodwin 1994). Differential access to information in turn moderates the behavior of actors. A similar dynamic is proposed here, in which a network of prior alliances shapes the likelihood

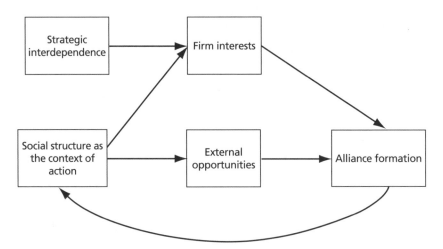

Figure 3.2. Social structural theory of alliance formation (adapted from Burt 1982)

that participating firms will enter future alliances. I discuss the effects of proximate and more distant components of networks and the network resources they generate in greater detail below, labeling them relational and structural embeddedness, respectively.

The feedback loop from action to social structure in Figure 3.2 indicates the dynamic and iterative relationship of these two factors over time in the current context: new alliances alter the social structure that influenced their creation. This feedback makes the ontological status of the emergent alliance network quite ambiguous and precludes conceptualizing it as either strategy or structure. Most likely, it involves both. I provide a more detailed account of this dynamic structure at the end of this chapter, when I discuss a follow-up study.

Given this dynamic interplay between firm action and its social network, network resources can be considered resident within a firm but also within ties it has with others based on past interactions. At the firm level, a firm possesses network resources that arise from the sum total of ties it has with others and from its placement in the overall network. At the dyad level, those network resources are resident in ties with specific others resulting from intimate interaction with these others (Dyer and Singh 1998).

Two distinct components of network resources are relevant to this discussion: the relational component, made up of the direct relationships within which a firm is embedded, and the structural component, which encompasses the overall social network within which firms exist (Granovetter 1992). The relational component of social structure provides direct, experience-based knowledge about current and prior alliance partners; the structural component provides indirect knowledge about potential partners that firms obtain from prior partners, from these allies' partners, and so on. Both the relational and structural components of social structure are influential in alliance formation and affect the search costs and moral hazard concerns associated with the formation of alliances.

Relational factors

The relational component of network resources results from closer ties between firms that provide each firm with information about the other. This first-hand information is particularly effective because (a) it is cheap, (b) individual firm members have a cognitive bias toward trusting first-hand information, (c) partnering organizations have an economic incentive to be honest and to prevent jeopardizing future ties, and (d) close interfirm ties become suffused with social elements that enhance the likelihood of trustworthy behavior (Granovetter 1985).

By providing access to information, the relational component of network resources serves two important functions, both of which are likely to enhance the possibility of further ties between firms. First, firms with relational connections are likely to have greater understanding of each other's needs and capabilities and are thus more likely than those without such connections to spot new opportunities for an alliance. Second, information about a partner based on prior interactions can reduce the hazards associated with future transactions and thus increase the parties' interest in future ties (Zucker 1986; Kogut 1989; Heide and Miner 1992; Gulati 1995*a*).

As indicated by one manager I interviewed, firm managers often embed their new ties by relying extensively on information from past partners (Gulati 1993):

> Our [past and current alliance partners] are familiar with many of our projects from their very inception and if there is potential for an alliance, we discuss it. Likewise, we learn about many of their product goals very early on and we actively explore alliance opportunities with them.

Such comments reflect the link between past alliances and new partnerships.

Several researchers have written about the evolution of partnerships between firms with prior relational ties. Levinthal and Fichman (1988) described dyadic interorganizational attachments that develop over time as firms accumulate experience through interactions. Granovetter (1973) distinguished strong and weak ties by the frequency of past interaction between actors. Along the same lines, Krackhardt (1992) described trusting relations between actors, which he called 'philos', as the outcome of positive effects of both their current and past interactions.

Scholars have also examined the incentives for firms to engage in exchange relations repeatedly. Cook and Emerson (1978) described a process of 'commitment', in which economic actors develop distinct preferences for engaging in subsequent exchanges with prior partners, a pattern inconsistent with conventional microeconomic visions of individual decision-making in an asocial market comprising many actors. Also, prior research on interorganizational relations among human service agencies discussed 'domain consensus' as an important prelude to new ties (Levine and White 1961; Litwak and Hylton 1962). Domain consensus refers to agreement among participants about the role and scope of ties. Thus, firms with prior alliances are more likely to have domain consensus than are others with more limited partnership experience. Hence, this literature suggests that such firms would also be more likely to form new ties. Along similar lines, Podolny (1994) argued that the greater the market uncertainty, the more likely firms are to engage in repeated market exchange with prior partners.

New ties between prior partners can also result from repetitive momentum—once two firms enter an alliance, they do so repeatedly in the future. Such repetitive behavior by organizations results from the establishment of organizational routines. A vast amount of empirical research supports this notion of repeated action (e.g. Miller and Friesen 1980; Amburgey and Miner 1992; Amburgey, Kelly, and Barnett 1993). In the dyadic context, two firms might develop specific routines for managing their interface, making it easier for them to initiate new alliances with each other (Cyert and March 1963; Nelson and Winter 1982). Furthermore, each organization's top managers could acquire mindsets that not only focus their attention on forming new alliances but also predispose them to making new ties with each other.

The theme across these explanations for repeated interorganizational ties is that prior ties create a strong social connection, which in turn leads to future interactions. From a focal firm's viewpoint, prior cohesive ties with other organizations provide channels through which it and its partner can learn about the competencies and the reliability of the other, making strong past ties a network resource that can have beneficial consequences for the firm in the future. Through a close relationship, the firm may also become aware of new opportunities for cooperation that would be difficult to identify outside of a partnership. Thus, a history of cooperation can be viewed as an important resource as it becomes a unique source of information about the partner's capabilities and reliability and increases the probability of new alliances with a specific prior partner. The following, then, can be hypothesized.

Hypothesis 2a: The higher the number of past alliances between a focal firm and a particular partner, the more likely they are to form new alliances with each other.

The above hypothesis assumes a positive monotonic effect of prior ties and the network resources they generate on alliance formation. This assumption is incompatible with two ideas. First, it conflicts with the notion that the number of possible alliances between two firms is limited, a notion akin to carrying capacity in population ecology (Baum and Oliver 1992). Even when two firms are distinct and share numerous arenas for collaboration, such a limit probably exists—due to finite opportunities for collaboration or one or both partners' fears of overdependence. An additional discrepant notion is that the marginal increment of information provided to firms entering multiple alliances with each other diminishes with each new partnership. These issues suggest that network resources may have diminishing marginal returns and that strategic considerations may place limits on the benefits accruing from network resources. As a result, the growth in network resources resulting from a firm's past ties with a particular partner may be followed by reduced alliance activity between those two firms in the future.

Hypothesis 2b: There is an inverted U-shaped relationship between the number of past alliances a focal firm shares with a particular partner, and the likelihood of their forming new alliances with each other.

Temporal dynamics can also play a role in alliance formation. Temporal elements include the accumulation of prior alliances over time and the amount of time that has passed since the initiation of the last alliance a focal firm entered with a particular partner. Several researchers studying the dynamics of organizational change have suggested that organizations have short memories: they are more likely to engage in activities similar to those of the recent past, but the likelihood of an action diminishes as the time elapsed since the last similar action increases (e.g. Amburgey, Kelly, and Barnett 1993). This view is consistent with the notion that routines drive organization action (Cyert and March 1963); recently applied routines are more salient in driving firm behavior than those utilized in the more distant past. Together, these ideas suggest that network resources of a firm may deplete and thus diminish in influence over time.

Hypothesis 3: The likelihood of an alliance between two firms diminishes as the time elapsed since they last entered an alliance increases.

Structural factors

In many instances, the indirect connections of a focal firm with other firms through common partners can also become an important network resource and in turn mobilize its entry into new alliances. This can occur for the two reasons highlighted earlier: first, the resources resulting from network ties promote awareness and reduce search costs and second, network resources can reduce moral hazard concerns for firms that reside within close proximity in a network. Thus, beyond direct ties, the overall structural context in which a firm is placed can also generate network resources that in turn influence its choice of new alliance partners. The example of the conference hosted by DEC discussed in the introduction illustrates such a dynamic.

As this example suggests, although the role of direct ties in fostering new alliances is intuitively compelling and clearly visible, indirect connections through common partners are also components of network resources that can play an important role in the formation of new alliances. Like that gained through previous direct ties, information gained through third-party ties can also be a valuable resource for a focal firm by serving two purposes. First, by serving as effective referral networks, indirect ties make a focal firm aware (or more aware) of potential partners (Van de Ven 1976). Second, as highlighted by both economists and sociologists, a given firm can leverage common ties as an important basis for enforceable trust (Kreps 1990; Raub and Weesie 1990; Portes and Sensenbrenner 1993; Burt and Knez 1995). The anticipated utility of both a tie with a given partner and those with shared partners motivates good behavior. Each partner's knowledge that the other has much to lose from behaving opportunistically enhances its confidence in the other.

Indirect ties can also influence alliance formation for technological reasons. In sectors such as industrial automation, compatibility between firms across product lines can be extremely beneficial to firms. To ensure compatibility across their product lines, a focal firm may prefer an alliance with another firm with whom they share many common partners. This reasoning is akin to the 'network externalities' argument made by economists, in which considerations of compatibility lead firms to participate in the same or competing networks (Katz and Shapiro 1985).

The simplest form of an indirect tie is the sharing of a third partner. A shared contact of a dyad (i, j) is any firm in direct contact with both firms i and j. A focal firm is likely to have access to more information about an indirectly tied firm (and vice versa) than about a firm with no such connection, and the larger the number of third partners the focal firm shares with another firm, the more information these two firms are likely to have about each other.[1]

To isolate the role of the structural from the relational context and their concomitant network resources, I examine whether the presence of common ties enhances the likelihood of an alliance between two firms, in the absence of prior direct ties:

Hypothesis 4: In the absence of prior direct ties between a focal firm and potential partners, the larger the number of their common third-party ties, the more likely they are to form new alliances with each other.

So far, I have assessed the possibility that direct and one-level-removed ties between a focal firm and its potential partners increase the likelihood of their entering an alliance together. In network terms, these are ties of path distance one and two, respectively. Extending the analytical frame of reference from dyads and triads to the whole social system of allied firms raises the question of whether indirect ties beyond the first level also generate network resources that shape the formation of new alliances. In other words, I assess whether the network resources a focal firm possesses result not only from its proximate ties but also from the overarching networks in which it is placed. If firms use the shortest available routes to gain information, which is reasonable to assume given the costs associated with indirect information access and the

---

[1] Having common third-party ties is different from structural equivalence (Burt 1976) because the logic behind each construct and their basis of influence is different (Marsden and Friedkin 1993; Mizruchi 1993). Two actors are structurally equivalent to the extent that they have a similar pattern of relations in a system and are thus equally tied to the same other actors. Two actors who occupy the same structurally equivalent position in their social structure are expected to be of similar status and to develop similar perceptions of the utility of pursuing a given behavior (Burt 1987). Common third-party ties, by contrast, emphasize cohesion—behavioral communication between ego and alter—instead of status-based processes. Operationally, as well, structural equivalence and sharing common third-party ties are not identical. Although by definition two structurally equivalent firms will have a number of common connections, the reverse need not be true. Two firms with many partners in common are not necessarily structurally equivalent. More generally, although the third-party argument focuses on the information benefits and the trust-enhancing properties of common ties, the structural equivalence argument focuses on the status-formation value of similar relational profiles. In the cohesion-based framework here, a firm is likely to enter an alliance with its partner's partner, regardless of the status of the third player.

diminishing value of indirect referrals, the distance between two firms in an alliance network should affect the likelihood of their forming an alliance:

Hypothesis 5: The shorter the path between a focal firm and potential partners in a network of prior alliances, the more likely they are to form new alliances with each other.

SOCIAL STRUCTURE AND STRATEGIC INTERDEPENDENCE

I have postulated additive effects of strategic interdependence and network resources and assumed in the hypotheses that network resources are equally efficacious in influencing alliance formation in both interdependent and non-interdependent dyads. However, alliances may be more likely to result from simultaneous strategic interdependence. Specifically, indirect ties are likely to be more effective in facilitating alliances for interdependent firms than for noninterdependent firms. That is, common ties are likely to amplify the possibility of alliances between interdependent firms more than they would between other firms. I assess the possibility of this relationship for firms with common third-party ties and those with a greater path distance.

Hypothesis 6a: Pairs of interdependent firms with common third-party ties will be more likely to form new alliances with each other than noninterdependent firms with similar third-party ties.

Hypothesis 6b: Pairs of interdependent firms connected through indirect ties of a given path distance will be more likely to form new alliances with each other than non-interdependent firms with indirect connections of similar distances.

Empirical research

METHOD

I tested the above hypotheses with comprehensive cross-sectional time-series data on alliances within the industrial automation, new materials, and auto-motive sectors among American, European, and Japanese firms between 1970 and 1989 (details in Appendix 1, as described in the 'Alliance Formation Data-base'). Although this was a large-sample study, it had qualitative antecedents. Because I was interested in understanding how firms come to enter alliances, I initiated the research with extensive field interviews conducted at eight firms that had numerous alliances. At each firm, I asked ten to twenty managers actively engaged in forming new alliances about some of the considerations underlying their recent alliance decisions.

I examined the factors that affect the likelihood that a pair of firms will enter an alliance at a given time. The unit of analysis was a dyad, with behavior assessed over time. The opportunity set of potential alliances included all feasible dyads in a given year. Given this initial set, I inquired into the factors that increased the likelihood that firms in a particular dyad entered a strategic alliance. I compared the alliance behavior of a panel of dyads during 1981–9, a period that saw unprecedented growth in alliances. This panel design allowed me to draw causal inferences and to assess the dynamics underlying alliance formation. To compute network measures, I constructed adjacency matrices representing the relationships between firms, with separate matrices for each industry for each year. For each matrix, I included all alliance activity among industry panel members up to the prior year (details in Appendix 1 under the section labeled 'Constructing the Social Networks').

Each dyad-year record was dichotomously coded for a dependent variable indicating whether the pair of firms entered an alliance with each other in the given year. No dyad entered more than one alliance in a given year. Each dyad-year record included various attributes of both firms as well as a number of social structural measures based on the cumulative alliance activity within the industry until the end of the year prior to the given year. Details on measures of interdependence can be found in the source article.

To address concerns of heterogeneity, I employed a random-effects panel probit model, developed by Butler and Moffitt (1982), for the statistical analysis. Details are provided in Appendix 2. To ensure the robustness of findings, I compared my results with those obtained with a fixed-effects model (Chamberlain 1985). I employed a random-effects model for two reasons. First, estimates based on fixed-effects models can be biased for panels over short periods (Heckman 1981a, 1981b; Hsiao 1986; Chintagunta, Jain, and Vilcassim 1991). This is not a problem with random-effects models. As all the dyads in my sample were present for only nine years, random effects was clearly the favored approach. Second, fixed-effects models cannot include time-independent covariates, a limitation that would have meant excluding interdependence, the key indicator for hypothesis 1, and the dummy variables for sector. An analysis without these variables would have been severely limited.

Much like dyad-level heterogeneity, there is also the potential for firm-level heterogeneity, which can occur if individual firms in the dyads display differing time-constant propensities to engage in alliances that are not captured by any of the independent variables. This can further compound the problems of interdependence discussed below. To account for such a possibility, I included two control variables for each firm's history (alliance history, firm 1 and alliance history, firm 2). This is an effective method of controlling for firm-level heterogeneity (Heckman and Borjas 1980).

RESULTS

Table 3.1 presents descriptive statistics for and correlations among the variables.

Table 3.2 reports the models explaining alliance formation. The first column reports the effects of the various firm- and dyad-level covariates included as controls. In column 2, I include the measure of strategic interdependence. Columns 3–7 show sequential introduction of the social structural variables that assess the role of prior direct and indirect ties and the time elapsed since the last alliance. Columns 8 and 9 report the results for each of the postulated interaction effects. The results reported in Table 3.2 are based on a risk set that includes only dyads of firms that had both previously entered at least one other alliance. All analyses were also conducted with two additional risk sets: one comprised all possible dyads in each sector regardless of whether dyad members had ever entered an alliance; the other comprised dyads in which at least one member had entered at least one past alliance. Results for these risk sets were the same in terms of directionality and significance.

An assumption underlying such a dyadic analysis is that observations in each year are independent of each other. For the analysis of dyads, this assumption can be a concern because the presence of the same firm in multiple dyads in the same year can lead to interdependence, also known as the common-actor effect (Lincoln 1984). Such interdependence could in turn lead to inefficient parameter estimates and difficulty in rigorously assessing the statistical significance of results (cf. Fernandez 1991).

I treated the problem of interdependence as a sampling issue and considered multiple alliances by a firm in a given year as overrepresented. During model estimation, I employed standard weighting methods and discounted oversampled cases in proportion to their extent of oversampling (Hoem 1985; Barnett 1993). According to such an approach, if a firm entered k alliances in a given year, each record would be given a weight of i/k in the estimation. A complication stemmed from the possibility that both members of a dyad might have entered multiple alliances in a given year, which required weighting for each partner. For the dyadic context, I decided to weight each record by the average of the weights for each partner. The results reported in Table 3.2 include this correction. In Appendix 2, I discuss a number of additional tests undertaken to address concerns of interdependence.

Several conclusions can immediately be drawn from the results in Table 3.2. The positive and significant coefficient of the variable strategic interdependence introduced in column 2 supports hypothesis 1 and indicates that firms

Table 3.1. Descriptive statistics and correlation matrix, all spells

Variable	Mean	SD	Lowest	Highest	1	2	3	4	5	6	7	8	9	10	11	12	13	14	15	16	17	18	19
1. Alliance	.21	.09	0	1	—																		
2. Strategic interdependence	.74	.44	0	1	.01	—																	
3. Repeated ties	.12	.40	0	5	.09	.03	—																
4. Repeated ties × Repeated ties	.17	.63	0	25	.07	.02	.84	—															
5. Duration	.21	.88	0	8	.07	.02	.56	.29	—														
6. Duration × Duration	.82	2.58	0	64	.05	.02	.40	.19	.93	—													
7. Common ties	.56	1.21	0	9	.10	.06	.42	.15	.36	.26	—												
8. Distance	2.18	1.85	0	7	.08	.05	.33	.21	.22	.15	.55	—											
9. Strategic interdependence × Common ties	.47	1.15	0	9	.08	.64	.37	.14	.29	.20	.92	.49	—										
10. Strategic interdependence × Distance	1.77	2.15	0	7	.08	.67	.29	.19	.19	.13	.50	.86	.56	—									
11. Time	5.72	1.98	0	8	.00	-.04	.04	.03	.08	.07	.04	.12	.03	.09	—								
12. Sector 1	.44	.49	0	1	-.01	.10	-.06	-.04	-.02	-.01	-.15	-.20	-.13	-.15	-.02	—							
13. Sector 2	.23	.42	0	1	.00	.07	-.03	-.02	.00	.00	-.09	-.14	-.08	-.10	.05	-.51	—						
14. Total alliances	89.36	49.73	11	168	-.01	.09	-.04	-.03	.01	.01	-.14	-.16	-.13	-.13	.42	.44	-.14	—					
15. Alliance history, firm 1	3.00	2.79	0	16	.11	.09	.19	.13	.18	.13	.30	.28	.28	.27	.25	.04	-.04	.12	—				
16. Alliance history, firm 2	3.13	2.90	0	16	.08	.09	.16	.10	.17	.13	.24	.27	.23	.27	.28	-.07	-.14	.00	-.04	—			
17. Size	.27	.25	.09	.94	-.03	-.45	.06	.05	.05	.04	.08	.07	.02	-.05	.02	.02	.00	.02	.01	-.03	—		
18. Performance	.35	.29	.13	.90	.06	.02	.07	.03	.04	.02	.07	.01	.08	.01	-.01	-.03	.01	.08	-.04	.05	.04	—	
19. Solvency	.24	.19	.07	.88	.17	-.20	.03	.01	.02	.01	.05	.06	.03	.01	.03	.02	.02	.04	.04	-.01	.52	.20	—
20. Liquidity	.64	.22	.02	.80	-.09	-.36	.01	-.04	.03	.02	.03	.02	.03	.02	-.03	.09	-.07	.04	.04	.05	.05	.02	.07

Table 3.2. Random-effects panel probit estimates (time-changing covariates)[a]

Variable	1	2	3	4	5	6	7	8	9
Constant	-3.27* (.06)	-3.55* (.13)	-3.15* (.05)	-3.15* (.05)	-3.16* (.04)	-3.17* (.05)	-3.23* (.05)	-3.22* (.05)	-3.29* (.05)
Strategic interdependence	—	.26* (.08)	.26* (.08)	.30* (.03)	.30* (.03)	.28* (.03)	.25* (.03)	.36* (.03)	.35* (.03)
Repeated ties	—	—	.51* (.01)	.63* (.03)	.22* (.06)	.26* (.06)	.38* (.06)	.28* (.05)	.40* (.05)
Repeated ties × Repeated ties	—	—	—	-.04* (.01)	-.05* (.02)	-.03* (.01)	-.03* (.01)	-.03* (.01)	-.03* (.01)
Duration	—	—	—	—	.31* (.036)	.35* (.036)	.31* (.036)	.37* (.037)	.32* (.035)
Duration × Duration	—	—	—	—	-.04* (.005)	-.04* (.005)	-.04* (.005)	-.04* (.005)	-.04* (.005)
Common ties	—	—	—	—	—	.04* (.007)	.001 (.008)	.22* (.015)	—
Distance	—	—	—	—	—	—	-.07* (.005)	—	-.12* (.008)
Strategic interdependence × Common ties	—	—	—	—	—	—	—	.20* (.015)	—
Strategic interdependence × Distance	—	—	—	—	—	—	—	—	-.06* (.008)
Time	.13* (.018)	.13* (.018)	.11* (.005)	.11* (.005)	.11* (.005)	.11* (.005)	.11* (.005)	.11* (.005)	.11* (.005)
Sector 1	-.68 (.12)	-.07 (.12)	-.04 (.04)	-.05 (.03)	-.03 (.03)	-.003 (.03)	.08 (.036)	-.003 (.03)	.08 (.03)
Sector 2	.21 (.09)	.15 (.09)	.17* (.03)	.17* (.02)	.19* (.03)	.22* (.03)	.32* (.03)	.22* (.03)	.32* (.03)
Total alliances	.001 (.001)	.001 (.001)	.001* (3E-03)	.001* (3E-03)	.001* (3E-03)	.001* (3E-03)	.001* (3E-03)	.001* (3E-03)	.001* (3E-03)
Alliance history, firm 1	.16* (.009)	.15* (.009)	.15* (.004)	.15* (.004)	.15* (.004)	.15* (.004)	.15* (.003)	.15* (.003)	.15* (.003)
Alliance history, firm 2	.13* (.009)	.12* (.009)	.12* (.003)	.12* (.003)	.13* (.003)	.12* (.003)	.12* (.003)	.12* (.003)	.12* (.003)
Size	-.48* (.11)	-.72* (.11)	-.64* (.04)	-.64* (.04)	-.63* (.04)	-.61* (.04)	-.60* (.04)	-.60* (.04)	-.59* (.04)
Performance	8E-03 (.003)	8E-03 (.003)	.001 (.007)	.001 (.006)	.001 (.006)	.001 (.006)	.001 (.006)	.001 (.006)	.001 (.006)
Solvency	.06 (.10)	.04 (.10)	.03 (.04)	.03 (.04)	.001 (.04)	.03 (.04)	.02 (.04)	.03 (.04)	.013 (.04)
Liquidity	-.11 (.13)	-.12 (.13)	-.14* (.04)	-.14* (.04)	-.14* (.04)	-.15* (.04)	-.16* (.04)	-.17* (.04)	-.17* (.04)
Rho	.65* (.02)	.67* (.02)	.69* (.02)	.70* (.02)	.72* (.02)	.72* (.019)	.73* (.018)	.73* (.018)	.74* (.016)
n	7,266	7,266	7,266	7,266	7,266	7,266	7,266	7,266	7,266
Log-likelihood	-955.03	-948.74	-936.59	-935.17	-933.34	-932.16	-925.11	-924.95	-923.40
χ^2	31.97*	33.39*	54.18*	54.57*	59.72*	60.50*	60.70*	61.27*	61.83*

[a] Standard errors in parentheses.

*$p < .01$.

are more likely to seek alliances with partners with whom they share greater interdependence.

The control variables generally have the predicted signs. With dummy variables for each year, I observed no systematic temporal effects, but the linear term for time is positive and significant, suggesting a general increase in alliance propensity over time. The control variable for sector 1 is nonsignificant, while the one for sector 2 becomes significant in later models. This suggests that while there are no intrinsic differences in alliance formation between the new materials and automotive sectors, firms in industrial automation show a higher propensity for alliances than those in automotive. Because this finding does not reveal whether the main effects differ across the three industries, I estimated unrestricted models for each industry. The signs of the coefficients indicated that the postulated directionality and significance of the main effects observed in the pooled sample held up for each sector.

There is also support for the influence of mimetic behavior on alliance formation, as shown by the effects of total alliances formed in the industry in the prior year. This variable is nonsignificant in earlier models but becomes more significant later, suggesting a modest suppresser effect of the new variables added. The variables for each firm's history of alliances suggest that dyads with more experienced members are more likely to form an alliance. As discussed in Appendix 2, these variables also control for firm-level heterogeneity.

The ratios for dyad-member attributes show mixed results. Differences in performance and solvency across the two firms in a dyad did not affect alliance formation, but the negative and significant coefficients for size and liquidity suggest that firms that differ in amount of assets and liquidity are more likely to enter an alliance.

The results shown in columns 3–7 are by and large consistent with the hypothesized main effects of social structure. In column 3, the positive and significant coefficient of repeated ties, which indicates prior alliances between two firms, supports hypothesis 2a and suggests that firms with a history of alliances have a higher propensity to ally with each other repeatedly than do firms with no such history. Addition of the squared term for repeated ties in column 4 suggests there is indeed a diminishing effect: up to about four prior alliances positively influenced current alliance formation; additional alliances after that point were associated with a decline in the likelihood of alliance formation.

Column 5 shows the effects of the time elapsed since a last alliance on current alliance formation, considered in hypothesis 3. I also included here a quadratic term to test for the possibility of nonlinear influence of this variable. According to the linear and quadratic estimates, there is an inverted U-shaped relationship between the time elapsed since a prior alliance and the likelihood of a new alliance. The likelihood of two firms entering an alliance increases during the first 3.8 years (approximately) and then diminishes over time.

The positive and significant coefficient of common ties and the negative coefficient of distance in columns 6 and 7 support hypotheses 4 and 5 and suggest that having common third partners or even indirect connections enhances the probability that two firms will enter an alliance. The positive coefficient of common ties indicates that the larger the number of common third partners shared by two unconnected firms, the more likely they are to enter an alliance. The negative coefficient of distance in column 7 indicates that the more distant two firms are in an alliance network, the less likely they are to seek mutual alliances. In column 7, the variable for the number of common ties becomes nonsignificant when distance is introduced. Because common ties refers to a path distance of two between firms, while distance captures all distances of two or greater, this result is not surprising.

The effects of the interactions of interdependence with common ties and distance are introduced in columns 8 and 9. Hypotheses 6a and 6b predicted that connected firms would enter alliances more frequently if the firms were interdependent to begin with, implying that there would be interactions between interdependence and common ties and between interdependence and distance. The effects of the interaction terms are strong and significant. The coefficient of the interaction in column 8 supports hypothesis 6a, indicating that there is a higher likelihood of alliance formation between interdependent firms if they have numerous third-party connections. The negative and significant coefficient of the interaction in column 9 supports hypothesis 6b and indicates a lower likelihood of alliance formation between interdependent firms that are further apart in an alliance network. Taken together, the significant interaction effects suggest that prior indirect connections are more influential in alliance formation among interdependent dyads than among other dyads.

The random-effects models applied here generate a parameter rho, an indicator of heterogeneity. An estimate close to zero implies little heterogeneity, and all the time dependence in the alliance formation rate can be ascribed to the independent variables included in the models. A significant rho implies heterogeneity. Economists typically treat such heterogeneity as an exogenous factor indicating the personal propensity of a unit (here, the dyad) to engage in the activity characterized by the dependent variable (cf. Black, Moffitt, and Warner 1990). Thus, a significant coefficient here would suggest that observationally identical dyads display different alliance propensities that remain fixed because of permanent differences in their alliance preferences and other unobserved factors. These could include pairs of firms developing specific managerial routines for entering into and managing alliances with each other. Or, in the case of firms not forming alliances, it could indicate that some pairs of firms are separated by insurmountable barriers to their entering an alliance. Given the possibility of multiple and confounding interpretations of heterogeneity (cf. Granovetter 1988), I am cautious about drawing direct inferences from this coefficient. For my purposes, rho primarily indicates that heterogeneity exists and is accounted for in the panel model, and its significant coefficients do indicate that unobserved factors not completely captured by the independent variables are accommodated by the statistical model.

The dynamic evolution of interorganizational networks and the changing role of network resources

A subsequent article titled 'Where Do Interorganizational Networks Come From?' builds on the research reported in this chapter and examines in greater depth the development of the network resulting from cumulative prior alliances (Gulati and Gargiulo 1999). This study is distinctive in its focus on explaining the formation and development of interorganizational networks, an important issue that has received only limited attention in prior research because of the lack of longitudinal network data and because prior research has focused on interorganizational networks that are relatively stable over time. If network resources originating from the network of prior alliances are important in determining which firms enter alliances and with whom they enter alliances, then it is likely that such resources are a key factor in determining how the very alliance networks from which they emanate may evolve. The networks that result from the accumulation of prior alliances are clearly dynamic entities that can transform significantly beyond their original design, and the varying evolutionary paths can have varying consequences.

In this follow-up article with coauthor Martin Gargiulo, I explore in greater depth the development of strategic alliance networks and how the distribution of network resources among actors within them influences the subsequent evolution of this network. We propose that network resources should be viewed not only as resident within firms but also as being embodied in the cumulative network of prior ties in the industry context in which they operate. Thus, network resources can be embodied in the industry network as well when we consider their aggregate level and distribution available to actors within it.

Building on the work cited in this and the previous chapter, this article proposes that as more ties are created in an industry and more internalized information is available about potential partners, organizations are more likely to resort to that network for cues to their future alliance decisions, which are thus more likely to be shaped by this emerging network. In turn, these new alliances engender additional network resources that further increase the informational value of the network, further enhancing its effect on subsequent alliance formation. In this iterative process, new partnerships modify the previous alliance network, which then shapes the formation of future cooperative ties.

Thus, we model the emergence of alliance networks imbued with network resources that can be tapped by participating firms in a dynamic process driven by exogenous interdependencies that prompt organizations to seek cooperation and by endogenous network embeddedness mechanisms that help them determine choice of partner. Our model shows how the entry of firms into alliances can lead to the growing structural differentiation of the industry network as a whole. This progressive differentiation in turn enhances the magnitude of the resources available to firms within the network and shapes their actions. As a result, the effect of a firm's proximate-tie-based network resources on its proclivity to enter alliances and choice of partners is moderated by the extent of differentiation of the overall network as well. Interorganizational networks are therefore the evolutionary products of embedded organizational action in which new alliances are increasingly embedded in the very same network that has shaped the organizational decisions to form those alliances.

To empirically test these claims, this article develops a model that specifies the mechanisms through which the existing alliance network enables organizations to decide with whom to build new alliances and shows how the newly created ties can increase the informational content of the same alliance network, enhancing its potential to shape future partnerships. The results show the emergence of alliance networks and the concomitant availability of network resources as a dynamic process driven by exogenous interdependencies that prompt organizations to seek cooperation and by an endogenous network formation process that influences partner choice. In other words, the model shows how network resources shape behavior by both their presence in a firm's proximate ties and their distribution across all members of the network itself. Such resources provide essential information that significantly influences the formation and evolution of strategic alliance networks. The growing structural differentiation of the network enhances the magnitude of the network resources available to firms within the network and in turn shapes their actions. In this instance, the very actions studied here—formation of alliances—shape the network from which they emerge. The model provides a systematic link between the social structure of an organizational field—understood in network terms—and the behavior of organizations within the field. This link is bidirectional. On one hand, the emerging social structure progressively shapes organizational decisions about whether and with whom to create new ties. On the other hand, this social structure is produced by the (structurally shaped) decisions to establish interorganizational ties. We show that interorganizational networks result not only from exogenous drivers such as interdependence but also from an endogenous evolutionary dynamic triggered by the very way in which organizations select potential partners. In this model, actors react to conditions they have helped create and in the process reproduce and change those very conditions.

Conclusion

The primary study in this chapter provides an important bridge between network and resource dependence theorists studying interorganizational ties and demonstrates the role of network resources in shaping not only the proclivity of a firm to enter into new alliances (Chapter 2) but also its choice of partners. More broadly, this chapter also contributes to the growing literature on interorganizational networks. Network theorists have established the importance of social structure in guiding firm behavior but have paid less attention to the origin and perpetuation of interorganizational relations. Resource dependence theorists have examined the critical contingencies guiding the creation of new ties but have assumed that those ties are created in a social vacuum. They admit that significant unexplained variance remains in resource dependence accounts of tie formation and that additional explanations for this variance should be explored (e.g. Pfeffer 1987). This study unites and extends these two perspectives, exploring the role of both critical contingencies and social structural factors in guiding the formation of interfirm ties.

By focusing on the dyad as the unit of analysis, this study provides empirical support for the importance of network resource and strategic interdependence factors in bringing firms together as alliance partners. It demonstrates that the social context resulting from cumulative prior partnerships influences alliance formation between firms. It also shows that interorganizational networks are valuable conduits for information about specific organizational practices and that they provide an important impetus for guiding the choice of partners.

The results of this empirical study suggest that of all the possible dyads of focal firms and potential partners that could enter alliances over a ten-year period, those with many prior direct ties, or with more third-party ties in common, or with greater proximity in the network of prior alliances were more likely to result in alliances. Simply stated, this study documents the role of network resources in bringing firms together as alliance partners. Clearly, network resources resulting from cumulative prior alliances influence alliance formation between firms by providing information about specific organizations' needs, resources, capabilities, and behavior, and thereby guide firms in their choice of alliance partners.

The observed effects of network resources result from both the direct and indirect ties firms have. Previously allied firms are likely to engage in further alliances. This finding for the role of direct previous ties supports Larson's observation (1992) (from an inductive field study) that firms entered alliances with each other repeatedly. An important catalyst for repeated alliances is the availability of information to each partner. Significant information about another firm's reliability as a partner, its operations, and possible alliance opportunities becomes available only after an alliance is in place. Hence, over time a firm acquires more information and builds greater confidence in its partners, increasing the likelihood of a new alliance.

Although prior ties between a focal firm and its partners constitute a form of network resources that leads to new alliances, the results of this study suggest that beyond a certain point, additional alliances between firms diminish the likelihood of future alliances. This confirms the notion of carrying capacity, implying that there are limits to the number of alliances two firms can sustain (Baum and Oliver 1992). Fears of overdependence may also truncate the number of ties two firms will seek. Additionally, at some point the informational benefits of a durable shared history reach a peak as alliances run their life courses.

The study also shows that the time elapsed since a previous alliance influences new alliance formation, and the effect is inverse and U-shaped. A repetitive-momentum argument would suggest that as the duration since the last alliance increases, the likelihood of the organization engaging in the initial action again diminishes (Amburgey, Kelly, and Barnett 1993). In the dyadic context, however, for the first several years after an alliance forms, the firms' enhanced mutual awareness actually increases the likelihood of their forming another alliance. Over time, this effect gives way to diminishing information as past alliances end, and the momentum for forming new alliances declines.

Ultimately, the study provides evidence of the impact of a firm's network resources on its proclivity for new alliances and choice of specific partners. I demonstrate that the informational benefits of indirect ties between a focal firm and its possible partners, both one-level-removed ties of path distance two and more distant ties, affect the likelihood of their entering a new alliance. A focal firm is more likely to enter into an alliance with previously unconnected firms if they have common partners. Furthermore, the greater the distance between a focal firm and a potential partner in a social network of prior alliances, the less likely they are to ally. These findings suggest that a firm's social network of indirect ties is an important constituent element of the network resources it possesses and serves as an effective referral mechanism for bringing it together with potential alliance partners. The results also indicate that dense colocation between a focal firm and potential partners in an alliance network enhances mutual confidence as firms become aware of the possible negative reputational consequences of their own or others' opportunistic behavior.

The results also suggest the relevance of dyadic interdependence in guiding alliance formation, confirming prior research on ties between human services agencies (Litwak and Hylton 1962; Hage and Aiken 1967; Schermerhorn 1975; Paulson 1976; Schmidt and Kochan 1977; Whetten 1977) and suggesting that focal firms are more likely to seek out as alliance partners those with whom they share interdependence. The role of interdependence is further confirmed by several financial attributes of focal firms entering alliances. The results suggest that firms tend to seek out partners who differ from them in size. Not only does the effect of size differences highlight the role of interdependence, but it is also consistent with ecologists' notion of size-localized competition, according to which firms compete most intensely with others of similar size (cf. Baum and Mezias 1992; Wholey, Christianson, and Sanchez 1992). In addition, the relative liquidities of firms affect their decision to enter an alliance. The greater the difference in liquidity, the more likely they are to enter an alliance. Differences in performance and solvency had no influence on alliance formation.

Finally, the interaction results suggest interesting dynamics between interdependence, network resources, and alliance formation, implying that strategic interdependence and social structural explanations for alliance formation are not mutually exclusive and could simultaneously affect alliance formation. Common third-party ties more effectively influence alliance formation in interdependent dyads than in others. Similarly, distance has a negative effect on the likelihood of an alliance among interdependent dyads. Consequently, this study provides an important bridge between network and resource dependence theorists studying interorganizational ties. Network theorists have focused on establishing the importance of social structure in guiding firm behavior but have paid less attention to the origin and perpetuation of interorganizational relations. Resource dependence theorists have looked at the critical contingencies guiding the creation of new ties but have assumed that those ties are created in a social vacuum. They admit that significant unexplained variance remains in resource dependence accounts of tie formation and that additional explanations for this variance should be explored (e.g. Pfeffer 1987). This study unites these two perspectives, exploring the role of both critical contingencies and social structural factors in guiding the formation of interfirm ties.

The social structural context studied here is unique in that it is dynamic and closely linked to firm action. Thus, the formation of ties in a given year modifies for subsequent years the very social structure that stimulates it. Observed over time, the dynamics between social structure and alliance formation suggest a dialectic of mutual influence between action and social structure. This vividly illustrates Giddens's notion (1984) of structuration in the interorganizational context and suggests that within the studied organizational fields there is an emergent social structure that influences firms' behavior. Or, as White (1992) suggests, within industry disciplines networks establish identities of their own as they grow and expand.

From a managerial standpoint, this research indicates that history matters when firms make alliance decisions. In a seminal book, Penrose (1959) argued that present investment decisions put a firm on an irreversible path-dependent trajectory of future development. Penrose's concern was the irreversibility of firms' financial and technological resource outlays. Their alliance choices appear to have similar ramifications: today's choice of an alliance partner shapes the availability of future network resources that in turn affect tomorrow's alliance choices. This historical effect is further complicated by the fact that the underlying social network is modified by the prior alliance decisions of other firms. Hence, both a firm's own past alliances and those of other firms in a network interact to shape the network resources available to the firm, which influence its future actions. Thus, in Penrose's terms, the path dependence of alliance decisions is not based only on economic resources, but is also influenced by network resources. Thus, neither traditional resource-based arguments nor network-resource-based ideas should dominate the discussion of alliances—in the final analysis, explanations for firm behavior must encompass both.

4 The contingent role of network resources emanating from board interlocks in alliance formation

While the last two chapters focused on prior alliance networks as a source of network resources, this chapter considers how additional interorganizational networks may also provide network resources that in turn influence the formation of strategic alliances by selectively channeling information and resultant opportunities to organizations. This additional source of network resources may not only shape the alliance behavior of firms but also beget more network resources by increasing firms' proclivities for alliances. One such source is the network of board interlocks, whose influence on firm behavior has been considered in a wide variety of settings, none of which include the formation of alliances. Director boards are unique formal mechanisms that create network resources by providing an opportunity for corporation leaders to exchange information and observe the leadership practices and style of their peers, along with the consequences of those practices. Thus, board ties to other firms have a strong influence over corporate policy and strategy decisions. Because of this influence, the board interlock network can be considered an important element of network resources and an ideal arena in which to develop and test the role of such resources in shaping firm behavior.

By considering the possibility that an interorganizational network arising from board interlocks may contribute to a firm's network resources and in turn shape the formation of new alliances, this chapter suggests the possibility that network resources may result from a complex multilevel interweaving of different types of interorganizational ties with bidirectional influence on one another. In this instance, one set of ties that contribute to a firm's network resources can shape the creation of another set of ties that in turn can influence

This chapter is adapted from 'Cooperative or Controlling? The Effects of CEO–Board Relations and the Content of Interlocks on the Formation of Joint Ventures' by Ranjay Gulati and James D. Westphal published in *Administrative Science Quarterly* © 1999, (44/3): 473–506, by permission of Johnson Graduate School of Management, Cornell University.

the network resources of those firms. Thus, network resources beget more network resources. Some of these ideas are assessed here by considering the role of one form of ties (board interlocks) in the creation of another (strategic alliances), while others are posed as important directions for future research.

In assessing the interplay among network resources here, this chapter also extends prior research by taking seriously the importance of the content of network ties in shaping the quality and quantity of network resources available to firms and their impact on firm behavior. Content here implies the specific nature of the relationship and behavioral processes underlying a connection between two actors. Although research in the governance literature suggests that relationships between top managers on corporate boards may be characterized by independence and distrust in some cases (Westphal 1999), in the interlock literature all ties are generally treated as equally positive connections that facilitate social cohesion and the exchange of information between firms. This treatment ignores potential heterogeneity among interlocks and the extent to which they create network resources that channel information and engender trusting relations among board members. This issue is also important for broader research on the embeddedness of ties, in that the presence of ties alone does not explain behavior and thus specifying the composition and content of ties is imperative.

This chapter explores how board interlocks serve as network resources that can affect alliance formation. It isolates these board interlock effects while controlling for the resources that may be generated by a firm's prior alliance ties. It also provides a more comprehensive and nuanced account of the constituent elements of network resources by specifically examining the influence of heterogeneous social processes that underlie interlock ties—and the moderating effects of indirect network ties—on the creation of strategic alliances. Some ties may promote the creation of new alliances, while others could actually reduce their likelihood, depending on the behavioral content of the tie. As a result, there may be both advantages and disadvantages to embeddedness in interorganizational relationships.

While the previous chapters focused on how prior alliance networks create resources that provide valuable information to potential partners about each other's reliability, capabilities, and needs, this chapter examines the role of alternative networks in creating network resources and guiding the formation of new alliances.[1] Specifically, this chapter considers how a focal firm's network resources result from both its direct and indirect board interlocks

---

[1] This chapter examines the role of board interlocks, focusing on a subset of alliances known as joint ventures, which entail the creation of a separate legal entity in which the parent firms take equity. In this chapter, I use the term 'alliance' to refer specifically to joint ventures. Such alliances typically entail a considerable outlay of resources and create enduring and irreversible commitments between partners, which can make the influence of the board interlock network on their formation even more important.

and the content of those ties, and how these resources in turn influence the firm's choice of future partners. Studying the effects of direct and indirect ties allows me to develop a more nuanced and comprehensive account of the constituent elements of network resources. While the focus of this study is on the behavior of pairs of firms (dyads), it is important again to clarify that network resources, while ultimately resident in individual firms, can be understood by considering the connections those firms build with specific other firms. Thus, a relationship with another firm is an important element of a firm's network resources.

Theory and hypotheses

CONTENT OF INTERLOCK TIES AND EFFECTS ON ALLIANCES

Empirical studies of the consequences of interlocking directorates have typically viewed interlock ties in broad terms as a mechanism for resolving uncertainty for top management decision-makers (Galaskiewicz 1985a). In doing so, scholars have emphasized the value of direct communication between managers and directors in reducing uncertainty about the implications of adopting specific business practices. From this perspective, information from fellow corporate leaders is particularly influential because it comes from a trusted source (Davis 1991; Haunschild 1993). Along the same lines, it is also likely that interlock ties can help resolve uncertainty for top management decision-makers regarding the implications of forming strategic alliances— in terms of the adoption of strategic alliances in general and the choice of a specific partner. While prior research has typically described interlocks as conduits of information about administrative innovations, it is reasonable to expect that board members also communicate information about their respective parent organizations. One way this can influence a firm's choice of alliance partners is by reducing uncertainty regarding the motives and capabilities of these organizations. Board interlocks can also provide information in a timely manner, which can be important when a firm seeking attractive alliance partners must approach them at the right juncture and pre-empt their seeking alliances elsewhere.

By serving as conduits for valuable and timely information, then, board interlock ties may be viewed as important constituent elements of network resources for firms that allow them enhanced access to opportunities. This suggests an initial, baseline hypothesis on the effect of interlock ties on alliance formation.

Hypothesis 1: An interlock tie between two firms will increase the likelihood of subsequent alliance formation between them.

INDEPENDENT BOARD CONTROL AND ALLIANCES

The discussion thus far has assumed that interlock ties involve positive social contact between top managers and outside directors of the focal firm. However, as interlock researchers have generally recognized, there is considerable variation in the nature of management–board relationships, although the consequences of this heterogeneity have yet to be systematically examined (Herman 1981; Johnson, Hoskisson, and Hitt 1993; Mizruchi 1996). The nature of management–board relationships can range from positive and relatively cohesive to negative and independent, with very different consequences for the likelihood of venture formation. As a result, not all interorganizational ties can be considered positive and reinforcing elements of network resources.

According to agency perspectives, while top managers are responsible for ongoing decision management, the board of directors is responsible for decision control, which involves monitoring and evaluating management decision-making and performance (Fama and Jensen 1983). In effect, the board is viewed as an efficient control device that can help align management decision-making with shareholder interest (Beatty and Zajac 1994). For instance, to the extent that managerial preferences regarding executive compensation, corporate diversification, or other strategy and policy issues conflict with the interests of shareholders, boards can intervene to protect shareholders' interests (Hermalin and Weisbach 1988; Hill and Snell 1988). Moreover, from this perspective outside directors in particular are critical to the board's ability to exercise control because, as nonemployee directors, they are formally independent of management and thus better able to evaluate management decisions and actions objectively on behalf of the shareholders.

In prior years, this agency model of the relationship between the CEO and the board was dismissed as an anomaly. Organization theorists have typically suggested that while outside directors are in a position to exercise independent control over management, various behavioral factors effectively limit the social independence of outsiders, diminishing their ability and willingness to exert control. For instance, because CEOs traditionally dictate the selection of new directors, several authors have suggested that chief executives can appoint personal friends or other individuals with whom they have preexisting social ties (e.g. Finkelstein and Hambrick 1988; Wade, O'Reilly, and Chandratat 1990; Cannella and Lubatkin 1993). Such ties are thought to inhibit the board's willingness to contradict management's preferences on behalf of shareholders. Moreover, organization theorists have long maintained that generalized norms of support among managerial elites enforce a passive role for outside directors in strategic decision-making (e.g. Herman 1981; Whisler 1984). From this perspective, boards have little potential to serve as independent agents of control and, in line with the assumptions of interlock theorists, management–board ties are characterized by social cohesion.

However, recent research on boards of directors has provided some evidence that widespread norms about the role of corporate boards may be changing. Useem (1993) and Westphal and Zajac (1997) have documented changes in board structure, composition, and executive compensation over the past fifteen years. These suggest a trend toward increased board control over management at large corporations. This shift may have originated as a response to external criticism from institutional investors and other stakeholders and the threat of lawsuits over perceived negligence in protecting shareholder interest (Kesner and Johnson 1990; Davis and Thompson 1994). External constituents have demanded evidence that boards are willing to challenge management's decisions on their behalf, perhaps motivated in part by recent public scandals such as those at Enron, Tyco, and NYSE, and backed by the passage of the Sarbanes-Oxley Act. In this new environment, boards have been told to expand the search for new directors beyond the CEO's close circle of friends and to alter board structure and processes in ways that limit the CEO's direct control over board meetings (Kaplan and Harrison 1993; Daily 1996). In effect, boards have been pressured to adopt a role characterized by more independent monitoring and control over management. Nevertheless, there remains considerable variance across boards in the extent to which they have adopted this orientation.

Given our understanding of board ties as constituent elements of network resources that impact alliance behavior, there are several possible effects of independent board control on the prospects of alliance formation between the focal firm and those of its manager-directors. On one level, a CEO–board relationship characterized by monitoring and control simply entails lower cohesion, or the absence of a strong tie, which limits the amount of network resources that a focal firm has in that relationship. On another level, independent board control over management may actually produce a negative relationship between the CEO and the board, characterized by a lack of mutual understanding and distrust, leading to the depletion of the network resources woven into that relationship. When benevolence and support toward the CEO is replaced with independent control over the CEO, leaders of the firm can divide into separate groups: decision managers (i.e. the CEO and other top managers) and decision controllers (i.e. outside directors) (Fama and Jensen 1983). The literature on intergroup relations has provided consistent evidence that dividing a single group of individuals into two or more separate groups has a variety of negative effects on relations between the groups (Brewer and Miller 1996). Empirical studies have demonstrated that when individuals are divided into separate groups, attitudes about out-group members become significantly more negative (Gaertner et al. 1989; Messick and Mackie 1989). Out-group categorization, which in the case of interlocks occurs when CEOs view outside directors as controllers rather than supporters or fellow managers, can promote distrust with respect to both the capabilities of the other party (task-based trust) and the fear that they might limit their contributions to the relationship (relational trust) (Creed and Miles 1996). This out-group bias occurs even when the basis for group categorization is arbitrary or minimal (Brewer 1979). Moreover, Kramer (1994, 1996: 224) and others (Fenigstein and Vanable 1992) have found evidence that 'a pattern of exaggerated mistrust' may develop when individuals are subjected to 'evaluative scrutiny' or control by out-group members.

In the CEO–board context, then, distrust can be expected to arise when outside directors assert themselves as an independent group of controllers accountable to shareholders rather than to management. Whereas outside directors on passive and supportive boards are effectively insiders with regard to their orientation toward management, they adopt the perspective of an independent outsider on controlling boards. As a result, the perception of a division between insiders and outsiders can reinforce a generalized sense of distrust across groups and lead to escalating cycles of distrust when outgroup members exercise control (Sitkin and Stickel 1996). This intergroup bias would lead each party of the management–board relationship to view members of the other group as less trustworthy in both professional and personal terms, reducing interest in various forms of cooperation.

Intergroup bias resulting from independent board control (as opposed to passive support) can affect network resources by diminishing both task-based and relational trust. Indeed, one might expect that when directors have asserted themselves as an independent group responsible for controlling managers rather than supporting them, CEOs may view them as less trustworthy alliance partners. Board independence can also prevent top managers and manager-directors from becoming familiar with each other's management and decision-making styles and developing a professional rapport. Moreover, given that distrust toward an independent, controlling group is a basic and powerful human response (Fenigstein and Vanable 1992; Kramer 1994, 1996), independent board control may have a particularly strong negative effect on alliance formation between top managers and manager-directors. In such situations, we would expect that board ties actually deplete network resources in those ties rather than reinforcing it.[2] As a result, it is likely that:

Hypothesis 2: The greater the board's control over the CEO, the lower the likelihood of subsequent alliance formation between the focal firm and outside directors' home companies.

---

[2] This study is not suggesting that independent board control, by depleting network resources, is necessarily bad for organizations as a whole. As recent events suggest, having such control may be beneficial to shareholders. We are simply focusing here on the ability of such interlocks to generate network resources by creating rich conduits of information that may in turn propagate the formation of new alliances between those firms. Hence, we are exploring the potential for controlling boards to create environments that do not provide as rich an informational context as those of cooperative boards. Future research should explore such trade-offs in further detail.

CEO–BOARD COOPERATION AND ALLIANCES

While empirical research on boards has typically assumed that board involvement in corporate affairs entails independent monitoring and control by outside directors (Johnson, Hoskisson, and Hitt 1993), the larger literature on boards suggests another form of involvement. In his classic qualitative study, Mace (1971: 179) concluded that while boards often do not challenge management's final decisions, they may nevertheless provide advice and counsel to management on strategic issues during the decision-making process. Pfeffer and Salancik (1978: 170) also considered the provision of advice and counsel a different form of board administration than board control (see also Mintzberg 1983). In a large-sample empirical study, Westphal (1999) found support for this general classification—factor analysis showed that CEO–board relationships could be classified into three categories: independent monitoring and control, close cooperation (i.e. advice and counsel), or inaction. Moreover, qualitative and survey evidence suggests that advice and counsel is typically provided at the CEO's request (Lorsch and MacIver 1989; Demb and Neubauer 1992). Thus, rather than remaining independent of top managers to permit objective monitoring and evaluation of managerial decision-making, some boards enter closer working relationships with CEOs by providing advice and counsel at the CEO's request. In such cases, CEOs direct a cooperative form of board involvement in which boards work closely with them to govern the firm, rather than at a distance in a principal–agent relationship.

Cooperative CEO–board relationships may influence the quality of information transmitted through those ties and hence affect the magnitude of network resources embodied in those ties, which can impact alliance formation between the focal firm and manager-directors' home companies in several ways. One way in which CEO–board cooperation should enhance network resources is by facilitating trust between top managers and outside directors by fostering social interaction. Simmel's theory (1964) of trust emphasized how the mere occurrence of social interaction builds trust or the expectation of faithfulness, and other theorists have suggested that more frequent interaction increases trust by enhancing mutual affect and familiarity (Laumann, Galaskiewicz, and Marsden 1978; Gulati 1995a; Creed and Miles 1996). Accordingly, the heightened social interaction resulting from greater CEO–board cooperation (e.g. advice seeking) should reinforce relational trust between CEOs and outside directors.

The network resources created through cooperative interactions in CEO–board relationships and the extent of trust between managers can also be illuminated by considering some of the evidence from research on intergroup relations. According to this literature, cooperative interactions between group members make common goals more salient, which builds mutual trust and respect (Gaertner et al. 1990, 1999). Thus, while independent board control may reduce trust by effectively splitting top managers and outside directors into separate groups, CEOs seeking advice from the board should enhance trust by drawing outside directors into a collective decision-making team. In effect, just as negative affect and distrust toward an independent, controlling group is a basic and powerful human response, cooperation between group members can engender in-group biases that lead to positive affect and higher, even excessive levels of trust between individuals (Fenigstein 1979; Kramer 1996). As a result, in those instances characterized by cooperative interactions, we would expect that the presence of ties reinforces network resources embodied in those ties. Given the importance of intermanagement trust in alliance formation, cooperative CEO–board relationships and the network resources resulting from them should promote alliances between a focal firm and those of outside directors by enhancing confidence in each other's reliability and managerial capability and lowering the perceived risk of opportunism.

Hypothesis 3: The greater the cooperation between the CEO and the board, the higher the likelihood of subsequent alliance formation between the focal firm and outside directors' home companies.

THE ROLE OF INDIRECT TIES

While little empirical research has examined how broader social structural factors moderate the effects of dyadic interlock ties and the resultant network resources between firms, qualitative evidence suggests that managers may have access to indirect information about directors through managers' appointments on other boards (Useem 1984). An indirect or third-party tie could be an important source of network resources that provides top managers with information about outside directors who sit on their boards. For example, CEO A is exposed to second-hand information about outside director B on his or her board when A has a common appointment on another board with director C, who sits on B's board. These indirect ties are particularly relevant in light of recent evidence suggesting that third-party ties can affect the level of trust between individuals or organizations (e.g. Raub and Weesie 1990; Burt and Knez 1995; Gulati 1995b; Gulati and Gargiulo 1999).

It is typically assumed that third-party ties will enhance trust between parties in a relationship by increasing the reputational costs of noncooperative behavior (Van de Ven 1976). For instance, if A is cheated by relationship partner B, and A has third-party ties to B through C, A can impose reputational costs on B by spreading the word to C that B cannot be trusted. Given this threat, A can trust B not to defect from cooperative exchange (Kreps 1990). The claim that third-party ties enforce cooperation through reputational effects assumes that noncooperative behavior is illegitimate or nonnormative, like cheating a friend (Granovetter 1992). In many cases, however, noncooperative behavior involving competition or control is not normatively proscribed in the larger social structure, or the related norms are ambiguous. As several authors have noted, norms governing CEO–board relationships have become uncertain: it is not clear whether independent board control is any more normative or legitimate than CEO–board cooperation (Lorsch and MacIver 1989; Useem 1993). Accordingly, noncooperative behavior, such as exercising independent control, does not necessarily have negative reputational consequences for the participants. Thus, third-party ties between a CEO and his or her board members may not necessarily reduce the likelihood of noncooperative behavior in CEO–board relationships and hence fail to enhance network resources.

While traditional perspectives on indirect network ties may not apply to board interlocks, recent research on third-party ties suggests a more germane perspective. Burt and Knez (1995, 1996) have extended existing theories on how social structure affects trust by proposing that third-party ties amplify existing trust or distrust in professional relationships (see also Labianca, Brass, and Gray 1998). They showed empirically that when the immediate relationship between managers tends to foster trust, third-party ties further enhance this trust. At the same time, third-party ties amplify any distrust already in the relationship. Thus, they concluded that third-party ties influence the intensity but not the direction of trust in managerial relationships. In developing their theory, Burt and Knez suggested that managers exchange information about third-party ties with other managers, and the social dynamics underlying such interactions lead third parties to reaffirm whichever predisposition managers have toward their colleagues. This is consistent with anthropological and social psychological research on network gossip, which suggests that people gossip with third parties in a search for affirmation of their feelings and beliefs about other individuals in their network; in the process, gossip also serves to reaffirm the values that underlie those beliefs (Cox 1970; Haviland 1977; Besnier 1989). Moreover, by validating ego's trust or distrust, a third party strengthens his or her relationship with ego (Byrne, Clore, and Worchel 1966). Such behavior can be motivated by political self-interest or simply by the desire to maintain social cohesion for its own sake (Cox 1970; Burt and Knez 1995).

We can extend the previous hypothesis by considering that third-party ties between a CEO and his or her board members resulting from appointments on other boards may amplify the effects of these different relationships on trust between CEOs and outside directors and thus impact the magnitude of network resources embodied in those ties. As noted above, qualitative research on boards suggests that the relationship between CEO A and outside director B is influenced by third-party ties when A has a common appointment to another board with director C, who sits on B's board. From the third-party gossip perspective, when A and C discuss B (or A's relationship with B), the social dynamics underlying such interactions will lead C to confirm A's predisposition by drawing on his or her experience with B. For example, if A expresses doubt to C about whether B can be trusted to support A's decisions, C will tend to affirm A's distrust, either by providing explicit information or by 'replicating accounts' of B's behavior or through more subtle affirmations or nonverbal signals (Cox 1970; Burt and Knez 1995: 260). Such interactions are especially likely now because top managers have become increasingly concerned in recent years about whether they can count on the loyalty and support of their outside directors (Lorsch and MacIver 1989). These findings and theories suggest additional hypotheses as follows:

Hypothesis 4: Indirect interlock ties between the CEO and outside directors through third-party directors will interact with the content of the focal CEO–board tie to predict alliance formation between the focal firm and outside directors' home companies.

Hypothesis 4a: The more indirect interlock ties there are between the CEO and outside directors through third-party directors, the stronger the negative relationship between board control over the CEO and the likelihood of subsequent alliance formation between the focal firm and outside directors' home companies.

Hypothesis 4b: The more indirect interlock ties there are between the CEO and outside directors through third-party directors, the stronger the positive relationship between CEO–board cooperation and the likelihood of subsequent alliance formation between the focal firm and outside directors' home companies.

Empirical research

METHOD

The data-set used in this study is described in Appendix 1, under the heading 'Board and Alliance Database'. Alliance formation was measured with a dichotomous variable coded 1 if the two firms in a dyad entered into an alliance during the two-year period following the survey date (i.e. 1995–6). Two separate analyses were conducted with alliance formation measured over one year (1996) and over the period 1993–4. For each of these separate analyses, results for the hypothesized relationships were very similar to the results presented below, suggesting that the findings are robust for different periods.

Board interlocks were measured as directional ties created by individuals who are principally affiliated as officers or owners with the firms they connect (Davis 1991; Haunschild 1993; Palmer et al. 1993). Thus, two firms, A and B, are coded as having an interlock tie when at least one officer or owner from firm A serves as an outside director at firm B, or vice versa.

A pretest involving in-depth pilot interviews with twenty-two top managers and board members was used to refine and reword the survey items
of a survey conducted by my coauthor Jim Westphal (cf. Fowler 1993: 102).
Board control and CEO–board cooperation were measured with two multi-
item scales from the CEO survey that were carefully validated with responses
from the outside director survey and also with archival measures of board
characteristics. Items in the Control scale assessed key behavioral elements of board control that have been theorized to entail board independence
from management, including the board's tendency to monitor and evaluate
CEO decision-making and performance and the frequency with which directors challenge the CEO's position on strategic issues, rather than deferring
to the CEO's judgment. Items in the Cooperation scale were based on prior
qualitative research about how CEOs may engage in ongoing collaboration
with outside directors by seeking their advice and counsel on strategic issues,
as discussed above.

A confirmatory factor analysis using LISREL was conducted and estimated
cooperation and control factors were estimated using the Bartlett method.
Interrater reliability was assessed by comparing CEOs' and outside directors'
responses on the board control and cooperation items. We used the kappa
correlation coefficient, which corrects for the level of correlation that would
be expected by chance.

Convergent validity for the board cooperation and control measures was
also tested. First, an archival measure of each construct was developed, including multiple aspects of board structure and practice that are thought to facilitate controlling behavior by boards: the use of stock to compensate directors,
institutional ownership, and the presence or absence of the specific committees listed above (Hoskisson, Johnson, and Moesel 1994; Belliveau, O'Reilly,
and Wade 1996; David, Kochhar, and Levitas 1998). Institutional ownership
was measured as the percentage of total common stock held by pension funds,
banks and trust companies, savings and loans, mutual fund managers, and
labor union funds (Hansen and Hill 1991). The dichotomous measures were
combined into a Guttman scale and then combined with institutional ownership using principal components (Jackson 1991).

The archival measure of cooperation was a composite of three variables: joint tenure of the CEO and directors, complementary functional
backgrounds of the CEO and directors, and CEO stock ownership. The
organizational demography literature has provided consistent evidence that
higher joint tenure increases the level of task-related communication and
problem-solving behavior among group members (Zenger and Lawrence
1989; O'Reilly, Snyder, and Boothe 1993; Smith et al. 1994; Williams and
O'Reilly 1997). Moreover, the upper echelon perspective would suggest that
directors are more valuable to CEOs as a source of strategic advice and counsel
if they have a complementary base of functional expertise and experience
(e.g. if the CEO has a financial background and directors have marketing

backgrounds) (Hambrick, Cho, and Chen 1996). Functional background was measured using Hambrick and Mason's classification (1984), calculated as the percentage of directors who had functional backgrounds complementary to the CEO. Finally, given that stock ownership aligns CEOs' interests with shareholders' interests, it may motivate CEOs to engage the cooperation of board members in the strategic decision-making process (Murphy 1986; Jensen and Murphy 1990). These three variables were combined into a composite measure using principal components.

Indirect ties between CEOs and outside directors through third-party directors (third-party ties) were measured for each dyad as the number of board appointments shared by the CEO and board members of the outside director's home company board, excluding the focal board. The hypothesized interaction effects between third-party ties and the focal CEO–board ties were tested using the product-term approach (Jaccard, Turrisi, and Wan 1990).

To ensure the robustness of the results, a number of control variables were included that were considered to influence the formation of ventures between firms. To capture the role of resource considerations, the approach here built on Burt's measure (1983, 1992) of market constraint to capture the degree of resource interdependence between firms. Our approach followed Mizruchi (1992) in reducing the various operationalizations of constraint used by Burt and subsequent researchers to a single variable using principal components analysis. Mutual interdependence between firms in a dyad was then measured as the total amount of constraint between them. This measure is highest when both firms are in highly concentrated industries with a heavy flow of transactions between them.

Because constraint is measured at the industry level, the analyses here also controlled for industry overlap, measured as the percentage of total sales between the two firms made to the same industry, to assess strategic complementarity at the firm level (Mowery, Oxley, and Silverman 1996).

We included a number of measures that prior research suggests may be important strategic and economic drivers for the creation of new ventures: (a) size, measured as the log of total sales; (b) performance, measured as a composite of return on assets and market-to-book value, which were combined using principal components analysis; (c) solvency, measured as the total amount of long-term debt divided by current assets; (d) research and development (R&D) intensity, measured as research and development expense divided by total sales of the focal firm; (e) advertising intensity, measured as advertising expense divided by total sales of the focal firm; and (f) diversification, measured with the entropy variable, which takes into account the number of segments in which a firm operates and weights each segment according to its contribution to total sales (Palepu 1985). Each variable was measured using data from the prior year.

The analyses here also controlled for the firms' prior alliance history (Gulati 1995*a*, 1995*b*; Powell, Koput, and Smith-Doerr 1996). Thus, controls for the number of prior alliance ties between firms in the dyad were included. To control for the historical propensity of each firm to initiate alliances, variables indicating the total number of prior alliances initiated by each firm in the dyad were included. To compute this measure as accurately as possible, alliance activity from 1980 to 1994 was recorded and tested against varying periods. These two sets of measures serve as useful controls for unobserved heterogeneity that results from unobserved propensities by the actor to engage in those activities in the future (Heckman and Borjas 1980).

Controls for two other kinds of board ties that could influence CEO–board relationships and alliance formation were included. First, controls for common board appointments (common appointments) held by the CEO and the outside director on other boards were included. A common tie exists if CEO A and an outside director B on the focal board both serve as outside directors on another board. Second, we controlled for the total number of appointments (total appointments) held on other boards by the CEO and the outside director. As discussed above, the measure of third-party ties effectively includes indirect ties with a distance of two links: if CEO A sits on another board with C, who sits on outside director B's board, A and B are separated by two links. When this measure is held constant, the control variable for total appointments captures the effect of indirect ties of greater length (i.e. three links or more).

Given that alliance formation could also be influenced by the content of sent interlock ties (i.e. relationships between top managers and manager-directors at the latter directors' home company boards, which are not included in measures of cooperation and control), controls for reciprocated appointments were included, coded as 1 if a top manager serves on the home company board of an outside director who is on the focal firm's board.

Finally, controls were included for several other possible exogenous influences on management–board relationships. A survey measure of friendship ties was included, indicating the portion of the board composed of the CEO's personal friends. In separate analyses in which cooperation and control were measured for each CEO–director dyad, friendship ties were also measured at the dyad level.

ANALYSIS

Descriptive statistics and bivariate correlations are provided in Table 4.1. Maximum-likelihood logit regression analysis was used to test the effect of interlock ties on the likelihood of alliance formation (Aldrich and Nelson 1984; Hosmer and Lemeshow 1989). Because the appropriate risk sets to test

Table 4.1. Descriptive statistics and Pearson correlation coefficients for analyses of board control and CEO–board cooperation[a]

Variable	Mean	SD	1	2	3	4	5	6	7	8	9	10	11	12	13	14	15	16	17	18	19
1. Alliance	.15	.36	—																		
2. Interlock tie	.01	.11	.06	—																	
3. Board control	.00	.88	-.26	—	—																
4. CEO–board cooperation	.00	.82	.31	.16	-.16	—															
5. Third-party ties	2.79	2.03	.12	.05	.05	.06	—														
6. Prior alliance activity, firm 1	5.98	5.57	.29	.05	.07	.09	.11	—													
7. Prior alliance activity, firm 2	6.35	5.94	.34	.07	.08	.09	.11	.02	—												
8. Prior alliance ties	.09	.31	.23	.18	-.17	.21	.14	.17	.15	—											
9. Constraint	.00	1.33	.17	.17	.18	.13	-.02	.12	.10	.14	—										
10. Size	7.69	1.50	.02	-.05	-.04	-.08	.03	.06	.03	.01	-.08	—									
11. Performance	.00	1.01	-.23	.05	-.08	-.04	-.01	-.13	-.08	.03	-.04	-.06	—								
12. Solvency	.38	.31	-.08	-.01	-.05	-.01	.01	.02	.05	.04	-.11	.36	.17	—							
13. R&D intensity	.02	.02	-.18	.06	-.03	.00	.04	-.11	-.10	-.12	.03	-.31	.14	.27	—						
14. Advertising intensity	.02	.03	-.14	.02	.02	.06	.02	-.05	-.08	-.05	.01	-.09	.10	.05	-.18	—					
15. Diversification	.74	.56	-.05	.08	-.12	-.17	.00	-.04	-.07	-.06	-.09	.26	-.03	-.12	.16	.15	—				
16. Industry overlap	.09	.25	.22	.25	-.10	.20	.04	.03	.03	.14	-.32	.18	-.03	-.06	.02	-.02	-.09	—			
17. Common appointments	1.23	1.01	.09	.15	-.08	.07	.18	.04	.03	.16	.05	.08	.01	.10	.07	.00	.13	.16	—		
18. Total appointments	8.21	5.31	.07	.11	-.05	.02	.37	.01	.03	-.01	-.04	.04	-.02	.00	.05	.45	.08	-.11	.45	—	
19. Reciprocated appointments	.11	.31	.03	.29	-.09	.17	.03	.02	-.01	.04	.19	.06	.05	.04	.06	-.01	.03	-.02	.01	.00	—
20. Friendship ties	.37	.34	.16	.02	-.18	.21	.04	.03	-.02	.17	.10	-.04	.09	.06	.03	.10	.04	.01	.06	-.07	.05

[a] Descriptive statistics and correlation coefficients are calculated for the sample of interlocked firms (n = 898), except statistics for interlock ties, which are calculated for the larger sample of all possible dyads (n = 73,510).

each of the hypotheses differ somewhat, a number of additional analyses were conducted to ensure consistency across the findings. Because hypothesis 1 examined the effect of interlock ties on alliance formation, the risk set for this analysis included all possible dyadic combinations between each of the focal firms in the final survey sample and all firms in the total sample frame (73,510 dyads). Because hypotheses 2–4 assume that an interlock tie exists, because board control or cooperation only occur when there is an interlock, the risk set narrows here from all possible dyads to only those dyads for which there was an interlock tie between the two firms. Thus, to test the effects of board control versus cooperation on alliance formation, as well as the moderating effects of third-party ties, an initial set of analyses was conducted using logit regression on the sample of dyadic combinations between the focal firm and each of the home companies of CEO–directors on the board ($n = 898$). Moreover, for the sample of possible dyadic combinations that included a responding outside director, the analyses also examined whether individual CEO–board-member relationships mattered by estimating separate models using each responding director's assessment of his or her individual relationship with the CEO ($n = 412$ dyads).

In addition, Heckman selection models were estimated to ensure that logit estimates were not biased by any unmeasured differences between the smaller sample of CEO–director dyads and dyads in the larger sample frame used for testing hypothesis 1. This approach uses the larger risk set to assess hypotheses 2–4 (i.e. $n = 73,510$). The Heckman model is essentially a two-stage procedure that estimates the likelihood of interlock ties with probit regression and then incorporates estimates of parameters from that model in a second-stage regression model to predict alliance formation among dyads with an interlock tie; the second-stage model is also estimated with probit regression (van de Ven and van Praag 1981). More details on this are provided in the first section of Appendix 2 on unobserved heterogeneity.

RESULTS

Table 4.2 provides the results of the logistic regression analysis of alliance formation, and Table 4.3 gives the Heckman selection model results. The hypothesized effects are in bold. Model 1 in Table 4.2 tests hypothesis 1 that an interlock tie between two firms will enhance the network resources available to them and thus increase the likelihood of subsequent alliance formation between them. The results in model 1 do not support this hypothesis: after controlling for the extent of market constraint (i.e. resource interdependence) between firms, as well as other financial and strategic factors, the existence of an interlock tie is not significantly related to subsequent alliance formation.

Table 4.2. Logistic regression analysis of alliance formation[a]

Independent variable	1		2		3	
Interlock tie	.44	(.047)				
Board control			−.391*	(.149)	−.589*	(.203)
CEO–board cooperation			.575*	(.183)	.757*	(.249)
Third-party ties	.006	(.005)	.094	(.080)	.098	(.080)
Third-party ties × Board control					−.199*	(.074)
Third party ties × CEO–board cooperation					.227*	(.073)
Prior alliance activity, firm 1	.002*	(.0005)	.037*	(.009)	.037*	(.010)
Prior alliance activity, firm 2	.003*	(.0007)	.041*	(.009)	.040*	(.009)
Prior alliance ties	.057*	(.018)	1.678*	(.552)	1.701*	(.555)
Constraint	.022*	(.008)	.289*	(.109)	.290*	(.109)
Size	.002	(.004)	.034	(.092)	.045	(.092)
Performance	−.013*	(.005)	−.292*	(.132)	−.288*	(.132)
Solvency	−.032	(.021)	−.463	(.442)	−.491	(.438)
R&D intensity	−.323*	(.161)	−9.490	(4.837)	−8.682	(4.850)
Advertising intensity	−.377*	(.159)	−10.389*	(4.169)	−10.507*	(4.176)
Diversification	−.013	(.011)	−.177	(.257)	−.195	(.256)
Industry overlap	.047*	(.017)	1.330*	(4.92)	1.356*	(4.95)
Common appointments	.010	(.007)	.139	(.127)	.168	(.127)
Total appointments	.002	(.002)	.053	(.036)	.051	(.036)
Reciprocated appointments	.011	(.050)	.018	(.428)	.008	(.428)
Friendship ties			2.839*	(1.022)	2.906*	(1.029)
Constant	.041	(.045)	1.977	(1.011)	1.928	(1.017)
n	73,510		898		898	
x^2	104.18*		118.44*		140.36*	

[a]Standard errors are in parentheses. Hypothesized effects are in bold.

*p < .01.

Model 2 in Table 4.2 tests hypotheses 2 and 3, which address the influence of management–board relationships on subsequent alliance formation between the focal firm and outside directors' home companies. The results for board control and CEO–board cooperation shown in model 2 provide strong support for these hypotheses. Consistent with hypothesis 2, board control over the CEO depletes the network resources available to them and is thus negatively related to the likelihood of forming an alliance between the focal firm and outside directors' home companies. The results also support hypothesis 3: CEO–board cooperation enhances the network resources available to those firms and is thus significantly and positively related to subsequent alliance formation. The hypothesized effects of board control and cooperation were also supported in Heckman selection models of alliance formation, as shown in model 1 of Table 4.3.

In summary, the first set of results indicates that the mere presence of a board interlock tie between firms does not predict the formation of strategic alliances between firms; instead, such ties may either increase or decrease the availability of network resources and the concomitant likelihood of alliance formation, depending on the nature of the CEO–director relationship that

Table 4.3. Heckman selection models of alliance formation ($n = 73,510$)[a]

Independent variable	1		2	
Board control	−.480*	(.184)	−.678*	(.266)
CEO–board cooperation	.581*	(.201)	.767*	(.270)
Third-party ties	.142	(.114)	.139	(.113)
Third-party ties × Board control	—		−.259*	(.097)
Third-party ties × CEO–board cooperation	—		.268*	(.092)
Prior alliance activity, firm 1	.034*	(.010)	.035*	(.010)
Prior alliance activity, firm 2	.037*	(.010)	.036*	(.010)
Prior alliance ties	1.627*	(.564)	1.594*	(.567)
Constraint	.312*	(.116)	.311*	(.116)
Size	.044	(.096)	.041	(.096)
Performance	−.342*	(.138)	−.333*	(.138)
Solvency	−.419	(.460)	−.424	(.460)
R&D intensity	−10.756	(5.718)	−9.383	(5.760)
Advertising intensity	−11.085*	(4.881)	−10.691*	(4.893)
Diversification	.156	(.267)	.179	(2.70)
Industry overlap	1.330*	(.492)	1.346	(.494)
Common appointments	.071	(.134)	.089	(.137)
Total appointments	.050	(.040)	.052	(.040)
Reciprocated appointments	.018	(.428)	.011	(.428)
Friendship ties	2.799*	(1.101)	2.882*	(1.113)
Constant	2.446	(1.077)	2.386	(1.081)
x^2	132.45*		151.22*	

[a] Standard errors are in parentheses. Hypothesized effects are in bold.

*$p < .01$.

underlies the tie. The greater the extent to which an interlock tie results in cooperation between top managers of different firms in strategic decision-making (i.e. at the focal firm), the greater the network resources available to those firms and the concomitant likelihood of subsequent strategic cooperation between the focal firm and the outside director's home company. At the same time, the greater the extent to which an interlock tie results in an independent control relationship between top managers of different firms, the lower the network resources embodied in those relationships and the lower the likelihood of subsequent strategic cooperation between them.

The next set of results tests hypothesis 4 that third-party ties resulting from appointments of focal-firm CEOs on other boards amplify the effects of independent board control and CEO–board cooperation on alliance formation. The interaction effects in model 3 of Table 4.2 support this hypothesis. Consistent with hypothesis 4a, the results show that as the number of third-party ties between the CEO and outside directors increases, the negative relationship between board control over the CEO and the likelihood of subsequent alliance formation between the focal firm and outside directors' home companies becomes stronger. The results also support hypothesis 4b: as the number of third-party ties between the CEO and outside directors increases, the positive relationship between CEO–board cooperation and the likelihood of subsequent alliance formation between the focal firm and outside directors' home companies also becomes stronger. The hypothesized interaction effects were also supported in Heckman selection models of alliance formation, as shown in model 2 of Table 4.3.

Results for several of the control variables provide further insights. For instance, the degree to which firms are mutually constrained by resource inter-dependence, as indicated by resource flow between their respective industries, is positively associated with subsequent alliance formation, consistent with the traditional resource dependence perspective on alliance formation. While this effect has previously been observed only at the interindustry level, the results demonstrate that such effects for resource dependence occur at the dyad level as well. Results also show that friendship ties between CEOs and outside directors are positively and significantly related to subsequent alliance formation between the focal firm and outside directors' home companies in each of the models. In contrast, common appointments to other boards are not significantly associated with alliance formation, nor are the main effects of third-party ties significant. In general, the various network variables do not have independent effects on alliance formation; instead, network effects are contingent on the content of CEO–director relationships.

While the theoretical argument presented in this chapter suggests that trust in the CEO–board relationship can explain how control and cooperation affect alliance formation, the primary analysis did not explicitly model the mediating effect of trust. Thus, one might question whether other, related social processes mediate these relationships. For instance, cooperation might be associated with political influence processes such as ingratiation, which could affect the likelihood of alliance formation between the focal firm and manager-directors' home companies by enhancing directors' affect toward the CEO, without necessarily enhancing trust in the relationship. Similarly, cooperation could increase the board's approval of the CEO's performance and thus increase the likelihood of alliance formation independent of CEO–board trust. To assess the relative importance of these different social processes in explaining how control and cooperation affect alliance formation, we conducted further exploratory analyses using survey measures of trust, political influence (ingratiation), and board approval of the CEO. As shown in models 3 and 4 of Table 4.4, CEO–board trust has a strong and positive relationship with alliance formation, while the effects of ingratiation and board approval are nonsignificant. In addition, when trust is added to the models, the effects of cooperation and control become nonsignificant, suggesting that CEO–board trust mediates the effects of cooperation and control on alliance formation (Baron and Kenny 1986). Moreover, the effects of ingratiation and board approval of the CEO are nonsignificant in all models.

The results are not consistent with the view that preexisting trust in the CEO–board relationship leads to cooperation, which then facilitates alliance

Table 4.4. Supplementary Heckman selection models of alliance formation (n = 73,510)[a]

| Independent variable | With archival measures of cooperation/control | | | | With measures of CEO–board trust | | | |
	1		2		3		4	
Board control	**−.322***	**(.120)**	**−.339***	**(.123)**	−.252	(.185)	−.330	(.266)
CEO–board cooperation	**.603***	**(.230)**	**.568***	**(.233)**	.311	(.203)	.433	(.268)
CEO–board trust		—			**.605***	**(.167)**	**.599***	**(.167)**
Third-party ties	.139	(.113)	.126	(.113)	.141	(.114)	.139	(.114)
Third-party ties × Board control		—	**−.161***	**(.073)**		—	−.173	(.097)
Third-party ties × CEO–board cooperation		—	**.268***	**(.100)**		—	.119	(.094)
Prior alliance activity, firm 1	.034*	(.010)	.035*	(.010)	.035*	(.010)	.036*	(.010)
Prior alliance activity, firm 2	.036*	(.010)	.037*	(.010)	.037*	(.010)	.037*	(.010)
Prior alliance ties	1.566*	(.565)	1.590*	(.569)	1.589*	(.565)	1.601*	(.571)
Constraint	.310*	(.116)	.306*	(.115)	.309*	(.116)	.311*	(.117)
Size	.053	(.093)	.047	(.094)	.045	(.094)	.049	(.092)
Performance	−.290*	(.137)	−.332*	(.138)	−.339*	(.137)	−.330*	(.139)
Solvency	−.427	(.453)	−.431	(.460)	−.436	(.463)	−.434	(.462)
Research and development intensity	−10.729	(5.724)	−9.384	(5.772)	−10.192	(5.745)	−9.150	(5.788)
Advertising intensity	−10.937*	(4.845)	−10.625*	(4.875)	−11.677*	(4.911)	−11.392*	(4.909)
Diversification	.164	(.268)	.186	(.268)	.169	(.270)	.185	(.270)
Industry overlap	1.333*	(.494)	1.351*	(.497)	1.358*	(.500)	1.380*	(.503)
Common appointments	.071	(.133)	.093	(.136)	.070	(.134)	.091	(.136)
Total appointments	.041	(.039)	.051	(.040)	.050	(.040)	.051	(.040)
Reciprocated appointments	.022	(.427)	.019	(.429)	.019	(.425)	.019	(.426)
Friendship ties	2.804*	(1.103)	2.886*	(1.114)	2.810*	(1.103)	2.877*	(1.113)
Board approval	.124	(.208)	.116	(.208)	.118	(.208)	.114	(.209)
Ingratiation	.052	(.174)	.053	(.074)	.057	(.077)	.062	(.074)
Constant	2.500	(1.071)	2.363	(1.077)	2.565	(1.083)	2.366	(1.094)
x^2	125.16*		139.38*		130.01*		148.15*	

[a] Standard errors are in parentheses. Hypothesized effects are in bold.

*$p < .01$.

formation through some other mechanism. The findings suggest that trust mediates the effects of cooperation and control, not the reverse. We also measured trust using responses to the director survey, and results were substantively unchanged from results presented in Table 4.4. While researchers have typically viewed trust and distrust as one bipolar construct, Lewicki, McAllister, and Bies (1998) and others have suggested that these are separate constructs that may exist independently. Thus, we conducted further analyses using only items that refer to distrust. The results were nearly identical: distrust was strongly (and negatively) associated with alliance formation, and the control and cooperation variables became nonsignificant when distrust was added to the models, suggesting that distrust mediates the effects of control and cooperation on alliance formation. Thus, even if trust and distrust are viewed as distinct concepts, the results suggest that both predict alliance formation and mediate the effects of cooperation and control. Moreover, the CEO–board relationship appears to satisfy several of Lewicki, McAllister, and Bies' conditions (1998) for a high (negative) correlation between trust and distrust, including high value congruence and interdependence between the parties.

Conclusion

This study shows how board interlock ties can have qualitatively different effects on the magnitude of network resources they embody and in turn differentially impact alliance formation between firms, depending on the behavioral processes that underlie CEO–board relationships. In light of this book's larger discussion of how network resources impact alliances, this study shows how network resources are affected not only by the presence of ties but also by the specific valence (positive or negative) of those ties. By examining the interplay across different sets of ties (interlocks and alliances), this chapter highlights the likely multilevel nature of network resources that are shaped by different kinds of networks that influence each other as well as organizational behavior and outcomes.

The first set of results suggests that the mere presence of a board interlock tie between two firms does not appear to increase or decrease the magnitude of network resources as it does not affect their likelihood of entering a strategic alliance. Further results show that these aggregate effects of board interlock ties appear to mask more specific effects dependent on the content of the tie—there can be up- and downsides to the presence of a board interlock tie between two firms, depending on the underlying relationship. Thus, the extent of network resources embodied in a tie between two firms may vary depending on the nature of the tie. Higher levels of independent board control over management actually decreased the likelihood of subsequent alliance formation between them, suggesting that such ties may actually deplete network resources between those firms. Conversely, higher levels of CEO–board cooperation in strategic decision-making raised the likelihood that the two firms would enter an alliance, indicating that such ties positively contributed to the network resources between those firms. These results were confirmed with both survey-based and archival measures of board cooperation and control, and held true even after controlling for a variety of economic and strategic variables that could influence alliance formation. Thus, the first set of results demonstrates how the consequences of board interlock ties for network resources and the resultant strategic cooperation depend critically on the behavioral content of the tie.

Furthermore, the findings are consistent with the perspective that third-party ties primarily amplify whatever relational dispositions already exist among directly connected actors—they not only amplify trust resulting from cooperative interaction in CEO–board relationships but also amplify distrust resulting from independent board control. At the same time, such indirect ties did not have significant main effects on alliance formation. Thus, the results appear to support the proposition developed by Burt and Knez (1995) that third-party ties tend to reaffirm or amplify whichever predisposition managers have toward their colleagues (see also Labianca, Brass, and Gray 1998). These findings suggest that in order to fully grasp the multifaceted nature of network resources that arise from prior ties between firms, we need to take a more nuanced view and consider not only the content of those direct ties but also the indirect ties within which they are situated.

This reaffirmation or amplification resulting from third-party ties is not consistent with the view that third-party ties uniformly enhance trust between individuals by increasing the reputational costs of noncooperative behavior (Kreps 1990; Raub and Weesie 1990). Third-party ties are not effective in promoting cooperation when noncooperative behavior is normatively accept-able in the larger social structure. Consequently, the reputation of an outside director is not necessarily damaged by noncooperative behavior (i.e. exercising independent control over CEOs), and directors may even be increasingly rewarded for exercising independent control in the market for corporate directors. As a result, in the absence of reputational costs from noncooper-ation, third-party ties do not necessarily enforce such behavior. As we develop a deeper and fuller account of the multiple facets of network resources, we have to keep in mind the contingent nature of third-party ties in impacting them.

The results on cooperation among boards are consistent with the view that this behavior increases the magnitude of network resources and in turn the likelihood of alliance formation by increasing trust between top managers and manager-directors, while board control lowers network resources and the likelihood of alliance formation by reducing trust between them. Nevertheless, these additional analyses are merely exploratory, and further research should use alternative measures of trust and sociopolitical influence to verify more conclusively the social mechanism by which CEO–board interaction affects alliance formation. This could be further supplemented with studies that use alternative measures of cooperation and control. While this research is perhaps unique in demonstrating support for hypotheses about CEO–board relationships with both archival and survey measures of key constructs, there is a great need for research that uses alternative approaches to measuring cooperation, control, and other forms of CEO–board interaction as well as the network resources that they generate.

The control variable results also provide some valuable insights. The logit regression and Heckman selection model results show that previous ties between dyad members increase the likelihood of alliance formation. This is consistent with findings that show that prior alliance networks influence subsequent alliance formation (Kogut, Shan, and Walker 1992; Gulati 1995*b*, 1998; Powell, Koput, and Smith-Doerr 1996; Gulati and Gargiulo 1999). Variables indicating prior alliance activity also capture any unobserved propensities of the firms to enter alliances that are not captured by the independent variables; results for these here further attest to the robustness of our results (Heckman and Borjas 1980). Additionally, some of the resource dependence measures were significant, indicating that resource dependence was indeed an important consideration for the creation of new alliances. As expected, the measure for dyadic constraint was positive and significant: the greater the constraint, the greater the likelihood of alliance formation. Moreover, the significant effect of friendship ties between CEOs and manager-directors provides further evidence that positive links between CEOs and board members encourage alliance formation.

In delineating the critical role of tie content in moderating network effects and then showing how it may be moderated further by third-party ties, this study makes several related contributions to research on interorganizational networks. First, it considers the interrelationship across the multiplexity of interorganizational ties and the network resources that ensue from them by directly examining the influence of one such tie (board interlocks) on the creation of network resources that may be used to explain the formation of another set of ties (strategic alliances). In some ways, this indicates the reinforcing nature of network resources in which one kind of tie that constitutes a network resource enables the firm to accumulate other ties that in turn serve as constituent elements of such resources. The results also suggest that the influence of interorganizational network ties on the availability of network resources that in turn shape firm behavior is strongly conditioned by the content of those ties. In other words, ties alone do not automatically lead to the accumulation of network resources—their content must be considered.

Second, this chapter suggests that board interlocks are heterogeneous and goes on to demonstrate their positive and negative influence on the creation of network resources that in turn shape the formation of new strategic alliances between firms. Very little empirical research has examined when network ties may lead to more negative relations between individuals or organizations. By exploring how the content of network ties might diminish mutual trust between individuals and thus impede the creation of network resources, this study investigates what Burt and Knez (1995: 261) called the 'dark side' of social networks. This is further developed by showing that both negative and positive ties between dyads of firms are amplified by third-party connections in which firms are embedded.

Finally, the study highlights the importance of indirect, third-party ties in interorganizational networks on the accumulation of network resources and their subsequent impact on firm behavior. Research on social networks has typically treated network ties as exogenous; relatively little empirical research has examined the origin of organizational networks (Gulati 1998; Gulati and Gargiulo 1999). Thus, it is important to recognize that both interlocks and JVs are interorganizational relationships that accumulate into a social network. This study considers how the creation of interorganizational networks of strategic alliances may be influenced in significant ways by the social networks of board interlocks in which firms are placed. As a result, it examines the multiplexity of ties in which firms are embedded and the relationship between those ties: new social networks result from a social process in which preexisting ties shape their creation in an iterative dynamic. This research is distinctive because it examines simultaneously two networks that exist at different levels of analysis: the relationships between corporate leaders that make up board interlocks are interpersonal ties, while strategic alliances occur across firms. Very little empirical research has considered how social ties between individuals can influence a different kind of network tie at the interorganization level (for exceptions, see Galaskiewicz 1985b; Zaheer, McEvily, and Perrone 1998). Thus, the findings have implications for cross-level perspectives on the accumulation of network resources and the formation of interorganizational networks by showing how the microcontent of network ties between individual leaders can play an important role in the development of organization-level ties.

Part II

Network Resources and the Governance Structure of Ties

5 Network resources and the choice of governance structure in alliances

In Chapter 2, I discussed how firms entering alliances face considerable hazards because of the potential for unpredictable partner behavior. Network resources minimize these risks by providing information about the reliability of potential partners. Moreover, firms with a positive reputation in these networks and more connections with others through direct and indirect ties are more likely to be identified as reliable alliance partners. As the network of alliances itself grows, it becomes an expanding repository of network resources and in turn asserts a greater influence on firm behavior. In Chapter 4, I also considered the interplay among different kinds of network ties including board interlocks and alliance networks in shaping firm behavior.

It is important to note, however, that the influence of network resources extends beyond the identification of new alliance opportunities and potential partners. Network resources can also affect the specific governance structure used to formalize those alliances. Simply stated, the network-resource-based familiarity and trust between two firms that may bring them into an alliance in the first place are also likely to alter their choice of governance structure in the initial and subsequent alliances.

In this chapter, I examine how the familiarity gained through prior alliances provides firms with valuable information about each other and hence constitutes a network resource that engenders interorganizational trust. This reduces the need for hierarchical controls in future alliances, thereby influencing the choice of the governance structure used in those alliances. As a result of this process, cautious contracting gives way to looser practices as partners become increasingly embedded in a social network of prior ties. Although most research on this issue has followed a static logic, my research looks at contracting between firms over time and demonstrates the role of emergent network resources in dynamically influencing choice of governance structure

This chapter is adapted with permission from 'Does Familiarity Breed Trust? The Implications of Repeated Ties for Contractual Choice in Alliances' by Ranjay Gulati published in *Academy of Management Journal* © 1995, (38/1): 85–112.

in alliances. While the focus here is on the nature of contracts between particular pairs of firms, with the dyad as the implicit unit of analysis, the underlying
logic easily translates to the firm level as this study explores how the network
resources that firms accrue through their prior ties can shape the kinds of
contracts they use to formalize new alliances.

Organizational scholars studying governance structures within and across
organizations tended to view hierarchical structures as mechanisms for managing behavioral uncertainty. Prior research on contract choices in alliances
and the extent of hierarchical controls they employ had been carried out primarily by transaction cost economists, who focused on alliance-based appropriation concerns that originate from contracting hazards and behavioral
uncertainty at the time of alliance formation (e.g. Pisano, Russo, and Teece
1988; Pisano 1989; Balakrishnan and Koza 1993; Oxley 1997). These economists have suggested that hierarchical controls are effective responses to such
concerns. The logic for hierarchical controls in this circumstance is their
facilitation of control by fiat, monitoring, and incentive alignment. Hence,
just as appropriation concerns and the perceived need for hierarchical controls
can influence a firm's decision to make or buy a component, transaction
cost economists have suggested that these same considerations are at play
in exchange relations characterized by strategic alliances—and consequently,
they also shape the specific choice of governance structure for those alliances.
That is, the greater the appropriation concerns, the more hierarchical the
governance structures for organizing the alliance will be.

A number of researchers have challenged this view of hierarchical governance as occurring primarily as a reflection of associated transactional
attributes. For example, Zajac and Olsen (1993) found that transaction cost
accounts focus in general on single-party cost minimization, yet alliances are
inherently dyadic exchanges, which raises the question of whose costs are min-
imized by a particular governance structure. They also claimed that the structural emphasis of transaction cost economics leads to the neglect of important
process issues resulting from the ongoing nature of alliances. More specifically,
I suggest here that alliances are usually not one-off transactions but rather relationships with ongoing exchange and adjustments, as a result of which process
issues become salient (Khanna, Gulati, and Nohria 1998). Perrow (1986)
echoes similar concerns when he suggests that transaction cost perspectives
grossly overstate the regulatory potential of hierarchical mechanisms.

A consideration of the history of interaction between firms and the possible
role of network resources in mitigating risks calls into question the primary
focus of transaction cost economists on transactional attributes and the associated appropriation concerns as primary drivers of governance structure
choice. Unfortunately, much prior research on the governance structure of
alliances ignored the role of network resources in facilitating trust and diminishing risks.

My research here demonstrates that interorganizational trust gained from network resources originating in past partnerships reduces the appropriation concerns of potential alliance partners with such ties and thus independently influences choice of governance structure. The presence of network resources and concomitant interfirm trust is an extraordinary lubricant for alliances because firms with prior network connections are likely to have greater awareness of the rules, routines, and procedures each follows. Both knowledge-based trust resulting from mutual awareness and equity norms and deterrence-based trust arising from reputational concerns create 'self-enforcing' safeguards in an exchange relationship and can substitute for contractual safeguards (Bradach and Eccles 1989; Powell 1990). Consequently, familiarity and trust gained from network resources can enable firms to work together even in the absence of formal hierarchical controls.

Theory and hypotheses

GOVERNANCE STRUCTURE: EQUITY AND NON-EQUITY ALLIANCES

The specific governance structure of alliances, primarily communicated in the form of a contract, is important for a number of reasons. First, such a contract is an important mechanism by which firms protect themselves from a partner's opportunism. Evidence suggests that firms entering alliances are potentially vulnerable to the opportunistic behavior of their partners ('Corporate Odd Couples' 1986; Reich and Mankin 1986; Kogut 1988*b*, 1989; Hamel, Doz, and Prahalad 1989). In the face of the hazards associated with alliances, the contracts used reflect potential risks (Ring and Van de Ven 1992). Second, a contractual agreement serves as a framework for cooperation between partners. Although alliance partners may not follow their initial contract to the letter, it provides a set of normative guidelines: 'The major importance of a legal contract is to provide a framework . . . a framework [that is] highly adjustable, a framework which almost never accurately indicates real working relations, but which affords a rough indication around which such relations vary, an occasional guide in case of doubt, and a norm of ultimate appeal when the relations cease in fact to work' (Llewellyn 1931: 736–7). Third, the recent availability of an array of innovative contractual arrangements opens up the possibility of new interfirm cooperative agreements. The dramatic increase in the use of arm's length contracts, which do not involve shared ownership, is particularly noteworthy in this respect.

Transaction cost economists have typically classified the governance structures of alliances in terms of their use of equity ownership (e.g. Pisano, Russo, and Teece 1988; Pisano 1989). Equity alliances, as defined by transaction cost economists, take one of two forms: they may be organized either as an equity JV, which involves the creation of a new and independent jointly owned entity, or as an arrangement in which one of the partners takes a minority equity position in the other partner or partners. Transaction cost economists justify treating equity JVs and minority equity investments as a single category on the grounds that 'a direct equity investment by one firm into another essentially creates an equity JV between one firm's existing shareholders and the new corporate investor' (Pisano 1989: 111). In both types, the effective shared equity stakes of the firms vary case by case. The important point is that beyond a certain threshold, the shared ownership structure effectively deters opportunistic behavior.

Equity-based ventures are considered hierarchical to the extent that they more closely replicate some of the features associated with organizational hierarchies than do other alliances. Nonequity arrangements, in contrast, do not involve the sharing or exchange of equity, nor do they usually entail the creation of a new organizational entity. In the absence of any shared ownership structure, nonequity alliances are more akin to arm's length market exchanges on the continuum of market to hierarchy. Members of the partner firms work together directly from within their own organizational confines. Nonequity alliances include unidirectional agreements, such as licensing, second sourcing, and distribution agreements, and bidirectional agreements such as joint contracts and technology exchange agreements.

From a transaction cost economics standpoint, quasi-market ties such as nonequity alliances are the default mode for organizing alliances, and the use of equity must be explained. The explanation offered is that firms use equity alliances when the transaction costs associated with an exchange are too high to justify a quasi-market, nonequity alliance. Researchers have identified two sets of governance properties through which equity alliances effectively alleviate transaction costs (Pisano et al. 1988). The first are the properties of a 'mutual hostage' situation in which shared equity helps align the interests of all the partners. Not only are the partners required to make *ex ante* commitments to an equity alliance but also their concern for their investment reduces the possibility of their behaving opportunistically over the course of the alliance (Williamson 1975, 1991). In the case of alliances that involve sharing or developing new technologies over which property rights are difficult to enforce, equity ownership also provides an effective means for allocating such rights. Issues related to the ownership of intellectual property developed in the venture are sidestepped because the property belongs to the venture itself.

The second set of properties are those of the administrative hierarchy that not only oversees the day-to-day functioning of an alliance but also addresses contingencies as they arise. In equity JVs, a hierarchy of managers serves this function; in the case of direct equity investments, hierarchical supervision is created when the investing partners participate in the board of directors of the partner that received the investment. This participation is the mechanism by which partners exercise their residual rights of control (Grossman and Hart 1986).

The benefits of equity alliances, however, must be weighed against their costs. Equity alliances not only take a long time to negotiate and organize but can also involve very high exit costs. Furthermore, significant administrative costs can be associated with a hierarchical system of supervision. Similar pros and cons must be assessed for nonequity alliances. One advantage of nonequity alliances is that they can be negotiated rapidly and require only limited investments from each partner. One disadvantage, however, is that both partners are more vulnerable to each other's opportunistic behavior, and one may find it difficult to persuade the other to make significant alliance-specific investments in light of this increased vulnerability (Joskow 1987). A further difficulty may arise in alliances formed to share or develop new technologies; here, significant disagreements on the allocation of property rights may arise. Even when there is agreement, it may be difficult to transfer tacit knowledge across loosely connected firms (Hennart 1988; Badaracco 1991). Furthermore, such agreements entail a fair amount of management effort, albeit of a different nature than that required by equity alliances.

As in prior research on alliance governance, I chose to focus on the dichotomy between equity and nonequity alliances. My primary goal was to examine the factors underlying the use of equity in alliances. I looked at equity for numerous reasons. First, its use in partnerships is a highly visible feature that offers a means to distinguish most alliances. Most other classifications are not based on such a readily measured feature, making alliances more difficult to place on proposed scales. Second, the use of equity is an important measure with which partners, especially first-time partners, address their concerns about malfeasance. My previous fieldwork at firms entering alliances corroborates this practice (Gulati 1993). Third, prior research by transaction cost economists on these issues has focused on the use of equity, so an explanation of the dichotomy between equity and nonequity alliances allows the present findings to be compared directly to past results.

R&D ALLIANCES

A primary basis on which transaction cost economics has examined the costs of alliances has been the activities involved with R&D. Prior research suggests that transactions involving the sharing, exchange, or codevelopment of knowledge can be somewhat problematic because of the peculiar character of knowledge as a commodity (Arrow 1974). Many of these problems result from the inability to accurately assess the value of the commodity being exchanged as well as from concerns about opportunism resulting from poor monitoring possibilities in such exchanges (Balakrishnan and Koza 1993). The challenge of transferring R&D know-how across organizations compounds these problems (Hennart 1988; Badaracco 1991). Because of these issues, alliances with an R&D component are likely to have higher transaction costs than those that do not involve joint R&D.

Transaction cost theorists claim that alliances involving R&D will most likely be organized as equity-based partnerships because of the significant transaction cost burden. Shared equity can align the interests of partners and limit opportunistic behavior by focusing their attention on equity stakes in the alliance. Furthermore, such alliances are usually accompanied by an independent administrative structure, which fosters information flow and provides for ongoing coordination.

In a study of the telecommunications industry, Pisano et al. (1988) explicitly tested the impact of transaction costs on alliance structure. They predicted that the greater the hazards associated with an alliance, the more likely it will be equity based. Their findings supported these predictions. Pisano (1989) observed similar results in the biotechnology sector. In both studies, high transaction costs were measured as the presence of an R&D component in the alliance. In a study of US–Japanese alliances, Osborn and Baughn (1990) followed similar reasoning and showed that alliances encompassing joint R&D were more likely to be equity-based. Thus, I propose the following:

Hypothesis 1: Alliances are more likely to be equity-based if they have a shared R&D component.

THE ROLE OF INTERFIRM TRUST AND NETWORK RESOURCES IN ALLIANCES

Numerous researchers have been critical of transaction cost economics' narrow focus on transaction attributes and its implicit treatment of each transaction between companies as an independent event (e.g. Doz and Prahalad 1991; Ring and Van de Ven 1992). This assumption is particularly inappropriate when firms enter recurrent transactions. As I have discussed in previous chapters, network resources resulting from the cumulation of prior ties between firms are key factors in reducing both search costs and associated moral hazards concerns. Because they foster trust, network resources also play an important role in a firm's choice of governance structure for its alliances. The term 'trust' has widely varying connotations (for excellent reviews on the topic, see Luhmann 1979; Barber 1983; Gambetta 1988; and Kramer and Tyler 1996). In this context, I conceived of trust as 'a type of expectation that alleviates the fear that one's exchange partner will act opportunistically' (Bradach and Eccles 1989: 104). This definition is akin to Simmel's notion (1978: 379) of mutual 'faithfulness' in social relationships. Gambetta gave this cogent definition of such forms of trust:

Trust . . . is a particular level of the subjective probability with which an agent assesses that another agent or group of agents will perform a particular action both before he can monitor such action . . . and in a context in which it affects his own action. When we say we trust someone or that someone is trustworthy, we implicitly mean that the probability that he will perform an action that is beneficial or at least not detrimental to us is high enough for us to consider engaging in some form of cooperation with him. (1988: 217)

Can there be trust between two organizations that are simply agglomerations of individuals? Intuitively, trust is an interpersonal phenomenon. Some sociologists have argued that although expectations of trust do ultimately reside within individuals, it is possible to think of interfirm trust in economic transactions (Zucker 1986). At the organizational level, observers point to numerous examples of preferential, stable, obligated, and bilateral trading relationships to illustrate that firms develop close bonds with other firms through recurrent interactions (Sabel 1993; Zaheer and Venkatraman 1995). Accounts of industrial districts such as the modern woolens center at Prato, Italy, the injection moulding center in Oyannax, France, the cutlery industry in Sheffield, England, and the nineteenth-century Swiss watch-making region (Piore and Sabel 1984; Weiss 1984, 1988; Sabel and Zeitlin 1985; Sabel 1993) support this argument. Similar evidence has been observed from subcontracting relations in the Japanese textile industry (Dore 1983), the French engineering industry (Lorenz 1988), the American construction industry (Eccles 1981), and the Italian textile industry (Johnston and Lawrence 1988). A variety of terms have been used to describe this development of trust through repeated interactions: Williamson (1985) labeled it as relational and obligational contracting; Eccles (1981) as quasi-firm arrangements; Johnston and Lawrence (1988) as value-added partnerships; Dore (1983) as obligated relational contracting; and Zucker (1986) as process-based trust. Underlying all these accounts is a single notion: interfirm trust is built incrementally through recurrent interactions (Good 1988).

The link between trust and prior contact is based on the premise that through ongoing interaction, firms come to be embedded in a set of historical ties that serve as conduits of valuable information. This information in turn enables partners to learn about each other and develop trust around norms of equity, or 'knowledge-based trust' (Shapiro, Sheppard, and Cheraskin 1992). There are strong cognitive and emotional bases for such trust, which are perhaps most visible among individual organization members (Lewis and Weigert 1985). Macaulay, in a seminal essay, observed how close personal ties emerged between individuals in organizations that contracted with each other; these personal relationships in turn 'exert pressures for conformity to expectations' (Macaulay 1963: 63). Similarly, Palay (1985) found that the relationships between rail-freight carriers and auto shippers were characterized by close personal connections among members of those organizations. He described how these personal ties were important factors in the companies' use of informal contracts in a high transaction cost situation that would otherwise have demanded a detailed formal contract. Similarly, Ring and Van de Ven (1989) pointed to the important role of informal, personal connections across organizations in determining the governance structures used for their transactions.

Other theorists have made similar claims about the role of repeat alliances. In a survey-based empirical study, Parkhe (1993a) observed that the presence of a history of cooperation between two firms limited their perception of expected opportunistic behavior in new alliances and thus lowered the level of contractual safeguards employed in those alliances. Drawing on an inductive field study of seven pairs of firms in alliances, Larson (1992) observed that firms rely extensively on mechanisms of social control, as opposed to formal contracts, in the formation and maintenance of alliances, and that such relational factors become increasingly important as relationships develop over time (Nooteboom, Berger, and Noorderhaven 1997).

In this context, the emergent trust from prior ties between firms can be considered an important element of network resources. Interorganizational trust that results from each firm's prior alliances is inherently dyadic in nature. Through each of its dyadic ties, any participating firm is able to enter into looser contracts with its prior partners for future alliances. Such a resource can be the basis for speedier response to quick shifts in the marketplace and reduced governance costs. As a result, network resources resulting from their prior networks provide firms with the ability to build trusting ties with specific partners. Thus, it is no surprise that Kenneth Arrow once described trust as the most efficient mechanism for governing economic transactions (1974).

One of the reasons that network resources and the concomitant trust may enable firms to quickly execute new alliances is that the history of interaction and information-sharing alters each firm's perception of the potential transaction costs associated with new alliance opportunities. Trust counteracts fear of opportunistic behavior and, as a result, may limit the perceived transaction costs associated with an exchange. This process in turn should affect the governance structure of new alliances between these two parties. In other words, trust can substitute for hierarchical contracts in many exchanges by serving as an informal control mechanism (Bradach and Eccles 1989).

It is important to distinguish the aforementioned knowledge-based trust from deterrence-based trust, which also plays a role in repeat alliances

(Ring and Van de Ven 1989; Shapiro, Sheppard, and Cheraskin 1992). The latter emphasizes utilitarian considerations that may also lead to believing that a partner will behave in a trustworthy manner. Specifically, trust can arise when untrustworthy behavior by a partner can lead to costly sanctions that exceed any potential benefits of opportunistic behavior. Possible sanctions include loss of repeat business with the same partner, loss of other points of interaction between the two firms, and loss of reputation (Macaulay 1963; Granovetter 1985; Maitland, Bryson, and Van de Ven 1985). Thus, on strictly utilitarian grounds it is to the firm's benefit to behave in a trustworthy manner.[1]

Based on the above discussion, I propose that firms embedded in prior alliance networks are likely to trust each other more than other firms with whom they have had no alliances. Firms are less likely to use equity in repeated alliances than in a first-time alliance because interfirm trust resulting from network resources reduces the imperative to use equity. Actors are thus willing to take what Williamson (1993) calls 'calculative risks' because of their confident expectation that their counterparts will act responsibly. Thus:

Hypothesis 2: The greater the number of previous alliances between the partners in an alliance, the less likely the alliance is to be equity-based.

A question remains as to whether the character of firms' previous alliances affects the type of governance structure used for new alliances between the same parties. In other words, does a firm's perception of the transaction costs associated with a new alliance opportunity vary by the type of tie that a focal firm may have entered with the same partner in the past? It could be that two firms will prefer a nonequity alliance only when they already have worked together in an equity-based alliance. According to such logic, an equity alliance engenders greater network resources, in the form of trust, by creating a hostage situation that requires *ex ante* commitments by the partners and leads to partners' concern for the value of their investments. Once two firms share a hostage, the need for additional hostages is obviated. This is similar to what Williamson (1983) described as credible commitments. A singular focus on hostage-taking is, however, too narrow. As highlighted earlier, prior equity alliance situations represent more than simple hostages. They entail close interactions between the partners over prolonged periods, which can enhance trust through mutual awareness.

Such behavior could be a result of having a hostage in the form of an equity alliance already in place. However, informants also reported that the logic

---

[1] In recent years, there has been some debate on whether behavior with utilitarian motivations can really be described as trust (Williamson 1993). For my purposes, interfirm trust encompasses such utilitarian behavior, and I choose not to engage in this debate.

behind their use of loose contracts was based not so much on the existing equity alliance, but on their familiarity with their partners and the judgment that they were trustworthy (Gulati 1993).

An alternative to the above scenario is that two firms will prefer a nonequity alliance even when they already have a prior nonequity tie that may be easy to dissolve. This effect is likely to be less powerful than that based on the presence of prior equity alliances, which not only creates shared hostages but may lead to greater network resources and closer interaction among partners. Thus the following two hypotheses:

Hypothesis 3a: The greater the number of previous equity alliances between the partners in an alliance, the less likely an alliance is to be equity-based.

Hypothesis 3b: The greater the number of previous non-equity alliances between the partners in an alliance, the less likely the alliance is to be equity-based.

Looking beyond the history of alliances between given firms, I also expected firms to trust domestic partners more than international partners, not only because network resources available to a firm are likely to generate more information about domestic firms due to physical proximity but also because the reputational consequences of opportunistic behavior are greater in a domestic context (Gerlach 1992). Character-based trust, whereby firms trust others that are socially similar to themselves, may also be higher among domestic firms (Zucker 1986). Given such trust, I expect firms to be more willing to engage in loose, quasi-market alliances with domestic partners than with international partners:

Hypothesis 4: Alliances are more likely to be equity-based if they are among firms of different nations.

Research on group behavior suggests that beyond a certain threshold, an increase in the number of participants in any group can lead to dysfunctional behavior within the group and to a decline in its ability to perform assigned tasks (Steiner 1972; Hackman 1987). Within alliances, the presence of more than two partners heightens the possibility of stalemates and conflicts. Inasmuch as multilateral alliances pose larger organizational problems than bilateral alliances, I expected the former to more likely be equity based regardless of the network resources available to those actors from their prior ties.

Hypothesis 5: Alliances are more likely to be equity-based if they are among more than two firms.

Empirical research

METHOD

The data-set used in this study is described in Appendix 1 under the heading 'Alliance Announcement Database'. The dependent variable, mode of alliance, was coded '1' if an alliance involved the use of equity and '0' if it did not. The fundamental characteristic that distinguishes equity alliances from nonequity alliances is that equity sharing creates shared ownership and is, beyond a minimum threshold, effective in reducing exposure to opportunistic behavior.

Table 5.1 describes the variables included in the analysis and provides sign predictions based on the arguments made in this chapter. For consistency with prior empirical research, I defined high-transaction costs as the presence of an R&D component in an alliance (1 = R&D present, 0 = no R&D). R&D alliances included those that encompassed basic R&D, product development, or elements of both. Non-R&D alliances typically were those that involved joint production or marketing.

Hypothesis 2 concerns the relationship between the current type of alliance given partners share and their history of alliances. The variable repeated ties recorded the number of prior alliances two firms had had since 1970

Table 5.1. Definitions and predicted signs of variables

Variable	Definition	Prediction
Mode	Dummy variable indicating if alliance was equity based	Dependent variable
R&D component	Dummy variable indicating presence of an R&D component in the alliance	+
Repeated ties	Number of prior alliances between the firms	—
International alliance	Dummy variable set to one if the firms are of differing nationalities (default domestic)	+
Multilateral alliance	Dummy variable set to one if the alliance has more than two partners (default bilateral)	+
Repeated equity ties	Number of prior equity alliances between the firms (in the presence or absence of any nonequity alliances)	—
Repeated nonequity ties	Number of prior nonequity alliances between the firms (in the absence of any equity alliances)	—
New materials sector	Dummy variable set to one if firms are in the new materials sector (default biopharmaceutical)	No prediction
Automotive sector	Dummy variable set to one if firms are in the automotive sector (default biopharmaceutical)	No prediction
Year	A year value for each record ranging from 1 to 19	No prediction
Percentage of equity alliances	Percentage of equity alliances announced in the industry in the prior year	+

(0 = first-time alliance). I also calculated the variables repeated equity ties and repeated nonequity ties, respectively indicating the number of prior equity and nonequity alliances between two parties. These variables also took a zero value for a first-time alliance of the given type.

An important clarification is necessary here. Three alternative scenarios are possible in the history of alliances: (*a*) only nonequity past alliances, (*b*) only equity alliances, and (*c*) both equity and nonequity alliances. To which category should the third scenario be assigned? Because hypothesis 3a predicts the role of prior equity ties, in the presence or absence of other nonequity ties, repeated equity includes both the situation in which there are only prior equity alliances and those in which there have been mixed alliances. Hypothesis 3b, on the other hand, focuses on the effect of prior nonequity alliances in the absence of any other ties. Hence, repeated nonequity ties does not include situations with mixed alliances.

I included a dummy variable indicating whether an alliance was domestic or international (1 = partners of differing nationalities, 0 = partners of the same nationality).

To capture any effects of the number of partners in an alliance, I included it as a variable. Since the alliances in the sample were either bilateral or trilateral, this variable was recoded as a dummy variable with a value of '1' if an alliance was multilateral and a value of '0' if an alliance was bilateral.

I included two control variables to represent the three sectors studied. One dummy variable was coded '1' if an alliance was in the new materials sector, '0' otherwise, and the second was coded '1' if the alliance was in the automotive sector and '0' otherwise. The default sector was biopharmaceuticals.

Another control variable captured the percentage of equity alliances announced in an industry. I counted the number of alliances announced in an industry in the year prior and computed the percentage of those that were equity based. This variable broadly tested the institutionalist claim that firms mimic the contracts other firms in their industry use. This variable can also be interpreted as capturing the net effect of the various macroeconomic factors within an industry that may influence the formation of equity alliances (Amburgey and Miner 1992).

Finally, I included a dummy variable for each year to capture temporal effects and control for any temporal autocorrelation.

RESULTS

Table 5.2 presents descriptive statistics and correlations for all variables. These results reflect the diversity of alliances included in the pooled sample, in which over 500 of the approximately 2,400 alliances were repeat links between firms.

Table 5.2. Descriptive statistics and correlations

Variable	Frequency[a]		Means	SD	Minimum	Maximum	1	2	3	4	5	6	7	8	9	10
	0	1														
1. Mode	840	1,577	0.65	0.47	0	1	—									
2. R&D component	1,015	1,402	0.58	0.49	0	1	.17	—								
3. Repeated ties			1.40	0.98	0	9	-.08	.04	—							
4. International alliance	1,322	1,095	0.45	0.49	0	1	.02	-.19	.01	—						
5. Multilateral alliance	1,756	661	0.27	0.45	0	1	.05	.07	.06	-.22	—					
6. Repeated equity ties			1.18	0.85	0	9	-.15	.02	.75	-.01	.05	—				
7. Repeated nonequity ties			0.01	0.11	0	2	.01	.02	.12	.02	.00	-.05	—			
8. New materials sector	1,274	1,143	0.47	0.49	0	1	.05	-.04	-.13	-.09	.28	-.13	-.04	—		
9. Automotive sector	1,924	493	0.20	0.40	0	1	.06	-.15	.09	.06	.01	.07	.00	.48	—	
10. Year			14.50	3.62	1	19	-.08	.00	.08	.02	.06	.05	.03	.07	-.16	—
11. Percentage of equity alliances			0.35	0.15	0.13	1.00	.10	-.06	-.02	.00	.03	-.01	-.01	.14	.15	-.35

[a] Where no figure is given, value is a count. Totals = 2,417 except for the percentage of equity alliances, for which the total is 2,395.

The correlations show a few problems of multicollinearity. Notably, repeated equity ties is highly correlated with repeated ties ($r > .70$); the high correlation is no surprise because repeated equity ties is a nested subset of repeated ties. Because of the collinearity, I introduced these variables separately in a logit analysis.

A logit model was used to assess the effects of the independent variables on the likelihood that a given alliance would be equity-based (Aldrich and Nelson 1984). A variable's positive coefficient indicates its association with equity alliances.

Table 5.3 presents the logistic regression estimates. The first column reports the base model including all the control variables. The coefficients for the sector variables were significant ($p < .01$) in all cases. Although this finding suggests intrinsic industry differences in the likelihood of equity-based alliances (the constant terms for each of the industries differ), it does not reveal whether the main effects hypothesized differ across the three industries. More specifically, the positive signs indicate that both the automotive and new materials sectors were more likely to have equity-based alliances than the biopharmaceutical sector, once independent variables included in each model were controlled. I later estimated unrestricted models for each of the industries (results not presented here). The signs of the coefficients indicated that the postulated directions of the main effects were indeed observed in each sector.

My original estimations included a dummy variable for each year. For simplicity of presentation, I reestimated the models using a single variable,

Table 5.3. Results of logistic regression analysis[a]

Variable	Model 1		Model 2		Model 3		Model 4		Model 5	
Constant	−0.83**	(0.26)	−1.55**	(0.27)	−1.53**	(0.28)	−1.66**	(0.28)	−1.66**	(0.28)
R&D component	—		0.90**	(0.09)	0.99**	(0.09)	0.99**	(0.09)	0.99**	(0.09)
Repeated ties	—		—		−0.23**	(0.05)	—		—	
International alliance	—		—		0.33**	(0.09)	0.32**	(0.09)	0.32**	(0.09)
Multilateral alliance	—		—		0.12	(0.11)	0.15	(0.11)	0.15	(0.11)
Repeated equity ties	—		—		—		−0.97**	(0.13)	−0.97**	(0.13)
Repeated nonequity ties	—		—		—		—		0.11	(0.37)
New materials sector	0.36**	(0.10)	0.50**	(0.11)	0.47**	(0.12)	0.41**	(0.12)	0.41**	(0.12)
Automotive sector	0.42**	(0.13)	0.67**	(0.13)	0.69**	(0.14)	0.68**	(0.14)	0.68**	(0.14)
Year	−0.03*	(0.01)	−0.03*	(0.01)	−0.02	(0.01)	−0.02	(0.01)	−0.02	(0.01)
Percentage of equity alliances	0.90**	(0.30)	0.99**	(0.31)	1.03**	(0.31)	1.08**	(0.32)	1.08**	(0.32)
n	2,395		2,395		2,395		2,395		2,395	
−2 log likelihood	3,041.74		2,946.79		2,915.02		2,875.03		2,874.93	
χ^2	45.37**		140.31**		172.09**		212.08**		212.18**	
df	4		5		8		8		9	

[a]Standard errors are in parentheses.

*$p < .05$; **$p < .01$.

year, which ranges in value from 1 to 19, indicating each year. No differences in results for the other independent variables were observed in these two sets of estimates, and the results are mixed for year, which is significant in some models and not in others.

The positive and significant coefficient (p < .01) for the percentage of equity-based alliances announced in an industry in a given year suggests that this variable positively affects the use of equity alliances by firms in the industry in the subsequent year. This finding holds true in the remaining models as well and suggests that the form of contracts used in alliances may be linked to an industry's propensity to use equity alliances.

The second column in Table 5.3 shows results with the measure of transaction costs introduced into the model. The results are consistent with hypothesis 1: alliances involving R&D are more likely to be equity based than are non-R&D alliances, a relationship indicated by the positive coefficients of the variable R&D component (p < .01). This finding remains true in later models as well.

The third column shows results with the three measures of trust arising from its network resources and from contextual factors: the number of prior alliances by the same pair of firms, whether they were domestic or international, and the number of partners involved. Results suggest that the repetition of ties is a significant determinant of mode of alliance (p < .01). Specifically, the negative coefficient of the dummy variable repeated ties supports hypothesis 2 and indicates that the larger the number of prior alliances between partners, the less likely their current alliance is to be equity-based, even when the presence of an R&D component is controlled for. The positive and significant coefficient for international alliance supports hypothesis 4, which predicts that such alliances are more likely to be equity-based than domestic alliances. No support is found for hypothesis 5, however, which predicts that the use of equity is more likely in multilateral than in bilateral alliances. These results remain true in subsequent models.

Models 4 and 5 were estimated using the measures of prior equity and nonequity alliances. The variable for repeated alliances was omitted because of multicollinearity concerns. In both models, results suggest that the number of prior equity-based ties between two firms reduces the likelihood that a current alliance between them will be equity based, thus supporting hypothesis 3a.

Results do not support hypothesis 3b, which postulates that even in the absence of prior equity ties, the larger the number of nonequity alliances between two firms, the less likely their future alliance is to be equity-based. However, the number of alliances that actually fit this pattern was extremely small ($n = 23$). Thus, the nonsignificant finding may be the result of too few observations.

Table 5.4. Estimates of fit of logistic regression models

Observed	Predicted			Percentage correct
	No event	Event	Total	
Model 1				
No event	20	807	827	—
Event	15	1,553	1,568	—
Total	35	2,360	2,395	65.7
Model 2				
No event	125	702	827	—
Event	91	1,477	1,568	—
Total	216	2,179	2,395	66.9
Model 3				
No event	173	654	827	—
Event	119	1,449	1,568	—
Total	292	2,103	2,395	67.7
Model 4				
No event	199	628	827	—
Event	177	1,391	1,568	—
Total	376	2,019	2,395	66.4
Model 5				
No event	199	628	827	—
Event	178	1,390	1,568	—
Total	377	2,018	2,395	66.3

Looking at the overall fit of each of the models indicated by their log likelihoods and associated x^2, I observed that the introduction of R&D in model 2 significantly improved the fit of the base model. Another significant improvement occurred in models 3 and 4, with the introduction of the variables for repeated, international, and multilateral alliances and that for repeated equity ties.

Table 5.4 presents the classification tables corresponding to each of the models in Table 5.3. These tables highlight the association between predicted and observed responses for each model. All five models perform better than a random proportional chance model, which would have a 'hit rate' of $p^2 + (1 - p)^2$, where p is the probability of an event's having occurred (Bayus and Gupta 1992). On the basis of the observed proportion of events, I estimated p to be .65 (1,568/2,395). Thus, the classification accuracy for a random model is 54.25 percent. The percentage of correctly classified cases in the five models reported ranges from 65.7 to 67.7 percent, a rate clearly superior to the random model. The models also perform better than a simple model with only the intercept (which would predict all nonevents), albeit not by a large percentage difference. Although this pattern suggests a significant improvement over a random proportional chance model, it also indicates that I may have overlooked additional relevant variables.

Table 5.5. Elasticities[a] for logistic regression analysis results

Variables	Model 3	Model 5
R&D	37.73	38.36
Repeated ties	−14.13	—
International alliance	12.47	12.10
Multilateral alliance	5.74	7.46
Repeated equity ties	—	−13.70
Repeated nonequity ties	—	7.51

[a] Elasticity is the change in probability resulting from a unit change in an independent variable.

The relative magnitudes of raw logit coefficients are not directly interpretable because they refer to the increase in logarithmic odds resulting from a unit increase in a variable. In Table 5.5, I present elasticities for the key variables entered in two models shown in Table 5.3 (Ben-Akiva and Lerman 1985; Petersen 1985; Fernandez and McAdam 1988).[2] Elasticities indicate the percentage change in the probability of a hypothesized event for a one-unit change in an explanatory variable.

The results in Table 5.5 must be interpreted with caution because each variable has a different underlying measurement scale. In particular, for R&D, a unit change indicates that non-R&D alliances possibly had an R&D component. For repeated alliances, a unit change indicates the existence of one more prior alliance. Thus, Table 5.5 shows that if two firms had entered an R&D alliance instead of a non-R&D alliance, their likelihood of forming an equity JV would have increased by about 38 percent. If two firms entering an alliance had one more prior alliance of any kind, model 3 suggests that their likelihood of forming an equity JV would have declined by 14.13 percent. Model 5 suggests that one more prior equity alliance reduced the likelihood of forming an equity alliance by 13.70 percent. Similarly, the marginal effects of international and multilateral alliances are also reported.

Conclusion

The results of models 1 through 5 (Table 5.3) provide strong evidence for most of the present hypotheses. They show that (a) R&D-based alliances are more likely to be equity-based than non-R&D alliances, (b) the larger the

[2] I computed these elasticity scores by looking across all individual records as opposed to simply setting mean values for each independent variable and then looking at percentage shifts.

number of prior alliances between two firms, the less likely their subsequent alliances are to be equity-based, (c) the larger the number of prior equity alliances between two firms, the less likely their subsequent alliances are to be equity-based, and (d) international alliances are more likely to be equity based than domestic alliances. However, no support emerged for the claim that prior nonequity alliances alone reduce use of equity in new alliances. Also the number of partners in an alliance does not seem to affect the form of governance used. Taken together, the results suggest that firms select contractual forms for their alliances not only on the basis of the activities they include (R&D) but also according to information obtained through prior alliances and the resultant network resources. What emerges from this account is an image of alliance formation in which cautious contracting gives way to looser practices as partner firms build confidence in each other as they accumulate network resources. In other words, network resources based on prior ties propagate valuable information to embedded firms that in turn promotes familiarity between organizations that breeds trust, which impacts, in turn, their governance structures.

Consequently, this chapter demonstrates an important additional benefit of network resources. By engendering trust between a focal firm and its prior partners, network resources can be a powerful lubricant not only in fostering new alliances between them but also in enabling them to enter into increasingly more complex relationships using looser contracts. As a result, network resources can be a powerful catalyst for creating governance cost efficiencies. It is worth noting that while trust resides inherently in a dyadic connection, it is possible to envision how a focal firm can create diverse ties that cumulate into a network resource allowing more frequent alliances with past partners and looser contracts than the activities included within those partnerships might typically mandate. An important direction for future research would be to go beyond the dyadic level here to consider the role of additional sources of network resources discussed before, such as more distant alliance ties in the network and alternative ties such as board interlocks in shaping the governance structures of alliances.

In a review of the transaction cost economics literature, Bradach and Eccles (1989) argued that three primary control mechanisms govern economic transactions between firms: price, authority, and trust. They observed that, in equity alliances, firms rely on a mix of price and authority—price because of concern for the value of their equity and authority because of the hierarchy created. Such an approach, however, examines alliances in a static context, treating each transaction as independent, without taking into account how the relationships can evolve over time. Observing interfirm alliances over time suggests that repeated ties between firms engender trust that in turn shapes the form of the contracts used in subsequent alliances. Firms appear to substitute trust to some degree for contractual safeguards in their repeated alliances. Thus, trust is also an important component of the control mechanisms used within alliances.

The network resources a firm may possess and the concomitant trust in specific partners is most visible in the case of partners with whom equity alliances are already in place. My earlier discussion of some of the processes underlying interorganizational behavior suggests that prior equity ties are not simply mutual hostages that enhance each firm's ability to penalize partners that behave opportunistically but also network resources that provide information about partners, helping to build knowledge-based trust. The finding here that only having prior equity alliances leads to looser contracts could very well indicate that equity alliances foster closer interaction between partners than do nonequity alliances and thus are an avenue to greater network resources for those firms.

Although this study enhances our understanding of governance structure in alliances, it has broad implications for transaction cost economics as well. Building on the original insights of Coase (1937), this theory has reified the transaction as the unit of analysis, treating each transaction as an independent event. It has ignored the work of Commons (1970), Coase's contemporary, who also placed importance on transactions as the appropriate unit of analysis but offered a more process-oriented and temporally informed view of transactions (cf. Van de Ven 1993). Other scholars have offered similar exhortations (cf. Zajac and Olsen 1993), but organizational researchers have yet to take them up. This chapter, which is a step in this direction, suggests that transaction cost economics must explicitly incorporate the role of prior ties in its analytical framework. In particular, if the theory's emphasis on the transaction as the appropriate unit of analysis is to remain viable, the interdependencies that result from prior transactions should be included.

By highlighting a number of efficiency benefits that follow from network resources and the trust it engenders, this study has several practical consequences for interfirm alliance activity and interfirm cooperation. First, trust obtained from network resources can significantly reduce the costs of and time spent on detailed contracts. *Business Week* ('Corporate Odd Couples' 1986) reported that executives can spend as much as 23 percent of their time developing alliance plans and 19 percent of their time drafting legal documents, so savings could be significant. Another benefit of trust is that it enables firms to avoid detailed contracts that may stifle a partnership's adaptability to shifting environments. Trust may also expand the realm of feasible alliances and allow firms to enter partnerships that may otherwise have been deemed impossible, even with detailed equity contracts. Finally, firms in trusting relationships enjoy reduced search costs. An important concern for firms seeking new alliances is the availability of trustworthy partners, and considerable effort can be devoted to identifying them (Nohria 1992*a*). Through network resources, firms are able to more easily identify trustworthy partners, which can significantly reduce their search time and costs.

6 The architecture of cooperation: the role of network resources in managing coordination costs and appropriation concerns in strategic alliances

The last chapter detailed how choice of governance structures in alliances is influenced not only by appropriation concerns and moral hazards arising from the attributes of the specific transactions to be consummated within a particular alliance partnership but also by the network resources available to participating firms. It showed that the network of prior alliances provides firms with a valuable network resource in the form of familiarity with prior alliance partners that engenders interorganizational trust, which in turn reduces uncertainty and the need for hierarchical controls in new alliances between previously allied parties. In other words, trust produced by network resources is a distinct factor that obviates the need for hierarchical controls in alliances.

Still, while the appropriation concerns highlighted in the previous chapter and in much prior research on alliance governance structure are clearly important, firms face another set of concerns when they enter an alliance. These concerns relate to anticipated coordination costs at the outset, which can be extensive in some types of alliances. This chapter draws on an article I published with Harbir Singh. We introduced the notion of coordination costs

This chapter is adapted from 'The Architecture of Cooperation: Managing Coordination Costs and Appropriation Concerns in Strategic Alliances' by Ranjay Gulati and Harbir Singh published in *Administrative Science Quarterly* © 1998, (43/4): 781–814, by permission of Johnson Graduate School of Management, Cornell University.

to refer to the anticipated complexity of decomposing tasks among partners and the ongoing coordination of joint and individual activities across organizational boundaries, as well as any related communication and decision-making. Some of these ideas date back to much earlier research. For instance, Litwak and Hylton (1962: 399) noted that the specialized coordination in interorganizational relations is a challenge, 'since there is both conflict and cooperation and formal authority structure is lacking'. Given this reality, inter-dependence and the complexities of task coordination can create considerable uncertainty at the outset of an alliance, uncertainty that is distinct from appropriation concerns. For example, even if an alliance is formed between two firms that have complete confidence in each other and face no appropriation concerns, they must still coordinate the division of labor and the interface of activities and products between them. Consequently, they may still face considerable uncertainty regarding how activities will be decomposed and integrated and the extent to which there will be an ongoing need for mutual adaptation and adjustment. In many ways, the problems identified in the last chapter can be described as 'cooperation' issues while those discussed in this chapter are more focused on 'coordination'.

As with appropriation concerns, hierarchical controls can be an effective remedy for coordination uncertainty, especially in those cases where anticipated coordination costs are high. As noted by Barnard (1938), Chandler (1977), Thompson (1967), and others, an important basis for hierarchical controls is their ability to provide superior task coordination, especially in situations involving high interdependence and coordination. In the context of alliance relationships, interdependence refers to situations in which a firm has to rely at least partially on other firms for the attainment of its goals (Pfeffer and Salancik 1978). The degree of interdependence and associated coordination costs perceived by prospective partners are important determinants of the governance arrangement chosen for their alliance. Hence, the governance structure of an alliance reflects not only the appropriation concerns anticipated by managers at the outset but also coordination costs arising from the complexity of allocating and coordinating joint tasks between the partners.

This chapter proposes that the incorporation of hierarchical controls within the governance structure, or hierarchical control of an alliance is not only a method for managing appropriation concerns but also an effective mechanism for coordinating complex and interdependent tasks across partners. The results of the empirical study in this chapter validate that choice of governance structure is influenced not only by appropriation concerns, as previously suggested, but also by concerns about managing coordination costs. Furthermore, while the focus of the original article was primarily on coordination, I adapt those ideas here to show that network resources can be instrumental in shaping the choice of governance structure not only by influencing the magnitude of anticipated appropriation concerns but also by shaping firms' expected concerns regarding coordination.

This research has implications for the study of alternative bases of hierarchical control in alliances and for the study of organization design in general and is distinctive in several ways: (*a*) it specifies the concept of coordination costs, which highlights the importance of uncertainty resulting from task coordination across partners as a strong influence on the choice of governance structure in alliances; (*b*) by directly modeling the influence of anticipated coordination costs on the governance structure of alliances after accounting for concerns about appropriation, it provides a window into the multiple types of logic used by alliance participants in determining the governance structure of alliances; (*c*) it suggests a typology of alliance governance structures and provides details on the magnitude and type of hierarchical controls present in each; and (*d*) it shows that network resources and concomitant interorganizational trust can influence the chosen governance structure by mitigating concerns of both cooperation and coordination.

Theory and hypotheses

COORDINATION COSTS AND INTERDEPENDENCE AS AN ORGANIZING PRINCIPLE

As mentioned in the last chapter, the importance of behavioral uncertainty and appropriation concerns as rationales for hierarchical controls in exchange relationships are well understood. The role of anticipated coordination costs in influencing the use of hierarchical controls in exchange relationships, though less developed, may be equally important (e.g. Gulati, Lawrence, and Puranam 2005). Organizational sociologists have referred to hierarchical controls as superior information-processing mechanisms that have arisen from an increasing division of labor within organizations and the concomitant uncertainty originating from the need to coordinate interdependent subtasks (Galbraith 1977: 93). This concept can be traced to the work of others. Barnard (1938) noted the ability of organizational hierarchies to mitigate the uncertainty associated with the coordination and control of complex and interdependent tasks by enhancing cooperation among organizational members. Similarly, Chandler (1977) emphasized the significance of coordination in hierarchical structures. In more recent years, transaction cost economists have examined issues such as temporal specificity, or the importance of timing in receipt of goods or services, that are also related to coordination costs (Masten, Meehan, and Snyder 1991).

Concerns about anticipated coordination costs are particularly salient in strategic alliances, which can entail significant coordination of activities that must be managed without the benefit of some of the structure and systems available in traditional hierarchies (Litwak and Hylton 1962; Gulati, Lawrence, and Puranam 2005). Some observers have described alliances as a hybrid organizational form between the extremes of market and hierarchy (Williamson 1991). Coordination concerns arise in such hybrid forms from the complexity associated with the ongoing coordination of activities to be completed jointly or individually across organizational boundaries and from the difficulties associated with decomposing tasks and specifying a precise division of labor across alliance partners. The extent of such coordination concerns in an alliance is a function of the level of 'interdependence' necessary for the alliance partners to complete tasks (Thompson 1967). Interdependence here refers to the extent to which partners need each other to accomplish the agreed-on joint tasks. At one extreme, partners in an alliance may anticipate minimal interaction; while at the other, extensive coordination may be necessary. Many researchers have testified to the complexities associated with the interdependence of activities across partners in strategic alliances (Hamel, Doz, and Prahalad 1989; Ring and Van de Ven 1992), yet the implications of anticipated interdependence and coordination costs for the governance structure of interfirm alliances remain unexplored.[1]

The concept of interdependence, a fundamental principle defining the costs of coordination within organizations, dates back to the early work of systems theorists (Ashby 1956; Katz and Kahn 1966) and was further developed by Thompson (1967) and others.[2] Scholars have primarily applied interdependence to studying the internal design features of organizations and have devoted considerable effort to its elaboration and measurement. Organization design scholars have in fact referred to the challenges posed by interdependence as 'coordination costs' (McCann and Galbraith 1981). As interdependence increases, information-processing costs may rise (Galbraith 1977), as may pressure for faster responses (Emery and Trist 1965) and, ultimately, conflict; this can lead to a decline in performance (Pondy 1970).

---

[1] Davis, Kahn, and Zald (1990) connected governance structure and interdependence in the context of interactions between nation-states by using interorganizational ties as an analog to illuminate how nation-states behave. Gerlach and Palmer (1981) looked at changing levels of sociopolitical interdependence to explore the antecedents of interdependence and its consequences for the emergence of new governance institutions.

[2] Teece (1992: 8) acknowledged that an innovator's quest for complementary assets can lead to varying degrees of interdependence and cospecialization, but he focused on the relative degree of mutual dependence resulting from specialization of assets for the alliance; the greater the mutual dependence, the larger the cospecialization. In contrast, our usage of interdependence focuses on the partners' anticipation of the extent of complexity in decomposing tasks and the degree to which it will entail ongoing mutual adjustment and adaptation to accomplish joint tasks, which is akin to Teece's discussion of 'coupling'.

The anticipated extent of interdependence between partners at the time they form an alliance can vary substantially and depends on the tasks included and the likely division of labor in the partnership, all of which are a function of the strategic rationale for the alliance. At one extreme, interdependence may be minimal, such as those cases where an alliance has a simple division of labor and little perceived need for ongoing adjustments and the sharing of information to achieve alliance objectives. At the other extreme, interdependence can be extensive, resulting from the anticipation of a complex and overlapping division of labor that will entail continuing mutual adjustments between partners and require each partner to coordinate specific activities with other partners closely and regularly. The higher the anticipated interdependence between alliance partners, the greater the magnitude of expected coordination costs. While the anticipated interdependence in an alliance may also influence the extent of the appropriation concerns partners experience (Stinchcombe 1985), the primary interdependence-based concerns are the administrative challenges of task coordination. Consequently, the greater the need for ongoing task coordination and joint decision-making between the partners in an alliance, the higher the anticipated level of interdependence and coordination costs.

As highlighted in the previous chapter, alliances can be formalized using an array of governance arrangements. While the previous chapter highlighted how governance structure can be a powerful vehicle for addressing appropriation concerns in alliances and hence reflects the level of such concerns regarding an alliance at the outset, this chapter suggests that the governance structure may also be a function of the anticipated coordination costs at the outset. Each form of alliance governance structure provides differing degrees of control over and coordination of activities in a partnership. As a result, firms will seek the governance structures for alliances that provide the necessary ongoing oversight and coordination that they anticipate needing at the time they form the alliance. The higher the likely interdependence among partners, the greater the amount of information they must process while the alliance is in place (Galbraith 1977). Partners in such alliances must evolve mechanisms through the governance structure to process the requisite information. Alliances with more hierarchical controls are capable of providing greater coordination and information-processing capabilities than those with fewer controls.

HIERARCHICAL CONTROLS IN STRATEGIC ALLIANCES

Contractual relationships such as alliances can include several embedded hierarchical elements in their structures (Stinchcombe 1985): (*a*) a command structure and authority systems to put it in place, as well as systems for certifying which communications are authoritative; (*b*) incentive systems that facilitate performance measurement and link rewards to performance; (*c*) standard operating procedures that enable quick decisions by anticipating those decisions in advance; (*d*) dispute resolution procedures that bypass courts and markets by specifying a hierarchy of entities or individuals to which appeals can be made; and (*e*) nonmarket pricing systems, such as cost-plus systems, that enable greater precision in remuneration when specifications change. These hierarchical elements are present to varying degrees in different governance structures for alliances. While incentive systems and nonmarket pricing highlight some of the agency features of hierarchical controls, other elements concern the coordination capabilities of hierarchical controls in alliances. For instance, the command structure, authority systems, and standard operating procedures help partners coordinate tasks by clarifying decision-making procedures and anticipating issues before they arise.

Hierarchical elements in alliances can effectively alleviate anticipated coordination costs resulting from interdependence because they coordinate tasks, formalize partner interaction, and designate partner roles. The standard operating procedures, command structure, and authority systems in hierarchical governance structures in alliances typically include planning, rules, programs, or procedures, which March and Simon (1958) identified as key means for task coordination. Planning involves presetting schedules, outcomes, and targets, while rules, programs, and procedures emphasize formal controls in the form of a priori decisions for various likely scenarios. All of these serve the common purpose of streamlining communication, simplifying decision-making, reducing uncertainty about future tasks, and preventing disputes (Pondy 1977).

Hierarchical controls also formalize the interactions and roles of partners, which makes the division of labor and the interactions between partners more predictable and allows joint decisions to be made more by rules than by exceptions. Furthermore, if division of labor and task coordination conflicts do arise, hierarchical controls may also include procedures for resolving disputes. These procedures anticipate potential disputes and try to bypass adjudication by the courts by specifying a hierarchy of avenues for resolution. Such alternative forums not only limit the scope of disputes but also allow partners to discover joint solutions to more effective coordination.

Hierarchical controls in alliances also exist in the form of incentive systems and pricing mechanisms that can simplify the contribution of partner resources. Both of these hierarchical controls typically occur in alliances that create autonomous entities, such as JVs. Creating a separate entity makes it easier to monitor each party's contributions and the performance of joint activities while also aligning incentives for each of them. It also reduces ongoing market price haggling between partners by locating all resources and expenses within a single entity that is jointly owned. The creation of an autonomous entity can also simplify coordination in alliances. Such alliances provide a high level of discretion to the entity in which joint activities are being conducted, which provides a dedicated management with a mandate to make decisions that optimize the activities contributed by each partner toward the accomplishment of joint goals. An autonomous alliance such as a JV thus echoes Galbraith's notion (1977) of self-contained tasks because the discrete entity is provided with its own set of resources to perform the assigned task. Such alliances address anticipated coordination costs by limiting future discussions between partners on the precise division of labor and focuses attention on the outputs because the inputs have already been agreed on at the outset.

Because such hierarchical controls are effective in alleviating coordination costs in alliances, we propose the following hypothesis:

Hypothesis 1: The greater the anticipated interdependence (coordination costs) in an alliance, the more hierarchical the governance structure used to organize it.

APPROPRIATION CONCERNS AND THE GOVERNANCE STRUCTURE OF STRATEGIC ALLIANCES

The term 'appropriation concerns' is used here in the context of alliances to refer to a firm's concern about its ability to capture a fair share of the rents from the alliance in which it is engaged. Such concerns arise from the uncertainties associated with future specifications, cost uncertainties, and problems in observing partner contributions, all of which increase the potential for moral hazards. As outlined in the previous chapter, these appropriation concerns occur to varying degrees in most alliances. As shown earlier, the anticipation of appropriation concerns at the time an alliance is formed is linked to the specific governance structure used to formalize the alliance, suggesting that the greater the potential concerns, the more hierarchical the contract used. According to this logic, concerns about appropriation can vary with the specific circumstances of an alliance at its inception and arise because of the difficulty of writing complete contracts. This difficulty is exacerbated when technology exchange or sharing is involved and the limits of the technology transacted are difficult to specify (Merges and Nelson 1990; Oxley 1997; Anand and Khanna 2000*a*, 2000*b*).

The previous chapter looked at one condition that can influence the extent to which such concerns arise: the presence of a technology component in the alliance, as represented by R&D. However, an additional factor that may shape the magnitude of such concerns is the appropriability regime in the industry. Both factors can independently and jointly influence the extent of appropriation concerns of firms entering an alliance by presenting challenges associated with specifying property rights and monitoring and enforcing the agreement. Because the first factor was discussed in the last chapter, this chapter focuses primarily on the second factor, appropriability regime, and then turns to addressing the role of network resources as an important catalyst that reduces appropriation concerns and in turn impacts the selection of governance structure in exchange relationships.

TECHNOLOGY IN ALLIANCES

A primary factor that prior researchers have examined in regard to concerns of moral hazards and appropriation in alliances is the presence of a technology component (e.g. Pisano, Russo, and Teece 1988; Pisano 1989). Technology-based issues generally increase the extent of possible monitoring problems and the possibility of unobserved violation of contracts. Monitoring problems in technology alliances result from the ambiguity surrounding two key issues: the technology being transferred and the limits to its use (Anand and Khanna 2000a, 2000b). In alliances that encompass technology, circumscribing, bounding, monitoring, and codifying the knowledge to be included within the alliance can be difficult, which may lead to concerns about free riding and possible appropriation of key technology by the partner. Such concerns are further compounded by the peculiar character of knowledge, the commodity value of which is difficult to assess accurately without complete information from all partners, some of whom may not want to reveal such information because it is proprietary (Winter 1964; Arrow 1974; Teece 1980: 28). This dilemma, which is called the knowledge paradox, can further aggravate concerns about appropriation of rents resulting from poor monitoring possibilities in such exchanges (Barzel 1982; Hennart 1988; Balakrishnan and Koza 1993). The difficulty of transferring tacit R&D know-how across organizations inflates these problems (Teece 1980; Silver 1984; Mowery and Rosenberg 1989).

Coordination costs can also be a concern in technology alliances, but they are likely to be salient only in the subset that involves bilateral exchange or joint development. The primary concern of participants entering alliances with a technology component, then, has to do with anticipated appropriation issues. Thus, firms entering an alliance with a technology component are likely to prefer hierarchical alliances:

Hypothesis 2a: Alliances with an expected technology component are more likely than those without a technology component to be organized with more hierarchical governance structures.

APPROPRIABILITY REGIME IN ALLIANCES

Another factor likely to influence the level of appropriation concerns is the strength of the appropriability regime of the industry, which is the degree to which firms are able to capture the rents generated by their innovations (Anand and Khanna 2000*a*, 2000*b*). In a tight appropriability regime, firms can retain the profits they earn from their proprietary resources, while in a loose regime, these profits are subject to involuntary leakage or spillovers to other firms. The strength of the appropriability regime of an industry is related to patent strength, the value of first-mover advantage, and the ability to maintain the secrecy of an innovation (Teece 1986; Levin et al. 1987). For alliances, a firm's concerns about appropriation will vary depending on the industry in which the alliance occurs and the degree to which the appropriability regime in the industry is tight or loose (Teece 1986). If participants in an alliance believe that the appropriability regime is strong—because patent protection is significant, or they can keep trade secrets, or their first-mover advantage is sufficiently large—they are likely to be less concerned about appropriation in an alliance, and this will be reflected in the formal governance structure used for the alliance.[3] As a result, there should be a relationship between the appropriability regime of the industry and the governance structure of alliances, with more hierarchical structures expected in industries with weak appropriability regimes.

Hypothesis 2b: Alliances in an industry in which appropriability regimes are weak are more likely to be organized with more hierarchical governance structures than are alliances in an industry in which appropriability regimes are strong.

The effects of a given industry's appropriability regime are strongest for alliances with a technology or other knowledge-sharing component. As a result, partners in technology alliances are likely to experience concerns related to appropriability regimes more acutely than those in alliances without a technology component. More specifically, the appropriation concerns anticipated are likely to be amplified when potential partners consider a technology alliance in an industry with a weak appropriability regime. Thus, the effect of the appropriability regime on the governance structure of alliances is likely to be moderated by the presence of a technology component in the proposed alliance.

---

[3] It is likely that the strength of the appropriability regime in an industry may be shaped by the distribution of network resources in that sector. In sectors with dense sets of ties among firms and easy access to network resources, the appropriability regime is likely to be stronger due to the creation of reputational circuits in which participating firms are less likely to engage in malfeasance due to reputational concerns. This intriguing idea is not tested in this study but is put forward as an exciting arena for future research.

Hypothesis 2c: The negative relationship between the strength of the appropriability regime in the industry and the extent of hierarchical governance structures of alliances will be stronger for alliances with a technology component than for those without one.

TRUST, NETWORK RESOURCES, AND GOVERNANCE STRUCTURE

As discussed in the previous chapter, network resources resulting from a firm's network of prior ties are likely to grant it greater confidence in the predictability of its alliance partners' actions and thus decrease appropriation concerns related to a potential alliance. So, the presence of network resources at the time of an alliance announcement can help firms address appropriation concerns by making it easier to assess likely partner behavior. Network resources can also help firms preserve intellectual property rights by creating reputational circuits whereby partner malfeasance results in reduced prospects for future alliance relationships among network participants.

In addition to mitigating appropriation concerns, network resources can alleviate anticipated concerns about coordination costs. They do this by fostering the development of interfirm trust, which can be an extraordinary lubricant for alliances that involve considerable interdependence and task coordination. Firms that trust each other are likely to have a greater awareness—or at least a stronger willingness to become aware—of the rules, routines, and procedures each follows. Furthermore, because the interorganizational trust associated with network resources typically arises from prior alliance relationships between given firms, these firms may already have developed efficient joint routines. Thus, interconnected firms may have greater competence in transacting with each other, which makes the interface between them easier to manage and the information-processing requirements associated with anticipated coordination costs more easily addressed (Dyer and Singh 1998).

While the presence of network resources and resulting trust may not allow us to discriminate between coordination-cost and appropriation concerns, trust is distinct in its ability to address both types of concerns. As a result, the presence of trust between partners is likely to promote fewer hierarchical controls in the alliances between them, not only because concerns of appropriation and behavioral uncertainty are effectively addressed by trust but also because coordination costs are more easily managed in the context of trust.

Hypothesis 3: Alliances in which there is less trust between partners are more likely to be organized with more hierarchical governance structures than are those in which there is greater trust.

CLASSIFYING GOVERNANCE STRUCTURES: JOINT VENTURES, MINORITY ALLIANCES, AND CONTRACTUAL ALLIANCES

Research presented in the previous chapter was consistent with prior research that has generally classified the governance structure of interfirm alliances in terms of their hierarchical components and has differentiated alliances by the presence or absence of equity, with alliances involving equity considered more hierarchical than nonequity exchanges (e.g. Hennart 1988; Pisano, Russo, and Teece 1988; Pisano 1989; Teece 1992). Equity alliances comprise any exchange agreement in which the partners share or exchange equity, including agreements in which partners create a new entity in which they share equity as well as those in which one partner takes an equity interest in the other. Equity has been considered an indicator of hierarchy because it is considered to be an effective mechanism for managing the rent appropriation concerns associated with partnerships (Pisano, Russo, and Teece 1988; Parkhe 1993*a*; Moon and Khanna 1995). Thus, Teece (1992: 20) suggested, 'Equity stakes provide a mechanism for distributing residuals when ex ante contractual agreements cannot be written to specify or enforce a division of returns.' In JVs, this occurs by creating a mutual hostage in the form of shared equity that helps align the interests of all the partners, inasmuch as each partner is concerned about the value of its equity in the alliance. In minority equity investments, the investing partner has an interest in the value of its equity holdings, while the recipient of investments can be legally required to furnish certain verified information to its investors. In equity alliances, the effective shared equity stakes of the firms vary, but beyond a certain threshold the shared ownership structure is expected to provide an effective hierarchical control over the exchange.

While such categorization is parsimonious, it masks differences in hierarchical controls across different types of structures and ignores the original basis for classifying the governance structure of alliances: degree of hierarchical controls. Also, because this typology considers the presence of equity sharing a heuristic to indicate hierarchical controls, there has been little serious consideration of the specific governance structures of each alliance type or their precise levels of hierarchical controls and how these manifest themselves. For instance, JVs and minority investments provide varying levels of hierarchical control in a partnership, with JVs incorporating more hierarchical elements than minority investments. To varying degrees, each includes several 'mechanisms for collecting information, deciding, and disseminating information to resolve conflicts and guide interdependent actions' (Galbraith 1977: 40). In contrast with JVs, minority investments typically do not have a separate organizational and administrative structure and are thus relatively limited in their capacity for activity coordination. In addition to the exchanged equity, JVs entail separate administrative entities, each with its own management structure. Thus, separating out these different types of alliances may allow a more fine-grained assessment of the factors that drive choice of governance structure.

This chapter departs from prior efforts and further refines the typology used in the last chapter by presenting a typology of alliance structure that does not treat the presence of equity as synonymous with hierarchical controls but, rather, defines three distinct types of alliance governance structures—JVs, minority investment, and contractual alliances—and the types and magnitudes of hierarchical controls typically present in each of them. Earlier in this chapter, I noted that hierarchical controls in alliances typically include the following: command structure and authority systems, incentive systems, standard operating procedures, dispute resolution procedures, and nonmarket pricing systems.

Together, these dimensions encompass both the agency and coordination features of hierarchical controls that are likely to be part of various types of alliances. Each of the three types of governance structure is typically associated with a specific level and form of hierarchical control, though there may be some variation. This typology of alliance structures is the basis for testing the hypotheses on the factors influencing choice of governance structure and extent of hierarchical control.

At the hierarchical end of the spectrum are JVs, in which partners create a separate entity of which each owns a portion of the equity. In such alliances, a separate administrative hierarchy of managers oversees day-to-day functioning and addresses contingencies as they arise. This provides an independent command structure and authority system with clearly defined rules and responsibilities for each partner. The autonomous unit enables creation of an incentive system because each partner is concerned about the value of its equity in the JV. Furthermore, pricing discussions are internalized by the JV, which simplifies much of the input and output resource flows between the partner organizations. As part of creating a JV entity, partner firms also typically establish standard operating systems and dispute resolution procedures. Together, these features provide JVs with considerable hierarchical controls.

Minority alliances, in contrast, include partnerships in which the firms work together without creating a new entity. Instead, one partner or a set of partners takes a minority equity position in the other (or others). Such alliances introduce a weaker form of hierarchical control, between that of JVs and that of contractual alliances (Herriott 1996). Hierarchical supervision is typically created by the investing partner's joining the board of directors of the invested-in partner. This board membership introduces a fiduciary role into the relationship and is also a vehicle for hierarchical controls. Because boards ratify most major decisions, the presence of an individual from the investing organization on the investee board ensures that the investor has some form of command and authority system. A concern for the value of its equity provides appropriate incentives for the investor. Furthermore, disputes may be easier to resolve through board member intervention. Finally, while there may or may not be many standard operating procedures with such alliances, board representation does create a forum in which both partners exchange information and can initiate and ratify decisions on a regular basis. Beyond board-level interactions, day-to-day activities are jointly coordinated by the partners and negotiated on an ongoing basis.

Alliances in the third category, contractual alliances, do not involve the sharing or exchange of equity, nor do they entail the creation of new organizational entities. Lacking any shared ownership or administrative structure, contractual alliances are considered more akin to arm's length market exchanges. Members of the partner firms work together directly from their own organizational confines. Few if any command structures, authority systems, incentive systems, standard operating systems, dispute resolution procedures, or nonmarket pricing systems are necessarily part of such arrangements. Ongoing activities are jointly coordinated, and new decisions are negotiated by the partners. Contractual alliances include unidirectional agreements such as licensing, second-sourcing, and distribution agreements, and bidirectional agreements such as joint contracts and technology exchange agreements. While some of the hierarchical elements discussed earlier may occur in some contractual alliances, they are not widespread and do not occur on a systematic basis.

Empirical research

METHOD

The data set used in this study is described in Appendix 1 under the heading 'Alliance Announcement Database'. This study does not treat the presence of equity as the sole indicator of whether hierarchical controls are present within an alliance relationship. To assess more accurately the factors explaining the degree of hierarchy in alliances, this study was conducted with three categories of alliances, arrayed in increasing order of hierarchical controls (*hierarchy*): contractual alliances (coded 0), minority equity investments (1), and JVs (2).

The focus here was on assessing the levels of interdependence the partners in an alliance anticipated at the outset, when the alliance was announced. Using Thompson's distinction (1967) between pooled, sequential, and reciprocal interdependence offers a clear methodology for classifying the degree of interdependence in alliances that underlies coordination costs. These three types of interdependence, although previously discussed in the intraorganizational context, can also be seen in the context of interfirm coordination of activities (Borys and Jennison 1989). Pooled, or generalized interdependence, denotes situations in which 'each part renders a discrete contribution to the whole, and each is supported by the whole', is 'coordinated by standardization, and is least costly in terms of communication and decision effort' because it does not require any serial ordering of activities (Thompson 1967: 54, 64). It exists in alliances when organizations pool their resources to achieve a shared strategic goal, the common benefits arise from combining resources into a shared pool, and each partner uses resources from the shared pool. These relatively small interdependencies entail low coordination requirements but provide partners with benefits from the pooled resources.

In situations of sequential interdependence, the activities of each partner are distinct and are serially arrayed so that the activities of one partner precede those of another, resulting in a higher degree of coordination relative to pooled interdependence. Coordination in a sequentially interdependent alliance thus goes beyond the pooling of resources to include the order in which the product or service moves from one organization to the other. The partner producing the original product or service has to perform the task as laid out in plans for the alliance, and the subsequent activities in the alliance then have to be performed in a coordinated fashion for the overall strategy to be successful.

Reciprocal interdependence occurs when units come together to exchange outputs with each other simultaneously. Such exchange entails a pooling of resources by different units, but in addition, each unit is simultaneously dependent on the other because its outputs are the other's inputs. In contrast to pooled interdependence, reciprocal interdependence is more interactive and requires ongoing mutual adjustment by both units and continuous adaptation to each other's circumstances. Each unit must continually anticipate the other's output stream and communicate its own production schedule to the other. These efforts require both units to work closely together to ensure that there is requisite mutual adaptation and adjustment. These three types of interdependence can be arrayed on a scale, with reciprocal interdependence encompassing the highest coordination costs due to the need for extensive coordination across the partners (Thompson 1967). Somewhat less uncertainty is associated with sequential interdependence. The least amount of uncertainty is associated with pooled interdependence, in which close ongoing coordination is not essential, and coordination demands are limited to broadly aligning the activities of the partners toward joint success.

Consistent with prior research, the anticipated interdependence in an alliance relationship at the time of its inception was identified from its underlying logic of value creation (Borys and Jennison 1989; Zajac and Olsen 1993). Alliances are usually formed to create value in a way that each partner alone could not. Different logics for value creation require distinctly different levels of coordination between the partners and hence are indicative of different types of interdependence (Borys and Jennison 1989: 241). For instance, an alliance in which two partners seek to create value by one of them distributing the other's products is likely to have lower coordination and interdependence than another in which the logic for creating value involves both partners coming together to develop a new product. In Thompson's classic (1967) formulation as well, interdependence among units in an organization was embedded in the logic by which they created value through interacting with each other. That is, the logic for value creation led to distinct levels and types of interaction between adjacent units in a value chain and indicated the level of interdependence between those units.

The anticipated presence of reciprocal, sequential, or pooled interdependence in an alliance was gauged from the strategic rationales given by each partner for its participation in the alliance. The rationales provided by each partner for an alliance at the time of its announcement are an excellent indicator of the interdependence they anticipate because each rationale suggests a distinct logic for value creation that is associated with a specific level of interdependence necessary for accomplishing the rationale. From an extensive review of the alliance literature, we identified eight rationales that provided a comprehensive picture of all the value creation logics of firms that entered alliances: (*a*) sharing costs/risks, (*b*) access to financial resources, (*c*) sharing complementary technology, (*d*) reducing the time span of innovation, (*e*) joint development of new technology, (*f*) access to new markets, (*g*) access to new products, and (*h*) sharing production facilities (Contractor and Lorange 1988; Hagedoorn 1993). We then identified which of these rationales were stated by alliance participants (in our data-set) in their public announcements—and coded them separately for each partner in each alliance. In most instances, multiple alliance announcements were examined in a variety of public sources, including industry-specific trade journals, to gauge this measure accurately. The eight categories are not mutually exclusive, and an alliance could include multiple strategic objectives for any partner. Each alliance was coded as involving reciprocal, sequential, or pooled interdependence, using the classification scheme discussed below. Two dummy variables, *reciprocal* and *sequential*, capture this distinction and were used to test hypothesis 1. The default category included instances of pooled interdependence. A comparison of the coefficients of the two dummy variables allowed us to look at the differences in effects across reciprocally and sequentially interdependent alliances.

Alliances were classified as reciprocally interdependent if the strategic rationales of the partners included sharing complementary technology, jointly reducing the time needed for innovation, or joint development of new technology. Such alliances include those in which the partners are actively seeking to learn from the alliances to broaden or deepen their skills or to develop new skills jointly, all of which require crucial ongoing inputs from all partners and involve high levels of interdependence. Reciprocally interdependent alliances overlap with but are not synonymous with alliances encompassing a technology component. For instance, not all technology alliances are bilateral learning ties, and some can thus include a unilateral transfer of technological know-how that does not create reciprocal interdependence. Also, reciprocally interdependent alliances may involve the joint development of marketing or distribution skills and not include any technology component.

Sequentially interdependent alliances include partnerships in which the output of one partner is handed off to the other, for whom it is an input. An alliance was classified as involving sequential interdependence both when one partner sought to expand its market access or tap into new markets and did so through an alliance with a partner that had marketing and distribution prowess in those markets and when an alliance involved one partner gaining access to new products provided by the other.

Pooled interdependent alliances exist when alliance partners do not depend on each other for inputs or outputs but, rather, pool resources toward shared activities that need not be coordinated on a regular basis. Alliances were classified as involving pooled interdependence when partners came together to share high costs and risks, to share financial resources for expensive endeavours, or to build joint production facilities.

Because the unit of analysis here is the individual alliance and not the firm, and all partners usually have a voice in determining the alliance's formal governance structure, the goal was to capture the highest level of interdependence anticipated by the partners entering the alliance. Each alliance was therefore conservatively coded with the highest level of interdependence anticipated by either partner within it. Alliances in which a partner had multiple strategic rationales or in which the partners had differing rationales were thus placed in one of the three categories according to the highest level of interdependence among them. As a result, an alliance was classified with elements of both reciprocal and sequential interdependence as reciprocal, one with sequential and pooled interdependence as sequential, and so forth. This coding is consistent with Thompson's notion that the three types of interdependence can be arrayed on a scale in which reciprocal interdependence may include elements of sequential and pooled interdependence, and sequentially interdependent situations may also have some pooled elements.

To ensure that the findings were robust, estimations were also done by coding this variable with alternative specifications in which all eight original dimensions were arrayed on a single ordinal scale of interdependence. This was done by first constructing a single variable that took values from 1 to 8 and, second, by introducing seven dummy variables for the eight categories. The results were consistent with those obtained using Thompson's three-way typology.

Separate measures were included for each facet of appropriation concerns that partners are likely to anticipate at the time they are forming an alliance: presence of a technology component in the alliance and appropriability regime of the industry. Following prior empirical research the measure R&D was included to capture the presence of a technology component within the alliance (1 = technology component, 0 = no technology component). R&D alliances included those that encompassed a technology component in the agreement. They could involve exchange, unilateral transfer, sharing, or codevelopment of technology or elements of all the above. Such alliances could encompass basic R&D, product development, or any other technology-related efforts. Non-R&D alliances typically included those that primarily involved production, distribution, or marketing. This variable was used to test hypothesis 2a on the role of appropriation concerns resulting from the presence of a technology component in determining the governance structure of alliances.

The magnitude of appropriation concerns was assessed by including measures to capture systematic differences in appropriability regimes across industries. Sector differences were controlled with two dummy variables, *new materials* and *automotive*; biopharmaceuticals was the default sector. These variables allowed us to test hypothesis 2b on the role of appropriation concerns resulting from the appropriability regime of the industry in determining the governance structure of alliances. Prior research suggests that biopharmaceuticals has the strongest appropriability regime and automotives the weakest, with new materials lying in between (Levin et al. 1987; Arora and Gambardella 1994). While it is possible that the strength of appropriability regimes may have changed over the twenty-year observation period, discussions with experts suggests that there have been no dramatic changes in any of these industries to alter the relative levels of appropriability regimes across them. Thus, while there may have been shifts in the absolute levels of the strength of appropriability regimes, relative differences across the three seem to have remained stable. Since the concern here is with the relative differentiation across the three, any changes over time should not affect the findings.

Interaction terms were used between the presence of technology and industry participation to test hypothesis 2c, which predicted that the presence of a technology component in an alliance would moderate the effect of appropriability regimes on the structure of the alliance.

Several measures were included to capture interorganizational trust and test hypothesis 3, which suggests that trust can reduce the likelihood of hierarchical controls in alliances. One mechanism, which has been discussed extensively, through which such trust built is through prior alliances and the network resources they create (Ring and Van de Ven 1992; Gulati 1995a; Gulati and Gargiulo 1999). The idea of trust emerging from prior contact is based on the premise that through ongoing interaction, firms learn about each other and develop trust around norms of equity, or knowledge-based trust (Shapiro, Sheppard, and Cheraskin 1992). Prior ties can also promote deterrence-based trust, resulting from viewing prior ties as possible hostages, which deters partners from untrustworthy behavior because they are concerned about potential sanctions, including the dissolution of prior alliances and loss of reputation. Firms having prior alliances with each other will trust each other more than partners who have no history with each other. Although it is possible that an experience may be a negative one, those firms with bad experiences are unlikely to form subsequent alliances with each other. In fact, entering a repeated tie can be a way to mitigate adverse selection problems because the firms have reliable firsthand information on each other from prior interactions (Balakrishnan and Koza 1993). Thus, repeated interaction between two firms can be considered one reasonable indicator of trust between them.

Consequently, an indicator, *repeated ties*, was used to record the number of prior alliances the two firms had entered into since 1970 to test hypothesis 3 (0 = first-time alliance). The models also examined whether the nature of prior ties (i.e. if they were JVs, minority equity investments, or contractual alliances) influenced the governance structure chosen in subsequent alliances. Since this measure could also be capturing experience-related effects resulting from the partners developing routines for working with each other, several other measures for trust were included as well (Nelson and Winter 1982).

The discussion of trust in alliances has been extended to comparisons of international and domestic and multilateral and bilateral alliances and is used here to further test hypothesis 3. One rationale for a different level of trust between two domestic firms compared to two firms from differing regions of the world is that individual firms may enjoy greater network resources in their domestic market than they enjoy in the broader international market— and this differential in network resources could lead to a greater level of trust between two domestic firms than would exist between two potential partners from different regions. Furthermore, prior research indicates systematic differences in the behavior of participants in alliances involving partners of different nationalities (Parkhe 1993b) and also in choices between modes of entry into new geographic markets (Kogut and Singh 1988; Singh and Kogut 1989). Recent evidence also suggests systematic differences in the level of patent protection afforded by different countries (Mansfield 1993). Researchers have also argued that cross-border alliances have greater obstacles for building trust and a concomitant higher potential for appropriation concerns than domestic alliances because the difficulties of specifying intellectual property rights, legally enforcing intellectual property, and monitoring partner activities are greater in cross-border alliances (Pisano 1990; Oxley 1997). As a result, greater trust is expected in domestic alliances than in others. To assess whether alliances between cross-regional partners are likely to have more hierarchical controls and to examine differences across local partner alliances in different global regions, three dummy variables were included—*United States, Europe,* and *Japan*—indicating whether an alliance was between partners in those regions. The default was a cross-region alliance (1 = partners of that region, 0 = partners of different regions).

Increasing the number of partners in an alliance can also limit the level of trust between alliance partners. Including more partners in an alliance can make identifying and realizing common interests more difficult, which complicates the task of ensuring trust between alliance partners (Parkhe 1993*b*). Furthermore, simply having more partners makes it less likely that all the partners will trust all others in the alliance. Monitoring each partner's contributions and introducing appropriate sanctions in the face of free riding is harder to implement when there is a large group of participants involved. This makes it difficult to introduce incentive structures that may foster trust. Another way to describe this would be that there are greater network resources in dyadic as opposed to multilateral alliances for some of the reasons suggested above. To capture any effects that arose from the number of partners in the alliance, that number was computed and recoded as a dummy variable, *multilateral*, with a value of 1 if an alliance was multilateral and a value of 0 if an alliance was bilateral.

Controls were introduced for temporal trends in alliances and included dummy variables for each year. The models included nineteen dummy variables for the twenty-year period covered in the study, with the default year being 1970. For simplicity of presentation, the results for these dummy variables are not reported in the tables. Two control variables, *percent joint venture* and *percent minority investment*, were also included to assess the influence of the frequency with which specific types of alliances had been announced in each industry on the choice of governance structure. The number of alliances announced in an industry in the prior year was counted and the percentage of those that were of each type was computed. *Percent joint venture* and *percent minority investment* capture the percentage of alliances that were JVs and minority equity investments, respectively, in the previous year. In a limited way, this calculation tests the institutionalist claim that firms may mimic the contracts other firms in the industry use to organize their alliances (Fligstein 1985; Davis 1991). An alternative interpretation of the variables is that they capture the net effect of the various macroeconomic factors within an industry that may influence the formation of particular types of alliances (Amburgey and Miner 1992).

Table 6.1 describes the variables included in the analysis and summarizes the predicted signs for the effects of each independent variable.

RESULTS

Table 6.2 presents descriptive statistics and correlations for all variables. The descriptive statistics indicate that of the alliances in the sample, 52 percent

Table 6.1. Definitions and predicted signs of variables[a]

Variable	Definition	Predicted sign
Hierarchy	Dependent variable, set to 1 if alliance was a minority equity investment and 2 if it was a joint venture (default: contractual alliance).	
Reciprocal	Dummy variable set to one if reciprocal interdependence is present (default: pooled interdependence).	+
Sequential	Dummy variable set to one if sequential interdependence is present (default: pooled interdependence).	+
R&D	Dummy variable indicating presence of a technology component (default: no technology component).	+
New materials	Dummy variable set to one if alliance is in new materials sector (default: biopharmaceutical).	+
Automotive	Dummy variable set to one if alliance is in automotive sector (default: biopharmaceutical).	+
Repeated ties	Number of prior alliances between the firms.	−
USA	Dummy variable set to one if firms are both American (default: cross-regional).	−
Japan	Dummy variable set to one if firms are both Japanese (default: cross-regional).	−
Europe	Dummy variable set to one if firms are both European (default: cross-regional).	−
Multilateral	Dummy variable set to one if alliance is multilateral (default: bilateral).	+
Time 1–19	A series of 19 dummy variables for each year, 1971–89 (default: 1970).	NP
Percent joint venture	Percentage of all alliances announced in the industry in the prior year that were joint ventures.	NP
Percent minority equity	Percentage of all alliances announced in the industry in the prior year that were minority equity investments.	NP

[a]NP = No prediction.

involved reciprocal interdependence, 24 percent involved sequential interdependence, and the remainder involved pooled interdependence. The total sample of 1,570 alliances included 769 alliances in the new materials industry, 345 alliances in automotives, and 456 alliances in biopharmaceuticals. There was considerable geographic diversity in the sample as well: 27 percent of alliances were among US firms, 13 percent among Japanese firms, 22 percent among European firms, and the remainder were cross-region alliances. Also, 32 percent of the sample involved more than two partners. Of the total alliances, 31 percent were JVs, 23 percent were minority equity investments, and the remainder were contractual alliances. Overall, the results point to the diversity of alliances included within the pooled sample of all three industries. The correlations show no significant problems of multicollinearity. The dependent variable is moderately correlated with both dummy variables capturing interdependence (*reciprocal* and *sequential*).

Table 6.3 presents the results of the multinomial logistic regression analysis as estimated with LIMDEP 7.0. This set of analyses examined the choice

Table 6.2. Descriptive statistics and correlations

Variable	Mean	SD	Low	High	1	2	3	4	5	6	7	8	9	10	11	12
1. Hierarchy	.89	.31	0	2	—											
2. Reciprocal	.52	.38	0	1	.59	—										
3. Sequential	.24	.23	0	1	.47	-.73	—									
4. R&D	.47	.42	0	1	.19	.25	.25	—								
5. New materials	.49	.50	0	1	.04	.11	-.04	.00	—							
6. Automotive	.22	.21	0	1	.06	-.19	.09	.27	-.50	—						
7. Repeated ties	1.46	1.04	0	9	-.13	.07	-.07	-.00	-.13	.12	—					
8. USA	.27	.34	0	1	.01	.09	-.05	-.17	-.04	-.20	-.10	—				
9. Japan	.13	.33	0	1	-.22	.16	-.14	-.09	.09	.02	.17	-.23	—			
10. Europe	.22	.40	0	1	-.03	-.03	-.04	.08	.11	.04	-.03	-.32	-.20	—		
11. Multilateral	.32	.42	0	1	.04	.15	-.21	.01	.31	.00	.05	.07	.14	.10	—	
12. % Joint venture	.28	.10	.15	.68	-.14	.21	-.13	-.10	.34	.35	-.03	.07	.08	-.07	.18	—
13. % Minority equity	.22	.08	.13	.31	-.10	.15	-.17	.01	.22	.24	.01	.02	.05	.01	.07	.33

Table 6.3. Multinomial logistic analysis of tendency to participate in minority equity investments and joint ventures[a]

	Model 1		Model 2		Model 3		Model 4	
Variable	Minority investment	Joint venture	Minority investment	Joint venture	Minority investment	Joint venture	Minority investment	Joint venture
Intercept	-1.37* (.33)	-2.41* (.49)	-1.74* (.53)	-2.16* (.68)	-1.63* (.58)	-2.03* (.59)	-1.82* (.60)	-2.26* (.47)
Reciprocal	—	—	.85* (.21)	1.55* (.28)	.67* (.22)	1.09* (.34)	.62* (.20)	1.01* (.35)
Sequential	—	—	.19* (.03)	.95* (.15)	.13* (.03)	.88* (.15)	.12* (.03)	.85* (.15)
R&D	—	—	—	—	.20* (.04)	.53* (.11)	.18* (.05)	.45* (.12)
New materials	—	—	—	—	.38 (.29)	.68* (.13)	.35 (.27)	.70* (.15)
Automotive	—	—	—	—	.27* (.09)	.73* (.22)	.20* (.05)	.88* (.23)
Repeated ties	—	—	—	—	-.32* (.05)	-.50* (.07)	-.28* (.05)	-.46* (.07)
USA	—	—	—	—	.48 (.34)	.16 (.14)	.46 (.34)	.15 (.14)
Japan	—	—	—	—	.16 (.09)	-.77* (.16)	.15 (.09)	-.65* (.18)
Europe	—	—	—	—	-.24* (.04)	-.41* (.05)	-.21* (.04)	-.38* (.05)
Multilateral	—	—	—	—	.57 (.46)	.73 (.59)	.54 (.45)	.66 (.57)
R&D × New materials	—	—	—	—	—	—	.42 (.33)	.31 (.28)
R&D × Automotive	—	—	—	—	—	—	1.24* (.21)	1.98* (.25)
% Joint venture	.08 (.10)	.06* (.02)	.07 (.11)	.05 (.03)	.07 (.10)	.03 (.07)	.07 (.10)	.04 (.07)
% Minority equity	.12* (.01)	.03 (.07)	.08 (.04)	.03 (.05)	.09 (.04)	.04 (.04)	.07 (.06)	.03 (.04)
Log likelihood	-1,342.21		-1,186.48		-994.35		-952.72	
x^2	774.72*		1,051.26*		1,289.52*		1,307.37*	

[a]Coefficients show effects of covariates for each alliance type relative to effects that the covariates have for the base category, contractual alliances. Standard errors are in parentheses. $n =$ 1,570. Coefficients for time 1–19 were included in all models.

*$p < .01$.

between JVs, minority equity investments, and contractual alliances. These results provide a detailed assessment of the choices firms make when entering alliances and the factors that may be guiding this choice. Each model estimates coefficients for the choice of minority equity investments and for JVs against the default category of contractual alliances. We later compared the sets of coefficients to examine the choice between minority equity investments and JVs. Overall, the directionality and significance of the coefficients are consistent with the hypotheses presented here. Furthermore, all models included have significant explanatory power, as demonstrated by the χ^2 test on the observed log likelihoods. The negative and significant coefficient for the intercept term suggests that, on average, minority equity investments and JVs were used less often than contractual alliances.

Model 1 in Table 6.3 includes the control variables only, and model 2 shows results with the addition of the two measures of interdependence, *reciprocal* and *sequential*. Alliances can be arrayed from low to high interdependence as pooled, sequential, and reciprocal. They can have contracts that vary from less to more hierarchical and that range from contractual alliances to minority investments to JVs. Tests of hypothesis 1 assessed whether alliances with higher levels of interdependence use more hierarchical contracts than those with lower levels by comparing the presence of the three alternative types of interdependence with the use of the three alternative types of governance structure. The results in model 2 support hypothesis 1, which predicted that alliances with higher interdependence are likely to be organized with more hierarchical contracts than are those with less interdependence. This result holds true in models 3 and 4 as well.

The positive coefficients for reciprocal in model 2 indicate that both JVs and minority equity investments are more likely than contractual alliances when interdependence is reciprocal than when it is pooled. A *t*-test of the difference between the coefficients for reciprocal under JVs and minority equity investments further supports hypothesis 1 and shows that JVs, which encompass the most hierarchical controls, are more likely than minority equity investments when interdependence is reciprocal rather than pooled. The results in model 2 suggest that hierarchical contracts such as minority equity investments and JVs are more likely for sequentially interdependent alliances than for alliances with pooled interdependence. The positive coefficients for sequential in model 2 indicate that both JVs and minority equity investments are more likely than contractual alliances when interdependence is sequential than when it is pooled. A *t*-test of the difference between the coefficients for sequential under JVs and minority equity investments further supports hypothesis 1 and shows that JVs are more likely than minority equity investments when interdependence is sequential rather than pooled. A comparison of the coefficients of reciprocal and sequential in model 2 under JVs and minority equity investments further suggests that reciprocally interdependent alliances (vs. those with sequential interdependence) will be more likely to take the form of JVs or minority equity investments than contractual alliances. Finally, a t-test to compare the coefficients of reciprocal and sequential for JVs and minority equity investments shows that JVs are more likely than minority equity investments when interdependence is reciprocal rather than sequential.

Overall, not only are the two interdependence indicators significant in predictable ways in the models, but the significant improvement in log likelihood and χ^2 statistics in model 2 indicates a much better model fit. This finding makes clear the added value of incorporating coordination costs and interdependence into the analysis.

Results of models 3 and 4 support hypotheses 2a–2c. The positive coefficient for R&D supports hypothesis 2a and shows that alliances with a technology component are more likely than those without one to be organized with hierarchical governance structures and, under such circumstances, firms will prefer JVs and minority equity investments to contractual alliances. A t-test of the difference in coefficients of R&D for JVs and minority equity investments shows further support for hypothesis 2a and suggests that firms prefer JVs over minority equity investments when an alliance includes a technology component.

The industry dummy variables, which indicate the appropriability regime, provide mixed support for hypothesis 2b. We expected more hierarchical controls for alliances in sectors with weaker appropriability regimes. The dummy variable for new materials, where the appropriability regime is of a strength between those of the other two sectors, suggests that compared with biopharmaceuticals, where the appropriability regime is stronger, JVs are more likely than contractual alliances in new materials, which is consistent with hypothesis 2b. Contrary to our expectations, however, there is no significant difference in the use of minority equity investments and contractual alliances between new materials and biopharmaceuticals. In the automotive sector, where the appropriability regime is the weakest, consistent with our expectations, both JVs and minority equity investments are more likely than contractual alliances when this sector is compared with biopharmaceuticals, where the appropriability regime is strongest. The inclusion of dummy variables for each sector does not reveal whether the remaining main effects differ across the industries. To assess if the other effects observed differ systematically across industries, we estimated unrestricted models for each industry separately (results not reported here). The signs of the coefficients indicated that the postulated directionality and significance of the other main effects observed in the pooled sample held true for each sector.

Model 4 introduced the interaction term between R&D and the dummy variables for industry to test hypothesis 2c and examine whether the effect of industrial sector was more salient for alliances with a technology component than for those without one. Hypothesis 2c predicted that hierarchical controls in alliances would be greatest when alliances have a technology component and are in an industry with a weak appropriability regime. As expected, the positive and significant coefficient for the interaction between automotive and R&D shows that technology-based alliances are more likely to be JVs and minority equity investments than contractual alliances in the automotive sector, where appropriability regimes are relatively weak, than they are in biopharmaceuticals, where appropriability regimes are stronger. Contrary to our expectations, the statistically nonsignificant coefficient for the interaction between new materials and R&D suggests that technology alliances in the new materials sector, which has an intermediate-level appropriability regime, are no different in their governance structures than technology alliances in the biopharmaceutical sector, where the appropriability regime is strongest.

Model 3 also includes several measures of the trust developed among alliance partners, and the associated amount of network resources. The negative coefficient for repeated ties, a measure of interorganizational trust and the associated network resources, supports hypothesis 3 and indicates that repeated ties are less likely than first-time alliances to be organized as JVs or minority equity investments than as contractual alliances. A comparison of the coefficients further supports hypothesis 3 and suggests that repeated ties are less likely to be organized as JVs than as minority equity investments. While we are not able to empirically separate the role of network resources and the associated interorganizational trust on coordination versus appropriation concerns, the results do suggest that it does matter in shaping governance.

The models also included dummy variables for nationality of partner and alliance multilaterality to further assess the effect of trust on governance structure, as predicted by hypothesis 3. The negative and significant coefficient for Japan and Europe in the second column of model 3 suggests that alliances involving firms from only those regions are less likely than cross-regional alliances to use JVs and minority equity investments than contractual alliances. This is consistent with our intuition that there is likely to be greater trust and associated network resources in alliances involving regionally similar partners than cross-regional partners, which in turn is reflected in the governance structure of the alliances. Contrary to our expectations, Japanese domestic alliances are no different from cross-regional alliances in their use of minority equity investments or contractual alliances. Similarly, the nonsignificant coefficient for the United States suggests that alliances between American partners are no different from cross-regional alliances in their governance structures and is contrary to hypothesis 3. Also contrary to hypothesis 3, the positive but nonsignificant coefficients for multilateral alliances across all models indicate that, compared to multilateral alliances are statistically no more likely than bilateral alliances to be JVs or minority equity investments than contractual alliances.

The first column of Table 6.3 also reports the base model including all the control variables. The estimations included a dummy variable for each year but one in all models. The results for these dummy variables (not reported in tables for ease of presentation) broadly confirm the growing frequency of minority investments and contractual alliances. In addition, the positive and significant coefficient for percent JVs and percent minority equity investments suggests that the use of these alliances within an industry positively affects firms' use of those types of alliances in that industry.

To assess the possible influence of firm-level attributes on choice of governance structure, a separate analysis was conducted with data on all alliances formed by a subgroup of firms. Given the diversity of firms in the sample—they were based in the United States, Europe, and Japan—it was not possible to collect financial information on all firms. For the subgroup analysis, we selected the fifty largest firms in each sector and collected information on their size, performance, liquidity, and solvency. We reestimated all the models with this sample and included variables to assess the role of partner differences by computing a ratio of the smaller to the larger financial item to assess the effect of differences across partners on their choice of governance structure. The results (not reported here) for coordination costs and appropriation concerns after controlling for these firm attributes were consistent with those based on the original sample. The persistence of the hypothesized findings increases the robustness of the results. Among the ratios themselves, the only significant one was size, indicating that the greater the difference in size between the partners, the more likely they were to use JVs or minority equity investments than contractual alliances.

Conclusion

This study sheds light on the factors that underlie how firms choose to govern their alliances. By using a typology of three types of alliance structure and the magnitude and type of hierarchical controls present in each, we found that both the anticipated extent of coordination costs and appropriation concerns at the outset in the formation of an alliance could predict the use of particular governance structures. Furthermore, we found that trust engendered by network resources is a powerful catalyst in shaping the governance structure in alliances. While this chapter does not empirically disentangle potential mechanisms of the effects of network resources and resultant trust on governance, it is likely that these affect both anticipated coordination costs and appropriation concerns. Thus, this study suggests that network resources may play an important role not only in shaping the likely appropriation concerns in interorganizational relationships but also in facilitating greater coordination among the partners.

While the study provides strong support for the importance of coordination costs in determining alliance governance structure, one particularly important finding was that the greater the anticipated coordination costs in relation to a new strategic alliance—as reflected by the anticipated level of interdependence between firms—the more hierarchical the governance structure used to formalize it. The findings confirm that reciprocally interdependent alliances are likely to have structures with greater hierarchical control than those with sequential interdependence, which in turn are likely to have more hierarchically organized alliances than those with pooled interdependence. This result suggests that the deliberations underlying the choice of alliance structure are not dominated by concerns of appropriation alone, as previously suggested, but that considerations associated with managing interdependence-based coordination costs are also salient.

The further examination of the role of appropriation concerns and behavioral uncertainty in alliance formation in this chapter provided mixed results. Consistent with previous work (Pisano 1989), alliances involving a technology component were likely to use more hierarchical structures than those that did not. Contrary to our expectations, however, differences across industrial sectors, which also reflect varying appropriability regimes, do not fully explain the choice of governance structure. This is problematic in the comparison of new materials alliances with those in biopharmaceuticals, and the results show that while JVs are more likely than contractual alliances in the former than the latter, there is no significant difference in the use of minority equity investments and contractual alliances. The interpretation of this null result is ambiguous, as it could be influenced by additional unmeasured factors, such as localized institutional norms, historical imprinting of behavior by industry participants, and the intensity, diversity, and niche-based dynamics of competition in those industries.

The results for appropriation concerns were also confirmed by looking at the simultaneous influence of the sector in which the alliance occurred and the presence of a technology component in the alliance. The results suggest that the presence of a technology component in alliances enhances the influence of the appropriability regime of the industry on the governance structure used. In particular, the combination of a technology component and an alliance in a sector with a weak appropriability regime increases the likelihood of firms choosing hierarchical governance structures.

Overall, the results for the effect of prior ties confirm that alliance networks and the resources they create strongly influence the governance structures of alliance. Network resources channel valuable information between firms that not only affects the frequency of new alliances and the choice of partners but also the specific structures used to formalize alliances. The analyses here used several measures to assess the influence of interfirm trust and associated network resources as another factor that can affect the choice of alliance governance structure. Results for the first indicator of trust, the presence of repeated ties, are consistent with our expectations: repeated ties diminish the use of hierarchical controls in alliances. This result holds true even after we separated out the history of alliances by specific type of alliance. Thus, a history between the firms matters, regardless of the type of prior alliance the firms entered. A topic for future research would be to explore more precisely the role of network resources in shaping appropriation versus coordination concerns and the resultant governance structure used in alliances.

The results for the regional origin of partners, which we also proposed would capture trust and network resources, reveal some interesting trends. The comparison between local versus cross-region alliances was broadly consistent with our expectations of greater trust in local than in cross-regional alliances, but breaking down local alliances by region suggests some provocative issues not fully explored here. While the results for European alliances are consistent with the predictions, contrary to our expectations, Japanese domestic alliances are no different from cross-regional alliances in their use of minority equity investments or contractual alliances, although they do differ in their use of JVs or contractual alliances. Even more remarkable is the absence of significant differences in the governance structure of American domestic alliances and cross-regional ones. While these results suggest some systematic differences in the level of trust between local and cross-regional alliances that is reflected in the governance structure of alliances, several alternative interpretations are possible for these results. These regional differences may be the result of appropriation concerns resulting from greater difficulties in specifying and enforcing property rights and monitoring problems in cross-regional alliances than in local alliances, or they may be due to the greater coordination challenges and coordination costs of cross-regional alliances than local alliances. Local alliances in each region may also be influenced by localized institutional contexts deeply embedded in normative practices and authority structures (Hamilton and Biggart 1988). Or perhaps there are historical and legal circumstances that mandate or encourage the use of particular governance structures for alliances. These results, along with those for sectoral differences, reveal some interesting patterns that remain to be explored more deeply.

The results for the control variables suggest that both the time trend and the frequency with which other industry participants used particular structures influence the choice of governance structure in alliances. The positive influence of frequency of prior alliances by industry participants on the choice of structure reflects the likely occurrence of imitation or of industry imperatives not captured by other variables included in the study (Westphal, Gulati, and Shortell 1997). This effect disappeared, however, once we introduced the hypothesized variables in the framework. The findings in this study help explain some of the reasons why the composition of structures used may have shifted over time from more to less hierarchical. In particular, the nonsignificance of most of the dummy variables capturing time, once we introduced the measures for interdependence, suggest that the time trend may have reflected the changing patterns in underlying interdependence in alliances. Thus, a likely explanation for the observed time trend may be that firms are entering alliances with lower levels of interdependence.

In this study, we have considered two perspectives that suggest differing factors that influence the extent of hierarchical controls in alliances: an economic approach, which highlights appropriation concerns, and an organizational approach, which emphasizes coordination costs. We have also considered the influential role of network resources and resultant trust in shaping choice of governance structure. Network resources directly affect governance by engendering trust, mitigating appropriation concerns, and shaping anticipated coordination costs.

Overall, the results presented in this chapter have several ramifications. First, they suggest that the formation of exchange relations between firms is not entirely dominated by appropriation concerns—coordination costs, arising from decomposing tasks between partners and the requisite ongoing coordination and management of tasks across partners, play at least an equally significant role. Underlying this study is the fundamental question of the relative importance of alternative bases for hierarchical controls in alliances. Both perspectives discussed point to the salience of bounded rationality and concomitant uncertainty as important considerations for the emergence of hierarchical controls. But each specifies the role of different facets of uncertainty experienced by alliance participants as important in their decision to introduce hierarchical controls in the formal structure. While one perspective highlights anticipated appropriation concerns resulting from contracting hazards and manifest behavioral uncertainty, the other points to uncertainty arising from the anticipation of the extent of ongoing task coordination and the complexity of decomposing the division of tasks.

Network resources and the associated trust they engender cut across both these distinct facets in that it is likely they shape both the anticipated appropriation and coordination costs, which in turn impact choice of governance. This chapter does not claim that coordination costs can explain all the variance in hierarchical controls in alliances; rather, it investigates the simultaneous influence of both coordination- and appropriation-related costs. Yet these two factors often overlap. As a result, it can be difficult to distinguish between their influences empirically. While it may be difficult to isolate the occurrence of each in its pure form, as was true with the hypothetical example discussed earlier, we empirically demonstrate the distinct role of coordination costs in guiding the choice of governance structure in alliances while also considering the independent influence of appropriation concerns and network resources.

Second, the results here highlight the fundamental issue of the origin of hierarchical controls in alliances: whether they arise from a concern with coordination costs and interdependence across partners or result from anticipated appropriation concerns. These results show that both sets of factors along with the network resources that may shape them are important considerations for alliances. Firms choose governance structures both to manage anticipated coordination costs and to address appropriation concerns. This finding is consistent with the belief that hierarchical controls are more than mechanisms to control opportunism and provide incentive alignment across partners; they also provide an organizational context that determines the rules of the game and creates an administrative architecture within which the partnership proceeds. This architecture encourages alliance partners to use network resources to coordinate tasks and responsibilities between themselves in a way that meets their own needs for value creation and allays their particular concerns about the alliance.

While this study focused on the origin of hierarchical controls in alliances, its findings could spur an examination of the importance of coordination costs in answering the question of why firms exist. Efforts to question the singular importance of opportunism-based transaction costs economics have introduced the role of knowledge and its application to business activities as a basis for the existence of firms (Conner and Prahalad 1996). This work could easily be expanded to examine the role of coordination costs as an important basis for why firms exist and their influence on the scale and scope of firms. Further research could examine how network resources can be a powerful influence on coordination costs.

Part III

Network Resources and the Performance of Firms and Their Alliances

7 Network resources and the performance of firms

Do firms benefit from entering strategic alliances and reaping the network resources these generate? To answer this question, one must consider two dimensions of performance: the performance of a given alliance and the performance of the individual firms that enter it. This chapter, based on a study I conducted with Lihua Wang, relates to the latter dimension, with a focus on the performance consequences of alliances and the network resources generated for firms entering such partnerships. A study of these performance consequences is important because it allows us to assess the actual benefits of network resources emanating from the alliance networks in which firms participate.

Because the influence of other, nonalliance activities on firm performance makes empirically linking alliance activity and associated network resources with performance difficult, scholars have looked for a variety of direct and indirect ways to test the relationship between alliance activity and firm performance. The most common approach has been to conduct event study analyses of the stock market effects of alliance announcements (e.g. Koh and Venkatraman 1991). This approach has been further refined as scholars have examined the differential benefits firms receive from different types of alliances and how these benefits are influenced by the conditions under which the alliances were formed (e.g. Balakrishnan and Koza 1993; Anand and Khanna 2000a). Still, as stock market reactions portend the likely future outcomes of alliances, these results provide only a prospective estimate of the beneficial consequences of alliances for firms—and in many cases the resulting evidence has been mixed.

After controlling for other factors that may influence firm performance, several researchers have explained firm performance as a function of the extent of alliance activity. For example, in an early study of the chemical industry,

This chapter is adapted from 'Size of the Pie and Share of the Pie: Implications of Network Embeddedness and Business Relatedness for Value Creation and Value Appropriation in Joint Ventures' by Ranjay Gulati and Lihua Wang published in *Research in the Sociology of Organizations* © 2003, (20): 209–42, with permission from Elsevier.

Berg, Duncan, and Friedman (1982) found a negative relationship between joint venture incidence and firm rates of return but were unable to definitively establish a causal relationship. More recently, some researchers have narrowed the domain of performance that might be explained by alliances by focusing on the impact of technology alliances on the patenting activities of firms and for their overall performance (Hagedoorn and Schakenraad 1994; Mowery, Oxley, and Silverman 1996). This line of research has been extended by linking firm performance not only to the frequency of past alliances but also to the firm's position in interorganizational networks (Ahuja 2000a). Researchers have also used a similar approach to examine the relationship between the extent to which firms are embedded in alliances and the likelihood of their survival. Thus, firm survival has been considered a tentative proxy for performance (e.g. Baum and Oliver 1991, 1992; Uzzi 1996). The alliances studied in regard to firm survival have included those with vertical suppliers and with key government institutions in the environment. The results of these studies suggest that such ties are generally beneficial in enhancing survival chances. Still, this relationship may not always be true and numerous contingencies that may alter the relationship between alliances and firm survival have also been proposed (e.g. Mitchell and Singh 1996). The challenge in this research has been to isolate the factors beyond embeddedness that may also have an influence on survival and to examine all relevant factors longitudinally.

While past studies have tried to link the alliance behavior of firms to various facets of firm performance, they have not invoked nor focused on network resources as the conceptual anchor for their theoretical and empirical assessments. Despite its insights, the aforementioned body of research has also largely overlooked the influence of overarching networks and the resources they offer firms beyond immediate ties.

This chapter assesses the likely impact of such network resources on firm performance by detailing an event study of stock market reactions to new alliance announcements. The study examines the effects of a specific form of strategic alliance that typically requires substantial investment and that is likely to have a measurable impact on firm performance: the joint venture (JV). Prior research has typically assessed the value creation potential of JVs by using an event-study methodology to examine stock market reactions to JV announcements (Anand and Khanna 2000a). Because accurate data that quantify the value created by JVs are difficult to collect, scholars have looked at investor expectations regarding how much value a new JV will create value for its parent firms as a reasonable estimate of the value that a joint venture will generate. As a result, their judgment of whether a JV is expected to create value for parent firms and how the created value will be divided between partners is believed to incorporate all available information.

As mentioned earlier, one of the weaknesses of prior research has been its limited recognition of the impact of network resources that firms may possess on alliance outcomes. As previous chapters have demonstrated, prior alliance ties generate network resources that are conduits of information, which in turn engender trust and alter subsequent behavior. Given this impact, investors may expect the network resources possessed by each firm entering a new JV to affect the total value creation of the new JV and the relative value appropriation between partners. While network resources may ultimately reside within individual firms, this study accounts for such resources by looking at the prior direct and indirect ties that exist between joint venture partners. Furthermore, we assess the impact of these network resources on investor perceptions of the benefit of firms entry into new joint venture relationships. In other words, we explore the extent to which the market reaction to the announcement of a new alliance between two firms is influenced by each firm's existing network resources based on prior direct and indirect ties.

Building on prior research, this chapter focuses not only on the total value creation for both participating firms (e.g. Koh and Venkatraman 1991) but also on the factors that may influence the relative value appropriation among the partners when a JV is announced. This approach is supported by theoretical accounts of alliances which have suggested that both total value creation and relative value appropriation for each partner in a joint venture are important (Hamel 1991; Gulati, Khanna, and Nohria 1994).

To gain a better understanding of the effect of network resources on firm performance, we specifically examine the influence of network resources on the stock market returns that firms realize when a new joint venture in which they are involved is announced. The expectation is that firms with greater network resources are likely to extract greater value from their new joint ventures than firms with limited access to such resources. Because new joint ventures contribute to a firm's existing pool of network resources, another way to state this would be that the effects of new ties on the performance of participating firms will be contingent on the amount of existing network resources that they have at the outset of their new relationship. The greater the existing stock of such resources, the greater the benefits a firm can extract from its new partnerships.

In addition to examining the role of firms' existing network resources on the total value creation associated with a new JV relationship (i.e. the size of the total pie for all firms), this chapter also studies the impact of such resources on the relative value appropriation (i.e. the share of the pie for each firm) for the firms entering JVs. The results of this event study of stock market reaction to JV announcements by the largest US firms during the 1987–96 period suggest that network resources affect the total value creation of joint ventures but not the relative value appropriation of each partner in a JV.

This study also considers the role of firms' material resources and complementary capabilities by looking at the effect of 'business relatedness' among JV partners in shaping their alliance outcomes. Business relatedness refers to the similarities in products, markets, and technologies among business units within a diversified firm (Rumelt 1974) and the similarities in products, markets, and technologies between acquiring and acquired firms (Datta and Puia 1995). In the analyses here, this concept refers to the similarities that exist in the products, markets, and technologies of JV partners and their joint venture. In particular, we consider the effects of business relatedness on both the total value created by the JV and the relative value appropriated by each JV partner.

Theory and hypotheses

NETWORK RESOURCES AND TOTAL VALUE CREATION IN JOINT VENTURES

Total value creation refers to the stock market's expectation of the total value a JV is going to create for all partners collectively. As a separate entity created by partners, a JV is usually an enduring arrangement for a certain period in which two or more firms combine their resources in order to achieve some common objectives (Lewis 1990). As in many negotiation situations, it is not only the share of the pie that each party receives in such arrangements but also the total size of the pie that is important (Thompson 1998).

Prior studies of the total value creation of joint ventures at the time they are announced have typically assumed that investors are only concerned with the economic antecedents of the new JV and have used firm attributes (i.e. size) or dyad attributes (i.e. business relatedness of two firms) as proxies for these factors. As previous chapters have shown, however, network resources that arise from prior alliances also play a significant role in the formation and functioning of such relationships. As a result, they can have a large impact on the total value created by a joint venture. One way they can do this is by providing firms with information regarding the reliability, specific capabilities, and trustworthiness of current and potential partners, information that can serve as an important basis for trust between firms in a new JV. The knowledge obtained from firms' prior network ties enables the JV partners to have more accurate expectations of each other and also makes their behavior more predictable. Furthermore, the circulation of information within the network also establishes accountability by communicating reputational concerns for the firms and deterring them from acting opportunistically (Gulati 1995b). For example, if both firms in a new JV have a previous JV with a common third party, either partner's behavior can be reported to the third party and this information may spread through the wider network. The anticipation of future interaction with firms in this network and the desire to develop long-term relationships with existing partners will thus prevent firms from engaging in opportunistic behavior that could be communicated across the wider social network.

NETWORK RESOURCES, RELATIONAL EMBEDDEDNESS, AND TOTAL VALUE CREATION

As discussed in Chapter 3, there are two distinct components of network resources: the relational component, made up of the direct relationships within which a firm is embedded, and the structural component, which encompasses the overall social network within which firms exist (Granovetter 1992). The relational component of social structure provides direct experience-based knowledge about current and prior alliance partners; the structural component provides indirect knowledge about potential partners that firms obtain from prior partners, their partners' partners, and so on. Both of these elements may influence investor perceptions of the total value to be created by new joint ventures.

One reason why relational ties can affect the total value created by a joint venture is that such ties provide valuable information to partner firms that can make interactions in new joint ventures less uncertain and costly by limiting different types of transaction costs such as monitoring and negotiation costs. Monitoring costs may be reduced because prior direct interactions promote interfirm trust that reduces the incentive for opportunistic behavior (Gulati 1995a; Gulati and Sytch 2006b). Negotiation costs are reduced because the partner firms develop deeper knowledge of each other in terms of their interests, needs, and capabilities through prior connections, and information exchange can be more efficient. Moreover, the trusting relationship of the partners facilitates open communication and private information exchange. As prior research suggests, communication and information exchange are considered keys to reducing the negotiation costs and increasing the chance of integrative solutions (Thompson 1998).

Relational ties between firms can also make a new JV more product-ive by reducing coordination costs. As detailed in Chapter 6, coordination costs encompass the anticipated complexity of (a) decomposing tasks among partners, (*b*) ongoing coordination of activities to be completed jointly or individually across organizational boundaries, and (*c*) managing relevant communication and decision-making (Gulati and Singh 1998; Gulati, Lawrence, and Puranam 2005). As partners build up experience with each other, they not only have more information about each other's strategies, culture, and capabilities but also develop shared norms of behavior and routines of joint decision-making and coordination (Walker, Kogut, and Shan 1997). As a result, coordination costs are reduced.

Finally, prior direct ties may enhance prospects for joint learning, which is perhaps one of the most important sources of value creation in JVs (Dyer and Singh 1998; Khanna, Gulati, and Nohria 1998). The ability of a firm to recognize and assimilate valuable knowledge from a particular ally can be referred to as a kind of partner-specific absorptive capability that should be heightened as firms develop joint work routines (Cohen and Levinthal 1990; Dyer and Singh 1998).

Given the various benefits JV partners may realize from the network resources originating from their prior direct ties, we hypothesized the following:

Hypothesis 1a: The degree of relational embeddedness between new JV partners has a positive relationship with the total value creation of the JV.

While network resources gained from prior direct ties are indeed beneficial, it is possible that when the number of direct ties between two firms grows beyond a certain point, collaboration opportunities may reach a limit (Gulati 1995*b*). Indeed, two firms that have many prior direct ties may be at risk of overdependence on each other through significant investments in relation-specific assets. The increasing interdependence between the two firms places them in a vulnerable situation if the priorities of one or both change. As research has shown, when a firm is overly dependent on its partners, especially in an asymmetric way, be they customers, suppliers, or collaborators, the very source of competitive advantage from the collaborative relationship may adversely affect the performance of both firms if the technology of one of the firms becomes obsolete or the environment of one or both abruptly changes (Lorenz 1988; Afuah 2000).

Network resources originating from direct ties can also encourage the two firms to keep investing in those relation-specific assets to reap immediate benefits—at the expense of investing in new opportunities with partners with whom they have no experience. Unlike a JV between firms with prior ties, a new JV between firms that have no prior direct ties may also be important for firms' levels of competitive advantage by allowing them to extend their reach and explore new and unique rewarding opportunities. Although risky at the outset, new relationships can enhance each firm's opportunity set in the long run by creating network resources that provide access to the other party's information sources for new deals with additional partners. Such relationships also give each firm new opportunity for referrals to rewarding opportunities within its newly expanded network (Gulati 1998).

New JVs between firms with no prior direct ties may also benefit participants by providing opportunities for sharing complementary resources or for pooling common resources to enhance economies of scale and scope (Ahuja 2000a), while also allowing them to acquire new and unique skills that could potentially be used in their own activities beyond the JV (Khanna, Gulati, and Nohria 1998). Finally, new JVs between firms with no direct ties can create potential future opportunities for the two firms to cooperate and further exploit the benefit of collaboration.

The discussion above indicates that as the number of direct ties between two firms increases, the benefits accrued to partners from a new JV might increase to a certain point and then diminish. Consequently, as two partners become more relationally embedded, they may become overly dependent on each other and under-explore new opportunities. Hence, while firms may accumulate network resources by repeated interactions with the same partners, the rate of accumulation of such resources from repeat ties may diminish over time. This argument is consistent with the trade-off between exploration and exploitation suggested in the literature on organizational learning (March 1991). Exploration refers to the behavior of a firm trying to discover new information about alternatives to improve future returns, while exploitation refers to the behavior of a firm using current information to improve present returns. Koza and Lewin (1998), who have applied these concepts to the study of JVs, suggest that the formation of an alliance is an indication of a firm's adaptive choice between exploration and exploitation. On one hand, exploration of new alliance opportunities by participants with no prior direct interactions may be more risky, but such behavior may also be more beneficial. On the other hand, exploitation of cooperative relationships between participants with prior direct ties may be safer now but less beneficial in the future. Given these considerations, investors may expect that new JVs between firms with an intermediate number of direct ties will balance exploration of new opportunities with exploitation of existing ones.

The above rationale calls for the following alternative relationship between network resources based on relational embeddedness and the total value creation of a JV:

Hypothesis 1b: The degree of relational embeddedness between new JV partners has an inverted U-shape relationship with the total expected value creation of their new joint ventures, with the highest value occurring at an intermediate degree of relational embeddedness.

NETWORK RESOURCES, STRUCTURAL EMBEDDEDNESS, AND TOTAL VALUE CREATION

As previously mentioned, in addition to a relational component, network resources also entail a structural component that encompasses the overall social network within which firms exist. In many instances, a firm may not have prior direct ties to a potential partner, but it may be linked to that firm by indirect ties through common partners. Here we consider the simplest case, where two firms with no prior direct ties share direct ties with a common third firm. When these two firms announce a JV, investors are likely to consider two benefits of their indirect-tie-based network resources in enhancing the value creation potential of the new partnership: information and reputation. The indirect tie in this example promotes information exchange by allowing each prospective partner to query the common partner regarding the reliability, trustworthiness, and capabilities of the other firm. This information can reduce uncertainty about the behavior of each partner and serve as the basis for interfirm trust (Burt and Knez 1995; Gulati 1995*b*). The mere fact that the two firms have entered a JV may signal to investors that both are considered by the third party as suitable and trustworthy. In such cases, investors are likely to expect that such JVs have a high probability to create value for both firms. Therefore, a positive relationship between the degree of structural embeddedness of JV partners and the total value creation of the JV can be expected:

Hypothesis 2a: In the absence of relational embeddedness, the degree of structural embeddedness between two JV partners has a positive relationship with the total value creation of the JV.

Nevertheless, it is possible that as two partners become more structurally embedded and accumulate more indirect ties, the rate of growth of network resources and the concomitant information-based benefits may diminish as the information becomes more redundant and less valuable (Coleman 1988; Burt 1992). Multiple common third parties may have similar information about partners and the value of the information may not increase proportionally with an increase in indirect ties between partners. In terms of reputation concerns, as two firms have more common partners and the local network becomes extremely cohesive, behavioral constraints in the form of standard norms of behavior may develop across the network. These norms may constrain the firms' abilities to execute their joint strategies (Baum and Oliver 1991). Based on this argument, an alternative hypothesis suggests that the degree of structural embeddedness of two partners may have a diminishing positive relationship with investors' estimates of the total value expected from a new JV:

Hypothesis 2b: In the absence of relational embeddedness between two firms, the degree of structural embeddedness between two firms has a positive diminishing effect on the investors' expectation of the new JV's total value creation.

NETWORK RESOURCES AND RELATIVE VALUE APPROPRIATION IN JOINT VENTURES

The relative value appropriation of each partner in a JV refers to the relative proportion of total value creation that each partner extracts from the JV. It is important because the ultimate goal of each partner is to extract its own value from the JV. Hamel (1991) was one of the first to highlight the importance of relative value appropriation. Several recent studies have built on these ideas by examining how interfirm partnerships may turn into learning races in which each partner hopes to gain the greatest benefits from the alliance (Khanna, Gulati, and Nohria 1998; Khanna, Gulati, and Nohria 2000). Still, in spite of its importance, few empirical studies have examined the factors that affect the relative value appropriation between partners in a JV. This study attempts to examine this issue by looking at the relationship between the relational and structural embeddedness of partnering firms and the relative proportion of total value creation they are likely to seek from new JV relationships.

The relational embeddedness resulting from prior direct partnering experiences between two firms serves as an important basis for a trusting relationship to develop (Gulati 1995a; Gulati and Sytch 2006b). This trust between two partners encourages reciprocity and consideration of mutual benefits. As a result, firms with previous or current direct ties should be more likely to consider not only their individual costs and benefits but also their mutual costs and benefits when dividing the potential value of a new joint venture. Consequently, they should be less likely to emphasize the pursuit of specific individual economic returns in light of their interest in maintaining a harmonious and mutually fruitful relationship. When two firms are relationally embedded, they are more likely to view the JV transaction as part of a long-term relationship, and this orientation should reduce the desire for the firms to seek asymmetric returns (Dyer 1997). Given this expectation of firm behavior, we would expect that investors would also anticipate symmetric returns for both partners entering a JV.

While prior direct ties between two partners provide each first-hand information about the other, prior indirect ties that indicate structural embeddedness provide similar types of information through common third parties. Third parties are important go-betweens in new relationships, enabling individual firms to transfer their expectations from well-established relationships to others in which adequate knowledge or partnership history may not be available. Because both firms have direct interaction with the third common party, the common party passes on information about the trustworthiness of the two firms, and this information provides a basis for a trusting relationship. Investors considering the announcement of a JV are likely to expect that prior indirect ties promote trust between the parent firms and encourage cooperative behavior. This trust and the cooperative behavior it fosters should lead to parity in the benefits each party extracts from the JV.

In contrast, two firms that have no direct or indirect ties lack accurate information about each other and are more likely to consider the relationship with private costs and benefits in mind and view the relationship in terms of power and dependence. Thus, private benefits are likely to be emphasized over mutual gains. Furthermore, because firm managers may feel uncertain about the strategic intent of their JV partners, they are more likely to engage in learning races to extract the most private benefits in the quickest possible way (Khanna, Gulati, and Nohria 1998). In these situations, investors are likely to expect that the relative value extractions of the two firms are more likely to depart from an equal sharing of the expected total value created. The discussion above suggests the following:

Hypothesis 3: As two firms are more relationally embedded, the relative value appropriation to each partner in the JV becomes more symmetric.

Hypothesis 4: As two firms are more structurally embedded, the relative value appropriation to each partner in the JV becomes more symmetric.

MATERIAL RESOURCES, ASYMMETRY OF PARTNER BUSINESS RELATEDNESS, AND THEIR IMPACT ON TOTAL VALUE CREATION AND RELATIVE VALUE APPROPRIATION

Business relatedness has been widely studied in the literature on diversification strategy and mergers and acquisitions by firms. In these two literatures, the term refers, respectively, to the similarities in products, markets, and technologies among business units within a diversified firm (Rumelt 1974) and the similarities in products, markets, and technologies between acquiring and acquired firms (Datta and Puia 1995). Current research suggests that a high level of business relatedness vis-à-vis a target firm is beneficial to firms both for diversification and for mergers and acquisitions because it creates value for firms by enhancing economies of scale or scope, increasing market power, and providing access to necessary technology in familiar industries (Seth 1990; Datta and Puia 1995).

The concept of business relatedness has also been extended to the study of JVs, where the term is synonymous with market or technology overlap between partnering firms. Recent research suggests that greater overlap between firms in a JV positively affects each firm's capacity to learn from its partner and, in turn, increases the economic rent the partners can extract from their collaboration (Mowery, Oxley, and Silverman 1996; Dyer and Singh 1998). Stuart (2000) suggests that technology overlap facilitates effective collaboration among firms in an alliance because (*a*) the firms are better at evaluating and internalizing each other's technologies because they share knowledge of technologies and market segments and (*b*) the firms provide high value for each other in terms of information exchange and cost sharing, especially in a crowded technological area.

Because JVs involve the creation of a third, neutral entity, not only the overlap between two partners but also the overlaps between each of the parent firms' core activities and the activities undertaken by the JV are important. In a JV, each partner's business operation can be either related or unrelated to that of the new partnership. When the business of a focal firm is related to the JV, it is likely that the firm can more effectively use its core competencies in the operation of the JV and further exploit any potential economies of scale with its current resources. Relatedness is also likely to increase the market power of the focal firm (Pfeffer and Nowak 1976). In addition, this overlap provides potential opportunities for spillover effects that allow the focal firm to apply the skills learned from the new JV to its other activities and thus fully exploit new learning opportunities (Hamel, Doz, and Prahalad 1989). It is also likely that firms that are closely related to their JV operations may have greater absorptive capacity for knowledge coming from the areas of development in the JV, and this is reflected in a greater ability to recognize the value of the new knowledge, assimilate it, and apply it for their economic benefits (Cohen and Levinthal 1990).

Building on the research in individual learning, studies on absorptive capacity suggest that a firm's absorptive capacity is closely associated with the extent to which the firm possesses prior related knowledge of the technology being developed outside its boundaries. Applying this logic, a firm operating in areas related to the JV has prior related knowledge, is familiar with the JV operation, and thus is likely to have the ability to recognize and absorb the new knowledge from the JV and exploit it in its operations. The business relatedness between the firm and the JV thus not only provides the firm with potential opportunities for exploiting economies of scale and scope, as well as with learning opportunities, but also provides conditions that enhance the ability of the firm to realize such opportunities.

When assessing the potential value creation of a JV, the business relatedness of each of the parent firms to the JV's activities becomes significant.

Specifically, asymmetry of business relatedness for each of the partners with the JV may negatively affect the investors' expectations about the future cooperative relationship between the partners and thus the total value created in the JV (Harrigan 1988; Borys and Jennison 1989). When one partner's business is related to the JV and the other partner's is not, the partners themselves are likely to value the JV differently because the benefits of economies of scale, scope, and learning opportunities from the new JV are not symmetric. Investors may expect that the firm more related to the JV may extract private benefits that it can use in its own operations before both firms are able to obtain any common benefits (Khanna, Gulati, and Nohria 1998). In addition, in such asymmetric JVs, the abilities of the two partners to learn and absorb the new knowledge are also likely to be asymmetric. This may cause the advantaged firm to race with its partner to learn its partner's skills from the JV operation before the other party realizes its learning objective (Khanna, Gulati, and Nohria 1998). The asymmetry of knowledge transfer benefits between the two partners may lead to shifts in the bargaining power within the JV, which may discourage knowledge-sharing between partners and thus reduce the joint value created by the JV (Inkpen 1998; Chi 2000). Moreover, asymmetry also encourages both partners to expand resources to learn as much as possible from the other partner for private benefit while making fewer efforts to take advantage of the potential synergy between them to generate common benefits (Chi 2000).

The firm that receives fewer benefits may not be able to achieve its strategic goals and may become dissatisfied with the JV. The likely unequal and possibly unfair relationship in an asymmetric JVs may cause investors to expect that the future cooperative relationship between the partners will not be fruitful and that the JV may not perform well. Therefore, investor expectations of the total value creation of a JV may be lower if the partnership includes asymmetry of business relatedness:

Hypothesis 5: Asymmetry of business relatedness of the parent firms with the JV is negatively related to the total value creation of the JV.

As mentioned above, the asymmetry of business relatedness of two firms with the JV is likely to contribute to the partners' extracting different levels of value from the JV. Firms whose activities are more closely related to the JV are more likely to extract greater value from the JV than their partners. As a result, investors may expect that the asymmetry of business relatedness of the two partners with the JV will promote greater differences in the likely value extracted by the two partners. When the two partners both have similar relatedness to the JV operation, however, their potential opportunities to extract value are more likely to be similar. Based on the above discussion, the following can be hypothesized:

Hypothesis 6: Asymmetry of business relatedness of two partners with the JV is associated with greater departure from an equal share of the created value of the venture.

Empirical research

METHOD

The data-set used in this study is described in Appendix 1 under the heading 'Joint Venture Announcement Database'. The most widely used market model was used, based on residual analysis, to calculate the firm's abnormal return, which was the expected return that the market believed the firm would capture by participating in a JV (Fama et al. 1969). The event (JV announcement) date was designated as $t = 0$. Accordingly, $t = -10$ if the date is 10 trading days before the announcement date and $t = 10$ if the date is 10 trading days after the announcement and so forth. Daily data were used on the stock market returns of each firm over a period 241 days prior to the event day (250 days before the announcement of the JV until 10 days before the announcement of the JV) to estimate the market model:

$$r_{it} = a_i + \beta_i r_{mt} + \varepsilon_{it}$$

where r_{it} is the common stock return of firm i on day t, r_{mt} is the corresponding daily market return on the equal-weighted S&P 500, a_i and β_i are firm-specific parameters, and ε_{it} is the error term.

Estimates from the above model were used to predict the daily returns for each firm i over a two-day period and a 21-day period surrounding the event date using the following equation:

$$\hat{r}_{it} = \text{estimated } a_i + \text{estimated } \beta_i * r_{mt}$$

where the $\hat{r}_{it}$ is the predicted daily return and the estimated a_i and estimated β_i are the model estimates.

Next, the daily firm-specific abnormal returns are calculated as:

$$\text{Estimated } \varepsilon_{it} = r_{it} - \hat{r}_{it}$$

The cumulative abnormal return of firm i during the event period was calculated by summing the daily abnormal returns of the firm over the event period, i.e.

$$\text{CAR}_i = \sum_t (\text{Estimated } \varepsilon_{it})$$

where t is either from -1 to 0 or from -10 to 10.

Total return and relative return were used to measure total value creation and relative value appropriation, respectively. Total return refers to the aggregated abnormal return of the two firms involved in a JV and reflects the total anticipated stock market gain of the two firms from the JV. Relative return compares the abnormal returns of the two participating firms entering the JV. It reflects the asymmetry of the two firms' abnormal returns from the JV participation. Both variables were calculated from the firms' abnormal returns.

The literature describes two ways to calculate the value creation of a new JV to the partners—equal-weighted single security and value-weighted single security (Anand and Khanna 2000*a*). The value-weighted single security approach aggregates the abnormal return of the participating firms, using the market value of the firms as weights, while the equal-weighted single security approach gives each participating firm equal weights. The approach here follows McConnell and Nantell (1985) in using the equal-weighted approach. In those studies in which the value-weighted approach was used, one of the major interests was to find out the absolute total dollar value creation from the announcement of JVs. Total return was calculated as the simple addition of the two firms' cumulative abnormal return over the event period. That is:

$$\text{Total return} = (\text{CAR1} + \text{CAR2})$$

where CAR1 and CAR2 are firm 1's and firm 2's respective cumulative abnormal returns over certain event period (we use 2-day and 21-day event periods in this study).

Relative return was calculated by first taking the exponential of the two firms' abnormal returns and then using the ratio of the absolute difference of the two transformed returns and the addition of the two transformed returns to represent the relative return:

$$\text{Relative return} = \frac{\{\exp(\max(\text{CAR1}, \text{CAR2})) - \exp(\min(\text{CAR1}, \text{CAR2}))\}}{\{\exp(\min(\text{CAR1}, \text{CAR2})) + \exp(\max(\text{CAR1}, \text{CAR2}))\}}$$

The transformation corrects for the problem of a possible mixture of positive versus negative cumulative returns for the two firms entering the same JV. For example, if firm 1's cumulative abnormal return is −.02 while firm 2's cumulative abnormal return is .001, then the absolute difference .021 is not very intuitive. Thus, I used the exponential of their cumulative abnormal returns to transform them into positive numbers. For example, if firm 1's transformed return is $\exp(-.2) = .82$, and firm 2's transformed return is $\exp(.01) = 1.01$, then the relative return is the absolute difference of the two transformed returns, i.e. 0.19.

This absolute difference, though, treats the difference between a return of .01 and .02, for example, the same as the difference between .49 and .50. To correct this problem, the absolute difference of the two above transformed returns is divided by the addition of the two transformed returns. To continue the above example, the final calculation of the relative return is:

$$\frac{.19}{(.82 + 1.01)} = 0.104.$$

When the value of relative value appropriation is 0, the investors expect equal shares of the pie for the two firms. The larger this value is, the less equal the share of the pie for the two firms.

Relational embeddedness is indicated by the number of prior direct JV ties between two firms while structural embeddedness is indicated by the number of common third-party ties (indirect ties with the distance of two) between two firms. The number of prior direct ties is measured by counting the number of JV ties between two firms from 1970 to the year prior to the JV announcement. The number of indirect ties is calculated by counting the number of common third firms with which both parent firms have had a JV from 1970 until the year before the JV was announced. This includes those common third firms outside the sample.

The first two digits of the primary Standard Industrial Classification (SIC) codes of the two firms and the primary SIC code of the JV were used to calculate their respective business relatedness with the JV. The business relatedness of firm A with the JV equals 1 if the first two digits of the primary SIC code of firm A are the same as the first two digits of the primary SIC code of the JV. The asymmetry of business relatedness of two firms with the JV equals 1 if only one of the partner firms has the same SIC code as the new JV and equals 0 if both or neither firm has the same SIC code as the new JV. The reliance on the first two digits of the SIC code to indicate business relatedness is consistent with that of Palepu (1985). Although subject to criticism, there is evidence that the congruence between this approach and finer-grained approaches is very high if the sample size is large (Montgomery 1982).

Some economic variables and firm characteristics were included as control variables. First, the analyses here controlled for the business relatedness of two parent firms using a binary variable with a value of 1 if the two parent firms have the same two-digit primary SIC codes and 0 otherwise. Firm size and performance indicators (return on assets and solvency) were also included as control variables, lagged by one year. Firm size is indicated by total sales; solvency was calculated as long-term debt/current assets. Because the unit of analysis was a dyad, control variables were created for total size by summing across the two partners' total sales and taking a log. Control variables were also created for total return on assets (ROA) and total solvency

Table 7.1. Frequency of positive and negative cumulative stock market reaction for all partners (658 pairs and 1,316 firm cases)

Reaction	Frequency	Percentage (%)
Positive	605	45.97
Negative	609	46.28
Missing	102	7.75

as the simple sums of the respective return on assets and solvency of the two firms.

The three control variables mentioned above were used when the dependent variable was total return. Relative size, relative return on assets, and relative solvency were used, respectively, when the dependent variable was relative return. Relative size was calculated as the ratio of the smaller firm's size to the larger firm's size. Relative performance was calculated as the ratio of the exponential of the smaller value of return on assets (or solvency) between the two firms to the exponential of the bigger value of return on assets (or solvency) (Gulati and Gargiulo 1999). Data from input–output tables were used to capture the possible effect of such a resource dependence on the value creation of the JVs. The sum was used to compute total dependence and the ratio to compute relative dependence. The first digit of the SIC code of each firm in a JV was also used as an additional control variable because the value creation and appropriation across different economic sectors could vary (Madhavan and Prescott 1995).

Finally, to capture any unobservable time effect, dummy variables were created for each year from 1987 to 1996 to control for the time effect in all regression analyses. Some firms were also involved in more JV activities than others. Firms involved in more than one JV create interdependence across these cases. Although the event-study methodology controls for the firm-specific characteristics in the calculation of firm abnormal returns, and thus partially takes care of this problem, dummy variables for the top fifteen firms with the most JV activities were also included as control variables.[1]

RESULTS

Table 7.1 presents the distribution of positive and negative cumulative stock market reactions for all participating firms (658 pairs and 1,316 firm cases). In 45.97 percent of the cases, the abnormal returns are positive, in 46.28 percent

---

[1] Results for these control variables are not reported here.

Table 7.2. Descriptive statistics of the major variables

Variable	n	Mean	SD	Min	Max
1. Total value creation	570	0.001	0.043	−0.240	0.282
2. Relative value appropriation	570	0.012	0.013	0	0.126
3. The degree of relational embeddedness (number of direct ties)	658	0.716	1.696	0	15
4. The degree of structural embeddedness (number of indirect ties)	658	1.125	2.295	0	13
5. Asymmetry of business relatedness of two firms with the JV	658	0.351	0.478	0	1
6. Business relatedness of two firms	658	0.347	0.476	0	1
7. Log (total size)	630	10.450	0.805	8.395	11.982
8. Total return on assets	630	0.084	0.098	−0.432	0.411
9. Total solvency	504	1.147	1.019	0.006	5.836
10. Total dependence of two firms	658	0.108	0.164	0	0.748
11. Relative size	630	0.410	0.275	0.010	1
12. Relative return on assets	630	0.942	0.058	0.552	1
13. Relative solvency	504	0.388	0.302	0	1
14. Relative dependence of two firms	658	0.374	0.430	0	1

of the cases, they are negative (the data for the remaining 7.75 percent of the cases are missing).

Tables 7.2 and 7.3 provide descriptive statistics and the correlation matrix among variables. The correlation matrix indicates that total value creation is highly correlated with all major independent variables (degree of relational embeddedness, degree of structural embeddedness, and asymmetry of business relatedness of two firms with the JV). Relative value appropriation, however, is highly correlated only with degree of relational embeddedness. In addition, degree of relational embeddedness and degree of structural embeddedness are highly correlated (r = .582). We do not include the two variables simultaneously in any model, so this correlation does not pose a problem.

Tables 7.4 and 7.5 present the results of the regression models using total value creation and relative value appropriation as the dependent variable, respectively. Models 1–8 use total value creation as the dependent variable. Model 1 is the baseline model, including only control variables. Model 2 introduces the degree of relational embeddedness between two firms into the regression equation to test hypothesis 1a. The result indicates that there is a positive relationship between the degree of relational embeddedness between two firms and total value creation. Hypothesis 1a is supported. The total value creation from announcing a new JV is .342 percent more with an additional prior direct tie between two firms. For example, for two firms with total current value of $4 billion dollars, the benefits from having an additional direct tie is $13.68 million. Model 3 tests hypothesis 1b, which predicts that the degree of relational embeddedness (indicated by the number of prior direct

Table 7.3. Correlation matrix of the major variables (n = 436)

Variable	(1)	(2)	(3)	(4)	(5)	(6)	(7)	(8)	(9)	(10)	(11)	(12)	(13)	(14)
(1) Total value creation	1.00	—	—	—	—	—	—	—	—	—	—	—	—	—
(2) Relative value appropriation	0.190*	1.00	—	—	—	—	—	—	—	—	—	—	—	—
(3) The degree of relational embeddedness	0.116*	0.104*	1.00	—	—	—	—	—	—	—	—	—	—	—
(4) The degree of structural embeddedness	0.107*	0.065	0.582*	1.00	—	—	—	—	—	—	—	—	—	—
(5) Asymmetry of business relatedness of two firms with the JV	-0.144*	0.012	-0.053	-0.112*	1.00	—	—	—	—	—	—	—	—	—
(6) Business relatedness of two firms	0.057	-0.018	0.120*	0.111*	-0.536*	1.00	—	—	—	—	—	—	—	—
(7) Log (total size)	0.070	0.026	0.274*	0.330*	-0.073	-0.066	1.00	—	—	—	—	—	—	—
(8) Total ROA	-0.088*	-0.086*	-0.101*	-0.158*	0.101	-0.097*	-0.139*	1.00	—	—	—	—	—	—
(9) Total solvency	-0.034	-0.020	-0.221*	-0.332*	-0.006	-0.030	-0.104*	-0.188*	1.00	—	—	—	—	—
(10) Total interdependence	0.061	0.052	0.189*	0.232*	-0.351*	0.727*	0.026	-0.170*	0.009	1.00	—	—	—	—
(11) Relative size	-0.038	-0.120*	-0.161*	-0.142*	-0.015	-0.005	-0.423*	0.077	0.126*	-0.069	1.00	—	—	—
(12) Relative ROA	-0.011	-0.093*	-0.159*	-0.160*	-0.004	0.005	0.096	0.302*	0.131*	-0.054	0.033	1.00	—	—
(13) Relative solvency	-0.047	-0.093	-0.130*	-0.125*	-0.083	0.038	-0.002	-0.051	0.032	-0.043	0.110*	0.251*	1.00	—
(14) Relative interdependence	0.035	-0.009	0.108*	0.135*	-0.362*	0.647*	-0.028	-0.138*	0.120*	0.731	-0.004	-0.009	0.037	1.00

*p < .05.

Table 7.4. Regression analysis using total value creation (%) as the dependent variable

Variable	Model 1	Model 2	Model 3	Model 4	Model 5	Model 6	Model 7	Model 8
The degree of relational embeddedness (number of direct ties)	—	0.342**(0.151)	0.515*(0.282)	—	—	—	0.376** (0.151)	—
The degree of relational embeddedness (number of direct ties) squared	—	—	−0.019 (0.026)	—	—	—	—	—
The degree of structural embeddedness (number of indirect ties)	—	—	—	0.183 (0.228)	0.220 (0.480)	—	—	0.169 (0.227)
The degree of structural embeddedness (number of indirect ties) squared	—	—	—	—	−0.005 (0.063)	—	—	—
Asymmetry of business relatedness of two firms with the JV	—	—	—	—	—	−1.128** (0.556)	−1.267** (0.555)	−1.411** (0.618)
Business relatedness of two firms	0.573 (0.666)	0.415 (0.666)	0.388 (0.668)	0.409 (0.728)	0.411 (0.730)	−0.102 (0.742)	−0.357 (0.744)	−0.431 (0.811)
Log (total size)	−0.075 (0.470)	−0.059 (0.467)	−0.058 (0.467)	0.054 (0.502)	0.050 (0.505)	−0.070 (0.468)	−0.052 (0.465)	0.065 (0.498)
Total return on assets	−2.732 (2.700)	−1.890 (2.712)	−1.743 (2.721)	1.199 (3.252)	1.164 (3.283)	−2.674 (2.689)	−1.739 (2.698)	1.272 (3.227)
Total solvency	−0.393 (0.268)	−0.325 (0.268)	−0.316 (0.268)	−0.484*(0.288)	−0.482*(0.289)	−0.387 (0.267)	−0.311 (0.267)	−0.471 (0.286)
Total dependence	1.933 (1.944)	1.935 (1.935)	2.064 (1.944)	3.232 (2.106)	3.227 (2.110)	2.300 (1.945)	2.348 (1.933)	3.553* (2.094)

(continued)

Table 7.4. (cont.)

Variable	Model 1	Model 2	Model 3	Model 4	Model 5	Model 6	Model 7	Model 8
Period 88	1.294 (1.282)	1.169 (1.277)	1.133 (1.279)	2.190 (1.365)	2.194 (1.368)	1.274 (1.277)	1.135 (1.271)	2.135 (1.355)
Period 89	1.627 (1.336)	1.525 (1.330)	1.505 (1.331)	1.739 (1.413)	1.737 (1.415)	1.486 (1.333)	1.357 (1.326)	1.708 (1.402)
Period 90	2.693** (1.201)	2.571** (1.196)	2.548** (1.197)	2.895** (1.230)	2.895** (1.232)	2.607** (1.197)	2.463** (1.191)	2.763** (1.221)
Period 91	−0.615 (1.114)	−0.684 (1.109)	−0.718 (1.110)	−1.002 (1.143)	−1.007 (1.147)	−0.722 (1.111)	−0.811 (1.104)	−1.154 (1.136)
Period 92	1.280 (1.096)	1.190 (1.091)	1.144 (1.094)	0.962 (1.176)	0.956 (1.180)	1.102 (1.095)	0.981 (1.089)	0.754 (1.170)
Period 93	1.368 (1.154)	1.166 (1.152)	1.083 (1.158)	1.199 (1.308)	1.192 (1.313)	1.191 (1.153)	0.946 (1.150)	0.902 (1.304)
Period 94	1.350 (1.092)	1.024 (1.096)	0.974 (1.099)	1.391 (1.153)	1.384 (1.158)	1.082 (1.096)	0.691 (1.100)	0.957 (1.160)
Period 95	1.313 (1.176)	0.934 (1.182)	0.878 (1.185)	0.900 (1.293)	0.890 (1.301)	1.179 (1.173)	0.745 (1.178)	0.848 (1.284)
Period 96	1.986 (1.357)	1.385 (1.376)	1.376 (1.377)	2.582* (1.527)	2.574* (1.533)	1.723 (1.358)	1.029 (1.377)	2.215 (1.523)
Industry sector of firm 1	−0.034 (0.283)	−0.030 (0.282)	−0.027 (0.282)	−0.224 (0.299)	−0.226 (0.300)	0.019 (0.283)	0.029 (0.281)	−0.155 (0.298)
Industry sector of firm 2	0.081 (0.288)	0.097 (0.287)	0.092 (0.287)	0.275 (0.294)	0.276 (0.295)	0.052 (0.287)	0.066 (0.285)	0.225 (0.293)
Constants	−0.169 (4.901)	−0.296 (4.876)	1.322 (4.879)	−1.454 (5.274)	−1.410 (5.309)	0.454 (4.891)	0.392 (4.860)	−0.670 (5.245)
Number of cases	436	436	436	300	300	436	436	300
R^2	0.101	0.112	0.113	0.194	0.195	0.110	0.124	0.210
Adjusted R^2	0.032	0.042	0.041	0.098	0.095	0.039	0.052	0.112

Notes: Fifteen dummy variables representing fifteen firms that participated in the most JVs are also entered as control variables for all models in Tables 7.4 and 7.5. For simplicity, the results are not shown in the tables. These firms are: Apple Computer, AT&T, Bell Atlantic, B. F. Goodrich, Digital Equipment, Dow Chemical, Du Pont, Eastman Kodak, General Electric, General Motors, HP, IBM, Intel, Motorola, and Sun Microsystems.

*p < .10; **p < .05.

Table 7.5. Regression analyses using relative value appropriation (%) as the dependent variable

Variable	Model 9	Model 10	Model 11	Model 12	Model 13	Model 14
The degree of relational embeddedness (number of direct ties)	—	0.062 (0.043)	—	—	0.063 (0.044)	—
The degree of structural embeddedness (number of indirect ties)	—	—	-0.0004 (0.073)	—	—	-0.0004 (0.073)
Asymmetry of business relatedness of two firms with the JV	—	—	—	0.015 (0.160)	-0.007 (0.161)	0.006 (0.193)
Business relatedness of two firms	-0.043 (0.174)	0.006 (0.176)	0.051 (0.206)	0.051 (0.194)	0.002 (0.196)	0.055 (0.233)
Relative size	-0.366 (0.256)	-0.373 (0.255)	-0.313 (0.320)	-0.366 (0.256)	-0.373 (0.256)	-0.312 (0.321)
Relative return on assets	-3.012** (1.261)	-2.831** (1.265)	-2.248 (1.523)	-3.011** (1.262)	-2.831** (1.267)	-2.248 (1.526)
Relative solvency	-0.033 (0.227)	-0.035 (0.226)	-0.115 (0.282)	-0.032 (0.228)	-0.036 (0.227)	-0.114 (0.284)
Relative dependence	-0.072 (0.192)	-0.064 (0.192)	-0.105 (0.229)	-0.073 (0.192)	-0.064 (0.192)	-0.105 (0.230)
Period 88	-0.260 (0.362)	-0.268 (0.362)	-0.260 (0.419)	-0.259 (0.363)	-0.268 (0.362)	-0.260 (0.420)
Period 89	-0.711* (0.373)	-0.711* (0.372)	-0.551* (0.431)	-0.709* (0.374)	-0.712* (0.373)	-0.550 (0.432)
Period 90	0.549 (0.339)	0.539 (0.338)	0.701 (0.376)	0.550 (0.339)	0.538 (0.339)	0.702* (0.378)
Period 91	-0.021 (0.312)	-0.022 (0.311)	-0.027 (0.349)	-0.020 (0.312)	-0.022 (0.312)	-0.027 (0.350)
Period 92	-0.078 (0.314)	-0.088 (0.314)	-0.138 (0.364)	-0.076 (0.316)	-0.089 (0.315)	-0.137 (0.365)
Period 93	-0.317 (0.333)	-0.348 (0.334)	-0.310 (0.407)	-0.315 (0.335)	-0.349 (0.335)	-0.309 (0.410)
Period 94	-0.406 (0.312)	-0.459 (0.314)	-0.388 (0.357)	-0.402 (0.315)	-0.461 (0.317)	-0.386 (0.362)
Period 95	-0.214 (0.331)	-0.272 (0.333)	-0.482 (0.395)	-0.212 (0.332)	-0.272 (0.334)	-0.482 (0.396)
Period 96	-0.598 (0.372)	-0.692* (0.377)	-0.464 (0.455)	-0.595 (0.374)	-0.674* (0.380)	-0.462 (0.459)
Industry sector of firm 1	0.075 (0.078)	0.076 (0.077)	0.064 (0.088)	0.075 (0.078)	0.076 (0.078)	0.064 (0.089)
Industry sector of firm 2	0.037 (0.079)	0.043 (0.079)	0.074 (0.088)	0.037 (0.079)	0.043 (0.079)	0.075 (0.088)
Constants	4.014*** (1.260)	3.867*** (1.263)	3.236** (1.516)	4.003*** (1.267)	3.872 (1.268)	3.231** (1.524)
Number of cases	436	436	300	436	436	300
R^2	0.141	0.146	0.167	0.141	0.146	0.167
Adjusted R^2	0.078	0.080	0.070	0.075	0.078	0.067

*p < .10; **p < .05; ***p < .01.

ties) between two firms has an inverted-U-shaped relationship with total value creation. The coefficient of the square term of the number of direct ties is not significant. Hypothesis 1b is not supported.

Models 4 and 5 examine the relationship between degree of structural embeddedness (indicated by the number of indirect ties between two firms) and total value creation. Because the effect of structural embeddedness could be confounded with the effect of relational embeddedness, we evaluate the effect of structural embeddedness only in the absence of relational embeddedness between the firms. Model 4 examines the linear relationship between degree of structural embeddedness and total value creation (hypothesis 2a). The result shows no linear relationship between these variables. Model 5 tests hypothesis 2b, which predicts a curvilinear relationship between degree of structural embeddedness between two firms and total value creation. The coefficient for this variable is also not significant. Hypothesis 2b is not supported.

Models 6–8 test hypothesis 5, which predicts a negative relationship between asymmetry of business relatedness of two firms and total value creation. Model 6 introduces only asymmetry of business relatedness of two firms with the JV in addition to the control variables. The result suggests that the asymmetry of business relatedness of two firms with the JV significantly discounts the investors' expectations of the total value created by a new JV, which supports hypothesis 5. If one firm is related to the JV operation while the other firm is not, the total value creation will be 1.128 percent lower than if neither or both firms are related to the JV operation. The result holds even when we include embeddedness variables in the equations (models 7 and 8). To further test the hypothesis, we divided all cases into three groups: (*a*) both partners' primary businesses are related to JV activities (*b*) both partners' primary businesses are not related to JV activities (*c*) one partner's primary business is related to JV activities while the other partner's primary business is not (in this case, asymmetry exists). We found that the total value creation amounts of the first two groups (symmetric case) are not significantly different, but they are significantly different from that of the third group, where the asymmetry of business relatedness between two firms and the JV exists (results not reported here).

Models 9–14 test the hypotheses using relative value appropriation as the dependent variable. Model 9 is the baseline model, with only control variables in the equation. The result indicates that the relative return on assets of the two firms has a negative relationship with relative value appropriation, indicating that JVs formed by partners with similar returns on assets are more likely to have similar abnormal returns. Model 10 introduces the degree of relational embeddedness (the number of direct ties) between two firms into the regression equation to test hypothesis 3, which predicts that as the degree of relational embeddedness increases, the value to each partner becomes more symmetric. The result is not significant, and hypothesis 3 is not supported. Model 11 tests the effect of structural embeddedness in the absence of relational embeddedness (hypothesis 4). This hypothesis predicts that the more structurally embedded the two firms are, the more likely they will have a symmetric value appropriation. The nonsignificant result does not support this hypothesis.

Models 12–14 test hypothesis 6, which predicts a positive relationship between asymmetry of business relatedness of two firms with the JV and relative value appropriation (i.e. asymmetry of business relatedness of two firms with the JV promotes unequal sharing of the pie). Model 12 adds asymmetry of business relatedness of two firms with the JV into the equation in addition to control variables. The result shows that asymmetry of business relatedness of two firms with the JV has no relationship with relative value appropriation. The results do not change as embeddedness variables are added into the equation (Models 13 and 14). Therefore, hypothesis 6 is not supported.

Conclusion

This chapter seeks to determine whether firms benefit from entering strategic alliances and whether those benefits are contingent on the existing network resources available to them at the time of entry. In answering this question, we have examined the effects of both network resources and business relatedness asymmetry on the total value created and the relative value appropriated by partners in a JV. Examining the influence of network resources on the stock market returns for JV-announcing firms and examining the antecedents of both total value creation and relative value appropriation has shown that both network resources resulting from the embeddedness of partners and the asymmetry of business relatedness of two firms with the JV affect the total value creation of all partners but not the relative value appropriation between partners.

This study used an event-study methodology to examine the conditions under which a new JV is expected to create value for the shareholders of all partners of a JV and how the value created is appropriated by each partner. The study of the dynamics underlying dyadic-level value creation and appropriation in JVs is important because any JV involves at least two firms (Zajac and Olsen 1993). This study also extends prior research by considering the importance of network resources in influencing the dynamics of value creation and appropriation in JVs. The results show that the magnitude of total value created in a JV is influenced by the extent to which the two partners are embedded in prior alliance networks and that the degree of network embeddedness between two parent firms creates network resources that have a positive effect on total value creation from their new alliances. The study also shows that the asymmetry of business relatedness of two firms with the JV negatively affects the total value creation of the JV. Relative value appropriation, however, was found to remain uninfluenced by either network embeddedness or the asymmetry of business relatedness of two firms with the JV.

An important finding of this study is that the degree of relational embeddedness and the network resources originating from ties between two firms have a positive relationship with the total value creation associated with a new JV. The results also indicate that there is no limit to the benefits a firm can extract from a relationship with another firm with whom it has a rich history of direct JV relationships. Investors expect that the more relationally embedded two firms are, the more likely that the new JV is going to create value. This finding is at odds with the arguments and the empirical evidence that the benefits of relational embeddedness may reach a limit beyond which an increase in relational embeddedness may not provide additional benefits for JV partners or may even become a liability, preventing firms from pursuing new opportunities, as hypothesis 1b suggested. It is possible that the sample is not large enough and the time horizon not long enough for the degree of the relational embeddedness between firms to reach the point of diminishing returns. Future research with a larger sample size and a longer time horizon could further test this hypothesis.

The study failed to find support for hypotheses 2a and 2b, two competing hypotheses on the relationship between the degree of structural embeddedness two firms share and total value creation. Unlike many prior studies showing the significant information and control roles provided by structural embeddedness and the network resources they generate in the formation of an alliance between firms or in the innovative capabilities of firms (Ahuja 2000a), this one suggests that investors do not look beyond relational embeddedness to search for cues about whether a JV will create more value for the parent firms.

Underlying both relational embeddedness and structural embeddedness is the creation of network resources that aid firms with information (learning) and reputation (control) effects on total value creation. The strengths of these effects, however, are likely to be different for relational and structural embeddedness. In terms of information effects, although both relational and structural embeddedness offer information about partners' characteristics, partners may value information resulting from relational embeddedness more than that from structural embeddedness. This is because the former is from direct past interactions while the latter is based on third-party interactions. Therefore, the former is likely to be considered more reliable, richer, and finer-grained than the latter. In terms of reputation and control effects, the effect of structural embeddedness may be more profound than the effect of relational embeddedness. Reputation effects arising from the structural embeddedness between partners spread to wider circles of partners and thus affect the reputation of partners in a broader network. Conversely, the effect of relational embeddedness is strongest between partners: thus if reputation is lost, the damage does not extend nearly as far. Our study suggests that investors do not look beyond the effects of relational embeddedness on total value creation. It is quite possible that this finding comes from the fact that indirect ties are not salient enough for investors to attend to signals resulting from them. It is also possible that investors believe that information carried through prior indirect ties may not be reliable and thus discount it.

Contrary to our expectations, the study did not produce any evidence that embeddedness and concomitant network resources play a role in influencing the extent of relative value appropriation between two partners. One possible explanation for the nonsignificant results is that the findings do not demonstrate whether the differences in value extraction by firms in a JV result from the anticipated relative contributions by the partners. Future research should investigate this issue with richer data on projected contributions by each partner.

However, the study did demonstrate that material resources shape alliance outcomes. In particular, we found that the asymmetry of business relatedness of the two firms is detrimental to total value creation in the JV. The extent of total value created does not differ between those JVs in which both partners are related to the new JV and those in which neither partner is related to the new JV. The asymmetry of business relatedness (one partner is related to the JV but the other partner is not) reduces the total value creation, and it is possible that the asymmetry of knowledge transfer benefits between the two partners may lead to shifts in the bargaining power in a JV, which may discourage knowledge-sharing between partners and thus reduce the joint value creation of the two partners from the JV (Inkpen 1998; Chi 2000).

Still, while the asymmetry of business relatedness of two firms in a JV plays an important role in total value creation of a JV, it does not affect how much of this value is appropriated by each partner. This is contrary to the expectation that differences in potential learning opportunities and in the absorptive capacity of the partners would cause investors to expect that the returns to each partner would vary. One reason for this outcome may be that investors expect the independent legal status of the JV to provide a buffer that prevents either partner from gaining a differential advantage over the other.

IMPLICATIONS FOR BROADER RESEARCH ON NETWORK AND STRATEGIC ALLIANCES

The findings in this chapter have important implications for broader research on network embeddedness and strategic alliances. Network researchers have long elaborated on how cohesion and bridging mechanisms play different roles for a variety of individual and organizational outcomes, such as job search, manager promotions, and alliance formation (Granovetter 1974; Burt 1992; Gulati 1995*b*). Extending these ideas to the arena of value creation in JVs shows that a cohesive relationship between partners resulting from a large number of prior direct JV ties creates network resources that assure investors that the new JV will create more value for partners. Investors seem to value new JVs between two firms with no prior connections less than those involving firms with previous ties. Research on exploration and exploitation indicates that firms try to balance the exploitation of current opportunities and the exploration of new ones (March 1991; Koza and Lewin 1998). This study suggests that firms may value the exploitation of safety benefits resulting from the relational embeddedness between partners more than the exploration of new opportunities in joint venture formation. Nevertheless, firms may value exploration of new opportunities over exploitation of existing ones in other contexts (Rowley, Behrens, and Krackhardt 2000).

More importantly, this study shows the value of recognizing interorganizational networks and the resources they create in alliance research. In trying to determine why firms differ in their conduct and profitability, researchers have typically chosen to view firms as autonomous entities striving for competitive advantage from either external industry sources (e.g. Porter 1980) or internal resources and capabilities (e.g. Barney 1991). However, the image of atomistic actors competing for profits against each other in an impersonal marketplace is increasingly inadequate in a world in which firms are embedded in networks of social, professional, and exchange relationships with other organizational actors (Granovetter 1985; Gulati 1998; Galaskiewicz and Zaheer 1999). Consequently, the conduct and performance of firms can be more fully understood by examining the network of relationships in which they are embedded and the network resources that they may accumulate as a result. Adopting a relational, rather than an atomistic, approach deepens our understanding of the sources of differences in firm conduct and profitability by highlighting how strategic networks create resources that provide a firm with access to information, resources, markets, and technologies. Conversely, a network approach should also account for the drawbacks of interorganizational networks by showing how networks may lock firms into unproductive relationships or preclude their entering other viable partnerships. In other words, firms do not always accumulate network resources monotonically, with an increasing number of ties. Such varying effects should be the subject of further inquiry.

8 The multifaceted nature of network resources

This chapter looks at how successful firms differ from less successful ones with regard to the architecture of their intra- and interorganizational relationships. An important component of this difference is that successful firms focus on developing and elevating an array of relationships with key stakeholders that in turn becomes a vehicle for them to accumulate network resources. This chapter defines network resources more broadly to encompass not just a firm's ties with its alliance partners but also those with its customers and suppliers and those that exist between its internal subunits. It further considers how the quality of ties with each of these key stakeholders may evolve and become richer in content that in turn will provide those firms with access to greater network resources.[1] This chapter shows that winning companies define relationships in a very consistent, specific, and multifaceted manner. They focus extraordinary enterprisewide energy on moving beyond a transactional mindset as they develop trust-based, mutually beneficial, and enduring relationships with key constituencies both inside and outside of their organizational walls.

Ironically, as top performers expand their scope of activities by reaching out to external partners and, in effect, rendering their borders more porous, they are simultaneously contracting their organizational centers and outsourcing increasing portions of their internal functions. They are shrinking their core by increasing focus on fewer activities while outsourcing the remainder to strategic partners. The firms in our study anticipated more benefits from outsourcing in the future than garnered in the past in a range of areas

This chapter is adapted from 'Shrinking Core, Expanding Periphery: The Relational Architecture of High Performing Organizations' by Ranjay Gulati and David Kletter published in *California Management Review* ©2005, (47/3): 77–104, by The Regents of the University of California. By permission of The Regents.

[1] In the original article, network resources were referred to as 'relational capital'. For our purposes, these two terms are synonymous and I have retained the term 'network resources' to be consistent with the main thrust of this book. It is worth noting, however, that while the focus of many of the previous chapters has been primarily on the benefits that accrue to firms through their alliances—and in a few chapters other ties like board interlocks—our usage of the term network resources is broader in this chapter and encompasses connections with suppliers and customers and between internal business units.

including human resources, finance, manufacturing, logistics, customer service, research and development, sales, and information technology.

At the same time that they are shrinking their cores, top-performing firms are expanding their horizons by trying to provide customers with greater sets of products and services, many of which may come through partnerships with other firms and are bundled together into what are loosely called customer solutions. This 'shrinking core, expanding periphery' phenomenon is evident across an array of industries and is one of the hallmarks of a new operating model in which multifaceted network resources come to play an important role for those organizations. The relational architecture that such firms create provides them with a pathway to profitable growth by allowing them to simultaneously focus on their top and bottom lines. They manage their costs by shrinking the core and enhance revenue streams by expanding their periphery. This is more challenging to execute than it sounds, and therein lies one of the ultimate differentiators of successful firms.

Take Starbucks, for example. The company has long understood the importance of relationship building, not only with its customers but also with its suppliers, alliance partners, and internal business units. Indeed, the 'Starbucks experience' is predicated on the creation of enduring, multifaceted relationships. While brewed from high-end Arabica beans, Starbucks coffee is ultimately a high-priced commodity in a reasonably competitive space. To retain its market leadership, the company needs a tie that binds consumers to its brand on a very personal level, and that tie is not just the coffee but also the relationship the local Starbucks barista enjoys with his or her daily customers. Starbucks focuses the bulk of its energies on solidifying that relationship. It creates a comfortable coffeehouse environment in which a 'My Starbucks' relationship can easily develop. It staffs its stores with well-trained, highly motivated baristas who enjoy one of the best compensation and benefits packages in the retail industry. Its line organization is closely aligned with internal staff units that support it. It searches the world for the highest quality coffee beans and pays a more-than-fair price to the subsistence farmers who produce it. It allies with or acquires partners who can supplement its brand experience with music or ice cream or a flight to Chicago. In short, it develops a multidimensional relationship with its customers, which in turn rests on the multiple relationships it cultivates as a company with and between its internal subunits, suppliers, and alliance partners (Gulati, Huffman, and Neilson 2002).

To explore the ways in which relationship-centered organizations are developing in today's business world, and to discover the lessons that we can learn from these developments, we conducted a survey of Fortune 1000 companies. One hundred twelve CEOs and other senior executives from Fortune 1000 companies across a range of industries responded to a questionnaire comprising 115 questions on the organizational challenges and imperatives companies perceived in their markets. Of these firms, one hundred that were on the Fortune 1000 list in both 2000 and 2002 were retained for the remainder of the analyses reported in this chapter. We then stratified the performance of Fortune 1000 firms into quartiles based on their total returns to shareholders for the five years from 1995 to 2000 and 1997 to 2002 in order to isolate those attributes that differentiated top quartile respondents from the others, as well as to control for the market bubble in the late 1990s. The calculation of total shareholder return included both share price appreciation and dividend yield of the relevant stock. Needless to say, the gap in the valuations assigned top- and fourth-quartile respondents in 2000 is dramatic, with a less dramatic gap in 2002, driven by the overall market decline. The goal of our analysis is to elucidate the attributes of the firms that were sustained performers—that is, in the top quartile in both 2000 and 2002.

In addition to sending out the survey, we conducted a number of interviews with top-quartile firm leaders who were willing to discuss their responses in more detail. We also conducted a workshop on best practices in which we invited all participating firms to send a representative.

Leveraging network resources

As companies refocus around their core businesses and build a simultaneously expanding and shrinking firm, they have become increasingly reliant on their network resources based on ties to four sets of critical stakeholders that span both vertical and horizontal axes: customers, suppliers, alliance partners, and intraorganizational business units. Such resources are not only dependent upon the existence of ties to and between each of these constituents but also on the quality of those ties (see Chapter 4 for a discussion on the importance of tie content). As firms involve customers in product/solution development, share more and more information with vendors, and build wider and longer bridges with existing alliance partners (sometimes forging new ones), they are also developing more collaborative relationships among organizational subunits, at every level. Indeed, the relationship 'wave' sweeping successful companies exhibits the classic ripple effect visually depicted in Figure 8.1 as a move outward from the center on one or more of the four dimensions. On each of these relationship dimensions, successful firms work their way up a ladder in which they intensify their collaborative efforts with that particular constituent. Together these four dimensions and the quality of ties they encompass constitute the different types of network resources that a firm may come to possess.

Along each of these four dimensions, the relationship progresses from transactions at one end to collaboration until, in an ideal world, a company

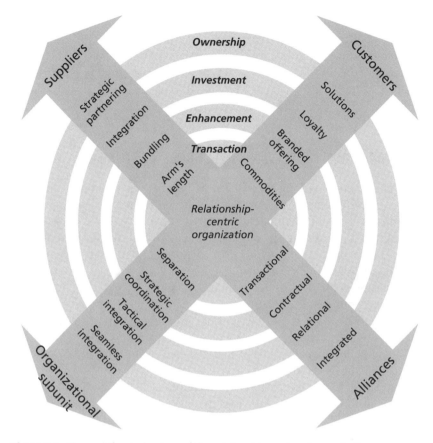

Figure 8.1. The multifaceted nature of the relationship-centered organization

and its key stakeholders all have a vested interest in the continued health and productivity of their relationship. What may start as an arrangement entailing minimal coordination and cooperation quickly expands into one of synchronous coordination and active cooperation. Suppliers are strategic partners, internal subunits are mutually aligned collaborators, alliance partners are part of a mutually reinforcing constellation of business relationships, and satisfied customers are collaborators on solutions. Thus, network resources are a function not only of the number of ties a firm may have on each of these dimensions but also of the quality of those ties.

A network-resource-rich organization with the relational architecture depicted in Figure 8.1 is a networked, agile, and highly adaptive entity that transcends traditional boundaries as it develops deep and collaborative relationships with internal subunits, customers, suppliers, and alliance partners. Such organizations appreciate that their competitiveness in today's marketplace and their achievement of profitable growth hinge on their ability to leverage their network resources by extracting full value from various partners—both internal and external, spanning vertical and horizontal boundaries—and they are creative and consistent in this endeavor. This chapter examines the four facets of network resources represented in Figure 8.1— customers, suppliers, alliance partners, and internal units—in greater detail.

FIRST DIMENSION OF NETWORK RESOURCES: CUSTOMERS

While customers have long been hailed by bumper sticker slogans and corporate values statements as the 'boss', their central role in sustaining the economic fortunes of the modern enterprise is being freshly acknowledged. No longer is the customer merely the someone who buys your product or service. Rather he or she is the someone whose problem your organization exists to solve (Day 1999; Hammer 2001; Kumar 2003).

And customers' expectations are on the rise. While 59 percent of our survey respondents found meeting customer expectations to be a significant challenge in the past, 84 percent now consider it to be a significant challenge in moving forward. Sixty-eight percent of the companies we surveyed project that it will be increasingly difficult to access new customers, and 52 percent believe it will be difficult to access new geographical markets. Underlying this drive to cement high-value customer connections is the recognition that while retaining customers remains far easier than acquiring them, ultimately both are important. In our survey, network-resource-rich organizations joined their poorly performing peers in acknowledging the difficulties associated with attracting new customers and entering new markets in the current business environment. An important element underlying the challenges of serving customers profitably is the growing pressures of commoditization, one result of which is increased competition on price. Through the confluence of an array of factors ranging from growing international competition and maturing technologies to open standards and reduced willingness of customers to pay for premium products, many industries face emerging pressures of commoditization. These can be particularly deadly in technology-intensive industries where firms must generate enough of a surplus to invest in innovation and development (Gulati et al. 2004).

What distinguishes successful organizations is their reaction to these mounting challenges and expectations and their focus on developing network resources through close ties with their customers to address these issues. More than two-thirds of the top-quartile firms we surveyed devote primary strategic focus to meeting customer expectations and building long-term customer relationships, a much higher percentage than the bottom-quartile companies, which tend to be far more focused on cutting costs and shedding underperforming assets. Relationship development, as one might expect, thus takes a back seat when the question of corporate survival arises.

Not only do successful firms develop a greater number of customer relationships, but they also invest heavily in increasing the quality of those ties. Hence, at the same time that winning companies are building new relationships, they are also strengthening the ones they have already formed by climbing a ladder of increasing mutual responsibility and commitment within these customer relationships. This becomes particularly important for those firms seeking ways to differentiate themselves by extending their products/services into a broader array of customer solutions. As companies ascend these ladders together with customers, each party shares more of the burden of sustained collaboration and realizes more of the mutual benefit (see Figure 8.2).

On the lowest rung of the customer relationship ladder, no significant relationship exists between buyer and seller, as products are only commodities, bought and sold transactionally, and are not differentiated from each other in the marketplace. In order to move one rung up from this state, companies must strengthen the relationship between their customers and their products. This is achieved by forming a set of expectations about a product in the customer's mind and creating a brand that represents the company's implicit promise to deliver against those expectations in the future. The relationship here is between the customer and the product, not between the customer and the seller; the relationship would thus be expected to move with the product if, for example, the brand were sold to another company. On the third tier of the ladder, the two parties invest in one another's success by creating a 'switching cost', which creates a bond of loyalty between them. This could take many forms, including physical (e.g. colocation or establishing facilities in close proximity), intellectual (e.g. sharing and/or licensing intellectual property), personnel-based (e.g. dedicating staff to work the interface across the companies), and monetary (e.g. use of 'gainsharing' or other financial rewards for mutual success). At the highest rung of the ladder, the customer–seller relationship is strongest, transcending and redefining the traditional boundaries of the two companies. Here the seller takes ownership for success of a portion of the customer's business, offering a solution to a problem that the customer faces, and receives compensation not based on the volume of products or services but on a successful outcome from the buyer's standpoint. Of course, a given company may operate at multiple points on the ladder simultaneously. Many leading companies have effectively segmented their customer base and created offerings tailored to different customer segments, with differing depths of relationships.

Our survey and field interviews supported our contention that top-quartile companies are ahead of their peers in moving their relationships with customers up this ladder. But how are they accomplishing it? Survey responses and follow-up interviews revealed that winning companies are more engaged

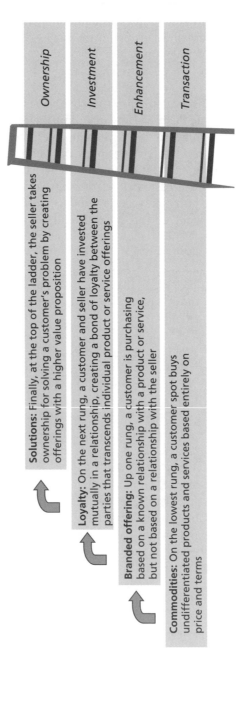

Figure 8.2. Customer relationship ladder

Ownership

Investment

Enhancement

Transaction

Solutions: Finally, at the top of the ladder, the seller takes ownership for solving a customer's problem by creating offerings with a higher value proposition

Loyalty: On the next rung, a customer and seller have invested mutually in a relationship, creating a bond of loyalty between the parties that transcends individual product or service offerings

Branded offering: Up one rung, a customer is purchasing based on a known relationship with a product or service, but not based on a relationship with the seller

Commodities: On the lowest rung, a customer spot buys undifferentiated products and services based entirely on price and terms

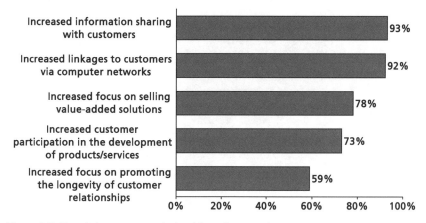

Figure 8.3. Trends in customer relationships, all respondents

in key collaborative behaviors with customers. Our survey results also suggest that deep customer connections and the network resources they generate have universal appeal for both top- and bottom-quartile firms, and both groups are using a common set of activities to develop such connections. These include the sharing of information with customers, the development of linkages to customers via computer networks, and increased involvement in customers' operations. They are also increasingly incorporating customer input into the development of products and services, and shifting their focus from selling products and/or services to selling 'value-added solutions' (see Figure 8.3). Across these five activities, we saw uniformly high levels of intent to share information with customers and link to them via computer networks among top- and bottom-quartile performers (responding at a level of 5 or greater on a 7-point scale). In fact, in 2002 the difference between the sustained performers and bottom-quartile performers was only 5 percent for information sharing, with 100 percent of sustained performers reporting to us that they planned to increase the amount of information they shared with customers, and 95 percent of bottom-quartile performers reporting to us that they planned to do the same. Furthermore, computer networks seem to be the medium of choice, with 100 percent of sustained performers reporting the plan to increase systematic connections using the Internet, and 95 percent of bottom-quartile performers reporting such plans.

The differences in practices between sustained performers and other companies in the survey were most pronounced in the shift from selling products and services to providing integrated solutions, in the degree that customers provide into the development of new products/services, and in their focus on longevity of customer relationships. We will elaborate on the shift to selling solutions in greater detail below (see Figure 8.4).

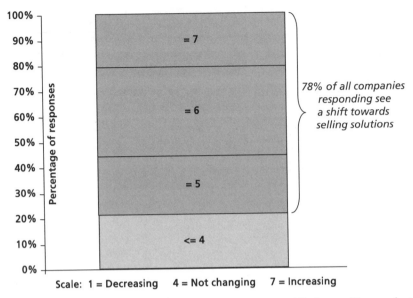

Figure 8.4. Survey question: To what extent do you see a shift from selling products/ services to selling value-added solutions?

From Selling Products to Providing Customer Solutions

As highlighted above, successful firms accumulate network resources not only by building a larger number of ties with their customers but also by enhancing the quality of those ties. An important consequence of the move by top-performing firms to pay greater attention to their customers and develop concomitant network resources has been the shift from selling products to selling what has loosely been described as customer solutions. In an increasingly competitive and transparent global environment where customer expectations are on the rise, it has become harder for many established companies to maintain their profit margins while selling traditional products and services. Established industry players are confronting the reality that product-based differentiation is more costly and difficult to maintain than ever before, and product differences are increasingly less meaningful. Value has, in effect, migrated downstream from suppliers toward customers. Rather than continuing to resist the inevitable, companies of all descriptions in diverse industries are looking for opportunities to develop higher-margin 'solutions' businesses (Foote et al. 2001; Sharma, Lucier, and Molloy 2002).

Our survey indicated that most companies are trying to climb the rungs of the customer relationship ladder as they move from a singular product/service orientation to a more blended solutions-driven approach (see Figure 8.4). A solution is not, despite what many believe, an extension of an existing product line or the mere bundling of services with products. It is instead a fundamentally new approach to *creating* incremental value for the customer and, by extension, for the solution provider. A solution is typically developed as a combination of products, services, and knowledge (e.g. risk management, performance guarantees, and customer consulting), and is a supplier's customized response to a customer's pressing business need. It is the logical next step in the customer value proposition, one that promises increased profits, stronger customer relationships, and greater competitive differentiation to those providers who get it right (see Figure 8.5 for some examples across a range of settings). For example, rather than selling simply lubricants, which may be tough to differentiate and may typically be purchased as commodities at the lowest available price, a company with a solution-focused value proposition could combine the products with deep expertise in the application of lubricants. This would reflect a shift from a pure 'product' sell, to selling a combined set of products and services that

Industry	Traditional Product	Value-Added Services	Traditional Value Proposition		Solution Value Proposition
Truck Manufacturing	• Trucks	• Financing • Service	"We sell & service trucks"	⇨	"We can help you reduce your life cycle transportation costs"
Chemicals	• Lubricants	• Product support • Application design • Materials analysis	"We sell a wide range of lubricants"	⇨	"We can increase your machine performance and uptime" • Maintenance Analysis • Performance guarantees
Pharmaceuticals	• Drugs	• Product support • Outcomes-driven information database	"We sell pharmaceuticals"	⇨	"We can help you better manage your patient base"
Telecom	• Phones	• Billing	"We can serve multiple needs (e.g. voice, data)"	⇨	"We can be your single-point connection to the world"
Pharmacy Benefit Management	• Benefit plan management • Mail order prescription delivery	• Administration • Breaking bulk	"We can lower your health care costs"	⇨	"We can be your single-source for all benefits management, including long-term care and disease management"

Figure 8.5. Evolution of solution value proposition

together enhance a customer's machine performance and guarantee the maintenance of the enhanced level of performance over time.

As companies transition from transacting in products and services to developing value-added solutions *in partnership with* their customers, the risks they naturally assume increase. A common lament among fledgling solutions providers is, 'Our customers are thrilled, but we're not making any money.' One of the critical distinguishing features of a true solutions relationship is that value is *not* reapportioned but rather new value is created—and shared. Hence, in structuring solutions, successful companies and their customers focus on the creation of value and on establishing performance-monitoring metrics that will both measure gains and distribute them equitably.

Moreover, top-performing companies make sure they build solutions with the customers that value them (Gulati and Oldroyd 2005). They also rigorously segment their customer bases according to relative cost-to-serve and profitability and account for such segmentation in their investment decisions. Successful companies want to focus their greatest efforts on enhancing the value proposition they offer to their most productive relationships because not every customer is interested in buying solutions. One of the companies we interviewed as part of our survey categorized customers as gold, silver, bronze, and lead, reserving special resources and attention for its gold and silver clientele—while encouraging the 'lead weight' to shop elsewhere. Examples abound of companies trying to advance their customer base up this value ladder. At the same time that they focus their attention on select customers, successful firms also seek to extend the duration of those relationships. One attribute on which top-quartile survey respondents differed was the degree of emphasis they placed on improving the longevity of customer relationships: 67 percent of sustained performer respondents thought it was critical, but only 50 percent of bottom-quartile firms thought it was critical (as indicated by a response of 5 or greater on a 7-point scale on the survey questions).

At the same time that successful firms focus their efforts on crafting solutions for select customers, they also see the value in engaging customers in this task (e.g. Prahalad and Ramaswamy 2004). As a result, another observed attribute that sets sustained performers apart from their peers is the willingness to incorporate customer input into product and service designs. Our survey showed that fully 92 percent of sustained performers planned to increase the amount of collaboration with customers during product development as compared to 73 percent of all survey respondents (as indicated by a response of 5 or greater on a 7-point scale on the survey questions).

The move toward selling solutions appears in different forms in different industries. In many traditional business-to-consumer markets, it takes the form of a shift from offering products to offering experiences or lifestyles, such as those purveyed by Starbucks or Harley Davidson. For instance, through its Riders' Edge program Harley Davidson tries to build closer relationships with customers. The company provides its network of independent dealers with all the tools and resources they need to get potential customers over the biggest hurdle to owning a Harley: securing a license to drive it. Harley Davidson, in partnership with state DMVs, has created an educational safety course to teach people how to drive a motorcycle. After teaching customers how to drive the bike, Harley dealers schedule them for road tests, transport them to the test sites, and even lend them bikes to take the test—all for US$250, which is credited toward the purchase of a Harley Davidson motorcycle.

But Harley Davidson's devotion to helping customers fulfill their dreams does not end there. It actively cultivates a network of Harley Owners Groups, or HOGs, across the country, with dues-paying chapters in 1,200 dealer communities. In fact, one of the responsibilities of a Harley Davidson dealer is to foster a local HOG by organizing rallies, rides, and other Harley-centric activities in the service area. Now 800,000 owners strong, HOGs do a lot to spread the Harley Davidson mystique. An active rental program also acts as a great feeder system for new purchases. Credit services, branded parts and accessories, and a full line of Harley Davidson attire and merchandise complete the portfolio of customer products and services. Harley Davidson does not pitch price or specs, but rather a way of life, or what the company calls a 'lifestyle'.

In many business-to-business markets where manufactured products are bought and sold, the focus on solutions manifests itself in the form of companies' attempts to combine a broader array of products with complementary services to create a more comprehensive offering for the customer. Many pure services firms have also embraced these ideas and offer solutions that encompass a broader array of services provided to customers in a more accessible manner. In all these instances, the solution provider uses a solutions approach to get closer to the customer and create meaningful differentiation between their offerings and those of others.

One example of such a company is Teradata, a division of NCR. In the mid-1990s, NCR began the process of consolidating a portfolio of hardware, database software, and services into a combined offering focused on customers, and soon began complementing its core database offering with complementary applications and services. Today, Teradata has consolidated and coordinated its entire company around providing such solutions, which are combinations of Teradata's portfolio of hardware, software, and services aimed at specific business problems in specific industries, such as Yield Management for airlines, Contract Compliance for the transportation industry, Customer Retention for retail banks, and Network Optimization for communications companies. The typical solution sale at Teradata is on average one-third hardware, one-third software, and one-third professional services. The goal is to make a solution greater than its individual parts, which can occur only when

Teradata develops a full understanding of customers' problems and creates an offering that can solve these.

A key component of Teradata's solution orientation arises from its close partnerships with customers, as evidenced by how it develops software. Rather than build isolated applications around its own internal expertise, Teradata forms partnerships with key customers to build integrated solutions for industry-specific problems, infusing key insights from select customers to create applications that fully leverage Teradata's key strengths. An example of this approach is National Australia Bank, which partnered with Teradata to develop Relationship Optimizer, an Analytical CRM solution that enables customer-oriented and personalized dialogs with hundreds of thousands or even millions of customers of major business-to-consumer businesses, such as retail banks. This application has allowed the bank not only to create an effective communication channel with its large number of customers but also to identify discrete individual customer events every day and react to them in a timely manner (not an event like a birthday, but an event like a deposit of more than 200 percent of the previous largest deposit a customer has made in the past twelve months, or the discontinuance of an automatic paycheck deposit for someone who is at least 55 years old, or the first time a specific person has ever made an ATM deposit, etc.). Such events in turn allow the bank to identify potential opportunities to contact the customer with product or service offerings in a proactive and timely manner. This joint project between Teradata and the National Australia Bank has resulted in a reliable and successful application, now in its fourth generation (Teradata CRM), leveraged by other industries worldwide.

In addition to partnering directly with select customers, Teradata also provides multiple forums to easily connect customers with each other and share knowledge and best practices. Along with its annual users conference where best-practice customers share their insights and experiences with others, Teradata regularly schedules 'webinars' throughout the year and invites customers and other experts to engage in interactive dialog with a business or technical user of a specific solution. The customer usually leads the dialog, not Teradata.

Because so many firms are now embracing a customer-focused perspective, perhaps the next logical question is: Are solutions also going to become table-stakes and commodities in the years to come?

SECOND DIMENSION OF NETWORK RESOURCES: SUPPLIERS

Another practice through which firms may accumulate network resources is the maintenance of strong and enduring ties with key suppliers. Many companies see the importance of building partnerships in this critical vertical dimension of the value chain as crucial to their success (e.g. Kumar, Scheer, and Steenkamp 1995; Zaheer and Venkatraman 1995; Dyer 2000; Gulati, Lawrence, and Puranam 2005). As firms realize the importance of cost-containment in increasingly competitive markets, they see the logic of 'shrinking their core' and begin to shift activities previously viewed to be core to their business to external suppliers and in doing so, hope to reap benefits from economies of scale or depth of specialization. The growing reach of manufacturing and services industries to distant outreaches of the globe have made it advantageous for firms to tap into local expertise on very economical terms. In doing so, they recognize that suppliers are an integral part of the value they offer their own customers, especially because complete solutions, which require more pieces from suppliers, now constitute a greater portion of their offerings.

As with customers, successful organizations are climbing a relationship ladder with suppliers with whom they wish to develop closer partnerships (see Figure 8.6). Suppliers have come to recognize the need to climb this ladder with their key customers as well: thus, they are climbing a customer ladder parallel to that described earlier. In doing so, each enriches the network resources available to them. The most basic form of relationship that a company can have with its suppliers is one in which the company purchases each product or service as an isolated transaction. In this case, interaction with the supplier occurs only to place the order, take delivery of product, and arrange for payment; in an increasingly electronic world, this 'interaction' may occur entirely between machines. Moving one rung up from this transaction level, companies work with their suppliers to leverage their knowledge and expertise. On this 'enhancement' rung, a richer and broader dialog occurs, including discussion of the company's objectives for the products and services, exploration of alternatives, and often a contractual agreement that formally establishes a relationship that transcends the transaction. This might include, for example, the establishment of a service agreement that coincides with the sale of a traditional product offering, an agreement designed to ensure that the company achieves the best possible results from the supplier's product.

On the third 'investment' rung, employees from the supplier become integrated into the company's operations and work as part of a team, side-by-side with the company's employees. This could be a temporary, project-based arrangement such as a product development effort or improvement initiative or, in the strongest case, part of ongoing operations. On the highest rung, the company turns part of its activities over to a supplier, who takes ownership of the successful execution of those activities. These could be mundane back-office transactions like payroll or entire business functions such as manufacturing or customer care. At this level of 'ownership', companies focus on what they do best, while accessing all other capabilities through their suppliers. In these relationships, the supplier is given the greatest amount of latitude in terms of how the activities are conducted. Success requires not only the 'soft' side of the relationship (i.e. trust and confidence) to be solid but also

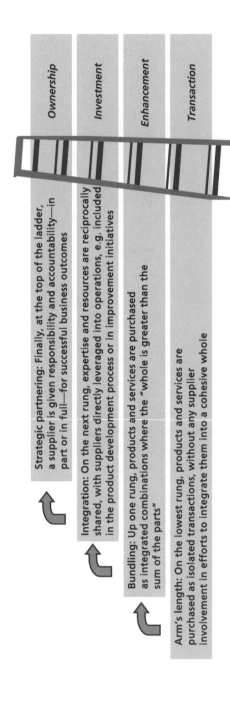

Figure 8.6. Supplier relationship ladder

the harder side: governance mechanisms that institute strong accountability by measuring and rewarding successful business outcomes. In the extreme, suppliers will in turn become solutions providers. It is important to note that a company will not have the same relationship with each of its suppliers and would therefore be likely to operate with them at several of the rungs simultaneously. Indeed, we observed that most firms maintain a portfolio of relationships that are on various rungs of the ladder. Firms may even operate simultaneously on multiple rungs with a given supplier, accessing different commodities or services within different operational contexts (Dyer 2000; Gulati, Lawrence, and Puranam 2006). Thus, a firm's network resources can include its multilevel connections with an individual supplier, as well as those across groups of suppliers. Some of these connections are deeper than others but together they provide firms with an array of choices and opportunities that may not be available to other firms.

Despite differences in the way a firm may ally with its suppliers, there were some consistent trends revealed by our survey (see Figure 8.7). A large percentage—88 percent—of survey respondents expected to increase information-sharing with suppliers, and the vast majority—92 percent—was experiencing a tightening of computer network linkages with suppliers, more supplier input into development, and more involvement in suppliers' operations (as indicated by a response of 5 or greater on a 7-point scale on our survey questions). All of these specific behaviors point to a more intimate relationship with suppliers overall where product specifications and cost drivers are increasingly shared. As companies pinpoint where on the value chain they want to play and shed noncore operations, their relationships with suppliers become increasingly vital, especially where critical components and complementary offerings are concerned. Winning suppliers have also recognized this

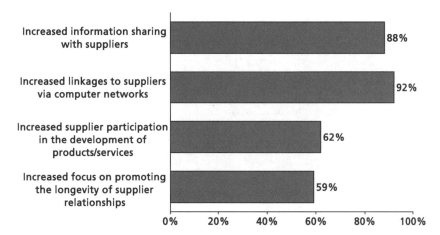

Figure 8.7. Trends in supplier relationships, all respondents

need among their important customers and have tried to work harder to climb this ladder with this group. Not only have they learned to develop close communication channels and dedicated client teams but in some instances have colocated staff on customer sites to simplify the coordination of tasks.

One of the ways for companies to strengthen supplier relationships, and to move them from the lowest 'transaction' level to one or more rungs up the ladder, is to develop and nurture trust with suppliers. Indeed, successful companies recognize the power of trust in all their business relationships, and they expend tremendous energy developing ways to institutionalize that trust, particularly in their procurement processes (Zaheer, McEvily, and Perrone 1998; Gulati and Sytch 2006*a*). Developing this level of trust is not easy, but some organizations are finding ways to breach traditional organizational boundaries and outsource activities closer and closer to the core. Sustained performers among our survey respondents try to build long-term relationships with their suppliers. The results show that while 59 percent of all respondents anticipated an increase in the longevity of supplier relationships, the difference between sustained performers and bottom-quartile companies was significant: 75 percent of sustained performers intended to increase the duration and strength of supplier relationships, while only 55 percent of bottom-quartile companies intended to do so.

When it works, outsourcing operations to suppliers—and the network resources this generates—offers compelling strategic and economic benefits. It results in lower costs, greater flexibility, enhanced expertise and discipline, and the freedom to focus on core business capabilities. At first confined to nonstrategic business activities such as cleaning, transport, and payroll, outsourcing now encompasses even such functions as manufacturing. Not surprisingly, top-quartile companies often lead by example. In their own dealings with customers, they model the sort of supplier behavior they have come to expect.

Sometimes value in partnerships with suppliers is measured by both entities not in terms of short-term individual gains but in long-term joint returns, and in other instances in terms of intangible (but equally remunerative) benefits such as reputational capital. Starbucks, for instance, has a great deal of brand equity invested in its reputation as a company focused on improving the economic, environmental, and social conditions of the Third World countries where its coffee originates. It works with Conservation International to develop environmentally sound sourcing guidelines designed to foster sustainable coffee farms. Moreover, it works with Fair Trade to help coffee growers form cooperatives and negotiate directly with coffee importers, who are also encouraged to foster long-term relationships with growers and to furnish financial credit. Starbucks pays Fair Trade prices for its Arabica beans regardless of market prices, which quite often fall below subsistence level. In fact, in October 2001 the company announced its intention to buy one million pounds of Fair Trade Certified coffee within the next eighteen months, a real commitment to improving the plight of coffee farmers who have sometimes seen the market price for their coffee decline as a result of oversupply.

Starbucks has also developed very clear standards and a rigorous process for selecting and maintaining its supply relationships with a wide range of vendors, from the farmers who grow its beans to the manufacturer of its cups. Specific criteria, robust training programs, regularly scheduled business reviews, and a high degree of information exchange all distinguish and guide the procurement process. Starbucks takes a holistic approach, engaging representatives from not only its purchasing operations but also its technical product development, category management, and even its business unit operations teams to understand, from an entire supply chain perspective, how a supply relationship will ultimately impact operations. Buck Hendrix, VP of Purchasing, says, 'We are looking for, first and foremost, quality; service is #2 on our priority list; and cost is #3. Not that we want to pay more than we should, because we negotiate very hard, but we are not willing to compromise quality or service in order to get a lower price.'

Once a supplier is selected, Starbucks works diligently to establish a mutually beneficial working relationship. If the relationship is strategic, senior management from both companies will meet face-to-face three or four times the first year and then semiannually afterward. 'Our biggest focus in these sessions is how to team with our suppliers', notes Buck Hendrix. 'We want to create a two-way dialog as opposed to dictating the conversation.' Discussions encompass not only Starbucks' expectations but also supplier concerns and suggestions about how to improve the productivity and profitability of the relationship.

According to John Yamin, VP of the Food division, 'We won't go into partnerships where the vendor won't make money or grow with us.' Michelle Gass, VP of Beverages, adds, 'Our vendors are willing to do what it takes to stay with us. I am amazed by the flexibility of our vendors, which is driven by our partnerships with them.' For example, Solo, Starbucks' cup manufacturer, bought a company in Japan and a manufacturing facility in the United Kingdom so they could supply the coffee retailer's operations there. In return, Starbucks has committed to a long-term global supply agreement with the disposable products company. It is this sort of give-and-take that characterizes top-quartile supply relationships, and that helps firms to establish network resources.

The benefits of leveraging network resources with one's supply base are manifold. In successful partnerships, both firms gain as they move up their industry's value chain together. Value is not reapportioned in such cases; rather, it is created and shared. The sharing is often the thorniest part. First of all, how do you fairly measure gains (from a total cost–benefit perspective) and split them so that both parties see a return on their investment?

Successful organizations that truly leverage this important facet of their network resources have wrestled with this central challenge longer than most and have developed best practices that help them establish win–win relationships with their suppliers. Ultimately, some form of 'open book' arrangements combined with joint mutual dependence in which both parties need each other may furnish the transparency necessary to ensure true gain-sharing (Gulati and Sytch 2006*b*). Building the trust that facilitates that sort of arrangement is not a 'feel good' exercise; it is a business imperative.

THIRD DIMENSION OF NETWORK RESOURCES: ALLIANCES

The third dimension of network resources—discussed extensively in previous chapters—arises from a firm's strategic alliances (e.g. Gulati 1998; Gulati, Nohria, and Zaheer 2000). The research underlying this chapter echoed some of the previous findings and also revealed that the vast majority of the firms surveyed placed a high level of importance on entering and carefully managing strategic alliances. For example, 70 percent of firms were forging increased linkages to their partners. Alliance partners were also reported to have increasing input into the development of products and/or services in 63 percent of the companies surveyed.

Such results suggest that successful companies are increasingly focusing on what they do best and 'alliancing' the rest. Thus, as firms 'expand the periphery' of their value proposition to customers, they increasingly rely on not only vertical connections with suppliers but also their connections with their alliance partners who may provide offerings complementary to their own to fill any gaps in their product or service offerings, thus rounding out their solutions packages. These partnerships can be not only along horizontal and vertical dimensions of the value chain but also diagonal, when partners from disparate industries come together to tackle new opportunities. The survey findings here indicate that while 59 percent of bottom-quartile firms expect to increase involvement of alliance partners in product development, fully 75 percent of sustained performers plan such an increase. As companies expand their network of alliances in this way, they move up a relationship ladder that parallels the customer and supplier ladders (see Figure 8.8). This ladder begins with one-off, mutually convenient agreements often sparked by a specific need or opportunity, but never evolving into anything greater. These 'transactional' relationships are often quite simple and may not even involve financial terms. The Maytag repairman who appears in a car commercial and talks about reliability can help build both brands—but the shared environment is unlikely to evolve into anything deeper between the two companies. At the next higher level, firms evolve toward creating 'contractual

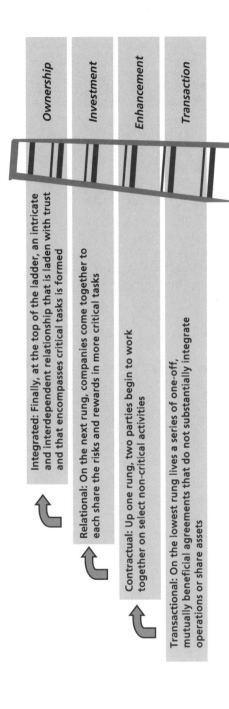

Figure 8.8. Alliance relationship ladder

coordination'—in which they agree to coordinate select, typically noncritical activities with each other. These 'enhanced' partnerships can take many forms, such as distributing one company's product through the other's channel.

At the third rung of the ladder, the relationship shifts from simple coordination of tasks to active cooperation in which the partners begin to rely on each other for more critical tasks. At the top of the ladder, in the 'trusted partner' stage, true partnerships form and are sustained, where each company shares resources with the other toward a purpose neither company could achieve alone, and they view each other as trustworthy partners.

As firms advance on this journey, they not only climb this ladder in their specific dyadic partnerships but also begin to create an intricate and interdependent web of collaborative entities, with each possessing a shared stake in the success of others and the combined whole. In some instances, entire industries form these relationship webs, most notably in the airline industry, where competition occurs among constellations such as Star Alliance, OneWorld, and SkyTeam (Nohria and Garcia-Pont 1991; Gomes-Casseres 1996). As with both the customer and supplier ladders, many companies will operate simultaneously on multiple rungs, forming different level alliances for different purposes.

As with the other ties that constitute a firm's network resources, its alliances may vary in strength. Not only are successful firms demonstrating greater propensities to enter into alliances, but the ties they are binding are also qualitatively different. They are more strategic, deeper, and more effective in leveraging network resources. Successful firms recognize that alliances enable them to do more with less. As they expand their peripheries, they need not do it all themselves and can instead leverage their partners' resource base much more broadly and effectively. As a result, they are becoming more creative in identifying alliance opportunities and potential partners with whom they can collectively serve certain target markets. The result is a constellation of business relationships populated with shifting alliances or webs that relate to one another in new and nonlinear ways.

Alliances that constitute a firm's network resources typically revolve around four distinct categories of partners that transcend horizontal and vertical boundaries: (a) the channel, (b) the licensee, (c) the complementer, and increasingly (d) the competitor. The implications of this expanded alliance building are profound in terms of organizational structure and behavior. The whole notion of 'in-house' becomes suspended as companies contend with organizational boundaries that are newly fluid, transparent, and, indeed, semipermeable. Web-based collaboration tools have accelerated this 'boundarylessness' and enhanced the channels of communication between partners (Welch 2001). Among the firms that responded to our survey, 68 percent are experiencing increased links to their partners via computer networks, and 63 percent are experiencing greater input from partners in the development of products and services. With the availability of new communication tools, alliance partners around the world can inexpensively share product specifications, opportunity alerts, blueprints, sales figures, expertise—all with the click of a mouse. And the sharing of this knowledge in turn accelerates value creation.

Companies in this new constellation context rely on external partners more and more, not only for cost reasons or to handle peripheral, narrowly circumscribed activities as in the past, but for strategic purposes, such as accessing new capabilities, improving quality, or sharing risk. New and powerful cooperatives are emerging, composed of multiple communities operating in a highly interdependent network and armed with a collective sense of purpose. At the extreme, we are witnessing unprecedented levels of cooperation between direct competitors, a phenomenon dubbed 'co-opetition' by some observers (Brandenburger and Nalebuff 1996).

While firms are exhibiting more enthusiasm toward alliances, there naturally remain hurdles to success. Like supplier relationships, governance and gain-sharing are two of the enduring challenges companies must address. In a world where the boundaries within and among firms are collapsing and your business is everyone's business, defining the 'rules of engagement' in alliances becomes a tricky issue. Previously guarded business processes are now open— either partially or entirely—to outside partners. Controls, operating protocols, and information technology standards must now be agreed on and embedded in the processes of all participants to create the electronically linked, real-time information-sharing network needed to ensure success. Leadership and accountability need to be clearly defined in this space; otherwise, multiple points of contact overwhelm the efficient functioning of the alliance. Thus, partners must fully understand their respective roles and responsibilities (Dyer, Kale, and Singh 2001; Gulati, Lawrence, and Puranam 2005).

For these reasons and others, several studies suggest that up to 70 percent of alliances ultimately fail. Most executives are not inclined to play those odds. However, underlying that discouraging figure, some companies are struggling with an abysmal track record, while others are enjoying an alliance success rate over 90 percent. For companies who discover and hone the right success formula, the alliance game becomes one of increasing the odds rather than simply playing the averages. That success formula is commonsensical and yet eludes many firms. It consists of careful partner selection, jointly articulated expectations, management flexibility, and performance incentives designed to secure a win–win outcome (Doz and Hamel 1998; Dyer and Singh 1998).

An example of a firm that has truly leveraged the network resources originating from its strategic alliances is, again, Starbucks. Over the years, Starbucks coffee has been served to millions of United, Horizon, and Canadian Airlines flyers as well as to Marriott, Sheraton, Westin, and Hyatt hotel guests through carefully constructed licensing agreements. Compass cafeterias, Barnes and Noble bookstores, HMS Host airports, and Safeway grocery stores all sell Starbucks coffee by the cup as *licensees*.

The company has also extended its product line in logical directions through *complementer* alliances and joint ventures. Its highly successful bottled Frappucino beverage is marketed, manufactured, and distributed through a 50/50 joint venture agreement with Pepsi. Its ice cream—the number 1 brand of coffee-flavored ice cream—is made and distributed by Dreyer's, and the packaged whole-bean and ground Starbucks coffees you see in supermarkets are marketed and distributed by an arch *competitor* in the at-home coffee consumption arena: Kraft.

In stark contrast to its domestic retail stores, which are all company-owned, Starbucks has expanded internationally through joint venture agreements with well-established local players. Today, they have expanded aggressively in disparate markets outside North America sporting the Starbucks name and logo.

Not all of Starbucks' alliances have been so successful. Its early attempts with Pepsi to produce a coffee-flavored carbonated beverage called Mazagran flopped. Attempts to diversify coffee ice creams to other flavors did not prove fruitful, and some of its more ambitious food-oriented ventures, such as the Café Starbucks and Circadia restaurant concepts, were not successful. Moreover, highly publicized plans to create a Starbucks destination/affinity portal on the Web with all sorts of lifestyle links came to naught.

But in each of these well-calculated risks was embedded a tremendously valuable lesson. The same joint venture that launched Mazagran produced Frappucino, a fabulously successful incremental revenue stream for Starbucks. The experiments with non-coffee-flavored ice cream and full-service restaurant concepts helped Starbucks establish parameters for customer perceptions of its brand. And while the Internet portal never came to pass, Starbucks used what it learned to design a wireless high-speed access network for its stores.

Maintaining these business alliances is, even at the best of times, a challenge, and Starbucks' approach has steadily evolved as its experience grows. According to Gregg Johnson, VP of Business Alliances,

Originally business alliances were intended to bring the Starbucks experience to places where retail could not go ... a fairly simple mission with a number of complex components. First, the alliances we build need to be profitable for both partners. Second, they need to be designed around delivering the experience, whether it's through a consumer product (e.g., packaged coffee) or on a United flight. If we are not confident that we can do that, we don't go to the next place. United, for example, had to replace the coffee-making equipment on all of its planes to meet Starbucks' exacting quality standards. Third, it has to be a place where the consumer expects to find us. Yes, people expect to find Starbucks in Hyatt hotels, but not at Motel 6 at this point. But what we see is a very natural expansion of those boundaries year after year as consumers become more comfortable associating Starbucks with places and products they did not a few years back.

Teradata is another firm in the business-to-business space that has also made alliances an important component of its network resources. In developing solutions for customers, Teradata frequently finds that it neither possesses nor desires to possess all the missing links that may be critical for a specific, industry-specific solution. In such instances, it seeks out alliance partners to provide key components of the solution. Some of its alliance partners include Siebel, SAS, Cognos, Fair Isaac, and Tibco. The offerings obtained from its partners can vary and include elements such as specific consulting services, specialized tools, or applications. Successful partnering is critical to Teradata's aggressive growth plans. As a result, even when there is conflict with partners, the company tries to retain focus on the bigger picture. And sometimes that takes sacrificing something for the greater good.

With the passage of the Sarbanes-Oxley Act, most companies have quickly learned that changing accounting processes alone will not address the resultant concerns sufficiently and that the timely availability of financial information on an ongoing basis across the enterprise is critical. To accomplish this, enterprises are turning to technology to make their financial information readily available, auditable, and analyzable. Teradata saw this opportunity but also realized that they did not have all the key applications to serve this market effectively. So they teamed up with Hyperion, a leading provider of financial applications, to develop a technology solution that could give customers greater insight into their financial performance. The agreement allowed businesses using a Teradata data warehouse and analytical solutions to link to Hyperion's Essbase XTD platform and applications. The partnership focused on two key goals: to drive core technology integration and optimization and to develop products that would enable customers to analyze their business results easier and faster. Since 2000 the companies worked together to integrate their respective products by building a Teradata Analytic Accelerator, a set of prebuilt analytics and reports centered on a subject area such as general ledger or accounts receivable. The objective of an Accelerator is to get analytics up faster and at less cost than by building analytic applications in traditional ways. A financial analyst can look at business results easily via graphs and reports at the summary level using information from the Teradata Enterprise Data Warehouse. Implementing an Accelerator can shorten the normal development and deployment of an analytic application by up to two months. The two companies have also worked closely on defining how they will support their joint customers in a coordinated manner. The support strategy involves having experts from both companies address customer issues through a single, coordinated point of contact. A customer contacts Hyperion for initial support for technical questions about the Accelerator. If these questions relate to certain specific technical aspects of the solution, an escalation process defines how they are conveyed within Teradata's support organization.

In some instances, it is a customer that forces two firms to work together. One such alliance is Teradata's partnership with Siebel systems to align their suite of applications and make them compatible with Teradata's data warehouse. Both shared a customer—DirecTV, who urged them to work together to deliver more convenience to the customer. As a result of these joint efforts, Siebel provides the analytic tools and related consulting while Teradata provides the data-oriented expertise and consulting.

FOURTH DIMENSION OF NETWORK RESOURCES: INTERNAL UNITS

Successful organizations typically follow the same relational instincts with their own business units as they do with customers, suppliers, and alliance partners, and often discover that the fourth dimension of network resources is in their very own backyards. This form of network resources results from promoting greater collaboration among the firm's own internal business units which in turn can lead to significant external benefits (Hansen and Oetinger 2001; Hansen and Nohria 2004; Gulati 2006). To optimize their core and offer customers complete solutions requires that firms create a seamless connection not only with their external suppliers and alliance partners but also with their internal business units and subunits that need to come together in a harmonious fashion to offer customers an integrated experience. Successful firms teach their subunits to treat their internal counterparts with the same respect and focus that characterize their relationships with customers, suppliers, and alliance partners. Hence, a similar ladder of increasing responsibility and commitment can be applied to internal relationships at high-performing companies (see Figure 8.9). In the weakest internal relationships, organizational subunits are treated as separate entities, perhaps even independent profit centers. There is little interaction among them, with limited sharing of intellectual or human capital. The relationship between the business units and the corporate core is more akin to those among divisions of a holding company. At the second rung the organizations operate in a largely independent fashion, but they come together for specific strategic initiatives, where focused pooling of capital and other resources facilitates the drive to a single corporate objective, after completion of which the constituent organizations return to a mode of independent operation.

On the third rung, business units are integrated, working toward a common corporate goal. They may have the power to independently define how they reach that goal and are often left by senior management to meet their targets using their own devices. But they are jointly accountable for corporate success, share capital, infrastructure, and talent, and communicate on a regular basis. The final rung represents a wholly integrated company with 'no walls'. Information, capital, and talent flow freely across any organizational boundaries.

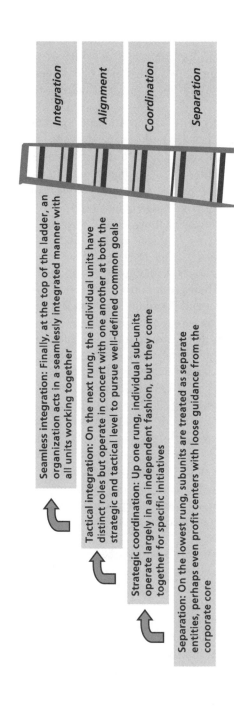

Integration

Alignment

Coordination

Separation

Seamless integration: Finally, at the top of the ladder, an organization acts in a seamlessly integrated manner with all units working together

Tactical integration: On the next rung, the individual units have distinct roles but operate in concert with one another at both the strategic and tactical level to pursue well-defined common goals

Strategic coordination: Up one rung, individual sub-units operate largely in an independent fashion, but they come together for specific initiatives

Separation: On the lowest rung, subunits are treated as separate entities, perhaps even profit centers with loose guidance from the corporate core

Figure 8.9. Organizational sub-unit relationship ladder

While the first two stages afford some basic levels of coordination, higher levels involve greater levels of active cooperation (Gulati and Singh 1998; Gulati, Lawrence, and Puranam 2005). The intensity of interaction increases, as does the interweaving of operations and outcomes across units. None of this comes easy, and common wisdom holds that sometimes cooperation with internal business units can be a greater challenge than with external partners.

Different levels on the ladder are appropriate for different companies, depending on their lifecycle stage and specific strategic goals. Furthermore, the level of interaction may vary among different business units of a single firm, depending on the nature of underlying synergy among their respective operations. In spite of these potential differences among firms, the survey data here show that the highest-performing organizations were those that fostered tighter connections across business units, regardless of size. Comparing high- and low-performing firms we find that among the former, business units communicate more with each other (58% vs. 36%) and best practices are deployed with greater frequency across groups/locations (83% vs. 55%) (as indicated by a response of 5 or greater on a 7-point scale). This elevated level of effective communication and coordinated action lays the groundwork for accelerated innovation, increasingly a requirement for success.

One example of a firm that discovered the benefits of network resources within its own intraorganizational units was Jones Lang LaSalle (JLL). In 2001, JLL was one of the largest commercial real estate services companies in the world. The product of a 1999 merger of London-based Jones Lang Wootton and Chicago-based LaSalle Partners, JLL was a global company with more than 680 million square feet of property and more than US$20 billion in real estate funds under management in the United States, Europe, and Asia. The previous few years had been financially difficult for JLL. By early 2001, the company's stock price warranted a market capitalization less than the valuation of either of the two original firms. And the economic downturn in the United States was further depressing sales. Senior management realized that change was needed to halt the slide in margins and boost revenue.

In the marketplace, corporate clients were beginning to demand more from their real estate service providers. On one hand, the trend toward globalization and heightened concerns about fees meant that the real estate marketplace was becoming increasingly commoditized. On the other hand, many customers were no longer satisfied with being sold just a product or service; they wanted a complete solution for their real estate needs. Some of JLL's largest customers— especially the prized global multinationals—sought more integrated services across the globe, often outsourcing their entire real estate operations.

Meeting such diverse requests strained JLL's historically independent business units, which offered disparate real estate services and operated autonomously. The company's management realized that significant changes to their traditionally silo-based organization were needed to compete successfully on price and to integrate their services. So, in 2001, JLL's Americas region underwent a dramatic reorganization, dividing its nine business units into two groups—Corporate Solutions and Investor Services—according to the types of clients they served. Along with bringing its disparate services targeted to large multinational clients under the one roof of Corporate Solutions, senior management created a new account manager function to better provide JLL's clients with integrated service solutions. By establishing a single point-of-contact for JLL's largest clients, along with shared accountability, senior management hoped to provide flexible and scalable resources for clients that spanned the full breadth of JLL's corporate service offerings. In establishing this new organizational arrangement, however, JLL had to tackle several critical internal issues. Most of these revolved around getting the internal business units to collaborate with each other and with the integrating unit that worked with the customers directly. Results so far have been excellent and they have been successful in attracting some of the largest firms in the United States as their clients including P&G, Microsoft, and Bank of America. Their success is a testimony to the efforts put into building a more collaborative internal environment.

Another company that has discovered the benefits of network resources built on greater intraorganizational coordination is, again, Teradata. In their efforts to differentiate themselves from the competition by providing customers with integrated solutions, Teradata has recognized the importance of aligning internal business units to create a seamless experience for the customer. To harmonize their internal efforts, they have shifted most resources, including technical specialists and industry specialists, into their sales organization. Further, they have devised what management calls a three-legged stool to approach customers in an integrated manner. The first leg of the stool is the sales account manager who owns the relationship with the customer organization and remains the point person for that firm throughout their interaction with Teradata. The second leg of the stool is the architectural technology specialist who helps specify customer needs and which components of Teradata's offering may make sense for that customer. The third leg is an industry specialist who also typically resides within the sales organization and is a specialist on applications for the customer's industry. This person helps define the industry-specific applications that would allow Teradata to customize the solution for the customer. While the sales account manager is the key point person, he or she works closely with the other two legs of the stool to ensure that the customer has a seamless experience. Along with incentive alignment to ensure that these disparate individuals work closely with customers, a customer-oriented culture also seems to be essential. As Bob Fair, Chief Marketing Office at Teradata suggests, 'The glue here is the culture.... Since we are trying to embark on a lifelong journey with our customers, we know clearly that the customer is critical and that we all need to work together to help solve the customer's problems.'

Combining the four dimensions of network resources

To achieve a shrinking core and expanding periphery, successful organizations recognize the mutually reinforcing nature of activities on each of the four dimensions of network resources discussed here. Hence, collaboration with customers on solutions necessitates working closely with alliance partners and suppliers, and among internal business units. As a result, what is noteworthy about relationships built by exemplar firms is their breadth and degree of integration. Winning organizations have moved beyond a single-minded focus on perhaps one or two facets of individual customer, supplier, or alliance relationships and are now developing a more holistic and multidimensional view of their entire network of relationships, one that takes into active account the other relationships the firm may have on different dimensions, creating exciting new opportunities for leverage and economies of scale. More and more, these companies' perspectives encompass a broader universe of involved and interacting players who move into and out of the organization with an unprecedented degree of freedom and flexibility.

In this new model, critical relationships along these three external dimensions—customer, supplier, and alliance partner—are no longer distinct and separate from the organization but rather are interconnected and synergistic. In developing a total solution for a customer, for example, a network-resource-rich organization will draw readily on such assets as the complementary capabilities of its alliance partners or its network of key suppliers. Recognizing that its internal subunits and the employees within them are ambassadors to customers, a network resource-centered organization will optimize the former to serve the latter. While many companies make varying attempts to leverage individual relationships, top performers build multifaceted relationships that are interdependent, and thus more than 'the sum of the parts'. And therein lies the difference.

Conclusion

This chapter sheds light on the particular strategies that top-performing network resource-centered organizations utilize to achieve superior performance by optimizing the architecture of their network of relationships.

While organizational theorists have long focused on individual relationships with, say, customers or suppliers, this chapter examined how four key relationships—with customers, suppliers, alliance partners, and among internal business units—work *together* in defining an organization and its success in the marketplace. In each of these four dimensions, survey results indicate that what clearly sets sustained performers apart from their peers is a higher willingness to engage these entities, and a greater focus on increasing the longevity of those relationships. That network resources are unleashed through collaboration is beyond dispute. Not only does collaboration within and between all constituencies improve operating performance, but its vehicles—be they solutions, strategic outsourcing agreements, alliances, or acquisitions—help companies leverage assets more effectively, expand into new markets, mitigate risk, and increase market agility. Together, these efforts shape their success by shrinking their cores and expanding their peripheries to achieve enhanced growth and profitability.

Our findings, based on both quantitative and qualitative research data, provide empirical support for a conclusion that many have already intuited: a relationship-driven architecture and the business strategies that it facilitates are inherently powerful. In addition, we can begin to build a more complex model that layers the 'how' onto the 'what' of successful organization-building. Already clear is the fact that no one relationship suffices to bring success in today's top competitive environment. Instead, it is a *combination* of distinct and critical relationships and the way they interact across a seamless and transparent organization as a *network* that leads to competitive advantage and value creation.

Ultimately, companies want to build operating models that enable customer orders to automatically trigger supplier orders or that appropriately leverage employees as conduits to the customer. Think of the Starbucks barista or the Harley Davidson dealer or the Jones Lang LaSalle account manager and you have a compelling image of the powerful circle of relationships that winning organizations create and foster. Organizations today are all too often impediments to their own long-term success because they create barriers rather than facilitating communication and coordination. The network resource-centered organization is, in contrast, moving toward becoming a friction-free facilitator.

It is important to reiterate that network resource accumulation is not a one-dimensional activity any more, but rather an integrated, four-dimensional campaign that encompasses relationships with suppliers, alliance partners, internal constituencies, and, of course, customers. Where the emphasis in recent years has typically been on a single dimension—such as outsourcing agreements with suppliers, joint ventures with alliance partners, vision and values exercises with employees to align goals of internal subunits and achieve greater synergy, or CRM tools for aligning with customers—top-performing organizations are now operating on all dimensions at once to build a coherent and enduring whole greater than the sum of its parts.

Gaining—and maintaining—competitive advantage through strategy alone is difficult, if not impossible. The universe of successful strategies is limited, and too many players pursue the most attractive options. The key to true differentiation lies in effective implementation, and the key to effective implementation is a winning organizational model. Based on survey data and fieldwork, this chapter has assembled a composite architecture of how successful organizations look and act. While the attributes and behaviors of the relationship-centered organization are by no means a guarantee of success, they do tend to differentiate the winners in many industries from the rest of the field. Just as companies manage, monitor, and measure their physical resources, so should they actively manage, monitor, and measure their network resources. Relationships are a mission-critical asset and should be treated as such. Relationship-centered organizations recognize this reality and organize in such a way to reflect it.

Part IV
Network Resources in Entrepreneurial Settings

9 The effects of network resources arising from upper echelon affiliations on underwriter prestige and performance

Research on entrepreneurship in technology-intensive settings is closely linked with research on alliances because partnering is a critical activity for high-tech start-ups. As in other arenas, interorganizational networks and the resources they create are a key factor in determining both the success of start-ups and the antecedent conditions that enable these firms to attract partners in the first place. Start-up enterprises in technology-intensive settings operate amidst considerable uncertainty and information scarcity. As a result, social networks in which such firms are embedded create valuable network resources that can provide information and thus influence both behavior and economic outcomes.

This chapter is based on joint research with Monica Higgins, and it examines the role of interorganizational networks in the entrepreneurial arena by focusing on the origin of one set of important ties that firms may have: interorganizational endorsements in the context of a company's IPO, one of the most critical events in a young firm's lifetime. Prior research has shown that securing the endorsement of a prestigious investment bank can be critical for IPO success (Carter and Manaster 1990). Firms that go public generally do so with the endorsement of a lead investment bank that underwrites the firm's security offerings. These investment banks act as intermediaries, providing certification of the value of new firms to potential investors, who rely on the

This chapter is adapted with permission from 'Getting Off to a Good Start: The Effects of Upper Echelon Affiliations on Underwriter Prestige' by Monica C. Higgins and Ranjay Gulati published in *Organization Science* © 2003, (14/3): 244–63, the Institute for Operations Research and the Management Sciences, 7240 Parkway Drive, Suite 310, Hanover, MD 21076 USA.

investment bank's evaluation of the quality of a firm when deciding whether to buy stock in a young company (Carter and Manaster 1990). Still, while the consequences of underwriter prestige for IPO performance have been examined (e.g. Beatty and Ritter 1986; Carter, Dark, and Singh 1998; Stuart, Hoang, and Hybels 1999), the antecedents to such critical endorsements have not. As a result, it is still unclear what factors may enable firms to attract the endorsements of prestigious underwriters during this critical event in their lives.

This chapter suggests that a network perspective can be effective in understanding how firms are able to secure endorsements from prestigious underwriters. Previous chapters have established that network resources are conduits of valuable information that help firms identify potential partners and reduce the risks of uncertainty and opportunistic behavior in alliances. Here, some of these ideas are extended by suggesting that network resources available to a firm not only facilitate the dissemination of information about a partner but also serve as indicators of firm quality. Such indicators can help young firms to establish an aura of organizational legitimacy more likely to attract prestigious endorsers. Hence, network resources can serve as substitute measures for less observable firm characteristics and at the same time provide the firm with valuable information that can help it achieve success.

This chapter extends my conceptualization of network resources described in prior sections of the book by including the amount and type of upper echelon experience as a component of such resources available to a firm. Along the lines of Chapter 4, I suggest here that network resources may originate not only in the interorganizational ties that firms enter into with other firms but also in the network connections that its upper echelons may have with others. Furthermore, just as Chapter 4 showed that network resources originating in interpersonal ties (board interlocks) can help firms to develop interorganizational ties (strategic alliances) that further contribute to their network resources, this chapter will delineate how another form of interpersonal ties (upper echelon prior employment and board affiliations) can help a firm to accumulate another important set of ties (connections with prestigious endorsement entities). I suggest that such resources reveal their value not only by mitigating uncertainty and reducing search costs but also by providing an important signal of a young firm's legitimacy to critical outsiders such as prestigious underwriters. The experience base of the upper echelon is conceptualized here as an indicator of the network resources that arise from the connections those individuals bring to the firm. This idea parallels the ideas in Chapter 4—which showed how network resources may emerge not only from interorganizational connections but also from those based on the interpersonal connections of its upper echelon—and builds on the other chapters in Part I, which demonstrated how network resources can beget further network ties that constitute alternate forms of future network resources.

I propose that the experience of a young firm's upper echelon constitutes network resources because it is indicative of (*a*) the connections those individuals can tap into for the benefit of this young firm and (b) the quality of the firm's management. Both of these factors make such resources a powerful signal to potential prestigious endorsers who must sift through a vast number of firms to identify promising candidates under conditions of considerable uncertainty.

This chapter also introduces a typology of network resources based on upper echelon experience that distinguishes between upper echelon upstream, horizontal, and downstream employment-based affiliations and suggests that these different types of upper echelon affiliations are each distinct facets of network resources that provide information and allay different types of endorser concerns regarding firm legitimacy, affecting the endorsement process. Furthermore, it includes the hypothesis that the relationships between network resources arising from upper echelon experience and investment bank prestige will be moderated by technological uncertainty.

These ideas were tested on a comprehensive sample of public and private biotechnology firms that were founded between 1961 and 1994 and went public between 1979 and 1996. Analyses of the five-year career histories of the over 3,200 executives and directors that make up the upper echelons of these firms show that firms with specific upper echelon affiliations are more likely to attract the endorsement of a prestigious investment bank. Specifically, the results suggest that upper echelon affiliations with prominent downstream organizations (i.e. pharmaceutical and/or health care companies) and with prominent horizontal organizations (i.e. biotechnology companies) help to attract the endorsement of a prestigious investment bank. The results also show that the greater the range of upper echelon affiliations across the categories of upstream, horizontal, and downstream affiliations, the more prestigious the firm's lead underwriter will be.

The research detailed in this chapter extends the previous sections on network resources in the following ways: (a) it elucidates the role of network resources that can originate from the experiences of a young firm's upper echelons, (b) it shows how network resources can be signals of legitimacy that shape the nature of interorganizational endorsement ties established by entrepreneurial firms, and (c) it provides a robust taxonomy of the network resources based on upper echelon affiliations.

Theory and hypotheses

SECURING AN IPO ENDORSEMENT

Research by Carter and Manaster (1990) has demonstrated that high-prestige investment banks are more likely to underwrite lower-risk IPOs than low-prestige investment banks. One explanation for this pattern lies in the relative levels of reputational capital associated with these endorsers (Beatty and Ritter 1986; Tinic 1988). The ability to generate substantial business enables prestigious underwriters to maintain their reputations (Hayes 1971), and the likelihood of future offerings is greater for firms issuing low-risk IPOs. Additionally, high-prestige banks prefer lower-risk IPOs because of the legal implications of underwriting risky deals; prestigious underwriters may have greater legal liabilities associated with due diligence, which dissuades them from engaging in speculative IPOs. Indeed, prestigious underwriters have become significantly less likely to underwrite risky issues since 1933, when the Security Exchange Commission Act imposed legal liabilities for lack of due diligence (Tinic 1988). Given these factors, a start-up is generally not in a position to decide which investment bank will endorse it. While the firm may seek out prominent underwriters, it may not ultimately attract such parties. This is somewhat similar to a job market situation: job-seekers may approach employers of their choosing, but it is not guaranteed they will receive any offers. In like manner, young firms must first sell themselves to secure the interest of potential endorsers.

The relationship with endorsers is also somewhat different from other types of interorganizational relationships, such as strategic alliances, because in this instance the partnership is short-lived and it is with an intermediary (the investment bank) evaluating the firm on behalf of others (the firm's investors). Still, in the case of start-ups, the firm is not a passive party to the endorsement process. Rather, IPO team members—a firm's top managers and board members—attempt to attract the attention of investment banks early in the firm's life. Promotional materials, including the backgrounds of the firm's managing officers and board members, profiles of the firm's research and technology, and publications, are sent to prospective investment banks in advance of the firm's filing with the SEC. Additionally, the CEO schedules appointments with investment bankers to 'pitch' the company, generally casting a broad rather than narrow net in its solicitations.

This matching process is also facilitated by investment banks, whose research analysts are dedicated to particular industries and, moreover, to specific industry segments such as biotechnology (Zuckerman 1999). After reviewing the information available—collected both through the bank's own efforts to scan and retrieve information and through the firm's initiative and marketing efforts—analysts identify certain firms as having greater potential. Following this initial evaluation period, these firms are then actively courted by interested investment banks; firms may be invited to annual conferences sponsored by investment banks, and the banks also engage in on-site due diligence with the firms.

Convincing a prestigious investment bank to endorse a young firm during its IPO is the primary responsibility of the firm's top managers and board members. Some have argued that the better the technological quality of the young firm, the easier it is for the firm to attract the attention of a prestigious investment bank and to obtain a sizable IPO (e.g. Deeds, DeCarolis, and Coombs 1997). But during the early stages of a young firm's lifetime, and particularly in industries in which the product's underlying technology is complex and uncertain, performance criteria are more obscure than clear. As a result, the use and control of symbolic information to create perceptions of firm legitimacy are extremely important (Feldman and March 1981).

One way to heighten the perceived legitimacy of a young firm is to show-case externally validated symbols of credibility. For example, highlighting the patents that a firm has obtained can increase perceptions of legitimacy by conveying competence and laying claims to valued intellectual property (Powell and Brantley 1992; Baum and Powell 1995). Unfortunately, external criteria of worth, such as patents, may be insufficient to assuage a variety of concerns held by the investment community regarding the 'social fitness' or legitimacy of the organization—especially in the biotechnology industry, in which product development cycles span many years into the future (Meyer and Rowan 1977). Indeed, in the present context, empirical studies have found that the number of patents held by a biotechnology firm has had mixed effects on investors' perceptions (DeCarolis and Deeds 1999).

In addition to relying on externally validated symbols of legitimacy, such as patents, a young firm may showcase other symbols of legitimacy that effectively communicate its potential. One such symbol is the experience base of the firm's upper echelons. Internal criteria of worth, such as upper echelon experience reflecting the 'most prestige' or 'latest expert thinking' can legitimate organizations with key stakeholders. This experience can also serve as an indicator of the access that senior management have to key outsiders via prior and current affiliations with other prominent organizations. Outside evaluators may assign worth to such credentials whether or not there is direct evidence that they contribute measurably to organizational outcomes (Meyer and Rowan 1977). The value of information in this case is symbolic. The benefit to young firms of using and citing such relevant information during the IPO process lies in the information's likelihood of inspiring confidence in key outsiders (Feldman and March 1981), thereby increasing perceptions of the firm's legitimacy. In this context, we can conceptualize upper echelon affiliations with prominent organizations as an element of network resources that can affect the perceived legitimacy of a young firm in the eyes of external parties. In this instance, network resources serve as enablers for firms, catalyzing connections with key others—prestigious investment banks that in turn provide access to greater resources.

A TYPOLOGY OF UPPER ECHELON AFFILIATIONS

This chapter proposes a typology of upper echelon experience (depicted in Figure 9.1) that builds from theory regarding the social organization of

Upper Echelon Affiliation Types	Elements of Legitimacy	Symbols of Legitimacy
Upstream	Product viability	Rank of membership in scientific profession
Horizontal	Competitive efficacy	Rank of membership in industry hierarchy
Downstream	Production/marketing efficacy	Rank of membership in product markets

Figure 9.1. A typology of upper echelon affiliations

attention and decision-making (Simon [1947] 1997; Ocasio 1997). Given the limited cognitive bandwidth of busy executives and the high level of ambiguity associated with evaluating young firms, investment bankers are constrained to focus their attention on a limited set of issues (March and Olsen 1976; Simon 1997; Thornton and Ocasio 1999). These issues may be structured in the form of 'logics' about appropriate firm behavior and how to succeed in an industry (Ocasio 1997). In the present context, the logic regarding what it takes to succeed in this industry centers on at least three questions: (*a*) Can a firm produce a scientifically viable product? (*b*) Can a firm compete effectively in the industry? (*c*) Can a firm bring a product all the way through the development cycle to market? Hence, this chapter conceptualizes legitimacy in this context as a multifaceted construct.

Recent studies have shown that an industry's institutional logics or rules of the game may be associated with membership in markets in professions, affecting executive attention (Thornton and Ocasio 1999; Thornton 2001). This chapter builds on this general idea that certain prevailing guidelines or logics may focus executive attention and affect decision-making—here, regarding the decision of an investment bank to underwrite a young firm. We also extend the idea that a firm's rank and membership in professions and markets may confer legitimacy that differentially affects executive attention and decision-making. In this case, we consider how upper echelon affiliations, which are a form of network resources, are akin to symbols of membership in professions, markets, and hierarchies (Powell 1990) that may confer different forms of legitimacy and thus affect endorser decision-making.

In this chapter, I propose that three different facets of network resources are represented by three distinct types of upper echelon affiliation, each of which touches on a specific issue relevant to the investment community's endorsement decision: (*a*) upstream: upper echelon affiliations with prominent research institutions (e.g. Dana Farber Cancer Institute) are symbolic of the firm's rank and membership in the scientific profession and can redress legitimacy concerns regarding technological viability; (*b*) horizontal: upper echelon affiliations with prominent biotechnology firms are symbolic of a firm's position and membership in the hierarchy of the industry, assuaging legitimacy concerns regarding a firm's ability to compete effectively in its specific market; (*c*) downstream: upper echelon affiliations with prominent pharmaceutical and/or health care organizations are symbolic of the firm's membership position in biotechnology product markets, allaying concerns that the firm will be able to bring its products to the marketplace.

Upper Echelon Upstream Affiliations

Upstream affiliations in the biotechnology industry, which are one form of network resources, originate in upper echelon members' employment affiliations with prominent organizations such as research institutions, think tanks, and/or universities. During the acquaintanceship period, when a firm seeks funding for an IPO, investment bankers are likely to interact with several members of the firm's upper echelon, including those in high-level research positions with the firm. In addition to calibrating the stage of the firm's products, discussions with upper echelon members with major research institution experience should bolster analyst confidence in the firm's ability to conduct high-quality research and manage the research process, assuaging legitimacy concerns regarding the technological viability of the firm's products. As one executive explained:

Getting the prestigious researchers was certainly part of the formula...scientists with lots of letters after their names. It gives you access to other research to broaden your net a little bit, not to be solely dependent upon one individual's work.

Organizational research on the biotechnology industry has shown that industry contact with academia enables the diffusion of technological knowledge extremely valuable to young biotechnology firms (e.g. Zucker, Darby, and Brewer 1994). During the acquaintanceship period a young firm and a potential underwriter share, resources such as the social networks alluded to in the prior quote may or may not be directly observable. Thus, at this point a young firm's upper echelon affiliations with prominent research institutions are highly valuable symbols. The firm's ability to garner support from individuals with externally validated credentials of high worth symbolizes its membership and position in the scientific professional hierarchy (Abbott 1981), which can allay endorser concerns regarding its ability to tap into the latest scientific thinking (Meyer and Rowan 1977; Baum and Powell 1995). By controlling and citing such information, the firm 'shows off' its criteria of worth, making its position more favorable and hence more legitimate in the eyes of key outsiders (Meyer and Rowan 1977; Feldman and March 1981).

Thus, firms that have IPO team members affiliated with prominent research institutions convey possession of greater network resources than firms without such affiliations and this, in turn, positions them better to attract the attention of a prestigious investment bank.

Hypothesis 1: The greater the number of upper echelon members with prominent upstream affiliations, the more prestigious the investment bank that underwrites the firm's IPO.

Upper Echelon Horizontal Affiliations

An upper echelon's horizontal affiliations in the biotechnology industry, another form of network resources, stem from upper echelon members' employment and board affiliations with prominent industry organizations. Such affiliations symbolize the firm's experience in the industry hierarchy, assuaging concerns regarding the firm's ability to compete effectively. In the biotechnology industry, competing effectively requires industry-specific knowledge to secure important resources such as cash, scientists, equipment, and laboratory space, as well as managerial means to structure, design, and run a biotech organization to maximize innovation and learning (Pisano and Mang 1993; Powell, Koput, and Smith-Doerr 1996). As one vice president described:

It was all about protein-based drugs, working with proteins—manufacturing expertise, operations knowledge . . . and an understanding of how biotech plays in the capital markets—meaning raise as much money as you can because it isn't always going to be there; when the window is open, put your hands out.

To a young firm, the symbolic value of having upper echelon members affiliated with major biotechnology companies is high, because these network resources assuage concerns regarding a firm's ability to compete (or even survive) in the industry. As recent research suggests, organizations can facilitate the transfer of valuable resources such as intellectual capital and ideas by recruiting individuals from well-established organizations in the firm's industry (Rao and Drazin 2002). During the firm's acquaintanceship period with potential underwriters, the transfer of such industry-specific knowledge by virtue of an IPO team member's affiliations may not be directly observable to the investment community. However, the symbolic nature of these affiliations can inspire endorser confidence, affecting the perceived legitimacy of the young firm. One executive described how this network resource is beneficial for a young firm:

The fact that experienced managers at larger [biotechnology] firms left to join a startup signals that there's something credible there—enough for that manager to take a risk.

The upper echelon's affiliation with a major biotechnology firm indicates that those with the latest expert thinking have essentially credentialed the young firm, enhancing the firm's reputation in its own industry hierarchy (Meyer and Rowan 1977). Thus, a firm's upper echelon affiliations with prominent biotechnology firms should be viewed as important network resources that signal a firm's capacity to compete and this in turn should attract the endorsement of prestigious underwriters.

Hypothesis 2: The greater the number of upper echelon members with prominent horizontal affiliations, the more prestigious the investment bank that underwrites the firm's IPO.

Upper Echelon Downstream Affiliations

In biotechnology, an upper echelon's downstream affiliations, which constitute a third form of network resources, originate in team members' affiliations with prominent pharmaceutical and/or health care companies. Downstream companies have valuable resources such as information, contacts, and funds that can help a young firm bring its core technology, product, and/or service to market (Pisano 1991). A young firm's reputation as a legitimate producer in its market can be enhanced through symbols of association with such firms. One former member of an IPO team described the beneficial effect of such associations:

People onboard from major pharmas are valuable for the [firm's] drug development process. They have experience getting a drug through clinical trials...as opposed to being just a group of academics—these guys can get the drug from the bench to the bottle...And, it's the ability to get in and meet with people from the big pharmas—connections—that can help make it all happen.

Unlike small biotechnology firms, prominent pharmaceutical companies are particularly well equipped to bring a product 'from the bench to the bottle'—they have experience testing products (e.g. clinical trials), gaining Food and Drug Administration (FDA) approval, marketing products, and selling technologies (Powell, Koput, and Smith-Doerr 1996). Consequently, upper echelon experience with such firms can assuage legitimacy concerns regarding the firm's ability to bring a product all the way through the seven- to ten-year product development cycle and successfully to market. In the biotechnology industry, signs of market legitimacy associated with bringing a product through the development stages and to the market are essential in garnering support from the investment community:

One of the issues is that you need to start with fundamental research but you need to quickly get away from that because no one is going to pay for fundamental research for an extended period of time. You need to be in the development game.

During the acquaintanceship period, meetings with executives who have experience at major pharmaceutical companies are likely to increase the underwriter's confidence in the firms' ability to be 'in the development game'. These affiliations constitute network resources that symbolize the firm's membership and position in the marketplace. Again, even if the networks or social resources that derive from an IPO team member's career experience are not directly observable to a potential underwriter during the acquaintanceship process, the perception conveyed by such affiliations is that the firm has gilt-edged qualifications that lend it legitimacy (Finkelstein 1992). Specifically, downstream affiliations have symbolic value in that they assuage outsider concerns regarding the firm's legitimacy as a producer in the biotechnology marketplace. Therefore, firms with upper echelon affiliations with prominent pharmaceutical and/or health care organizations can be viewed as having network resources that signal their capacity to bring a product to market and this in turn should attract the attention of prestigious underwriters.

Hypothesis 3: The greater the number of upper echelon members with prominent downstream affiliations, the more prestigious the investment bank that underwrites the firm's IPO.

UPPER ECHELON RANGE OF AFFILIATIONS

Thus far this chapter has argued that more of each of the three types of network resources emanating from upper echelon affiliations is better, enabling a young firm to allay all three types of legitimacy concerns: that it can produce a scientifically viable product, compete effectively in the industry, and bring a product to market. Upper echelon affiliations are network resources that have a direct impact on the concerns of endorsing organizations, collectively presenting a coherent and compelling story or social construction of the new firm's value (Berger and Luckman 1966). Consequently, the greater the range of affiliations represented by a firm's upper echelon, the greater the cumulative network resources available to it and the greater the confidence an endorsing organization should have in the firm's overall ability to deliver a return. Symbols in each of these areas should complement one another; they are not perfect substitutes because they tap into different legitimacy questions relevant to external evaluations of the firm's potential. A diverse set of affiliations conveys to outsiders both the breadth and depth of the firm's ability to develop viable technology, compete well in the industry, and effectively bring a product to market:

Hypothesis 4: The greater the range of prominent upstream, horizontal, and downstream affiliations of a young company's upper echelon, the more prestigious the investment bank that underwrites the firm's IPO.

MODERATING EFFECTS OF TECHNOLOGICAL UNCERTAINTY

In the IPO context and in the biotechnology industry in particular, a firm's top executives face significant challenges convincing outsiders to invest in their company. A young biotechnology firm's needs for resources are extraordinarily high, and payoff for investors is less clear than in other industries, as firms going public in this sector are typically several years away from initial product launches and steady revenue streams. Thus, the biotechnology IPO process is a highly uncertain context in which to study the network-resource-based antecedents of interorganizational endorsements. Within this context, there is considerable variance in the amount of uncertainty associated with individual firms. Because the function of network resources here is to mitigate uncertainty and thereby attract an endorsement from a prestigious underwriter, the importance of upper-echelon-based network resources will likely vary with the amount of uncertainty a young firm faces. In other words, the greater the uncertainty, the larger the influence of the network resources and the concomitant symbols of legitimacy associated with the affiliations of a firm's upper echelon.

In the biotechnology industry, a major source of uncertainty concerns a firm's scientific technology. Given the long product development cycles unique to this industry, it is particularly difficult for young biotechnology firms to convince outsiders that the firm will be able to produce a sound scientific product. Technological uncertainty is higher when a biotechnology firm has products in early stages of development. As organizational research on legitimacy suggests, symbols derived from the firm's use and control of information are especially important in establishing legitimacy when a firm's core technology is unclear (Feldman and March 1981; see also Baum and Powell 1995). More generally, studies have shown that firm affiliations with prominent others are particularly important during times of uncertainty (e.g. Burt 1992; Podolny 1994). This suggests that network resources arising from individual members' affiliations with prominent employers can be especially valuable in alleviating outsider concerns during times of high technological uncertainty. Thus, when externally validated symbols of legitimacy such as development milestones are not convincing to outsiders, the symbolic value of a firm's internal credentials is particularly important, and outsiders would be expected to look even more favorably on the amount and quality of experience possessed by the firm's IPO team.

Hypothesis 5: Technological uncertainty will moderate the effects of the upper echelon's affiliations with prominent upstream, horizontal, and downstream organizations on the prestige of the investment bank that a firm is able to attract such that upper echelon affiliations with prominent organizations will be particularly valuable when a firm's technology is relatively uncertain.

Empirical research

METHOD

The sample used for the findings reported in this chapter is described in Appendix 1 as 'Biotechnology Start-ups Database'. These data were collected by my coauthor Monica Higgins. The main variables were drawn from the career histories of the over 3,200 managing officers and directors who made up the upper echelons of the 299 public firms in our core sample, as found in the firms' final prospectuses. In filing with the SEC, firms are required to list the last five years of experience of the firm's managing officers and board members; additional information (e.g. educational background) may be listed but is not required by the SEC. We consulted additional sources such as Dun and Bradstreet for cross-verification.

Investment bank prestige was measured using an index developed by Carter and Manaster (1990) and then updated by Carter, Dark, and Singh (1998). Underwriter prestige information was available for all but twenty-five of the underwriters in our database. Mann-Whitney and Kolmogorov-Smirnov tests indicated that the firms for which this information was not available did not differ significantly on our main variables from those for which information was available. These prestige measures have been employed in recent organizational research on biotechnology firms that went public during the same period as our study (cf. Stuart, Hoang, and Hybels 1999); this scale has been cited widely by finance and organizational scholars (Podolny 1994; Bae, Klein, and Bowyer 1999; Rau 2000). The methods employed by Carter and colleagues to create the prestige scale are similar to those used by Podolny (1993) to analyze debt markets. In brief, Carter and colleagues' indices were created by looking at the hierarchy of investment banks as presented in the 'tombstone announcements' for IPOs that appear in the *Investment Dealer's Digest* or the *Wall Street Journal*. The highest integer rank (9) was assigned to the first-listed underwriter on the first announcement examined, the second highest integer rank (8) to the next-listed underwriter(s), and so on. On the second tombstone announcement, they checked to see if any underwriter *not* listed on the first one was listed above any underwriter that had been listed on the first one. If this was the case, the new, more highly ranked underwriter was assigned the rank of the superseded underwriter, and the superseded underwriter and all lower-ranked underwriters were shifted one point down on the scale. When more than ten categories became necessary to preserve the hierarchy presented on the tombstones, decimal increments were employed. The scale presented by Carter, Dark, and Singh (1998) is incremented in units of 0.125. Scores range from 0, indicating lowest prestige, to 9, indicating highest prestige. In our data-set, the mean score was 7.63. Carter and Dark's (1992) analyses suggest that these measures provide a finer-grained evaluation than a simpler market share alternative (e.g. Megginson and Weiss 1991). We obtained the name of the lead investment bank from the front page of each firm's final prospectus.

Upper echelon affiliations were assessed by manually coding the last five years of managing officers' and board members' employment and board memberships, as listed in the firms' final prospectuses. We assessed whether or not each upper echelon member had at least one tie to prominent upstream, horizontal, or downstream organizations during the year the company went public. We created indices of organizational prominence for each of our three categories, only looking at ties linking individuals with prominent organizations. Because the number of ties covaries with the size of the upper echelon, we divided upstream, horizontal, and downstream tie measures by upper echelon size, consistent with methods of other research in this arena (e.g. Geletkanycz and Hambrick 1997).

To gauge the prominence of downstream and horizontally affiliated institutions, we used the total of their domain-specific firm revenues as a proxy for prominence. To gauge whether upstream affiliations were with prominent organizations, we employed external evaluations of the research institutions.

For upper echelon *upstream affiliations*, we assessed the number of prominent research-based affiliations of members of a firm's upper echelon through board seats or employment (e.g. professorship). Seven consecutive editions of the *Gourman Report* (Gourman 1980, 1983, 1985, 1987, 1989, 1993, 1996) were used to compile eighteen lists of prominent research institutions—one for each IPO year. We coded academic institutions that appeared in the top ten in any of the following disciplines as prominent: microbiology/bacteriology, biochemistry, biology, biomedical engineering/bioengineering, molecular biology, cellular biology, molecular genetics, chemistry, and medicine. Gourman Report rankings are developed by examining an institution's performance in years prior to the publication of the report. For years in which a Gourman Report was not published, we used rankings from subsequent rather than preceding Gourman Report editions to code institutions. For example, codings for IPO years 1981 and 1982 were created from the 1983 Gourman Report. For each year, 19–24 institutions (depending on the degree of overlap created by institutions with multiple top ten rankings in differing disciplines) were coded as prominent. In addition, a number of national government institutions such as the NIH were added to these lists, as were nonuniversity research institutions that received a high amount of grant money per employee (e.g. the Salk Institute) ($n = 9$). The upper echelons in our sample generally had two individuals with at least one affiliation with a prominent research institution. Thus, upper echelon *upstream affiliations* was measured as the total number of upper echelon members with at least one affiliation with a prominent research organization.

For *horizontal affiliations*, we assessed the number of affiliations that members of a firm's upper echelon had to prominent biotechnology firms through employment and/or board memberships. We generated the list of prominent biotechnology companies by taking the list of worldwide revenues for the top thirty biotechnology companies in each of the years 1990–6, from POV Inc., 'Biotechnology's Top 50 in Pharmaceuticals and Diagnostics: A Competitive Analysis' (1997). We coded a biotechnology company as prominent if it appeared anywhere on this top-thirty listing at any time from 1990 through 1996.[1] Thirty-eight companies total were coded as prominent biotechnology firms; therefore, this was a relatively stable list. The firms in our sample generally had one or two individuals with an affiliation to a prominent biotechnology company. Upper echelon *horizontal affiliations* was measured as the total number of upper echelon members with at least one affiliation with a prominent biotechnology organization.

For upper echelon *downstream affiliations*, we assessed the number of affiliations that upper echelon members had to prominent pharmaceutical and/or health care institutions through prior employment and/or board memberships. To determine prominence, we used COMPUSTAT to generate eighteen lists of the top pharmaceutical and health care organizations by sales since 1979—one for each IPO year. International company rankings have appeared on COMPUSTAT only since 1988, so our rankings are based on the top thirty US organizations from 1979 to 1987 and on the top thirty US and international organizations from 1988 to 1996. We coded the top thirty organizations in a given year as prominent. We supplemented our lists with major pharmaceutical and health care companies that were private or based in Europe or Japan that were not listed in COMPUSTAT but were listed in PharmaBusiness and had comparable sales because many young biotechnology firms rely on international resources for support and talent. The firms in our sample generally had two to three team members with at least one tie to a prominent pharmaceutical or health care institution. Upper echelon *downstream affiliations* was measured as the total number of upper echelon members with at least one affiliation with a prominent pharmaceutical and/or health care organization.

We measured *range of upper echelon affiliations* in two ways. First, we used a variation of the Herfindahl-Hirschman index,

$$H = 1 - \sum_{i=1}^{3} p_i^2 \qquad (1)$$

in which H is the measure of heterogeneity or range and p is the percentage of individuals who have affiliations with prominent institutions in each of our

[1] Similar rankings were not available for the biotechnology industry prior to 1990. In looking at the employment affiliations in our data, we found that very few individuals had spent time at more than one biotechnology company prior to 1990, due in large part to the youth of the industry. Of those few individuals, the firms at which the overwhelming majority had spent time were already classified as prominent by the rankings we used.

three categories. This variable was set to equal 0 when the upper echelon had no relevant affiliations. This measure is equivalent to Blau's index of heterogeneity (1977). Second, we measured range as the count, 0 to 3, of the number of affiliation categories (upstream, horizontal, and downstream) covered by the career experiences of each firm's upper echelon. For example, a firm with an upper echelon with ten members, two of whom had worked for prominent pharmaceutical organizations, would receive a score of 1, while a different firm with a ten-person upper echelon that included one member who sat on the board of a prominent biotechnology company and another who had worked for a prominent pharmaceutical company would receive a score of 2.

We included a comprehensive set of control variables to ensure the robustness of our findings. First, to control for uncertainty associated with the stock market for biotechnology companies at the time our firms went public, we employed a financial index developed by Lerner (1994) and cited extensively in biotechnology industry research (e.g. Zucker, Darby, and Brewer 1994; Baum, Calabrese, and Silverman 2000) that gauges the receptivity of the equity markets to biotechnology offerings. Specifically, we used the value of Lerner's *equity index* at the end of the month prior to the IPO date for each of our firms.

In addition, we included a control variable for technological uncertainty: *product stage*. Because one of the most relevant thresholds for evaluation is the stage of clinical trials (Pisano 1991), our measure of *product stage* was based on a three-category classification: whether a company's lead product was in preclinical stages of development (coded as 1), clinical stages of development (coded as 2), or postclinical stages of development (coded as 3).

We also included controls for *firm size* and *firm age*, consistent with prior research on entrepreneurial firms and studies of IPOs. And, while not a direct indication of firm size, the amount of *private financing* the firm received prior to the IPO provides a reliable measure of its past success in securing financial capital and thus is an indicator of the firm's potential for growth as well. *Private financing* was calculated by summing the rounds of financing listed in the final prospectuses. This measure was adjusted to constant 1996 dollars and logged in our analyses.

We also coded geographic *location* of the firms. Young firms located in areas that are rich with industry-related activity will likely have greater access to resources—including qualified personnel, suitable lab space, and technology—that can give them an advantage. A dummy variable for *location* took a value of '1' if the company was headquartered in one of the areas consistently rated among the top biotechnology locations for the period of our study (Burrill and Lee 1990, 1993; Lee and Burrill, 1995): San Francisco, Boston, or San Diego. *Location* took a value of '0' otherwise.

In addition, we controlled for the total *number of alliances* a firm has with business and/or research organizations at the time of the IPO because prior research has demonstrated that strategic partnerships have important implications for organizational outcomes. And, given prior research on the important role of venture capitalists during initial public offerings (e.g. Gompers et al. 1998), we controlled for the *prominence of venture capital firms* at the time of the IPO. Firms were coded as 1 if any of the biotechnology firm's venture capital firms (with a minimum of a 5% stake) were listed among the top thirty venture capital firms on the list of prominent firms for the year prior to the firm's IPO date and 0 otherwise.[2]

We also included four variables that account for characteristics of the top management team (TMT), as opposed to the board, consistent with prior TMT research (e.g. Geletkanycz and Hambrick 1997). First, we included a variable for the *average prior position level* of TMT members that reflects the caliber of the prior jobs the executives held. We used a 0 to 5 ranking, from low to high, beginning with nonmanagement positions and ending with CEO/president, similar to that employed by Eisenhardt and Schoonhoven (1996) and then calculated the mean level of prior position for each TMT in our sample. Second, we controlled for the *average age of the executives*, which may be considered an indicator of the amount and breadth of experience of the TMT. Additionally, we assessed the amount of dispersion of TMT members' characteristics. We included a variable for the diversity of *tenure with the firm* among TMT members. Consistent with prior research, we used the coefficient of variation for the demographic variable of tenure in the group (Allison 1978; Bantel and Jackson 1989). And we included a variable for the *functional heterogeneity* of the TMT members. We classified the previous functional positions of all of the top managers in our dataset, based on an extension of categories used by Hambrick, Cho, and Chen (1996) that also included positions associated with younger research-based firms: chief scientific officer

---

[2] We investigated additional ways to code VC prominence, including, in particular, the age of the 'lead' VC firm at the time of a firm's IPO, in which 'lead' was considered the earliest investor (cf. Gompers 1996). In the present context, we found that such an approach was not possible to implement due to methodological and conceptual challenges. Methodologically, due to the significant funding requirements in biotechnology, many investors tend to come in prior to a firm's IPO, such that the initial seed investors often no longer hold a significant position when the firm goes public. Additionally, identifying the 'lead' VC firm from the final prospectus is difficult because entities that have the longest equity stake in a firm may not also have board membership and/or may not be recognizable VC firms (but rather are collections of individuals who raised a fund for the express purpose of starting a specific biotech firm). Conceptually, using the VC firm that was the oldest investor as the 'lead' VC and evaluating whether or not the VC firm was prestigious based on its age is problematic, since we want to capture the symbolic value associated with having any well-established VC firms on board at the time of IPO, irrespective of when they invested. Since the oldest firm may not have the largest equity stake at time of IPO and/or may not even be a recognizable VC firm, evaluating VC prominence based on the age of the oldest investing firm would miss the positive symbolic value associated with having the involvement of a well-established firm such as Hambrecht and Quist, which could have a sizable position by the time of IPO and yet not be the earliest seed investor. Thus, we chose to employ a time-sensitive measure of VC prominence, using one consistent data source (VentureXpert).

(CSO), founder, researcher, lab manager, and professor. Consistent with prior research, we used a variation of the Herfindal-Hirschman index.

Finally, we included a variable that accounts for the type of business the biotechnology company was in. From the main company descriptions in the prospectuses, firms were coded as being in therapeutics, diagnostics, both diagnostics and therapeutics, agriculture, chemical, or other. To verify the firm's business, we referred to the IBI database and BioScan. For *business type*, we dummy coded whether the company was in a core biotechnology field (i.e. therapeutics or therapeutics and diagnostics, or neither).

ANALYSIS

For each set of analyses, we used Heckman selection models to guard against the possibility of sample selection bias (Heckman 1979). In general, sample selection bias can arise when the criteria for selecting observations are not independent of the outcome variables. For example, studies of earnings and the status achievement of women can run the risk of sample selection bias if they do not account for factors that affect women's participation in the work-force. To correct for potential bias in such studies, sample selection models can be run that account for women's entry into the labor market and for the market rewards they receive (for a review, see Winship and Mare 1992).

Here, we are studying factors associated with upper echelon experience that influence the prestige of the investment banks that underwrite the firms' security offerings when a firm goes public. Therefore, to conduct analyses on our core sample of public firms, we need to first compare the sample of firms that did go public with a sample of private firms that were founded in the same period but were not able to go public. This way, antecedent conditions that impact a biotechnology firm's ability to go public are considered. Including these additional analyses (here, predicting whether a firm is able to go public) guards the researcher against the possibility that there is some other factor, in addition to those studied in the main analyses, that could be accounting for the effects observed.

Heckman's procedure generates consistent, asymptotically efficient esti-mates that can enable us to generalize to the larger population of biotechnol-ogy firms (cf. Heckman 1979). The Heckman model is a two-stage procedure that uses the larger risk set of public and private firms, including firms that ceased to exist as of 1996 in both categories ($n = 858$). Probit regres-sion was used to estimate the likelihood of completing an IPO during the first stage; estimates of parameters from that model were then incorporated into a second-stage regression model to predict prestige of investment bank (Van de Ven and Van Praag 1981). For the first-stage models, information available for both our public and private firms—geographical location, year of founding, and type of business—was used to predict likelihood of going public.[3] In the second stage, though the sample includes public and private firms, the standard errors reported reflect the smaller sample of firms ($n = 299$).

To account for the fact that the financial information spanned two decades, private financing estimates were transformed into constant 1996 dollars. In order to account for the time-varying market conditions firms faced when going public, the equity index variable described earlier was used in all analyses. The numbers were calibrated not just by the year but also by the month preceding the offering, which produces fairly fine-grained estimates.

RESULTS

Correlations between the main variables of interest are provided in Table 9.1. This table shows that the relationships between key variables of interest are in the directions predicted. Table 9.2 presents findings for the effects of upper echelon affiliations with prominent upstream, horizontal, and downstream organizations on the prestige of the firm's lead investment bank. In this main table, we begin with the selection equation variables and the firm and industry-level control variables, and then include the traditional upper echelon variables and core measures of upper echelon affiliations. The first-stage probit models predicting whether a company was able to go public in the first instance correctly classified 73 percent of our cases. As shown in the Heckman selection models, all of the selection variables were significant predictors.

Model 1 in Table 9.2 includes the control variables associated with the firm and the industry. As expected, the prominence of the firm's venture capital firms and the amount of private financing raised were positively and significantly related to the prestige of the young company's lead investment bank at the time of the IPO. Model 2 includes upper echelon variables that have been investigated in prior research. Here we find that the average prior position level of the upper echelon members and firm size are also positively related to investment bank prestige. Hypothesis 1 predicted that prominent upstream affiliations among upper echelons would be positively related to the prestige of a firm's lead underwriter. Model 3 shows that no support for hypothesis 1 was found. However, models 4 and 5 show support for

---

[3] Two-stage models do a particularly good job at estimation when there is at least one variable that may be considered an 'instrument' that is a good predictor in the first stage but not the second stage of the model; in this case, that 'instrument' was business type (see Winship and Mare 1992 for further discussion).

Table 9.1. Means, standard deviations, and correlations ($n = 299$)

Variable	X	SD	1	2	3	4	5	6	7	8	9	10	11	12	13	14	15	16
1. Equity index	3.78	0.96	—															
2. Firm age	4.90	2.89	0.08	—														
3. Firm size	85.64	120.85	0.02	0.08	—													
4. Location	0.50	0.50	0.15**	0.07	0.05	—												
5. Number of alliances	1.65	1.90	0.05	0.07	-0.02	-0.04	—											
6. VC prominence	0.32	0.47	0.17**	-0.01	0.05	0.33***	0.04	—										
7. Private financing[a]	6.92	0.77	0.19**	0.10*	0.28***	0.19**	0.23***	0.20**	—									
8. Product stage	1.84	0.85	0.04	0.25***	0.26***	0.05	-0.10†	0.03	0.14*	—								
9. Avg. prior position level	2.72	0.67	-0.00	-0.08	-0.08	0.01	-0.00	0.05	0.06	0.08	—							
10. Age of executives	47.60	4.56	-0.10†	0.12*	-0.02	-0.17**	-0.03	-0.27***	-0.07	-0.07	0.18**	—						
11. Tenure with firm	0.65	0.33	0.04	0.08	-0.00	-0.04	0.05	-0.05	0.06	-0.05	-0.02	-0.00	—					
12. Functional heterogeneity	0.79	0.10	0.01	0.11†	0.14*	0.09	0.04	-0.01	0.25***	0.17**	-0.39***	-0.01	0.10†	—				
13. Upstream affiliations	0.14	0.13	0.05	-0.09	-0.02	0.17**	0.03	-0.04	0.01	-0.20***	-0.12*	-0.05	-0.01	0.02	—			
14. Horizontal affiliations	0.12	0.15	0.03	-0.09	0.03	0.27***	0.07	0.17**	0.26***	-0.14*	0.04	-0.06	0.01	0.14*	0.10†	—		
15. Downstream affiliations	0.24	0.17	0.03	0.02	0.02	-0.01	0.03	0.07	0.24**	0.01	0.20**	0.13*	0.02	0.03	-0.07	0.10*	—	
16. Range of affiliations	2.18	0.86	0.10†	-0.01	0.12*	0.28***	0.13*	0.13*	0.40***	-0.03	0.09	-0.07	0.10†	0.24***	0.33***	0.58***	0.28***	—
17. Underwriter prestige[b]	7.63	1.95	0.14*	0.13*	0.22**	0.12†	0.18**	0.27**	0.41***	0.17	0.13*	-0.03	0.05	0.12†	-0.14*	0.27***	0.27***	0.33***

Notes: [a] Adjusted to constant 1996 dollars, then logged.

[b] $n = 244$ due to investment banks not ranked on Carter–Manaster scale.

*p < .05; **p < .01; ***p < .001; †p < .10.

Table 9.2. Heckman selection models of investment bank prestige at time of IPO[a]

	I		II		III		IV		V		VI		VII	
Control variables														
Equity index	0.06	(0.12)	0.06	(0.12)	0.08	(0.12)	0.08	(0.12)	0.08	(0.11)	0.05	(0.12)	0.08	(0.11)
Firm age	0.06	(0.04)	0.07†	(0.04)	0.07	(0.04)	0.07†	(0.04)	0.08*	(0.04)	0.08†	(0.04)	0.07†	(0.04)
Firm size	0.00†	(0.00)	0.00*	(0.00)	0.00*	(0.00)	0.00*	(0.00)	0.00*	(0.00)	0.00*	(0.00)	0.00*	(0.00)
Location	0.00	(0.26)	−0.05	(0.26)	−0.03	(0.26)	−0.17	(0.26)	−0.06	(0.26)	−0.18	(0.26)	−0.11	(0.26)
Number alliances	0.11†	(0.06)	0.11†	(0.06)	0.11†	(0.06)	0.11†	(0.06)	0.12*	(0.06)	0.10†	(0.06)	0.11*	(0.05)
VC prominence	0.81***	(0.25)	0.84**	(0.25)	0.80**	(0.25)	0.72**	(0.25)	0.70**	(0.24)	0.83***	(0.25)	0.71***	(0.24)
Private financing[b]	0.75***	(0.16)	0.63***	(0.17)	0.62***	(0.17)	0.54**	(0.17)	0.44**	(0.17)	0.49**	(0.17)	0.36*	(0.17)
Product stage	0.28†	(0.14)	0.22	(0.15)	0.19	(0.15)	0.28†	(0.15)	0.25†	(0.15)	0.27†	(0.15)	0.24†	(0.14)
Upper echelon variables														
Avg. prior position level	—		0.55**	(0.21)	0.52*	(0.21)	0.46*	(0.20)	0.41*	(0.20)	0.47*	(0.20)	0.36†	(0.20)
Age of executives	—		−0.01	(0.03)	−0.01	(0.03)	−0.01	(0.03)	−0.02	(0.02)	−0.01	(0.03)	−0.02	(0.02)
Tenure with firm	—		0.30	(0.33)	0.30	(0.33)	0.31	(0.32)	0.28	(0.32)	0.21	(0.33)	0.21	(0.32)
Functional heterogeneity	—		2.08	(1.42)	2.04	(1.42)	1.40	(1.41)	1.39	(1.38)	1.28	(1.42)	0.98	(1.38)
Upper echelon affiliations														
Upstream	—		—		−1.33	(0.83)	−1.31	(0.81)	0.99	(0.80)	—		−1.75*	(0.88)
Horizontal	—		—		—		2.37**	(0.78)	2.31**	(0.76)	—		1.35	(0.89)
Downstream	—		—		—		—		2.15**	(0.68)	—		1.77*	(0.70)
Range	—		—		—		—		—		0.45**	(0.14)	0.36*	(0.18)
Constant	0.77	(1.18)	−1.19	(1.85)	−0.66	(1.87)	0.08	(1.85)	0.81	(1.83)	−0.29	(1.84)	1.39	(1.84)
Selection equation variables														
Location	0.55***	(0.11)	0.55***	(0.11)	0.55***	(0.11)	0.55***	(0.11)	0.55***	(0.11)	0.55***	(0.11)	0.55***	(0.11)
Business type	1.23***	(0.11)	1.23***	(0.11)	1.23***	(0.11)	1.23***	(0.11)	1.23***	(0.11)	1.23***	(0.11)	1.23***	(0.11)
Year founded	−0.06***	(0.01)	−0.06***	(0.01)	−0.06***	(0.01)	−0.06***	(0.01)	−0.06***	(0.01)	−0.06***	(0.01)	−0.06***	(0.01)
Constant	119.96***	(21.53)	119.96***	(21.53)	119.96***	(21.53)	119.96***	(21.53)	119.96***	(21.53)	119.96***	(21.53)	119.96***	(21.53)
Wald χ^2	107.56***		118.98***		122.45***		135.29***		149.94***		132.44***		156.21***	
Rho	−0.02		−0.13		−0.20		−0.19		−0.07		−0.08		−0.10	
n	244		244		244		244		244		244		244	

Notes: [a]Unstandardized regression coefficients reported; standard errors in parentheses.

[b]Adjusted to constant 1996 dollars and logged.

*p < .05; **p < .01; ***p < .001 (two-tailed tests); †p < .10.

hypothesis 2—that prominent horizontal affiliations are positively related to investment bank prestige. In addition, support for hypothesis 3 was found: there was a significant and positive relationship between upper echelon affiliations with prominent downstream organizations and investment bank prestige.

The study also showed substantial support for hypothesis 4, as shown in model 6 of Table 2: upper echelon range of affiliations was significantly and positively related to the prestige of a firm's lead underwriter. Because range was constructed from the three forms of upper echelon affiliations, it is informative to present the results for range apart from the proportion of variance explained by our three types of upper echelon affiliations (as shown in model 6). The heterogeneity measure of range was highly correlated ($r > .90$) with the count measure of range. The final model (model 7) includes all upper echelon affiliation variables and shows a significant relationship between both downstream affiliations ($p = .011$) and range of affiliations and investment bank prestige. In this last model, the results also revealed an unexpected negative relationship between upper echelon upstream affiliations and investment bank prestige. It is likely that the loss of the significant effect for horizontal affiliations in this final model is due to the significant correlation between range and the other affiliation variables from which range was constructed.

Subsequent analyses revealed support for hypothesis 5, which predicted that technological uncertainty would moderate the effects of upper echelon affiliations on prestige of the firm's lead underwriter, such that upper echelon affiliations with prominent organizations would be particularly valuable when a firm's technology is relatively uncertain. Product stage was employed as the main indicator of technological uncertainty. The analyses tested for interaction effects between product stage and each type of upper echelon affiliation on investment bank prestige. Specifically, the results show significant negative interaction effects between product stage and upper echelon range of affiliations on investment bank prestige ($\beta = -0.3184$, $p < .05$). They also show significant and negative interaction effects between product stage and upper echelon horizontal affiliations on investment bank prestige ($\beta = -2.16$, $p < .05$).[4] These interaction effects are depicted in Figure 9.2.

An examination of the models in Table 9.2 reveals interesting patterns with respect to the control variables. First, the prominence of the company's venture capital firms and the amount of private financing the firm received prior

---

[4] In additional analyses, we recoded product stage into three dummy variables, one for each stage of product development, and reran the interaction analyses. The results remained consistent with the results we obtained using our 1-2-3 count measure of product stage. In particular, the strongest interaction effect was found between product stage and range of upper echelon affiliations. To be parsimonious, this chapter presents the results using the 1-2-3 variable.

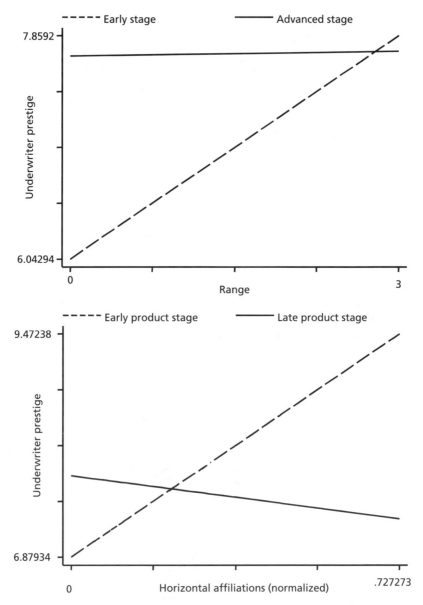

Figure 9.2. Interaction plots: The moderating effects of technological uncertainty

to the offering had significant and positive effects on underwriter prestige. In most instances, the results also suggest that larger firms tend to have more successful IPOs. Additional results also suggest that firms with prestigious strategic alliances received the endorsement of more prestigious underwriters.

Conclusion

The study detailed in this chapter suggests that network resources implicit in a young firm's upper echelon affiliations can be important signals of legitimacy to important intermediaries such as investment banks when they are deciding whether to endorse a young firm. This study also shows that the ability of firms to enter partnerships with prestigious intermediaries and to garner financial resources from these is influenced by the specific kinds of network resources that a firm possesses, which are directly associated with the career-based affiliations of a firm's upper echelon at the time of its IPO. This study further suggests that the greater the perceived legitimacy of a young firm, as signaled by its affiliation-based network resources, the greater the prestige of the investment bank that a firm will be able to attract as its lead IPO underwriter. This effect was examined for each facet of the proposed upper echelon affiliation typology of network resources, and it was found that young biotechnology firms with upper echelon affiliations with prominent pharmaceutical and/or health care organizations are better positioned to garner the support of prestigious underwriters. The study also provided some evidence that upper echelon affiliations with prominent biotechnology firms better position a company to secure the endorsement of prestigious underwriters. Finally, it showed that the greater the range of upper echelon affiliations with upstream, horizontal, and downstream organizations, the greater the prestige of the firm's lead investment bank.

Because our hypotheses centered on the symbolic value of upper echelon affiliations, the reported study also tested whether the effects were especially strong during times of high uncertainty. In particular, it tested whether having ties to prominent organizations was especially valuable to a firm when its lead product was in early stages of development. Results revealed significant and negative interaction effects between product stage and both upper echelon range and horizontal affiliations on investment bank prestige. These results lend support to our claims regarding the moderating role of technological uncertainty in the present context.

Surprisingly, this study did not find that network resources emanating from upper echelon upstream affiliations were significantly and positively associated with underwriter prestige. In fact, in one case, upstream affiliations were negatively associated with investment bank prestige. One possible explanation is that investment bankers look at alternative information to assess whether a firm's science is sound. Perhaps a firm's ties with scientific organizations are not fully represented in the firm's final prospectus, limiting the extent to which we were able to capture symbols of technological legitimacy associated with upstream affiliations. As an alternative explanation, it is also possible that upstream affiliations send negative signals by implying that the firm's products are in the basic research stages of development (cf. Baum, Calabrese, and Silverman 2000). Thus, perhaps upstream affiliations at the time of its IPO indicate to outsiders that a firm is trying to go public too early.

Results for the other independent variables included here yielded additional insights. In addition to amount of private financing, the prominence of a firm's venture capital partners was consistently and positively associated with the prestige of a firm's lead underwriter. There was also some evidence for a similar relationship between number of strategic alliances and underwriter prestige. Venture capital prominence was also significantly related to firm net proceeds.

Together, these results are consistent with the view that external parties look to the involvement of other firms when gauging whether to back a young firm. The present research supports the idea that the firm's affiliations with prior organizations affects subsequent alliance formation, as was discussed in Part I, and extends this research by suggesting the upper-echelon-based affiliations of firms are network resources that enable firms to partner with prestigious underwriters. In a following section of this chapter we see how such endorsements are themselves powerful network resources that enable firms to have successful public offerings.

The study detailed in this chapter focused on a novel set of interpersonal ties arising from a firm's upper echelons' prior employment and board affiliation ties. It assessed the role of such ties as network resources with strong symbolic value to other key constituents on which the firm may be dependent. Specifically, it showed how such ties can be a catalyst that enables firms to build endorsement relationships with prestigious underwriters. Thus, this study shows how one set of ties can enable a firm to accumulate other valuable ties. It echoes an earlier theme: network resources beget more network resources.

This study also contributes to organizational research on endorsements, legitimacy, and entrepreneurship in several respects. First, it considers the role of network resources emanating from a young firm's upper echelon experience in facilitating the establishment of endorsement ties. It further suggests that such resources can be beneficial to firms not so much by connecting potential partners, as was shown previously, but rather by serving as powerful signals of legitimacy that can be especially important when there is significant uncertainty surrounding a firm. It also provides a typology of such network resources and describes in detail how each type may influence outcomes for the firm.

Second, this study extends and further develops some of the research reported in earlier chapters by showing how network resources arising from a firm's upper echelon allow firms to form potentially advantageous new connections with other powerful intermediaries. Another way to conceptualize this is as an examination of the origins of critical intermediary ties in the early life stages of a firm. Whereas prior research has examined the role of third parties in helping a firm obtain much-needed resources from its environment (e.g. Stuart, Hoang, and Hybels 1999; Zuckerman 1999), the origins of these intraorganizational endorsements have been overlooked. The results suggest that the network resources arising from the type and quantity of experience of those who lead and manage a young firm can provide important symbols of legitimacy that affect the endorsement process. In mediated markets such as the primary market for IPOs, organizations have limited prior interaction patterns with one another. Further, there are ample 'questions in the minds of actors that [the firm] serves as the natural way to effect some kind of collective action' (Hannan and Carroll 1992: 34). In such contexts, symbols of legitimacy derived from network resources can be especially valuable to outsiders considering endorsement (Meyer and Rowan 1977; Feldman and March 1981).

Third, this study adds to the significant stream of research that has shown that affiliations with prominent institutions can yield beneficial consequences for firms (Podolny 1994; Podolny, Stuart, and Hannan 1996). Such research is based on the Matthew Effect, which refers to the tendency for credit or benefits to accrue to those who have already achieved success: as Merton (1973) argued in his study of elite scientists, prestige tends to beget prestige. Unlike prior research, which has focused attention on the benefits associated with having similarly prominent interorganizational ties, this study considers whether the type of tie a firm has affects its outcomes. The typology we employ introduces sharp distinctions between organizational affiliations, enabling a richer understanding of the conditions under which transfers of status are likely to occur. Also, focusing on one particular industry and on one critical event in the life of a young firm, the IPO, affords an in-depth look at how different types of prestigious affiliations associated with a firm's upper echelon may confer different symbols affecting outsider perceptions of a young firm's legitimacy in different ways.

Fourth, this study extends prior research on social networks and organizational legitimacy by arguing that a firm's upper echelon's experience base is a network resource that can provide powerful symbols of legitimacy to external parties, such as potential underwriters, who are considering endorsement. Thus, unlike prior IPO research, which has focused on outsider perceptions of firm quality that are based on specific resources that may transfer across firm ties (e.g. Stuart, Hoang, and Hybels 1999), this chapter's central argument is based on the notion that symbols of legitimacy arising from a firm's network resources can affect outsider perceptions of the firm. Thus, while an investment bank may be the final arbiter in the decision to endorse a young firm, the theory and conceptualization of the IPO process described in this chapter depicts the firm as an active rather than a passive player or 'pipe' through which resources flow (cf. Podolny 2001) during the IPO process. The firm's IPO team can use network resources to highlight organizational credentials, such as upper echelon backgrounds, in order to demonstrate the firm's organizational legitimacy.

Furthermore, the present study is distinctive because it revealed how network resources at the upper echelon level might allow firms to build valuable connections with other organizations that in turn constitute further valuable network resources. Empirical research has seldom addressed how individual-level affiliations can affect the formation of firm-level affiliations or how group-level ties embedded in members' employment and board memberships affect the formation of interorganizational ties. Thus, the findings of this study have important implications for research that links microlevel interorganizational affiliations to more macrolevel relationships (Coleman 1990) and to the growth of young firms (Burton, Sørensen, and Beckman 1998).

Finally, it is worth noting that the qualitative and quantitative findings of this research reached remarkable convergence. During the acquaintanceship stage between a young firm and an investment bank, a firm faces uncertainty on a host of fronts. During such times, important outsiders such as investment bankers and potential investors are likely to attend to signs that the firm shows promise and is a legitimate, collective entity (Hannan and Carroll 1992). Such symbols are valuable beyond other more purely objective indicators such as firm age, size, location, and product stage. Both empirical work and interviews revealed that the backgrounds of a firm's upper echelon may be instrumental in convincing outsiders that a young firm is getting off to a good start and is thus worthy of endorsement. While the findings do not suggest a specific formula for designing an ideal upper echelon for a young firm, they do suggest that the type and amount of network resources arising from this group's affiliations at the time of its IPO affect the company's ability to receive the endorsement of a prestigious third party. Consequently, because they provide valuable information that reduces uncertainty and grants legitimacy to start-up firms, upper echelon affiliations are indeed network resources key to the formation of strategic alliances between start-up firms and their underwriters.

Follow-up research

A follow-up study (Higgins and Gulati 2006) extends the findings reported in this chapter by suggesting that the composition of an entrepreneurial firm's

TMT can endow a firm with valuable network resources that can signal organizational legitimacy and thereby influence not only a firm's ability to attract prestigious underwriters but also its ability to influence investor decisions. The study examines the effect of firms' upper-echelon-based network resources on their IPOs. Specifically, it examines the effect of these network resources on a firm's ability to attract high-quality investors at the time it goes public. It proposes that the network resources implicit in the composition of a TMT have a symbolic role at the time of a firm's IPO, acting in concert with the more concrete operational activities of the team to affect the decisions of important resource-holders such as investors. As a result, this study refocuses attention on the symbolic role of top management and their concomitant network resources, a role that Pfeffer and Salancik (1978) proposed long ago but that has received only cursory consideration in recent empirical research on TMTs. The study also involves the context of entrepreneurial firms, where little attention has been given to the role of the TMT in relation to firms' IPOs.

This study proposes that young firms can influence investor decisions by signaling organizational legitimacy based on three key dimensions: the firm's access to *resources*, the firm's ability to fulfill key *roles*, and the firm's ability to attract the *endorsement* of prestigious partners. My coauthor and I developed this typology of legitimacy benefits to examine how each form of legitimacy may be associated with the composition of a young firm's TMT. Specifically, we propose that firms signal *resource* legitimacy through TMT employment affiliations, *role* legitimacy through the kinds of positions held by the seniormost members of the TMT, and *endorsement* legitimacy through a firm's prestigious partnerships. Our research examines how these multiple signals of legitimacy that ensue from a firm's network resources shape the quantity and quality of investors who take part in a firm's IPO.

As a result, this study assesses how different TMT structures influence investor decisions. It thus focuses on the ways in which firms strive to enhance perceptions of their legitimacy through TMT-based signals regarding firm resources, roles, and endorsement.

The ideas proposed in this study are tested with the same comprehensive data used in the previous study, which contains the career histories of 3,200 top managers who took biotechnology firms public between 1979 and 1996. At the time of IPO, nearly all biotechnology firms are several years away from generating revenues because it takes seven to ten years to bring a product from research stages to market and the average age of firms at IPO is four and a half years. Given this lack of profitability at the time such firms go public, investors face significant uncertainty regarding their decisions to invest, making this a particularly salient context in which to examine the role of network resources, signals, and organizational legitimacy.

Several important findings emerge from this study. One such finding is that investor decisions are affected by the employment affiliations and roles of TMT members and by a young firm's partnership with a prestigious lead underwriter. This suggests that network resources for a firm may emanate from its TMT affiliations and that the benefits of such resources may materialize in the form of greater legitimacy in the eyes of key stakeholders for firms. The findings specifically indicate that TMT employment affiliations with downstream organizations such as pharmaceutical companies are positively related to the number of quality institutional investors that decide to invest in young firms. No such effects were found for upstream or horizontal employment affiliations. The results also show that the greater the diversity of employment affiliations of a firm's TMT across these three categories, the greater the number and quality of institutional investors that take part in the initial public offering of a young firm.

A second form of organizational legitimacy arising from the network resources associated with upper echelon backgrounds was also introduced in this study: 'role legitimacy' refers to the extent to which the firm is able to fill top positions with individuals who have relevant role experience. This study proposes that the greater the match between the backgrounds of C-level managers and their roles at the time of IPO, the more likely investors would be to invest in the young firm. This study found that the background of one key top manager, the CSO, was related to investor decisions: specifically, having a CSO with similar experience was positively related to the number of dedicated institutional investors that invested in a young firm.

This study also considered a third form of legitimacy called 'endorsement legitimacy'. This type of legitimacy refers to the firm's ability to secure an endorsement from a prestigious partner by, for example, partnering with a respected underwriter for its IPO. Extending previous findings that have established a positive relationship between underwriter prestige and financial indicators of firm performance (e.g. Carter and Manaster 1990; Stuart, Hoang, and Hybels 1999), the results showed that underwriter prestige also affects the amount and quality of institutional investors that decide to invest in a firm undertaking an IPO.

This study also pointed to some interesting results when we included both underwriter prestige and TMT affiliations in the reported analyses. It was expected that investment bank prestige would mediate relationships between TMT backgrounds and investor behavior. Instead, the results showed that the effects of TMT backgrounds on investor decisions remained intact, even after accounting for underwriter prestige. These results suggest that institutional investors attend to multiple signals of a firm's legitimacy in the IPO context—those reflected in information about firm partnerships *and* top managers' backgrounds. Whereas prior organizational research on IPOs has focused on the importance of interorganizational partnerships for issuing firms (e.g. Stuart, Hoang, and Hybels 1999), the present research points to the possibility of an additional factor—signals associated with top manager backgrounds.

Focusing a lens on TMT research in this fashion affords not only empirical learning but also important theoretical insights. Rather than directing attention toward internal TMT processes and theory regarding information-processing and teamwork (e.g. Hambrick, Cho, and Chen 1996), this study focuses outward on the signaling value of the TMT to important external constituents and thus also builds on theories of organizational legitimacy (e.g. DiMaggio and Powell 1983). It further suggests that TMT affiliations can be viewed as contributing to a firm's network resources that in turn provide it with various forms of legitimacy benefits. This reorientation suggests not only that top managers take strategic actions that directly affect firm outcomes (e.g. innovation, Keck and Tushman 1993), as has been documented in the past, but also that their backgrounds can directly enhance their firms' legitimacy in the eyes of third parties.

This follow-up study extends prior research on upper echelons, network resources, and legitimacy by simultaneously examining multiple forms of legitimacy that originate from different types of network resources—those that stem from the TMT and those that arise from interfirm partnerships. Only a few recent studies of upper echelons have investigated the unique and pressing issues facing young firms as they strive to gain legitimacy in industries in which they have not yet developed reputations (Rao 1994; Eisenhardt and Schoonhoven 1996). Furthermore, prior TMT research has not examined whether or how top managers' backgrounds complement other sources of pre-IPO legitimacy, such as the endorsement of a prestigious intermediary. By considering different kinds of network resources and the legitimacy benefits they provide, we gain insight into how these resources affect the decisions of key outsiders. This approach opens avenues for future theory and research that considers more broadly how a firm can signal predictability through multiple means (Suchman 1995). Indeed, this study suggests that mixed signals yield anything but mixed messages. Perhaps, and as future research may show, legitimacy strategies that entail mixing signals can lead to positive 'success spirals', enhancing firm desirability to a magnitude beyond that reached via simple additive effects.

In addition to having implications for research, the findings presented in this study convey normative lessons, particularly for young firms contemplating an IPO. As one primer on IPOs explained, while going public may seem like a rather straightforward process—a new company simply pulls together the necessary documentation and a group of investment bankers to sell and distribute the offering, price the deal, and collect the fees—it is generally the case that companies 'walk a proverbial minefield in the path to completing their IPO' (Peterson 2001: 37–8). As this research suggests, while securing a reputable bank to underwrite the IPO deal is a crucial component of the IPO process, building an impressive team of managing officers is as important a lever for a firm to acquire organizational legitimacy.

10 The contingent effects of network resources

By focusing on the origin of interorganizational endorsements in the context of IPOs, the first chapter in this section showed how prior upper echelon affiliations engender network resources that are influential in helping start-up firms secure endorsements from prestigious underwriters by serving as powerful signals of legitimacy. I went on to suggest that such endorsement ties with important intermediaries can themselves be considered a form of network resource in turn beneficial to firms in other ways, especially at the time they go public. This chapter extends these findings by directly assessing the beneficial consequences for IPO-bound entrepreneurial firms of their endorser-based network resources and those based in other such ties.

This chapter shifts focus away from the role of interpersonal network resources arising from a firm's upper echelon to those generated by its interorganizational connections. Because the setting here is entrepreneurial firms at the time of their IPOs, the focus is on network resources based in organizational connections crucial at that time, including ties with investment banks and venture capitalists.

In addition to assessing the aggregate impact of different types of network ties on an entrepreneurial firm's IPO, this chapter also evaluates the possible contingent value of each type of interorganizational relationship. In other words, I consider which ties matter when for firms. Prior research has shown that network ties to prominent firms create network resources that can enhance new venture performance (Carter and Manaster 1990; Baum 1996) and signal a firm's quality to key external resource holders, which in turn affects IPO performance (Stuart, Hoang, and Hybels 1999). But there has been little exploration into whether and how these effects of various types of network ties on new venture performance vary.

A central theme here is that network ties are not uniform in their effects on firm outcomes, but rather vary across the different types of network ties a firm has. Further, the efficacy of network resources originating in different ties

This chapter is adapted with permission from 'Which Ties Matter When? The Contingent Effects of Interorganizational Partnerships on IPO Success' by Ranjay Gulati and Monica C. Higgins published in *Strategic Management Journal*, 2003, (24/2): 127–44, © John Wiley & Sons Limited.

would vary depending on the type of tie and the contingent factors that shape their efficacy. I refine this perspective by theorizing that the magnitude of the effect of each type of tie varies with the uncertainty associated with the equity market.

In assessing the contingent values of different kinds of ties, this chapter compares the effects of network resources resulting from prior strategic alliances with the effects of endorsement relationships with venture capital (VC) firms and investment banks. It proposes that under different equity market conditions, potential investors in an issuing firm attend to different types of uncertainty, which affects investor perception of the relative value of a young firm's different endorsements and partnerships and, hence, IPO success. In other words, different types of equity market uncertainty raise different kinds of investor concerns, and because different network resources (and the ties underlying them) provide different signals of a firm's potential, they become more or less important, depending on investor concerns in the specific market context. As a result, network resources based on different kinds of ties should vary in their levels of effectiveness, depending on the equity market context.

Theory and hypotheses

As discussed in the last chapter, interorganizational ties between a start-up and established firms provide network resources that mitigate uncertainty and establish the start-up's viability in the eyes of third parties (Stuart, Hoang, and Hybels 1999). Consequently, the value of a young firm's ties should not only vary by type of tie but also depend on the nature of the uncertainty the firm faces. Different types of uncertainty may raise different types of concerns for key outsiders, such as investors, affecting the value of a firm's risk-mitigating partnerships.

For public investors in entrepreneurial firms, uncertainty associated with a firm can arise due to characteristics associated with the firm itself, such as firm age or location (e.g. Sorenson and Audia 2000). Uncertainty can also arise from exogenous sources such as natural events, shifts in demand, or regulatory changes (Sutcliffe and Zaheer 1998). How favorable or unfavorable the market is for specific equity offerings is another critical aspect of uncertainty for investors. As research on the biotechnology industry has shown, the receptivity of the equity markets to biotechnology offerings has ebbed and flowed over the years, affecting the preferred timing of IPOs (Lerner 1994). When the market window is relatively open or 'hot' for equity offerings, the potential upside for both firms and investors is much greater than when the market window is relatively closed or 'cold'. Investor decisions to provide financial resources to a young firm are thus likely to be affected by the uncertainty associated with this window, or equity market uncertainty.

This chapter proposes that equity market uncertainty entails two over-arching types of investor concerns: investing in bad (low-potential) firms or missing good (high-potential) opportunities. Although both of these concerns surround any investment decision, investor attention shifts more toward one or the other, depending on the receptivity of the equity markets. When the equity markets are relatively hot for new issues, many firms try to go public, making the probability of and concern about investing in unworthy firms more salient. When the equity markets are relatively cold for new issues, few firms try to go public, making the probability of and concern about over-looking good firms more salient. Indeed, prior research has shown that when equity markets are relatively hot, investors are overly optimistic about the potential of young firms (Ritter 1984); thus, in this market context, investors' effective null hypothesis is that a given new company represents a profitable investment. At such times, investors are concerned about investing in firms when they should not (i.e. making a type II error). On the other hand, when the equity markets are relatively cold and few firms try to go public, investors are concerned about overlooking firms in which they should invest (i.e. mak-ing a type I error) (cf. Sah and Stiglitz 1986, 1988; Rosenthal and Rosnow 1991).

This perspective on investor decision-making is consistent with an attention-based view of the firm. As Ocasio (1997) describes, attention encompasses 'the noticing, encoding, interpreting and focusing of time and effort by organizational decision-makers' (189). In the present context, whether and how much investors decide to invest depends on the types of concerns to which they attend, which may be influenced by factors in the business environment (Ocasio 1997). Extending these ideas, it is likely that investors can resolve specific concerns by considering the different network resources implicit in the different ties of the focal firm. Here, we consider the network resources that arise from two types of ties: (*a*) endorsement relationships such as those with VCs and investment banks and (*b*) strategic alliance partnerships. I propose that each type of tie, with its attendant net-work resources, mitigates different types of uncertainty and thus varies in importance at different times.

ENDORSEMENT RELATIONSHIPS

In an endorsement relationship, an organization serves as an intermediary between the focal firm (i.e. the issuing firm) and a third party (i.e. public investors). Endorsement by powerful organizations can enable young firms to overcome the external liability of newness problems associated with the lack of a favorable reputation (Rao 1994; Thornton 1999). Securing such an endorsement is of particular importance for firms facing mediated markets, such as the primary market for IPOs, which are characterized by significant ambiguity regarding firm valuation and are heavily influenced by highly visible critics, such as investment analysts, who wield tremendous influence over investor behavior. In the present IPO context, endorsement relations include ties with VCs, accounting firms, law firms, and investment banks (Bochner and Priest 1993). Studies in finance and organizational strategy have demonstrated that two of these endorsement relations play a particularly significant role: VCs and investment banks (Carter and Manaster 1990; Jain and Kini 1995; Stuart, Hoang, and Hybels 1999). Relationships with both groups constitute important components of the network resources a young firm may possess at the time it goes public.

While prior research has established that ties to prominent organizations such as these can enhance IPO success in general, I suggest that the value of the network resources these ties create will be moderated in important and systematic ways by equity market uncertainty. In particular, I expect the signaling value of a tie to be the greatest when the information conveyed by that type of tie is the one most keenly attended to by the IPO market. Because ties to different types of partners signal different information that may be more or less valuable at different times, variance associated with the value of a new firm's ties can be expected. Thus, market context can significantly—and systematically—shift the effects of different types of network resources.

VENTURE CAPITAL ENDORSEMENT

Prior research has demonstrated that VC backing is a tie that increases the likelihood that a firm will have a successful IPO because VCs provide financial resources and expertise that can enhance the quality of new ventures (Megginson and Weiss 1991). Studies have also demonstrated that VC quality is associated with IPO performance. The greater the amount of monitoring by a VC, the lower the underpricing—the spread between issuing price and offering price shortly after public trading begins—which is one measure of IPO performance (Jain and Kini 1994; Lin 1996). Furthermore, VC endorsements not only help certify the present value of issuing firms but also signal the likelihood that firms will remain going concerns in the future. One reason for this is that empirical studies show that the presence of VCs improves a young company's chances of survival in the post-IPO period (Khurshed 2000). The logic behind this relationship is that in addition to providing financial experience to a young firm in the form of knowledge regarding incentive and compensation systems and deal structuring, VCs closely monitor their companies following their initial investments (Gorman and Sahlman 1989; Sahlman 1990). Therefore, the activities in which VCs are expected to engage in the future, such as recruiting senior managers and developing business strategy (Bygrave and Timmons 1992; Hellmann 1998; Hellmann and Puri 2000), should affect both post- and pre-IPO performance. In summary, a firm's partnership with a reputable VC is the source of valuable network resources for a firm that signals both the present and future quality of a young firm.

The research noted above assumes that the VC effect on firm IPOs is uniform across time. However, this may not always be the case: market swings may alter the effect. As described earlier, partnerships with high-quality VCs signal to the investment community that the new venture is a 'good bet' both at the time of IPO and in the future. Because VC ties alleviate uncertainty regarding the decision to invest in an IPO firm, it is also likely that the effects of such ties will vary depending on the types of uncertainty that surround the investment decision.

Recent research on the decision-making processes of VCs lends insight into how the signals associated with VC ties may differ depending on the uncertainty that characterizes the equity markets. During hot markets, 'too much money will chase too few deals' (*The Economist* 1997). As this quotation by Bill Hambrecht, chairman of well-known San Francisco VC Hambrecht and Quist, suggests, VCs are likely to be overly optimistic about the upsides of IPOs when the markets are favorable. And, with so many firms trying to go public during a hot market, the amount of information that a VC must process in deciding which firms to take public is likely to be greater than when fewer firms are considering IPOs. Indeed, extensive research has shown that precisely these two conditions—overconfidence and information overload—tend to undermine the accuracy of VC decision-making (Zacharakis and Meyer 1998; Zacharakis and Shepherd 2001).

These differences in how and when VCs carefully and accurately attend to the IPO market may affect investor perceptions of the value of VC partnerships. During a cold market, when VCs are not overwhelmed by the 'fools rush in' phenomenon of a hot market, investors are likely to attribute greater value to a focal firm's tie to a prominent VC. A cold market environment stands in contrast to the information-laden and hypercompetitive environment that can lead to lower attention spans and suboptimal VC decision-making during hot markets (for reviews of research on VC decision-making, see Zacharakis and Meyer 2000 or Fried and Hisrich 1994). The time and attention taken in the evaluation process during cold markets should result in fewer missed opportunities, or type I errors, made by VCs. Therefore, while the evaluation expertise underlying VC endorsements may, in general, signal firm quality to investors, investors will likely attribute greater value to such ties during cold markets.

Hypothesis 1: Endorsement by a prestigious VC should be particularly beneficial to the success of a young company's IPO when the equity markets are cold.

UNDERWRITER ENDORSEMENT

Prior studies have established a clear role for underwriter reputation in IPOs; these findings reinforce the notion that the underwriter endorsements can generate network resources for firms. Both finance and organizational scholars have demonstrated that firms with prestigious underwriters are more likely to have successful IPOs (Carter and Manaster 1990; Stuart, Hoang, and Hybels 1999). Additionally, finance scholars have demonstrated that high-prestige investment banks are unlikely to undertake speculative issues due to the legal liabilities and potential loss of reputational capital that can be associated with such deals (Beatty and Ritter 1986; Tinic 1988; Carter and Manaster 1990). Given this risk profile, prestigious investment banks generally prefer the seasoned equity market over the IPO market (Wolfe, Cooperman, and Ferris 1994; Bae, Klein, and Bowyer 1999). Moreover, when prestigious investment banks do engage in the IPO market, they tend to underwrite low-risk IPOs instead of high-risk ones (Hayes 1971; Tinic 1988), with the hope that such relationships will lead to opportunities for larger and more lucrative deals in the future.

These findings point to the tendency for prestigious investment banks to participate intermittently in the IPO market, depending on the receptivity of the equity market. Unlike prestigious VCs that specialize in a limited number of industries and often engage in new issues (Jain and Kini 1995), prestigious investment banks offer a wider range of financial instruments and thus have greater choice as to what types of deals they engage in (List, Platt, and Rombel 2000). Furthermore, unlike prestigious VCs that take public those firms in which they have previously invested, prestigious investment banks tend to be quite selective in picking firms at the IPO stage, because post-IPO deals tend to generate the most attractive returns for them. Thus, because prestigious investment banks are loath to incur significant risk, they are more likely to engage in deals in an equity market hot for new issues.

These differences in when and how extensively prestigious investment banks attend to the IPO market may affect the types of signals associated with their endorsements. Because prestigious investment banks attend most closely to the equity markets when the market is hot, a young firm's endorsement by a prestigious underwriter should be particularly helpful in alleviating investor concerns regarding the possibility of investing in bad deals, or making a type II error. Public investors, like investment banks, must choose between many possible firms to invest in when the equity markets are favorable because the pool of firms trying to go public is relatively large (Ritter 1984). And, as is also the case with investment banks, the number of firms that public investors can support is limited due to their own financial constraints (Puri 1999). During hot markets, then, considering the large number of firms seeking financial capital and the limited number that prestigious investment banks can actually underwrite, a young firm's partnership with a prestigious underwriter is a network resource that signals to potential investors that the issuing firm is a relatively good low-risk bet, reducing investors' concerns regarding type II errors. Indeed, because prestigious investment banks are extremely risk-averse (Beatty and Ritter 1986; Carter and Manaster 1990) and prefer to engage in postoffering deals (Wolfe, Cooperman, and Ferris 1994), investors may infer that the firm a prestigious underwriter chooses to endorse during a hot market has long-term potential—in short, that it is a worthwhile investment. Thus:

Hypothesis 2: Endorsement by a prestigious underwriter should be particularly beneficial to the success of a young company's IPO when the equity markets are hot.

Put another way, the hypothesis above suggests that the network resources generated by a firm's endorsement ties with a prestigious investment bank are likely to vary in efficacy depending on equity market conditions. They will be most beneficial to firms when the equity markets are hot as opposed to cold.

STRATEGIC ALLIANCES

In previous chapters, I have discussed how substantial research has examined the value of strategic alliances. Much of this research has focused on the performance implications of strategic partnerships among established firms (e.g. Mowery, Oxley, and Silverman 1996). This book, in particular, has examined how prior alliance networks influence the new alliances' formation, governance structure, and total value creation. In contrast, this chapter extends research that has explored the value of strategic alliances for entrepreneurial firms (e.g. DeCarolis and Deeds 1999; Baum, Calabrese, and Silverman 2000). For young firms in the biotechnology industry, strategic alliances with prominent pharmaceutical and health care organizations engender network resources that can send powerful signals to outsiders.

One of the biggest challenges for young biotechnology companies is the long product development cycle they must endure before generating revenues (Powell, Koput, and Smith-Doerr 1996). This is a major concern for investors as well. In the biotechnology industry, it takes seven to ten years on average for a firm to advance from basic R&D through clinical trials and the FDA approval process (Deeds, DeCarolis, and Coombs 1997). Due to these cycle times, along with capital needs in the hundreds of millions of dollars, biotechnology firms tend to be far from generating revenues when they try to go public (Pisano 1991). One way that biotechnology firms have tried to alleviate investor concerns regarding the viability of their products is to ally with major pharmaceutical and health care companies that have significant marketing and sales expertise as well as access to cash that can support firms through this lengthy process (Pisano 1990, 1991).

Because these types of alliances mitigate uncertainty for resource-holders, it is likely that the signal value varies with the types of uncertainty that characterize different market situations and the extent to which major pharmaceutical and health care companies actively engage in the evaluation of young biotechnology firms. During hot markets, a young biotechnology firm's concerns regarding its ability to sustain the long discovery and development process are not as acute as during cold markets, when the availability of funding is much more scarce. During cold markets, more young biotechnology firms seek interfirm collaborations, leading to closer scrutinization of their potential by prominent pharmaceutical and health care firms because so many firms approach them for resources at these times (Lerner and Merges 1996). These trends are likely to be transparent to investors.

This timing-based difference in how carefully potential partners evaluate new biotechnology ventures should affect the impact of the signal that is associated with their alliances. During cold markets, the signaling value of a strategic alliance is stronger, because well-established firms have carefully examined many young biotechnology firms to avoid missing a worthwhile investment (Pisano and Mang 1993), which is precisely the sort of type I concern that plagues investors during cold markets. Therefore, while a tie to a major pharmaceutical/health care organization may signal firm quality to outsiders, this should be particularly true when the signal-maker's attention is focused more intensely on evaluating the potential of young firms, as is the case during cold markets. This suggests that the efficacy of the network resources emanating from a firm's alliances with prominent pharmaceutical and health care companies may be contingent on the market context in which they occur.

Hypothesis 3: Strategic alliances will be especially beneficial to the success of a young company's IPO when the equity markets are relatively cold.

In summary, when examining the idea that interorganizational ties create network resources that have differential effects on IPO performance, this chapter considers two questions: (a) Which ties matter (network factors)?

Network factors: tie type

		Endorsement relations		Strategic alliances
		Venture capital firms	Lead investment bank	Downstream alliances
Contextual factors: equity market conditions	Hot	H1: Less positive	H2: More positive	H3: Less positive
	Cold	H1: More positive	H2: Less positive	H3: More positive

Figure 10.1. A contingency perspective on the effects of interorganizational partnerships on IPO success

(*b*) When do ties matter (contextual factors)? In this study of firms undergoing IPOs, the contextual dimension was operationalized as the extent to which the equity markets are favorable to new issues—in simplified terms, whether the equity markets are hot or cold for new issues. The network dimension was broken down into the following types of ties: VC partnerships, underwriter endorsements, and strategic alliances. Figure 10.1 depicts this 2 (hot vs. cold equity market) × 3 (tie type) contingency framework and summarizes the aforementioned predictions.

Empirical research

METHOD

The sample used for the findings reported in this chapter is described in Appendix 1 under the heading 'Biotechnology Start-ups Database'. The measure of IPO success was calculated based on four different financial measures. First, the value of a firm's net proceeds was obtained from the first page of its final prospectus. This is the amount of cash a firm received as a result of the offering, less costs incurred during the IPO process. Second, the premoney market valuation of each firm, an IPO-success indicator employed in previous organizational and strategic management research (Stuart, Hoang, and Hybels 1999), was calculated. The premoney market value is calculated as follows:

$$V^* = (p_u q_t - p_u q_i)$$

where p_u is the final IPO subscription price as indicated on the firm's final prospectus, q_t measures the number of shares outstanding, and q_i is the number of shares offered in the IPO. This is the firm's market valuation less the proceeds to the firm as a result of the IPO. V^* is therefore the market valuation of the biotechnology firm just preceding the first day of trading. Third and fourth, each firm's 90-day market valuation and 180-day market valuation after the IPO were calculated to gauge the early success of the firm's offering. The same formula that was used to calculate a firm's premoney market valuation was used to calculate these valuations, with substitutions of the post-IPO price at 90 days out and 180 days out for p_u in the formula. Because these four financial measures were highly correlated with one another (Cronbach α close to .90), these measures were standardized and averaged to create a composite financial indicator of IPO success.

Equity market uncertainty was measured with a financial index (Lerner 1994) widely used in finance and strategy literature (e.g. Zucker, Darby, and Brewer 1994; Stuart, Hoang, and Hybels 1999; Baum, Calabrese, and Silverman 2000), which gauges the receptivity of the equity markets to biotechnology offerings. Lerner's index (1994) was constructed using an equal amount of dollar shares of thirteen publicly traded, dedicated biotechnology firms. Lerner's findings (1994) imply that an industry-specific index is the preferred method for capturing the favorability of the equity markets, as times of high valuations vary across industries and do not always coincide with trends in the general market. The index included in these models is a finer-grained measure of market conditions than has been used recently in IPO-related research on the biotechnology industry (in which dummy variables for 'cold' market years were included) (e.g. DeCarolis and Deeds 1999). We used Lerner's index as our indicator of industry uncertainty at the time of the IPO. Specifically, we used the equity index value at the end of the month prior to the IPO date for each of our firms. The equity market measure thus ranges from low to high or from cold to hot (unfavorable to favorable).

VC partner prominence was measured by making lists of prominent VCs for each IPO year in the sample as follows: we obtained rankings of VCs from VentureXpert, a Securities Data Corporation database; rankings were based on total dollars invested by each VC in each of the eighteen years that made up the time frame of our dataset. Firms were coded as 1 if any of the biotechnology firm's VCs with at least a 5 percent stake were listed among the top thirty firms on the list of prominent VCs for the year prior to the firm's IPO date, and 0 otherwise.

Underwriter prestige was measured with an index developed by Carter and Manaster (1990) and updated by Carter, Dark, and Singh (1998). The measures are based on analyses of investment banks' positions in the 'tombstone' announcements for IPOs; this methodology has been cited widely in both finance and organizational and strategic management research (e.g. Podolny 1994; Bae, Klein, and Bowyer 1999; Stuart, Hoang, and Hybels 1999; Rau 2000). Information was available for all but 25 of the underwriters in the data-set (accounting for 55 of our firms), yielding rankings for 244 firms. Mann–Whitney and Kolmogorov–Smirnov tests indicated that the firms for which this information was not available did not differ significantly on any of our main independent variables of interest from those for which it was. Carter and colleagues' indices were created by examining the hierarchy of investment banks presented in the 'tombstone announcements' for IPOs that appear in the *Investment Dealer's Digest* or the *Wall Street Journal*. Please see the Empirical Research section of Chapter 9 for a more detailed description of how these indices were created. The name of the lead investment bank was taken from the front page of each firm's final prospectus.

The total number of strategic alliances that each firm had with prominent pharmaceutical and health care organizations was also calculated. To determine which institutions were prominent, eighteen lists were generated, one for each IPO year, of the top pharmaceutical and health care organizations by sales since 1979, using COMPUSTAT. International companies are only ranked by COMPUSTAT from 1988 onward, so the rankings used for this study were based on the top thirty US organizations from 1979 to 1987 and on the top US and international organizations from 1988 to 1996. For each year, the top thirty organizations in that given year were coded as prominent. These lists were supplemented with major pharmaceutical and health care companies that were private or based in Europe or Japan that were not listed in COMPUSTAT but were listed in PharmaBusiness and had comparable sales. The number of prominent *strategic alliances* was measured as the number of alliances with prominent pharmaceutical and/or health care companies the year prior to the offering, as defined above.

A number of control variables used here are similar to those used in the previous chapter, including measures for: *product stage* (of the most advanced product of the firm), *firm size*, *firm age*, amount of *private financing*, and *location* of firm. A control was also included for the type of business within the broad realm of biotechnology in which the firm operated. Additional controls accounted for characteristics of the TMT, including a variable for the size of a firm's upper echelon, because prior research has found this measure to be positively related to the success of entrepreneurial firms (Eisenhardt and Schoonhoven 1996; Higgins and Gulati 2003). For this measure, we used a count of the number of managing officers and outside board members who were listed on the firm's final prospectus. A variable for the *average prior position level* held by members of the firm's upper echelon, which reflects the calibre of the prior jobs the executives held, was also included.

RESULTS

Correlations between the main variables in this study are provided in Table 10.1. Table 10.2 presents the results from Heckman selection models in which the first stage predicted whether or not a company was able to go public and the second stage predicted IPO success. The first-stage probit models predicting whether a company was able to go public correctly classified 73 percent of the cases. As shown in Table 10.2, the analyses predicting IPO success begin with models that include firm and industry-level control variables, then main effects for firm partnerships and equity market uncertainty, then the interaction terms between equity market uncertainty and the specific forms of endorsement relations and strategic alliances, as suggested in hypotheses 1–3.

Hypothesis 1 predicted that having a prestigious VC partner when a firm goes public would be particularly beneficial to IPO success when the equity markets are cold for new issues. Model 3 in Table 10.2 tests this hypothesis. Because equity market uncertainty was operationalized as a continuous measure ranging from cold to hot, support for hypothesis 1 would be indicated if the results showed a significant and negative interaction effect between the equity market index and VC prominence. The findings reveal a significant and negative interaction, which supports hypothesis 1.

The results also support hypothesis 2, which predicted that underwriter prestige would be positively related to IPO success, particularly when the equity markets are relatively hot for new issues. As shown in model 3 of Table 10.2, the interaction term between equity index and underwriter prestige was positive and significant, as predicted. The main effect for underwriter prestige also remained significant and positively related to IPO success in all of our models, consistent with prior research (e.g. Carter and Manaster 1990). Model 5 of Table 10.2 included all of the interaction terms. The results supporting hypotheses 1 and 2 remained significant and in the directions predicted.

Hypothesis 3 predicted that prominent downstream strategic alliances would be positively related to IPO success, especially when the equity markets are relatively cold for new issues. This hypothesis was not supported; as shown in model 4 in Table 10.2, the interaction effect between equity market uncertainty and downstream alliances was not significant. In addition, no main effects for strategic alliances on IPO success were found.

With respect to the control variables, firm size and the amount of private financing a firm received prior to its IPO were significant, as was the size of

Table 10.1. Means, standard deviations, and correlations ($n = 299$)

Variable	X	SD	1	2	3	4	5	6	7	8	9	10	11	12	13	14
1. Firm age	4.90	2.89	—													
2. Firm size	85.64	120.85	0.08	—												
3. Location	0.50	0.50	0.07	0.05	—											
4. Product stage	4.65	2.82	0.23***	0.27***	0.07	—										
5. Private financing[a]	6.92	0.77	0.10†	0.28***	0.19***	0.12*	—									
6. Size of upper echelon	10.86	3.47	0.12*	0.29***	0.20***	0.11*	0.51***	—								
7. Average prior position of upper echelon	2.72	0.67	-0.08	-0.08	0.01	0.11†	0.06	-0.06	—							
8. Equity index	3.78	0.96	0.08	0.02	0.15**	0.02	0.19***	0.13*	-0.00	—						
9. VC prominence	0.32	0.47	-0.01	0.05	0.33***	0.04	0.20***	0.20***	0.05	0.17**	—					
10. Underwriter prestige[b]	7.63	1.95	0.13*	0.22***	0.12†	0.17*	0.41***	0.42***	0.13*	0.14*	0.27***	—				
11. Strategic alliances	0.52	0.88	0.09	0.05	0.05	-0.17**	0.24***	0.27***	-0.02	0.06	0.13*	0.20**	—			
12. Equity index × VC prominence	0.07	0.43	0.02	0.01	-0.02	0.01	-0.07	-0.05	0.01	-0.07	0.14*	-0.05	-0.02	—		
13. Equity index × Underwriter prestige[b]	0.25	1.99	0.10	-0.07	-0.13*	-0.08	-0.13*	-0.13*	-0.13*	-0.09	-0.05	-0.27***	-0.02	0.26***	—	
14. Equity index × Downstream alliances	0.05	0.82	-0.03	0.03	0.10	-0.06	-0.04	0.02	0.11†	-0.04	-0.02	-0.01	0.06	0.12*	0.20**	—
15. IPO success[c]	-0.01	0.87	0.18**	0.38***	0.25***	0.19***	0.58***	0.50***	0.04	0.17**	0.28***	0.54***	0.25***	-0.10†	-0.01	0.01

[a] Adjusted to constant 1996 dollars, then logged.

[b] $n = 244$ due to investment banks not ranked on Carter–Manaster scale.

[c] Based upon average standardized scores for firm net proceeds, pre-money market value, 90-day market value, and 180-day market value, adjusted to constant 1996 dollars and logged.

*$p \leq .05$; **$p \leq .01$; ***$p \leq .001$; †$p \leq .10$.

Table 10.2. The effects of interorganizational partnerships on IPO success[a,c]

	1		2		3		4		5	
Control variable										
Firm age	0.02	(0.01)	−0.01	(0.01)	−0.01	(0.01)	−0.01	(0.01)	−0.01	(0.01)
Firm size	0.00***	(0.00)	0.00***	(0.00)	0.00***	(0.00)	0.00***	(0.00)	0.00***	(0.00)
Location	0.08	(0.09)	0.01	(0.09)	0.06	(0.09)	0.00	(0.10)	0.06	(0.09)
Product stage	0.03†	(0.01)	0.02	(0.02)	0.02†	(0.01)	0.03	(0.02)	0.02	(0.01)
Private financing[b]	0.39***	(0.06)	0.28***	(0.06)	0.27***	(0.06)	0.06***	(0.06)	0.27***	(0.06)
Size of upper echelon	0.06***	(0.01)	0.04**	(0.01)	0.04**	(0.01)	0.04**	(0.01)	0.04**	(0.01)
Average prior position of upper echelon	0.07	(0.06)	0.04	(0.06)	0.06	(0.06)	0.03	(0.06)	0.06	(0.06)
Main effects										
Equity index	—		0.05	(0.04)	0.05	(0.04)	0.05	(0.04)	0.05	(0.04)
VC prominence	—		0.14	(0.09)	0.16†	(0.09)	0.14	(0.09)	0.16†	(0.09)
Underwriter prestige	—		0.12***	(0.02)	0.14***	(0.02)	0.12***	(0.02)	0.14***	(0.02)
Strategic alliances	—		0.05	(0.05)	0.05	(0.04)	0.05	(0.05)	0.05	(0.04)
Interaction effects										
Endorsement relations										
Equity index × VC prominence	—		—		−0.28**	(0.09)	—		−0.28**	(0.09)
Equity index × Underwriter prestige	—		—		0.09***	(0.02)	—		0.09***	(0.02)
Strategic alliances										
Equity index × Downstream alliances	—		—		—		0.03	(0.05)	−0.01	(0.04)
Constant	−03.03***	(0.43)	−1.93***	(0.49)	−2.00***	(0.47)	−1.94***	(0.49)	−1.99***	(0.47)
Wald χ^2	275.58***		272.08***		319.75***		272.70***		319.81***	
Rho	−0.49		−0.36		−0.31		−0.36		−0.31	
n	299		244		244		244		244	

[a] Unstandardized regression coefficients reported; standard errors in parentheses.

[b] Adjusted to 1996 dollars and logged.

[c] Based upon average standardized scores for firm net proceeds, pre-money market value, 90-day market value, and 180-day market value, adjusted to 1996 dollars and logged.

*p < .05; **p < .01; ***p < .001 (two-tailed tests); †p < .10.

a firm's upper echelon. And, as shown in two of the baseline models in the tables, firms with more advanced products tended to have more successful IPOs. With respect to the main effects, as expected, having a prestigious underwriter on board was consistently and positively related to IPO success. The main effect for VC prominence was marginally significant and positively related to IPO success as well. These latter results, when considered in tandem with the effects found for our interaction terms, highlight not only what types of ties benefit firms but also when such ties are particularly influential.

Conclusion

This chapter investigated the contingent value of interorganizational relationships and the network resources implicit in such ties at the time of a young firm's IPO, to determine which network ties matter when. While prior research has shown that network ties to prominent firms create network resources that can enhance new venture performance by signaling a firm's legitimacy to key external resource holders, the varying effects of such resources across tie type and market context have not been examined. The effects of various facets of network resources and the ties that generate them on firm outcomes are not uniform, but rather vary by tie type and level of uncertainty associated with the relevant equity market. This chapter demonstrates that different types of market uncertainty create different types of investor concerns and that signals from different network ties will be more or less influential in addressing those concerns based on the credibility and strength of those signals in the relevant market context.

Accordingly, results from our sample of biotechnology IPO firms show that young firms benefit from partnerships with prominent organizations in different ways and at different times: whereas partnerships with prestigious VCs positively affect IPO success when the equity markets are relatively cold for new issues, partnerships with prestigious underwriters positively affect IPO success when the equity markets are relatively hot. The results did not, however, yield significant effects for the contingent value of a new venture's strategic downstream partnerships on IPO success. The findings confirm the general thesis that network resources have effects that are contingent on both the nature of a firm's ties and on the uncertainty associated with the marketplace.

EXTENDING PRIOR RESEARCH ON INTERORGANIZATIONAL NETWORKS AND ENTREPRENEURSHIP

The present study extends prior research on interorganizational networks and entrepreneurship in several respects. First, it expands on the growing research in strategy and organizations on social networks. As discussed in previous chapters, examining the role of prior alliance networks and the resources they create provides a more social account of strategic alliances than traditional economic theories of firm behavior. This chapter not only assesses the multiple facets of network resources of IPO-bound entrepreneurial firms but also evaluates their impact on shaping the perceptions of investors at the time the firm goes public. Building on prior research, this chapter investigated the conditional effects of network resources. The contingency perspective built on theories of the social organization of attention and decision-making (Simon [1947] 1997; Ocasio 1997). Whereas prior research has suggested that certain prevailing industry-based logics may focus the attention of a firm's executives (Ocasio 1997; Thornton and Ocasio 1999), this study considers how the attention of external parties such as investors can be altered by the market context and how this, in turn, can affect firm performance. The results of this study showed that during cold markets, investor concerns center on avoiding type I errors (i.e. missing out on worthwhile investments) whereas during hot markets, investor concerns center on avoiding type II errors (i.e. investing in firms that are not worthwhile). Consequently, this chapter suggests that investors resolve these concerns by attending to the signals they receive based on network resources resulting from the endorsements and partnerships of the focal firm. The efficacies of these various ties are influenced by the market context at that time.

In addition to contributing to social network research, this study extends prior research on the sources and implications of uncertainty for new venture performance. Prior research has conceptualized uncertainty for start-up firms as associated with characteristics such as firm age and location (e.g. Sorenson and Audia 2000). This chapter extends these studies of endogenous sources of uncertainty by investigating the effects of uncertainty associated with the equity markets. Furthermore, by considering how the concerns investors face during a hot equity market differ substantially from those faced during a cold equity market, this chapter broadens previous unidimensional conceptualizations of uncertainty, which have tended to characterize the construct as either high or low (e.g. Stuart, Hoang, and Hybels 1999). The perspective put forth here is consistent with the view that uncertainty is a multidimensional phenomenon (Milliken 1987), which can alter the prevailing logic of strategic decision-making.

Finally, this study extends prior research on the implications of uncertainty for firm performance. Prior studies have focused on the effects of uncertainty on firms' strategic decision-making, such a firm's scope resulting from decisions regarding vertical integration (Sutcliffe and Zaheer 1998). This chapter, however, considered how the uncertainty impacting third-party stakeholders affects the performance of young firms. Thus, this study examined the implications of uncertainty for interorganizational perceptions that, in turn, affect firm performance.

Above all, this chapter demonstrates that network resources created from interorganizational ties are indeed a key factor in influencing the performance of entrepreneurial firms. Furthermore, the effects of network resources vary by type of tie and market context. By communicating valuable information regarding firm quality, network resources help start-up firms secure the endorsements and subsequent funding from investors necessary for success. Consequently, while the influence of network resources can vary with market environment and tie type, their role as sources and signals of valuable information is always notable.

11 Conclusions and future directions

The study of interorganizational networks has broadened significantly in the last decade, extending and building on past research that focused primarily on interpersonal networks. While early studies in this area helped to establish the role of networks in shaping organizational behavior and outcomes, recent research has explored nuances of the mechanisms underlying this interaction, delving into the contingencies around network effects. Along with this growth has come an explosion of new terminology, which, while seemingly related, often refers to somewhat distinct network constructs, making the accumulation of knowledge a greater challenge. The excessive use of jargon has now diluted the network metaphor almost to the point of irrelevance. In the introduction to his volume of seminal research on organizations and networks, Nohria (1992b) spoke to this issue when he pointed out the overinclusiveness of the network concept:

It is here that the failure to adopt a coherent network perspective becomes most problematic. It is precisely the lack of a clear understanding of a network perspective that has led to the rampant and indiscriminate use of the network metaphor to describe these new organizational forms (12).

In the decade and a half since this book was published, the explosion of research into firm-based networks has expanded this theme into new domains of organizational life. Despite the huge strides that have been made by the vast array of studies into a broad range of network-related phenomena, the aggregate contribution of this body of research toward the development of a coherent knowledge base has been limited by the rapidly growing catalog of network terms and constructs and the somewhat indiscriminate use of the network metaphor itself.

In this book, I have sought to illuminate the role of network resources to establish a conceptual anchor for this growing area of research. My hope is that scholars in the field may use this theme to develop and share a common vocabulary and to shape a more coherent body of present and future knowledge. Here, the term 'network resources' refers to valuable resources that stem from the ties a firm may have with key constituents outside its formal boundaries. In trying to bring together some of my prior research under this conceptual umbrella I was forced to be somewhat fluid with my definition of network resources. Furthermore, my research focus has primarily been on some of the informational advantages that accrue to firms from their network connections that in turn become valuable resources for those firms. As I highlighted at the outset, a firm's networks are conduits for not only valuable information but also material resources possessed by the partner firms. This is something I discuss in some of the last few chapters on entrepreneurial firms. A comprehensive account of the various aspects of network resources was not the focus of this book. My goal, however, was to delineate this core concept in both broad and specific terms, with the hope that such a treatment along with some concrete empirical illustrations of its application would serve as a prod and catalyst for future scholars to develop even sharper delineations and related taxonomies for this concept. Indeed, current research focuses on precisely this task (e.g. Gulati, Lavie, and Madhavan 2006; Lavie 2006).

This book has been unabashedly self-serving in that I have showcased only my own prior studies as exemplars of and building blocks for the core ideas underlying network resources. Because the chapters are based on articles published in the last decade, even the studies cited in those chapters are largely those that shaped my thinking at the time, and are in no way meant to reflect the current state-of-the art thinking in those realms. Numerous recent papers have explicitly embraced the term network resources or contributed findings that have a direct bearing on the core ideas that underlie the concept. I will not try to offer a comprehensive review of these ideas but will briefly highlight some of the papers that I have found beneficial as I have developed my own thinking on this concept. Thus, this chapter is organized around several key themes that highlight related research within the context of potential arenas for future inquiry.

Caveat emptor: The dark side of network resources

One of the obvious questions that arises from the overwhelmingly positive story that I have presented in this book is whether there are limits to the positive payoffs from the accumulation of network resources. This query could range from the narrow question of whether there are diminishing returns beyond a certain level of network resources, to the more extreme notion that such resources may generate negative returns or may even lead to more negative relations between individuals or organizations (e.g. Brass and Burkhardt 1992; Burt and Knez 1995; Labianca, Brass, and Gray 1998). Granovetter (1985) was perhaps the first to point out the possibility of limits to the benefits of networks when he suggested that extremely tight links between social actors present not only the prospect of great benefits but also ripe opportunities for malfeasance. The work of my colleague Brian Uzzi (1996, 1997) has also focused on the limits to the benefits of close connections and—in the extreme—the potential for such ties to negatively affect a firm's very survival. Subsequent research has also revealed that too-tight ties can restrict access to valuable information and otherwise create dysfunctional lock-ins in relationships (Gulati, Nohria, and Zaheer 2000; Li and Rowley 2002).

Chapter 4, which considers the role of board interlocks in the formation of new alliances, also hints at a specific cost associated with certain types of ties. In this chapter, I highlighted how board interlocks have a greater propensity to facilitate the formation of strategic alliances when board–management relations are characterized by cooperation. My examination of the differential implications of controlling versus cooperative boards, however, is not meant to imply that independent board control, which may deplete network resources in this particular context, is necessarily bad for a given organization as a whole. As recent events suggest, the presence of such control may be beneficial to shareholders. Because cooperative boards are more likely to serve as rich conduits of information regarding potential alliance opportunities, however, the potential dark side of controlling boards is their negative impact on the degree of information-sharing that takes place within a network of board interlocks. In delineating how specific types of network ties might diminish trust between individuals and groups, thus impeding alliance formation, this study investigates what Burt and Knez (1995: 261) termed the 'dark side' of social networks. This idea is also extended via the notion that both negative and positive ties between dyads of firms may be amplified by third-party connections in which the firms are embedded. Future research should explore the trade-offs between the governance benefits of controlling boards and the reduced trust and information-sharing that such boards engender in further detail.

The interplay between network and traditional resources

Generally, this book has shown how network resources can influence firm behavior and outcomes by enabling access to information and resources or by providing signals to key outsiders. These benefits in turn can lead to opportunities for firms to develop new ties, and can also affect various firm outcomes (Gulati 1993). One natural way to extend these ideas would be to conduct more research into the role that firms' network resources play in facilitating access to other, more traditional resources (e.g. Gulati, Nohria, and Zaheer 2000; Zaheer and Bell 2005). My focus in this book has primarily been on network resources that firms may accumulate by their participation in networks that are conduits of valuable information. As highlighted at the outset in this book, network resources may also result from a firm's channeling material resources that its partner makes available to it as well (e.g. Dyer 2000). I explicitly theorize about how network resources and the networks that engender them can provide firms with potential access to both information and material resources in Chapters 9 and 10 but am not able to empirically separate the flow of information from material resources through the networks. Such considerations are clearly important for a fuller account of network resources and the role they can play in shaping firm behavior and outcomes and are an important arena for future research.

A natural extension of this research would also be a deeper evaluation of how network resources can build on themselves and result in the accumulation of such resources. As I have suggested in several chapters of this book, research on social networks has typically treated network ties as exogenous; relatively little empirical work has examined the origins of sets of organizational ties that may in turn constitute a firm's network resources (Gulati 1998; Gulati and Gargiulo 1999). Chapters 2 and 3, in contrast, considered how prior ties may shape the creation of subsequent alliances, suggesting that social networks expand via an endogenous network dynamic. Similarly, Chapter 4 asserted that both interlocks (our key independent variable) and joint ventures (our dependent variable) are relationships that accumulate into a network of social resources. This latter study specifically examined the influence of board interlocks on the creation of strategic alliances. As such, it focused on the multiple types of ties in which firms are embedded and the relationships among these ties. The results of this study suggest that new networks can result from a social process that is initiated by preexisting ties. One reason why this study is distinctive is because the two networks considered exist at different levels of analysis: the relationships between corporate leaders that make up board interlocks are individual-level ties while strategic alliances are interorganizational relationships that occur across firms. The study featured in Chapter 9 is similar in that it also assessed the effects of individual-level variables (upper echelon's career history) on firm-level outcomes (affiliations with investment banks). Beyond these studies, however, there has been very little empirical research that has considered whether and how interpersonal ties influence interorganizational bonds (some exceptions include work by Galaskiewicz (1985b) and Zaheer, McEvily, and Perrone (1998)). Thus, the findings reported in Chapters 4 and 9 provide new impetus for additional research that links microlevel affiliations to macrolevel relationships (Coleman 1990).

Another important question that merits further investigation has to do with the interplay between network resources and those already resident within firms in shaping behavior and outcomes. Several studies have begun this effort by considering how network resources work *in combination* with resources that are already resident within firms to shape firm outcomes (e.g. Hagedoorn and Schakenraad 1994; Ahuja 2000a, 2000b; Chung, Singh, and Lee 2000).

In these studies, researchers have explicitly considered how material resources like R&D spending and a firm's network of connections can individually and together influence firm outcomes. In addition to the immediate synergies generated from combinations involving network resources and internal firm resources, firms may benefit by learning and internalizing network resources as well as from the appreciation in the value of their internal resources once network resources become available (e.g. Lavie 2006). Although these investigations have broadened our understanding of the complex interplay between network and other types of resources, there is still ample space for further research in this area. One way to extend such research would be to conduct a more detailed study, one that explicitly incorporates several types of resources and capabilities in an effort to understand the coevolution of network resources and other firm-level assets resident within their boundaries.

The heterogeneity of network resources

It is my hope that this book will motivate future researchers to more sharply delineate the types of networks that can shape organizational behavior and outcomes. This section promotes this objective by detailing some dimensions that can be used to distinguish between the various networks that contribute to a firm's accumulation of network resources. Heterogeneity in a firm's network resources can typically be described in terms of three different axes: (*a*) the *level of a firm's ties*, which would entail a consideration of both interpersonal and interorganizational links and their underlying mechanisms for influencing behavior and outcomes; (*b*) *the nature and types of a firm's ties*, requiring a more careful consideration of the content of past and current ties; and (*c*) the *types of partners* to which those ties connect the firm, requiring an understanding of the firm's partners' attributes.

THE LEVEL OF A FIRM'S TIES

With respect to the level of firms' network resources, this book was primarily focused on those resources that arise from firms' *interorganizational ties*. Yet we recognize that organizations are often connected not only by links at the organizational level but also by the numerous *interpersonal ties* among organizational agents. In this book, I considered some of the individual-level connections that link firms. In Chapter 4, for example, I discussed board of director interlocks as a network resource that is likely to shape firm behavior.

In Chapter 9, the interpersonal ties implicit in upper echelon affiliations were also considered network resources for entrepreneurial firms. Recent research has similarly expanded our understanding of interorganizational networks by specifically examining interpersonal ties such as those that exist within CEO networks (e.g. McDonald and Westphal 2003) and those of mid-level managers (e.g. Rosenkopf, Metiu, and George 2001). These studies have put forward the compelling argument that both the interorganizational ties of firms and the interpersonal ties of organizational agents shape the extent to which network resources are enjoyed by firms. Given the multilevel nature of ties that constitute firms' network resources, an important arena for future research is consideration of the independent and interactive effects of inter-personal and interorganizational ties on firm behavior and outcomes.

THE NATURE AND TYPES OF A FIRM'S TIES

Another way to distinguish between different network ties is to consider the specific types of connections that a set of ties represents and the underlying mechanisms through which they benefit participating firms. Ultimately, if we are to claim that a firm's networks give it access to network resources, it is important to clearly and fully explicate the exact nature of resources and information that are channeled through those ties and precisely how they may benefit participating firms. In recent years, several trends have contributed to scholars' increased focus on the diverse nature of ties from which firms accumulate their network resources. One such trend is researchers' increased motivation to explore the role of networks in the domain of entrepreneurial firms (see e.g. the introduction to the special issue of *Strategic Management Journal* edited by Hitt, Ireland, Camp, and Sexton 2001). Not only is this domain data-rich, but it is also one in which a broad variety of networks have become immensely consequential for firms. Given the relatively small size of most nascent firms and their significant vulnerability to environmental pressures, plausible linkages may be drawn between their network resources and immediate economic outcomes (e.g. Stuart, Hoang, and Hybels 1999; Baum, Calabrese, and Silverman 2000; Rothaermel 2001; Pollock and Rindova 2003). The investigations featured in Chapters 9 and 10 provide a window into the growing body of research on entrepreneurial firm ties, but represent only a fraction of the studies that have considered the network-resource-related ties of young firms. These connections range from those with other entre-preneurial firms to ties with large incumbents and financing entities, such as venture capitalists and investment banks, forcing researchers to consider a broad array of links that influence firm behavior and outcomes. Indeed, Chapter 10 highlights the richness of research opportunities in this area not only by looking at the diversity of ties entrepreneurial firms may enter but also by considering how their relative influence may vary based on market context, suggesting that the relative efficacy of network resources may be modulated by environmental factors. In spite of the number of studies that have been conducted in this space, this arena remains a fruitful area for future research, with a number of important questions still to be answered around both the antecedents and consequences of network resources for entrepreneurial firms.

Another trend spurring a closer look at the diverse types of firm ties that exist is the growing tendency of enterprises to redefine the scope of their operations and simultaneously enter into vertical partnerships (with suppliers of products and services) and horizontal alliances (with partners who may offer complementary goods and services). This development has forced researchers to more explicitly consider the heterogeneity of firm ties as firms enter alliances at distinct points in their value chain, with very different entities, and for widely different reasons (Gulati and Kletter 2005). As prior research suggests (e.g. Zaheer and Venkatraman 1995; Dyer 2000), not only may firms enter into ties at distinct points in their value chain, but the nature of those ties in terms of their quality of interaction is also likely to vary significantly, forcing researchers to confront the heterogeneity of ties and consider their varying implications for firms (e.g. Gulati, Lawrence, and Puranam 2005; Gulati and Sytch 2006a).

While early research on firm ties focused more on traditional joint manufacturing and marketing agreements under the rubric of interorganizational strategic alliances, the more recent focus on small entrepreneurial firms and the growing vertical and horizontal restructuring of large-firms architecture have now drawn researchers to consider the heterogeneity of various types of ties. One piece of evidence for this is that scholars have been more thorough and specific in distinguishing between component procurement (Gulati and Sytch 2006a), research and development (Powell et al. 2005; Sytch and Gulati 2006), venture capital funding (e.g. Lee, Lee, and Pennings 2001; Baum and Silverman 2004) and investment bank advisory ties (e.g. Stuart, Hoang, and Hybels 1999; Higgins and Gulati 2006), among others. While many still elect to group these studies together when discussing network research findings, it is essential for researchers to recognize that these distinct types of ties can give rise to differential portfolios of network resources and thus generate different consequences for firms. In Chapter 8, I point out this trend and propose that we maintain a holistic perspective on firm ties while at the same time respecting the heterogeneity of the connections that shape a firm's network resources. Each type of tie that a firm may enter may be further classified in terms of the intensity of interaction between the organizations that have formed them. Lastly, several other categories of firm ties remain to be examined in depth. For example, scholars may further broaden the array of interorganizational ties that constitute a firm's network resources by delving into its connections with nonprofit and government agencies. They may also examine the extent to which these different types of ties complement or substitute for each other as sources of network resources.

THE TYPES OF PARTNERS CONNECTED TO FIRMS

The third axis that can be used to describe a firm's network resources concerns the unique features of the partners to which the firm is connected. Before we even consider how the heterogeneity of partners may shape a firm's access to network resources it is important for researchers to more fully and clearly articulate whether network resources are resident in the ties themselves or primarily in the partners with whom firms are connected through those ties (e.g. Gulati, Lavie, and Madhavan 2006). This is a subtle yet important distinction since the former implies that to fully grasp network resources we need to delve deeply into the nature of the ties a firm enters while the latter implies a more detailed assessment of the partners to whom a firm may be connected through those ties. From the definition of network resources adopted here, it is clear that network resources accrue to firms because its networks are conduits of valuable information and resources from its partners. As a result, the type of partners a firm may have in its network is also likely to shape its cumulative network resource base. Prior work on status (e.g. Podolny 1993) and relational capabilities (Dyer and Singh 1998; Sytch and Gulati 2006) suggests that firms could build very distinct network resource bases that are contingent on their partners and the relative efficacies of these entities. Other characteristics of a firm's partners that could influence the formation and impact of network resources include its partners' technological expertise (Stuart, Hoang, and Hybels 1999) and the complementarity of their resource bases relative to those of the focal firm (e.g. Gulati 1995b; Gulati and Gargiulo 1999; Chung, Singh and Lee 2000). Given these findings, it would be immensely valuable for future researchers to build a taxonomy of partner attributes that are likely to influence a firm's access to network resources.

This multifaceted axis on which a firm's network resources could be assessed offers several valuable directions for future research. But such investigations will occur only when researchers explicitly embrace the diversity of ties that may shape a firm's access to network resources and begin to develop a shared vocabulary and taxonomy for these connections. Researchers have begun to make significant strides in this regard, with recent papers that explicate some of the conceptual underpinnings of such resources by drawing on the conceptual foundations of the resource-based view (Gnyawali and Madhavan 2001; Lavie 2006). In some follow-up research, my colleagues and I (Gulati, Lavie, and Madhavan 2006) seek to provide further clarity regarding the mechanisms by which networks may shape firm behavior and outcomes.

From individual ties to portfolios

As firms enter ties with external entities with growing frequency, many have found themselves with dozens of partnerships, if not more—especially in the case of larger companies. While issues concerning the management of individual ties are still important and merit further consideration, new issues around the management of a portfolio of ties have also arisen. Indeed, in recent years, researchers studying the formation of alliances in particular have invoked the 'portfolio' metaphor to suggest that the ties of a firm operate both independently and in aggregate (e.g. Stuart 2000; Bamford and Ernst 2002; Kale, Dyer, and Singh 2002; Parise and Casher 2003; Pinar and Eisenhardt 2005; Reuer and Ragozzino 2006).

The fact that a firm may have a wide array of ties suggests that it has to simultaneously manage this portfolio and address potentially conflicting demands from multiple partners. Furthermore, if the firm is centrally placed in a network, it must pay particular attention to a series of strategic and organizational issues (Lorenzoni and Baden-Fuller 1995). Thus, developing a more comprehensive portfolio perspective on ties that fully explicates how the sum of the parts resulting from individual ties aggregate or not to a whole is important—especially given the increasing number of firms that are facing these issues. There is also clearly room for further research to explicate the role that such portfolios may play in shaping a firm's access to network resources.

Consideration of how a firm's portfolio of ties can lead to the accumulation of network resources also opens up numerous questions about the cooperative capabilities of firms. For instance, evidence suggests that there may be systematic differences in the cooperative capabilities that firms build as they gain experience with alliances, and that the extent of this learning may affect their success with alliances and in turn shape their relative access to alliance-based network resources (Lyles 1988; Anand and Khanna 2000a; Hoang and Rothaermel 2005; Gulati and Sytch 2006b). This body of work poses questions about what these alliance-related capabilities are and what systematic tactics firms use to internalize them (e.g. Dyer and Singh 1998). Some of these capabilities appear to include: identifying valuable alliance opportunities and good partners, using appropriate governance mechanisms, developing interfirm knowledge-sharing routines, making requisite relationship-specific asset investments, and initiating necessary changes to the evolving partnership while managing partner expectations. There is still much room to expand on these ideas and to consider how firms can accumulate and aggregate their disparate ties into mutually reinforcing network resources while at the same time minimizing potential trade-offs that may arise with such aggregation.

Network resources within constellations of firms

The focus of this book has been on the relationship between firms' network resources and their behavior and relative success. In an increasingly networked world where competition occurs not only between firms but also among coalitions of companies (e.g. Nohria and Garcia-Pont 1991; Gomes-Casseres 1994, 1996), it is natural to ask whether influential network resources may also be possessed by agglomerations of firms. For example, a recent study by Venkatraman and Lee (2004) examined how the network structure of product platforms in the US video game industry impacts product launches. Along similar lines, Gomes-Casseres (1994) has looked at several industries in which networks, rather than firms, have become the organizing level at which firms compete. Such studies suggest that the performance of a firm is influenced by the networks to which it belongs. This line of work has been expanded to consider the relative success of competing networks of firms in particular geographic regions (Saxenian 1990; Gerlach 1992). While these researchers do not bring up network resources per se, their studies provide strong evidence that we could extend several network resource concepts from the domain of individual firms to the study of coalitions of firms.

Such network-focused approaches may be further refined by identifying specific network characteristics that are more likely to result in benefits for members of a network. For instance, in an ongoing study of hospitals and health care networks, my colleagues and I suggest that not all networks provide equal benefits to members (Westphal, Gulati, and Shortell 1997). We have identified several key network-based factors that shape the effects of network membership on firm performance—these may help explain why some networks provide greater benefits than others. A natural extension of these studies would be to look not only at the network characteristics but also at the positions of the individual organizations within the network. Such research could provide us with insights regarding the informational and control benefits that may result from particular locations in specific networks. Furthermore, it could help us to assess performance effects across the multiplicity of networks in which firms are embedded. Other possible lines of inquiry include who controls the network and why, and possible limits of network growth.

Network resources in institutional context

The unique features of the institutional environment in which firms reside are likely to influence access to network resources (e.g. Dacin, Hitt, and Levitas 1997). For instance, the strength of the appropriability regime of the industry, or the degree to which firms are able to capture the rents generated by their innovations, may have enormous implications for how firms elect to accumulate network resources and derive benefits from them (cf. Teece 1986; Oxley 1997; Gulati and Singh 1998). More interestingly, the relationship here could be reciprocal, as for instance the strength of the appropriability regime in an industry may be shaped by the distribution of network resources in that sector. In sectors with dense sets of ties among firms and easy access to network resources, the appropriability regime is likely to be stronger due to the creation of reputational circuits that make participating firms less likely to engage in malfeasance. Additionally, considerations of legitimacy may vary across institutional environments, at the extreme overshadowing the demands of the immediate task environment and leading firms in those environments to pursue unique stocks of network resources (cf. Meyer and Rowan 1977).

In my own research, I have uncovered interesting variations in the propensity of firms to pursue network resources, and such patterns may be linked to the institutional context. For example, in the study described in Chapter 2, I found systematic cross-industry differences in the propensity of firms to acquire new network resources (Gulati 1999). These effects were no longer significant once I included measures for network resources. This indicates that important differences in inherent propensities for alliances across sectors may be explained by systematic differences in network resources available to firms across those sectors.

My research summarized in Chapters 5 and 6 revealed intriguing results when comparing not only the variations in alliance contracts between industries but also the variations between domestic and cross-border collaborative ties of American and Japanese firms (Gulati and Singh 1998). The comparison of local and cross-regional alliances was broadly consistent with our expectations of greater trust in the former than the latter, but our breakdown of local alliances by region suggests some provocative issues not fully explored in the study. While the results for European alliances were consistent with our predictions, contrary to our expectations, Japanese domestic alliances were no different from cross-regional alliances in their use of minority equity investments or contractual alliances. Even more conspicuous was the absence of significant differences in the governance structures of alliances between American partners and cross-regional alliances. While these mixed results suggest some systematic differences in the level of trust between local and cross-regional alliances, as reflected by the types of alliance governance structure that were used, there are several alternative interpretations. The differences, at least for European alliances and some Japanese alliances, may stem from appropriation concerns resulting from greater difficulties in specifying and enforcing property rights and monitoring problems in cross-regional alliances relative to local ones, or they may be due to the greater coordination challenges and costs of cross-regional alliances. Local alliances in each region may also be influenced by geography-specific institutional contexts deeply embedded in normative practices and authority structures (Hamilton and Biggart 1988). Or perhaps there are historical and legal circumstances that mandate or encourage the use of particular governance structures for alliances. But it was beyond the scope of the study to examine fully the mechanisms underlying geography-based differences in alliance governance structure, as well as the lack of consistency in results by region. Thus, these areas of inquiry, along with those concerning sectoral differences, merit further exploration.

Network resources as explanations for behavior and outcomes

I have tried to demonstrate that network resources are powerful determinants of a firm's behavior and performance (for two excellent reviews of this burgeoning literature, see Kilduff and Tsai 2003; Monge and Contractor 2003). In the first half of this book, this idea was supported by studies that documented the relationship between a firm's current and prior ties and its propensity to enter into new ties. The rationale for the observed relationship was that a firm's current and prior network ties are conduits of valuable information that in turn expose it to new alliance opportunities and reduce the level of uncertainty that the firm faces regarding potential partner capabilities and behavior. While linking network resources to such organizational actions continues to be an important arena for future research, other important questions remain regarding the specific mechanisms that underlie such relationships.

There is also considerable room for further exploration of the role of network resources in shaping the governance structure of interorganizational relationships. In Chapters 5 and 6, I provide some evidence for the role that network resources play in shaping the contractual agreements used in new alliances. These ideas have since been refined and extended in subsequent research that has recast the selection of a governance structure as a choice that allows us to ask the broader question of whether or not formal and informal controls are substitutive or complementary in nature (e.g. Das and Teng 1998; Kale, Singh, and Perlmutter 2000; Poppo and Zenger 2002; Casciaro 2003; Gulati, Lawrence, and Puranam 2005; Gulati and Nickerson 2006; Gulati and Sytch 2006b). While most of these studies consider the antecedents of governance choice, few if any of them also consider and empirically assess the consequences of governance choice. Thus, this remains an important arena for future research (e.g. Gulati, Lawrence, and Puranam 2005). More broadly, consideration of how network resources may shape and be shaped by governance structures—and how such interactions may influence firm outcomes also remains a viable frontier for future research.

In the third section of the book, I focused more on the performance consequences of network resources—primarily by highlighting early research that I conducted in this area. There is now a growing body of research that does not allude to network resources per se, but does reveal how a firm's interorganizational ties may or may not have significant performance implications (e.g. Hagedoorn and Schakenraad 1994; Stuart 2000; Ahuja 2000a). These ideas have been further developed to include not only a firm's cumulative experience with alliances but also the specific nature of that experience (e.g. Reuer, Zollo, and Singh 2002; Hoang and Rothaermel 2005; Sytch and Gulati 2006) and of prescribed roles within those firms (e.g. Kale, Dyer, and Singh 2002). Others have extended the performance outcomes associated with network resources beyond proximate measures to more nuanced ones, such as the cumulative growth option value (e.g. Tong, Reuer, and Peng 2007).

Given the rich heterogeneity of network resources, scholars have also begun to explore how different facets of network resources shape firms' behavior and performance. Some researchers, for example, have examined how different types of ties have a differential impact on firm outcomes (e.g. Rowley, Behrens, and Krackhardt 2000). Others have sought to develop a more contingent argument that shows how different types of networks exert different effects on firm outcomes depending on the market context (Sarkar, Echambadi, and Harrison 2001; Gulati and Higgins 2003) or the firm's developmental stage (Lechner and Dowling 2003). Focusing on the potential transitivity of network resources, others have shown how ties formed in one realm may have beneficial consequences in others (e.g. Jensen 2003). Finally, some scholars have reframed the question to suggest that we consider carefully the very notion that networks of any kind are likely to shape firm behavior and outcomes (e.g. Rangan 2000).

Given these different streams of research, it is clear that linking network resources to concrete performance outcomes remains an important frontier for future research. A critical prerequisite for effectively analyzing the behavioral and performance impact of network resources, however, is to delve more deeply into the ties we know about and to delineate the precise behavioral mechanisms through which those ties shape behavior and outcomes (e.g. Gulati and Sytch 2006a; Hoetker, Swaminathan, and Mitchell 2006; Reuer and Arino 2006). If we are to move beyond using network resources as a crutch or catch-all for assessing the role of networks in economic life, we must be much more deliberate and precise in articulating the underlying mechanisms through which those network resources exert their effects. One line of thinking that scholars could consider in this regard is that network resources can simultaneously affect firms' abilities to appropriate *and* create value in various interorganizational collaborations (e.g. Gulati and Wang

2003; Gulati and Sytch 2006*a*; Sytch and Gulati 2006). Because the tactics for capturing a bigger share of the pie and those for expanding the pie itself have very different underpinnings and are often guided by different logics of action, they are also likely to have unique implications for firms' performance. One way to better understand these implications may be to study the dynamic interaction processes between alliance partners over time. Such processes may have a profound influence on the ongoing value creation and appropriation that occurs between firms and hence, shape each partner's respective access to the network resources generated by those ties (Ring and Van de Ven 1992, 1994; Doz 1996; Doz and Hamel 1998).

Finally, it is also likely that a firm's network resources not only influence the creation of new ties but also influence the performance of the ties themselves—and consequently, the performance of firms participating in such ties. Thus far, studies of how network resources impact firm behavior and firm performance have proceeded separately—yet such studies are interconnected and thus merit simultaneous consideration. For example, if network resources resulting from a firm's network of prior alliances have consequences for the relative success of individual alliances that the firm enters, then they may have long-term performance consequences for the firm as well. Furthermore, a natural extension of the study described in Chapter 4 could consider the implications of board interlocks not only for the creation of new alliances but also for organizational outcomes. One could examine, for instance, whether the nature of prior relationships (i.e. cooperative or controlling) between top managers and boards affects the likelihood of forming strategic alliances with other specific firms *and* the subsequent success of those strategies. In an insightful study, Baker (1984) suggested that distinct social structural patterns in the stock options market can alter the direction and magnitude of option price volatility. Similarly, the social structure of board interlocks that influence the creation of alliances may influence the relative terms of trade between alliance partners and also dampen the volatility that usually occurs in such partnerships. On one hand, good rapport between top managers involved in cooperative relationships on third-company boards may lead to more successful alliances between their companies by facilitating efforts to flexibly adjust the roles and responsibilities of alliance partners as environmental conditions change over time. On the other hand, in-group biases resulting from CEO–board cooperation may lead to excessive levels of trust between top managers, such that each party becomes overly optimistic about the capabilities and contributions of the other. Thus, empirical research could help determine how initial relationships between corporate leaders moderate the consequences of alliance formation. Such possibilities suggest that considering behavior and performance simultaneously is an important and fruitful direction for future research.

Managerial implications

By using the term 'resource' so centrally here I am clearly implying that networks have beneficial consequences for those firms endowed with them (notwithstanding the section titled 'Caveat Emptor'). Yet we must go beyond descriptive theory and empirical demonstrations of the benefits of network resources to articulating pathways for firms to secure such resources.

The growing recognition among managers that interorganizational ties are key strategic resources is partially offset by frustration that such ties are difficult to manage and carry a high failure rate. In response, a number of studies have considered in detail some of the behavioral dynamics underlying individual alliances and uncovered some of the managerial practices that may impact their relative success. The rich insights from these detailed clinical and theoretical accounts have significantly advanced our understanding of the dynamics within alliances (e.g. Ring and Van de Ven 1992, 1994; Gulati, Khanna, and Nohria 1994; Doz 1996). Nevertheless, the focus of these efforts has remained at the dyadic level of exchange, with a primary emphasis on interpartner dynamics. Similar behavioral patterns can occur within multifirm networks as well, but remain to be explored in detail (for an exception see Dialdin 2004).

There is now a parallel stream of research on some of the dynamics that underlie a firm's ability to manage its collection of interorganizational ties. Studies in this area have introduced the idea of 'relational capability', which denotes a number of related abilities including: effective integration and exchange of resources in interorganizational collaboration, identification of valuable alliance opportunities and good partners, use of appropriate governance mechanisms for ties, development of interfirm knowledge-sharing routines, appropriate investment in relationship-specific assets, initiation of necessary changes to the partnership as it evolves, and management of partner expectations (Dyer and Singh 1998; Kale, Dyer, and Singh 2002). Research on relational capabilities has come a long way, from a deeper assessment of the management of individual ties to a richer understanding of how firms leverage and coordinate their collection or portfolio of ties (e.g. Doz and Hamel 1998; Dyer 2000; Dyer and Nobeoka 2000; Gulati and Kletter 2005). Future research should consider in further detail some of the managerial processes that allow firms to accumulate such resources. Such capabilities could include scanning, screening, structuring, and managing interorganizational ties to minimize the costs of collaboration while maximizing the value created. On the cost side, in particular, recent studies have gone beyond looking at the costs associated with the risks of partner malfeasance to the costs associated with interorganizational task-coordination (e.g. Gulati and Singh 1998; Gulati, Lawrence and Puranam 2005). An important goal for future research would be to further disentangle these two costs in interorganizational ties and to consider how managerial practices focused on both types of costs may influence the efficacy of firm efforts to accumulate and develop network resources. Furthermore, more detailed studies could examine how firms cross-leverage different forms of network resources for maximum value creation.

Despite efforts by researchers to unpack a firm's relational capabilities, relatively little is known about the role of key individuals involved in the management of a firm's ties with disparate entities. For example, we know that interpersonal contacts between firms can affect intrafirm decision-making (Gulati 1993), as boundary-spanning individuals can have crucial influence on the decisions of their partner organizations (e.g. Kale, Dyer, and Singh 2002). Despite some advances we have made in this realm, a number of interesting arenas still remain for future research. For instance, when alliances entail the creation of new entities, such as joint ventures, they can also lead to conflicting identities for participating individuals, who may be torn between loyalties to the venture itself and to their parent organizations. Furthermore, when network-level decisions must be made among clusters of firms, specific multi-lateral negotiations and dynamics may be poorly understood. Firms may also use their network contacts to create control benefits proactively by utilizing their advantageous position in social networks to play one partner against the other. They may also seek to manage their networks to sustain advantages (Lorenzoni and Baden-Fuller 1995). Little is known about some of these intriguing behavioral dynamics that underlie complex interorganizational ties that generate network resources for those firms.

☐ APPENDIX 1 DATABASES

Alliance Formation Database (Used in Chapters 2 and 3)

The data for these studies were gathered from a variety of sources. Initially, I conducted field interviews with 153 managers in 11 large multinational corporations over a 2-year period (Gulati 1993). These managers typically had authority over alliance decisions. The open-ended interviews were unstructured and conducted to broadly understand the factors associated with decisions to enter new alliances. These interviews provided initial clues regarding the importance of a firm's network of prior ties in alliance formation, as well as insights into the mechanisms underlying this relationship.

The models in Chapters 2 and 3 were tested using longitudinal data on strategic alliances in a sample of American, European, and Japanese organizations in three industries from 1981 to 1989. Data were collected on a sample of 166 organizations operating in the new materials, industrial automation, and automotive product sectors. The selected panels included 50–60 of the largest publicly traded organizations within each sector, and I estimated an organization's size from its sector sales as reported in various industry sources. Industry panels were also checked with multiple experts to ensure they included all prominent competitors in each of the sectors. This design led to the inclusion of 62 organizations in new materials, 52 in automotive products, and 52 in industrial automation. Of these organizations, 54 were American, 66 Japanese, and 46 European.

For each organization, financial data were collected for each year between 1980 and 1989 from *Worldscope*, which provides detailed information about prominent organizations in a wide range of sectors. For organizations not reported in *Worldscope*, data were obtained from *COMPUSTAT* for US organizations, *Nikkei* for Japanese organizations, and *Disclosure* for European organizations. For a number of Japanese organizations, data were also obtained from *Daewoo Investor's Research Guide*.[1] Information identifying the industry subsegment in which each organization had expertise was also collected from numerous industry-specific trade journals about the subsegment of its industry within which it had expertise. To make sure that these classifications were correctly recorded, they were cross-checked with multiple experts from each of the industries.

---

[1] For a few organizations, financial data were available only for some years. The gaps typically resulted from the fact that *Worldscope* reports organization data in five-year continuous segments and omits some organizations from some volumes. One alternative for dealing with this problem would have been to use the 'available-case method', including only cases with the variables of interest in the analysis. Although such an approach is straightforward, it poses a number of problems, including variability in the sample base as the variables included in models change. Furthermore, it makes little sense to exclude entire cases simply because a single variable is missing. Thus, I chose to estimate the missing data using a time-trend-based imputation (Little and Rubin 1987). This procedure took into account that the financial outcome for an organization is the result of its own past actions as well as broad trends within its industry. I retained a dummy variable indicating imputation and later compared the results obtained with and without imputed values.

Information on the alliances formed in the three panels of organizations was derived from a much larger and more comprehensive dataset that includes information on over 2,400 alliances formed by American, European, and Japanese organizations in the three focal sectors from 1970 to 1989. More than half the data came from the Cooperative Agreements and Technology Indicators (CATI) database created by researchers at the Maastricht Economic Research Institute on Innovation and Technology (MERIT) at the University of Limburg. Additional alliance data were collected from numerous other sources, including industry reports and industry-specific articles reporting alliances. For the automotive industry, these sources included *Automotive News*, *Ward's Automotive Reports*, *U.S. Auto Industry Report*, *Motor Industry of Japan*, and the *Japanese Auto Manufacturers Forum*; for the industrial automation sector, *Managing Automation (1988–89)*; for the new materials sector, reports from the Office of Technology Assessment and the Organization for Economic Cooperation and Development; and for all sectors, Predicast's *Funk and Scott Index of Corporate Change*. In all instances, only alliances that had actually been formed were recorded. Consequently, the study excluded reports of probable alliances. The goal of this data collection was to compile the most comprehensive database of alliances within each focal sector that was possible, in terms of both depth and duration of coverage.

One concern with such a longitudinal design is left-censoring because many of the sample firms existed prior to the start of the alliance observation period in 1981. To avoid this problem, additional alliance data were collected for the alliance activity of this sample of firms for an additional eleven years, dating back to 1970. These data only confirmed what previous studies have reported, namely that alliance activity was only a trickle until 1980, when it surged (Harrigan 1986).

Constructing the Social Networks (Relates to Chapters 2 and 3)

To compute the social structural measures associated with these studies, adjacency matrices were constructed to represent the relationships between the actors in a network. Because the focus here was on alliances formed within industries, separate matrices were computed for each industry and year. Each matrix included all alliance activity among industry panel members up to the prior year. Additional data on alliances announced by the panel members between 1970 and 1980 were entered into the initial matrix for 1981 to minimize left-censorship effects. All matrices were entered into UCINET IV, a versatile software package that allows the computation of various network measures (Borgatti, Everett, and Freeman 1992).

To construct the social networks of past alliances, three choices were made about how to treat alliances. The first relates to the treatment of different types of alliances. Alliances range from equity joint ventures in which partners are closely intertwined, at one extreme, to arm's length licensing agreements at the other. Each type entails varying levels of organizational commitment and leads to differing levels of organizational interdependence. Thus, it is difficult to justify treating all alliances identically. In constructing the adjacency matrices, a decision was made to weight each type of alliance on the basis of the resulting relationship's strength. The weighting scheme, ranging from 1 (weak) to 7 (strong), was based on prior schemes used in alliance research (Contractor and Lorange 1988; Nohria and Garcia-Pont 1991). To ensure the robustness of the findings, the results were tested against those obtained using a simple dichotomous matrix that treated all alliances as the same.

The second methodological choice relates to the treatment of multiple ties between two firms over the observed time period. Three possible approaches were identified: (*a*) using an additive measure that yielded a higher score as firms made multiple ties, (*b*) adding the scores and normalizing them by the maximum score possible in that year, and (*c*) using a Guttman scale to capture the score of the strongest alliance the firms had formed. A Guttman scale was used for the final analysis, but the results obtained were compared against those yielded by the other two approaches.

The third choice relates to how long past alliances are likely to influence current alliance formation. One possibility was to include all past alliances in a social network, which meant assuming that any prior tie, no matter how long ago it occurred, would moderate firm behavior. Another possibility was to use a 'moving window', which implied that only the relationships formed in the previous few years affected current behavior. The first approach, which defined a social network of alliances to include all alliance activity that had taken place until the year before a given year, was used in Chapters 2 and 3. These results were compared against those obtained by using a five-year moving window because recent research suggests that the lifespan for alliances is usually no more than that length of time (Kogut 1988*b*, 1989). A follow-up study that I describe at the end of Chapter 4 (Gulati and Gargiulo 1999) uses a five-year moving window and, in that case, obtained results are compared against a network of cumulative ties.

Board and Alliance Database (Used in Chapter 4)

The research in this chapter is based on a sample of companies that included 600 firms selected from the Fortune and Forbes 500 indexes of US industrial and service firms. Both archival and survey-based data on these firms were collected. Archival information was collected on alliances formed, board interlocks and other board characteristics, strategic variables, and financial data. To measure board control and CEO–board cooperation, a questionnaire survey was distributed by my coauthor Jim Westphal in April 1995 to all CEOs of the 600 firms. In addition, to assess interrater reliability, another questionnaire was sent to individuals serving as outside directors at one or more companies whose CEO responded (*n* = 1,312 directors).

Surveys of top managers have notoriously low response rates. To ensure the highest possible response in this case, the following steps were taken by my coauthor (Forsythe 1977; Groves, Cialdini, and Couper 1992; Fowler 1993). First, an in-depth pretest was used to refine the format and length of the survey. Second, the cover letter linked the present study with prior surveys on top management issues that were conducted by a major business school, while noting that hundreds of their peers had responded to the prior surveys. The letter also highlighted the need for research on CEO–board relations, which also engaged respondents' natural interest in the topic (see Groves, Cialdini, and Couper 1992). Third, nonrespondents were sent a second letter with a new questionnaire about 21 days after the initial mailing. As a result of these efforts, 263 of the 600 CEOs in the sample frame responded, a response rate of 44 percent. Moreover, 564 of the 1,312 outside directors responded, yielding a response rate of

43 percent. These response rates are high compared with other top management surveys (Pettigrew 1992).

To check for nonresponse bias, respondents and nonrespondents were compared across a variety of firm characteristics using the Kolmogorov–Smirnov two-sample test (Siegel and Castellan 1988). This assesses whether significant differences exist between the distribution of respondents and nonrespondents for a given variable. The results of this test (not included here) suggest that respondents and nonrespondents came from the same population. We also assessed nonresponse bias according to the presence or absence of specific board structures and practices thought to indicate board control (cf. Hoskisson, Johnson, and Moesel 1994; Belliveau, O'Reilly, and Wade 1996). These analyses provided further evidence that nonresponse bias was not present in our data. In particular, a series of difference-in-proportions tests showed that respondents and nonrespondents were not significantly different with respect to the existence of (a) an executive committee on the board ($D = .018$; $p = .260$); (b) a nominating committee composed of outsiders ($D = .011$; $p = .585$); or (c) a management development and compensation committee ($D = .009$; $p = .649$). Moreover, respondents were not significantly different in their use (vs. nonuse) of stock compensation for directors ($D = .019$; $p = .212$), and CEOs of responding firms were neither more nor less likely to serve as an ex officio nonvoting director on the board ($D = .016$; $p = .435$).

Data were also collected on all alliances initiated by firms in the sample frame from 1970 to 1996. This sample included all interfirm partnerships that entailed the creation of a new legal entity in which both partners held equity, also referred to as joint ventures. These data were coded manually from the Predicast's *Funk and Scott Index of Corporate Change* and from *Lexis/Nexis*. Only joint ventures that had actually been formed were recorded. Hence, reports of probable joint ventures that never materialized were excluded. An effort was made to ensure that these data were comprehensive in covering all alliances during the previously mentioned time period. In this study, alliance formation was predicted over the two-year period following the survey date (1995–6), and the remaining historical alliance data were used to compute some key control variables that are described in Chapter 4. Data on board interlocks and board structure were collected for the period 1994–5 from *Standard and Poor's Register of Corporations, Directors, and Executives*, and the *Dun and Bradstreet Reference Book of Corporate Management*. To calculate measures of market constraint (discussed below), input–output data were obtained from the database created by the Interindustry Economics Division of the Bureau of Economic Analysis (cf. Burt 1992; Mizruchi 1992). Data on financial characteristics and other firm attributes were obtained from COMPUSTAT.

Alliance Announcement Database (Used in Chapters 5 and 6)

The unit of analysis used here was the transaction (i.e. each alliance). The dataset included information on all publicly announced alliances in the period 1970–89 in the biopharmaceuticals, new materials, and automotive economic sectors. The biopharmaceutical sector includes applications in therapeutics, vaccines, and diagnostics. The new materials sector includes metals, ceramics, polymers, and composites.

The automotive sector includes both manufacturers of finished automobiles and their suppliers. The data regarding alliances formed within these sectors originated from many of the same sources that were described earlier in relation to the Alliance Formation Database, including the CATI database, industry reports, and industry-specific articles. In the case of the biopharmaceutical sector, these latter sources also included: *Bioscan*, *Ernst & Young Reports*, and the *Biotechnology Directory*.

The goal of this data collection was to comprehensively include all alliances formed within the selected industries. While Chapters 2 and 3 examined only the alliances formed by a select panel of firms from each sector, for these chapters no size restrictions were placed on the firms included. As for the dataset referred to in Chapters 2 and 3, only alliances that had actually been formed were recorded. The complete dataset includes information on over 2,400 alliances among American, European, and Japanese firms. The goal was to create the most comprehensive dataset on alliances within each of the focal sectors that was possible, both in terms of the length of time included and the depth of coverage.[2]

As highlighted above, the alliance data used above in the 'Alliance Formation Dataset' were a subset of these data as they included all the alliances formed by the panel of firms to which that data-set was restricted. In this data-set, no such restrictions were placed.

The data segment acquired from MERIT (see Alliance Formation Database) included codes for the form of an alliance (equity based or not) and the activities it encompassed. The codings were based on precise criteria used to draw assessments from the public announcement of an alliance. To maintain coding consistency across the entire dataset, the same coding approach that was employed by MERIT was used to code the alliance data that did not originate from the CATI database. This coding required that the dichotomous choice process be carefully controlled by developing a list of synonyms for each choice. The explicit coding rules were clarified and refined using fifty nonsampled alliance announcements. The general rule was to code only explicit references to each choice. Multiple public announcements were consulted from a wide variety of sources described earlier. Because the dichotomous choices were clearly specified, the rules for coding were kept simple and straightforward, and multiple sources were consulted, the actual coding of alliances was not complex. In addition, the clear specification of categories and the simplified coding rules boosted the reliability of the coding. Attempts to assess this reliability were made by periodically recoding a small number of alliances after some time had elapsed since the original coding. Throughout the coding process, the recoding was almost identical to the original, with agreement rates ranging from .96 to 1.00. The reliability of the coding criteria was also assessed by asking two experts on strategic alliances to code a random sample of twenty-five alliances using the information that had been collected. There was complete coincidence in their coding and the coding that was independently performed subsequently. Overall, these results suggested that the alliance data were coded with a high degree of reliability.

---

[2] The number of alliances examined here far exceeds the numbers examined in previous studies: Nohria and Garcia-Pont (1991) reported 96 automotive sector alliances for the period 1980–9 vs. the 493 reported here; Pisano (1989) reported 195 biopharmaceuticals alliances vs. the 781 reported here.

During the coding process, an alliance was labeled as including R&D only if a public announcement clearly stated that the agreement encompassed joint product development or basic R&D. Similarly, an alliance was coded as equity based when a public announcement said that an equity joint venture had been created or that a firm had taken a substantive minority position in another company with the intent to pursue joint projects. Fortunately, most public announcements of alliances report detailed information on their governance structures, activities, and goals. When activities or governance structure were ambiguous, additional public records were identified that more clearly stated the goals of a partnership. For over 30 percent of the alliance records that were collected, multiple sources were consulted.

Joint Venture Announcement Database (Used in Chapter 7)

Our sample included all bilateral joint ventures that were formed among the 300 largest Fortune/Forbes firms (in 1988) from 1987 to 1996. We excluded from the analysis 20 firms that had no financial data available in the COMPUSTAT industrial firms database, leaving 280 firms. Among these, 186 had at least one JV with another firm in the sample, generating a total number of 658 JVs in the final sample.

Sample data were collected from a variety of sources. The longitudinal data on the announcements of bilateral JVs came from two major sources: Lexis-Nexis and Security Data Corporation (SDC). Rich descriptions of JVs in Lexis-Nexis were complemented and cross-validated by SDC data. We resolved duplications and contradictions between these sources by consulting additional sources, such as the *Wall Street Journal* index. Data on each firm's prior JVs during the 1970–86 period were also collected for all companies in the sample. These data, which were used to control for firm history, came from Lexis-Nexis, as SDC data only went back to 1986.

For all sampled firms, financial data were also collected for the 1986–95 period (inclusive) from COMPUSTAT. These financial data were lagged by one year (i.e. financial data from 1986 were used to predict the announcement of a JV in 1987, etc.).

Data on stock market reactions to JV announcements were collected from the Center for Research in Security Prices (CRSP). For each firm, we obtained data on stock market movements for that company over 241 days (from 250 days before the announcement until 10 days before the announcement) and over a two-day period (1 day before the announcement and the announcement day) as well as over a 21-day period (from 10 days before the announcement until 10 days after the announcement). Event periods (windows) are used in event studies to capture the possible stock market reaction to information leakage prior to the announcement of a JV and to additional information that becomes available to the market after a JV announcement (Datta and Puia 1995; Anand and Khanna 2000a). The most widely used 2-day event period (Datta and Puia 1995; Chan et al. 1997; Anand and Khanna 2000a) and a longer event period of 21 days were used (Bradley, Desai, and Kim 1983; Sicherman and Pettway 1987; Black and Grundfest 1988; Datta and Puia 1995) to capture the stock market reaction to JV announcements. The methodology is described in greater detail in Chapter 7.

Biotechnology Start-ups Database (Used in Chapters 9 and 10)

Our sample frame includes US biotechnology firms that were founded between 1961 and 1994. Of these 858 firms, 299 went public between 1979 and 1996. Approximately 86 percent of the public firms specialized in the development of therapeutics and/or human diagnostics; the majority of the remaining firms specialized in agriculture and/or other biological products, generally with the explicit intention of engaging in therapeutic applications in the future. The average time to IPO in our dataset was 4.87 years.

We compiled our data from both published and unpublished sources, striving to be as thorough as possible while remaining focused on true, dedicated biotechnology firms. Our primary list of public biotechnology firms was obtained from the *BioWorld Stock Report for Public Biotechnology Companies* in 1996 ($n = 281$). Unlike other sources (e.g. BioScan), this listing does not include large corporations (e.g. General Electric) that participate tangentially in the biotechnology industry; hence, ours is a narrower definition of biotechnology than that which has been employed by other researchers (e.g. Barley, Freeman, and Hybels 1992) and is in line with more recent research on the industry (e.g. Powell, Koput, and Smith-Doerr 1996).

To guard against sample selection bias, we also collected information on firms that went public in the same time frame as our sample but that had not survived in their original forms by 1996. To do this, we obtained information from biotechnology research organizations including BIO, the North Carolina Center for Biotechnology Information, Recombinant Capital (ReCap), and the Institute for Biotechnology Information. We also compared three editions of *Biotechnology Guide USA* (Dibner 1988, 1991, 1995). From these sources, we identified an additional 18 dedicated US biotechnology firms that had gone public but were not in existence in their original forms in 1996; they had merged, been acquired, or experienced name changes. These firms were founded in the same period and had gone public by the end of 1996.

We also collected information on biotechnology firms that were founded in the same time period as our sample but had not gone public by 1996 ($n = 468$), from the 1998 edition of the Institute for Biotechnology Information (IBI) database. We added to this list private biotechnology companies that were listed as 'dead', merged, or acquired in the first three editions of the *Biotechnology Guide USA* (Dibner 1988, 1991, 1995) and that had a founding date in the same period as our core sample ($n = 90$). Combining these private firms with our sample of firms that did go public yielded a final combined sample size of 858 firms.

The main variables of interest in the study described in Chapter 9, in particular, were drawn from the career histories of the 3,200 managing officers and directors that made up the upper echelons of the 299 public firms in our core sample. Information on these individuals and their firms was manually obtained from the firms' final prospectuses. The upper echelon was defined as the directors and managing officers listed in a firm's final prospectus. In filing with the SEC, firms are required to list the last five years of experience of the firm's managing officers and board members; additional information (e.g. educational background) may be listed but is not required by the SEC. We consulted additional sources such as Dun and Bradstreet for cross-verification.

Finally, we conducted field and ethnographic analyses at fourteen biotechnology firms in the United States, two investment banks, one venture capital firm, and one of the Big 6 audit firms. The individuals to whom we spoke at the service organizations were all intimately involved in various IPO deals in the biotechnology industry during the time period of our study and provided extremely helpful information about the complexities involved in taking a firm public. Among the biotechnology firms, we completed 12 formal interviews, ranging in length from 1.5 to 4.5 hours each. Five of those interviewed were in business-related positions (CEO, CFO, or chair of the board), while the other seven were in senior research positions. We gathered career history information through semi-structured interviews for all of the individuals in the biotechnology firms, as well as information on their roles in their firms and in the IPO process. In addition, we solicited ongoing input from one expert informant who has worked at two different biotechnology firms, one large and one small, and who was centrally involved in two IPO deals.

☐ APPENDIX 2 METHODS

Unobserved Heterogeneity (Used in Chapters 2, 3, and 4)

An issue that arises when analyzing data on a time series of cross sections, or panel data, is the possibility of unobserved time-invariant effects known as 'unobserved heterogeneity'. This is of particular concern with respect to the claim that a firm's prior history of alliances affects its future likelihood of entering an alliance. In the case of dyads, this issue arises when particular pairs of firms display a higher or lower propensity to enter into ties compared to all other possible pairings of firms. There are two distinct explanations for this empirical regularity, if it indeed occurs (Heckman 1981a, 1981b). One explanation is that a genuine behavioral effect exists whereby a firm's future preferences are altered by the prior alliances it has experienced. In econometric terms, such a behavioral effect is called 'state dependence'—the likelihood of an event is a function of the state of the unit.

If state dependence alone encapsulated the empirical reality, there would be no problem. But there is another possibility that could lead to spurious results if not accounted for: firms may differ in their propensities to enter alliances because of unobserved factors. In this instance, such unobservable effects could be based on permanent differences between firms in their preferences for alliances—differences which may not be captured by any of the independent variables. If this noise were systematic for the same unit over time, it could lead to a serial correlation among the error terms for those observations, which would yield inefficient coefficients, rendering any statistical testing inaccurate. Furthermore, prior alliance experience may appear to be a determinant of future alliance formation solely because it is a proxy for temporally persistent unobservable factors that determine alliance formation behavior. Improper treatment can lead to spurious effects when we attempt to assess the influence of experience on current decisions; this phenomenon is termed 'spurious state dependence' (Heckman and Borjas 1980; Heckman 1981a, 1981b; Hsiao 1986; Black, Moffitt, and Warner 1990).

In a statistical sense, the problem of unobserved heterogeneity relates to model specification (Petersen and Koput 1991). If a model is completely specified, no such problem occurs. Most statistical models, however, suffer from some degree of omitted-variable bias. Another way to think about this problem is to consider the appropriate risk set. In the experimental design associated with these studies, I include all firms within each industry for each year as the set of possible alliance partners. It is quite likely that some of these firms are in fact not likely to enter an alliance in some or all observation periods, while other firms have a high propensity to ally. This suggests the possibility of misspecification of the risk set unless adequate allowances are made for such unobserved differences in propensity. One way to deal with such a bias is to clean up the risk set by eliminating firms that are unlikely to engage in an alliance, a process analogous to removing men from pregnancy studies. The difference in propensity is frequently a result of unobservable factors, however, making it impossible to weed out records a priori from the sample without biasing the sample.

Two approaches frequently used to address problems of unobserved heterogeneity statistically are fixed- and random-effects models. Fixed-effects models treat the unobserved individual effect as a constant over time and compute it for each unit (i.e. each firm). In other words, the method entails estimating a constant term for each distinct unit and including dummy variables for each. This method is similar to that employed in least-squares-with-dummy-variables (LSDV) regression models (Hannan and Young 1977). Random-effects models treat the heterogeneity that varies across units as randomly drawn from some underlying probability distribution.

To address concerns of heterogeneity I employed a random-effects panel probit model developed by Butler and Moffitt (1982).[1] Subsequently, I tested the robustness of my findings with a fixed-effects model and found consistent results. My decision to employ a random-effects model was based on the following. First, estimates computed using fixed-effects models can be biased for panels over short periods (Heckman 1981*a*, 1981*b*; Hsiao 1986; Chintagunta, Jain, and Vilcassim 1991). This is not a problem with random-effects models. Because all the firm-year records in Chapter 2 and dyad-year records in Chapter 3 were present for only nine years, using a random-effects model was clearly the favored approach. Second, fixed-effects models cannot include time-independent covariates, a limitation that would have meant excluding several control variables. An analysis without some of these variables would have been severely limited. The random-effects models were computed using LIMDEP 6.0. The random effects approach used generates a coefficient Rho, which indicates the degree of overdispersion of the variance. Specifically, Rho is the proportion of the variance of the error term that is accounted for by the unobservable firm-specific variables in Chapter 2 and by the dyad-specific variables in Chapter 3. The significance of Rho suggests that observationally identical firms display different alliance propensities because of permanent differences in their alliance preferences and other unobserved factors.

Interdependence (Chapter 3)

A number of additional tests were conducted to address concerns of interdependence across observations resulting from the presence of the same firm across multiple dyads. First, a procedure akin to the Multivariate Regression Quadratic Assignment Procedure (MRQAP) routinely used by researchers studying dyads (Krackardt 1987, 1988; Manley 1992; Mizruchi 1992) was employed. My approach, however, differed from MRQAP in that a random-effects probit model, rather than OLS regression, was used for each iteration of the simulation.

In the primary study described in Chapter 3, 500 iterations of a completely specified random-effects model with a new randomized dependent variable (obtained by

[1] Within random-effects models, numerous alternatives are possible, depending on the choice of form for the distribution of unobservables. Although Butler and Moffitt specified a normal distribution, other functional forms are also possible. Some studies have moved away from functional specification of heterogeneity toward semiparametric random effects approaches that estimate the probability distribution directly from the data (cf. Chintagunta, Jain, and Vilcassim 1991).

random permutations of the rows and columns in the alliance matrix) were run (see Table 3.2, model 8). The coefficients obtained were compared with those obtained in the original formulation (also shown in Table 3.2). The percentage of frequency with which the independent variables exceeded their original values divided by the number of permutations plus 1 (in this case, 501) indicates the statistical reliability (pseudo t-test) of the original results. This test can be interpreted similarly to conventional tests of significance: a value of less than 5 percent (or even better, 1 percent) provides evidence that the original estimates are indeed accurate. The benefit of a randomization procedure is that satisfactory results can be obtained without requiring an assumption of independent observations, a random sample, or a specified distribution function. Use of this procedure enabled an assessment of the efficiency of the results, a primary concern given the potential for dyadic interdependence. The percentage frequency with which the results in the random sample simulations exceeded the original estimates was far less than 5 percent in all instances. Thus, it can be said with some confidence that for these data reasonable coefficients were obtained.

In the follow-up research reported at the end of Chapter 3 (Gulati and Gargiulo 1999), a variation and extension of this approach was used to assess the effect of structural differentiation and other network-level factors on the propensity for dyads to form new alliances. Similar to the study described earlier, 500 iterations of a completely specified random-effects model were run with a new randomized independent network variable that was obtained by random permutations of the rows and columns in each alliance matrix for each industry and year. The coefficients obtained were compared with those obtained in the original formulation in a manner similar to that described earlier.[2] The manner in which the network-embeddedness effects were specified made this model akin to the P^* logit models recently proposed by Wasserman and Pattison (1996). Building on the pioneering work by Holland and Leinhardt (1970) and Strauss and Ikeda (1990), P^* models produce pseudo-maximum-likelihood estimators of the probability of observing a binary tie x_{ij}, conditional on the rest of the data, without having to make the implausible assumption that the observations (dyads) are independent. Specifically, these models build into a logistic regression parameters that capture possible sources of interdependence between the observed dyads—such as reciprocity, transitivity, the in and out degree of each dyad member, and network density—and obtain estimators of the effect of these parameters on the conditional probability of $\{x_{ij} = 1\}$. Here, these models include network parameters similar to the ones of a typical P^* model—transitive triads, the degree of each dyad member, and network density—but the analyses here measured these parameters on the network at $(t - 1)$, while a strict pseudo-likelihood estimation requires parameters measured on the same network that contains the predicted tie. Because the inclusion of the $(t - 1)$ parameters cannot be considered an adequate safeguard against the potential effects of nonindependent observations, the aforementioned MRQAP-like procedure was used to test the robustness of the results and to limit concerns of interdependence. The percentage of frequency with which the results in the

---

[2] A more complete specification of this test would have entailed randomly extracting the 500 permutations from all possible ones for each industry (Mizruchi 1992), which was not feasible here due to the extremely large number of permutations that would be necessary for each industry and for each year.

random-sample simulations exceeded the original estimates was far less than 5 percent in all instances. Thus, it is possible to say with some confidence that for these data reasonable coefficients were obtained.

Across Chapter 3 the problem of cross-sectional dyadic interdependence can also be understood as one of model misspecification (Lincoln 1984). If a statistical model incorporated all essential nodal (organization-level) characteristics that influence alliance formation, no unobserved effects resulting from common nodes would remain. To capture any organization-level effects across dyads sharing the same organization, the analyses here controlled for each company's cumulative history of alliances. Organization history is an important factor that captures any residual organizational propensities to engage in alliances (Heckman and Borjas 1980; Black, Moffitt, and Warner 1990). As noted earlier, separate estimations were also run in which a host of financial attributes related to each organization in a dyad were retained, including firm size, performance, liquidity, and solvency. In addition to these controls, the models used here account for unobserved heterogeneity and adjust for such systematic biases resulting from missing variables. The expectation was that the unobserved heterogeneity term (ρ) would capture any residual dyad-level effects not included in the model.

Comparative Analyses (Chapter 3)

The primary theoretical basis for the use of network measures is that the links formed in an industry are not random but are driven by the structure of historical relationships. The models that included network variables were expected to be powerful predictors of alliance formation to the extent that (a) alliance formation among firms arises from the flow of information via networks of preexisting relationships, and (b) the specific structural models used to reflect these information flows cluster firms that are densely connected by such informational links (Friedkin 1984).

To verify the claim that the formation of interorganizational alliances is systematic in nature, the results for this study's sample were compared against results obtained with a sample in which the formation of alliances was assigned randomly. The implicit null hypothesis here is that an observed pattern in the data is due purely to chance. Such a comparative analysis serves as a valuable baseline (cf. Zajac 1988). Finding no differences in the predictive power of the independent variables for the actual and random dependent variables or finding greater predictive power for the random dependent variable would suggest that the postulated independent effects could have predicted the random occurrence of alliances just as well or better. As a result, the claims for systematic patterning of alliances would be moot.

The predictive ability of each model specified in this chapter was tested against random assignments on the dependent variable on the basis of its original distribution. The results indicated that none of the hypothesized effects are better predictors of randomly assigned alliances than those in the results tables in this chapter. Not a single independent variable is significant in all the models. This finding allows a rejection of the implicit null hypothesis and suggests that the postulated independent effects are not at all good predictors of the random occurrence of alliances. The exogenous interdependence and endogenous embeddedness effects explain the systematic pattern of alliances.

☐ BIBLIOGRAPHY

ABBOTT, A. (1981). 'Status and Status Strain in the Professions', *American Journal of Sociology*, 86/4: 819–35.

AFUAH, A. (2000). 'How Much Do Your Competitors' Capabilities Matter in the Face of Technological Change?' *Strategic Management Journal*, 21: 387–404.

AHUJA, G. (2000a). 'Collaboration Networks, Structural Holes, and Innovation: A Longitudinal Study', *Administrative Science Quarterly*, 45/3: 425–55.

——— (2000b). 'The Duality of Collaboration: Inducements and Opportunities in the Formation of Interfirm Linkages', *Strategic Management Journal*, 21/3: 317–43.

AIKEN, M. and HAGE, J. (1968). 'Organizational Interdependence and Intraorganizational Structure', *American Sociological Review*, 33: 912–30.

ALDRICH, J. H. and NELSON, F. D. (1984). *Linear Probability, Logit, and Probit Models*. Sage university papers series. Quantitative applications in the social sciences, no. 07–045; Beverly Hills, CA: Sage.

ALLISON, P. D. (1978). 'Measures of Inequality', *American Sociological Review*, 43: 865–80.

AMBURGEY, T. L. and MINER, A. S. (1992). 'Strategic Momentum: The Effects of Repetitive, Positional, and Contextual Momentum on Merger Activity', *Strategic Management Journal*, 13/5: 335–48.

——— DACIN, M. T., and SINGH, J. V. (1996). 'Learning Races, Patent Races, and Capital Races: Strategic Interaction and Embeddedness within Organizational Fields', in Joel A. C. Baum and J. E. Dutton (eds.), *Advances in Strategic Management*, vol. 13, Greenwich, CT: JAI Press.

——— KELLY, D., and BARNETT, W. P. (1993). 'Resetting the Clock: The Dynamics of Organizational Change and Failure', *Administrative Science Quarterly*, 38/1: 51–73.

ANAND, B. N. and KHANNA, T. (2000a). 'Do Firms Learn to Create Value? The Case of Alliances', *Strategic Management Journal*, 21/3: 295–315.

——— ——— (2000b). 'The Structure of Licensing Contracts', *Journal of Industrial Economics*, 48/1: 103–35.

ARGYRIS, C. and SCHON, D. A. (1978). *Organizational Learning: A Theory of Action Perspective*. Reading, MA: Addison-Wesley.

ARORA, A. and GAMBARDELLA, A. (1994). 'The Changing Technology of Technological Change: General and Abstract Knowledge and the Division of Innovative Labour', *Research Policy*, 23/5: 523–32.

ARREGLE, J. L., AMBURGEY, T. L., and DACIN, M. T. (1996). 'Strategic Alliances and Firm Capabilities: Strategy and Structure', Paper given at Strategic Management Society Conference, Phoenix, Ariz.

ARROW, K. J. (1974). *The Limits of Organization*, 1st edn. New York: Norton.

ARTHUR, W. B. (1989). 'Competing Technologies, Increasing Returns, and Lock-in by Historical Events', *Economic Journal*, 99/394: 116–31.

ASHBY, W. R. (1956). *Introduction to Cybernetics*. London: Chapman & Hall.

BADARACCO, J. (1991). *The Knowledge Link: How Firms Compete Through Strategic Alliances.* Boston, MA: Harvard Business School Press.

BAE, S. C., KLEIN, D. P., and BOWYER, J. W. (1999). 'Determinants of Underwriter Participation in Initial Public Offerings of Common Stock: An Empirical Study', *Journal of Business Finance and Accounting*, 26: 595–618.

BAKER, W. E. (1984). 'The Social Structure of a National Securities Market', *American Journal of Sociology*, 89/4: 775–811.

——(1990). 'Market Networks and Corporate Behavior', *American Journal of Sociology*, 96/3: 589–625.

BALAKRISHNAN, S. and KOZA, M. P. (1993). 'Information Asymmetry, Adverse Selection and Joint-Ventures: Theory and Evidence', *Journal of Economic Behavior & Organization*, 20/1: 99–117.

BAMFORD, J. and ERNST, D. (2002). 'Managing an Alliance Portfolio', *McKinsey Quarterly*, 3: 28–39.

BANTEL, K. and JACKSON, E. (1989). 'Top Management and Innovations in Banking: Does the Composition of the Top Team Make a Difference?' *Strategic Management Journal*, 10: 107–24.

BARBER, B. (1983). *The Logic and Limits of Trust.* New Brunswick, NJ: Rutgers University Press.

BARLEY, S. R., FREEMAN, J., and HYBELS, R. C. (1992). 'Strategic Alliances in Commercial Biotechnology', in N. Nohria and R. G. Eccles (eds.), *Networks and Organizations: Structure, Form, and Action.* Boston, MA: Harvard Business School Press.

BARNARD, C. I. (1938). *The Functions of the Executive.* Cambridge, MA: Harvard University Press.

BARNETT, W. P. (1993). 'Strategic Deterrence Among Multipoint Competitors', *Industrial and Corporate Change*, 2: 249–78.

BARNEY, J. (1991). 'Firm Resources and Sustained Competitive Advantage', *Journal of Management*, 17/1: 99–120.

BARON, R. M. and KENNY, D. A. (1986). 'The Moderator–Mediator Variable Distinction in Social Psychological Research: Conceptual, Strategic, and Statistical Considerations', *Journal of Personality & Social Psychology*, 51/6: 1173–82.

BARZEL, Y. (1982). 'Measurement Cost and the Organization of Markets', *Journal of Law and Economics*, 25/1: 27–48.

BAUM, J. A. C. (1996). 'Organizational Ecology', in S. Clegg, C. Hardy, and W. R. Nord (eds.), *Handbook of Organization Studies.* London: Sage.

——and DUTTON, J. E. (eds.) (1996). *The Embeddedness of Strategy.* P. Shrivastava, A. S. Huff, and J. E. Dutton (eds.), *Advances in Strategic Management*, vol. 13. Greenwich, CT: JAI Press.

——and MEZIAS, S. J. (1992). 'Localized Competition and Organizational Failure in the Manhattan Hotel Industry, 1898–1990', *Administrative Science Quarterly*, 37/4: 580–604.

——and OLIVER, C. (1991). 'Institutional Linkages and Organizational Mortality', *Administrative Science Quarterly*, 36/2: 187–218.

————(1992). 'Institutional Embeddedness and the Dynamics of Organizational Populations', *American Sociological Review*, 57: 540–59.

——and POWELL, W. W. (1995). 'Cultivating an Institutional Ecology of Organizations: Comment on Hannan, Carroll, Dundon, and Torres', *American Sociological Review*, 60: 529–38.

——and SILVERMAN, B. S. (2004). 'Picking Winners or Building Them? Alliance, Intellectual, and Human Capital as Selection Criteria in Venture Financing and Performance of Biotechnology Startups', *Journal of Business Venturing*, 19/3: 411–36.

BAUM, J. A. C., CALABRESE, T., and SILVERMAN, S. (2000). 'Don't Go It Alone: Alliance Network Composition and Startups' Performance in Canadian Biotechnology', *Strategic Management Journal*, 21/3: 267–94.

BAYUS, B. L. and GUPTA, S. (1992). 'An Empirical Analysis of Consumer Durable Replacement Intentions', *International Journal of Research in Marketing*, 9/3: 257–67.

BEATTY, R. P. and RITTER, J. R. (1986). 'Investment Banking, Reputation, and the Underpricing of Initial Public Offerings', *Journal of Financial Economics*, 15: 213–32.

———and ZAJAC, E. J. (1994). 'Managerial Incentives, Monitoring, and Risk Bearing: A Study of Executive Compensation, Ownership, and Board Structure in Initial Public Offerings', *Administrative Science Quarterly*, 39/2: 313–35.

BELLIVEAU, M. A., O'REILLY, C. A., III, and WADE, J. B. (1996). 'Social Capital at the Top: Effects of Social Similarity and Status on CEO Compensation', *Academy of Management Journal*, 39/6: 1568–93.

BEN-AKIVA, M. E. and LERMAN, S. R. (1985). *Discrete Choice Analysis: Theory and Application to Predict Travel Demand*. Cambridge, MA: MIT Press.

BERG, S. V., DUNCAN, J., and FRIEDMAN, P. (1982). *Joint Venture Strategies and Corporate Innovation*. Cambridge, MA: Oelgeschlager Gunn & Hain.

BERGER, P. L. and LUCKMAN, T. (1966). *The Social Construction of Reality*. Garden City, NY: Doubleday.

BESNIER, N. (1989). 'Information Withholding as a Manipulative and Collusive Strategy in Nukulaelae Gossip', *Language in Society*, 18/3: 315–41.

BLACK, B. S. and GRUNDFEST, J. A. (1988). 'Shareholder Gains from Takeovers and Restructurings Between 1981 and 1986', *Journal of Applied Corporate Finance*, 11: 71–8.

BLACK, M., MOFFITT, R., and WARNER, J. T. (1990). 'The Dynamics of Job Separation: The Case of Federal Employees', *Journal of Applied Econometrics*, 5/3: 245–62.

BLAU, P. M. (1977), *Inequality and Heterogeneity*. New York: Free Press.

BLEEKE, J. and ERNST, D. (1993). *Collaborating to Compete: Using Strategic Alliances and Acquisitions in the Global Marketplace*. New York: Wiley.

BOCHNER, S. E. and PRIEST, G. M. (1993). *Guide to the Initial Public Offering*, 2nd edn. New York: Merrill Corporation.

BOEKER, W. (1997). 'Executive Migration and Strategic Change: The Effect of Top Manager Movement on Product-Market Entry', *Administrative Science Quarterly*, 42/2: 213–75.

BORGATTI, S. P., EVERETT, M. G., and FREEMAN, L. C. (1992). *UCINET IV*, 1.00 edn. Columbia, SC: Analytic Technologies.

BORYS, B. and JENNISON, D. B. (1989). 'Hybrid Arrangements as Strategic Alliances: Theoretical Issues in Organizational Combinations', *Academy of Management Review*, 14/2: 234–49.

BOURDIEU, P. (1986). 'The Forms of Social Capital', in J. G. Richardson (ed.), *Handbook of Theory and Research for the Sociology of Education*. New York: Greenwood Press.

BRADACH, J. L. and ECCLES, R. G. (1989). 'Price, Authority, and Trust: From Ideal Types to Plural Forms', *Annual Review of Sociology*, 15: 97–118.

BRADLEY, M., DESAI, A., and KIM, E. H. (1983). 'Synergistic Gains from Corporate Acquisitions and Their Division Between the Stockholders of Target and Acquiring Firms', *Journal of Financial Economics*, 21: 3–40.

BRANDENBURGER, A. and NALEBUFF, B. (1996). *Co-opetition*, 1st edn. New York: Doubleday.

BRASS, D. J. and BURKHARDT, M. E. (1992). 'Centrality and Power in Organizations', in N. Nohria and R. G. Eccles (eds.), *Networks and Organizations: Structure, Form, and Action*. Boston, MA: Harvard Business School Press.

BREWER, M. B. (1979). 'In-Group Bias in the Minimal Intergroup Situation: A Cognitive-Motivational Analysis', *Psychological Bulletin*, 86/2: 307–24.

——and MILLER, N. (1996). *Intergroup Relations*. Buckingham, UK: Open University Press.

BURGERS, W. P., HILL, C. W. L., and KIM, W. C. (1993). 'A Theory of Global Strategic Alliances: The Case of the Global Auto Industry', *Strategic Management Journal*, 14/6: 419–32.

BURRILL, G. S. and LEE, K. (1990). *Biotech 91: A Changing Environment*. San Francisco, CA: Ernst and Young.

————(1993). *Biotech 94*. San Francisco, CA: Ernst and Young.

BURT, R. S. (1976). 'Positions in Networks', *Social Forces*, 55/1: 93–122.

——(1982). *Toward a Structural Theory of Action: Network Models of Social Structure, Perception, and Action*. New York: Academic Press.

——(1983). *Corporate Profits and Cooptation: Networks of Market Constraints and Directorate Ties in the American Economy*. Quantitative studies in social relations; New York: Academic Press.

——(1987). 'Social Contagion and Innovation: Cohesion Versus Structural Equivalence', *American Journal of Sociology*, 92/6: 1287–335.

——(1992). *Structural Holes: The Social Structure of Competition*. Cambridge, MA: Harvard University Press.

——(1996). 'Trust and Third-Party Gossip', in R. M. Kramer and T. R. Tyler (eds.), *Trust in Organizations: Frontiers of Theory and Research*. Thousand Oaks, CA: Sage.

——(2004). 'Structural Holes and Good Ideas', *American Journal of Sociology*, 110/2: 349–99.

——and KNEZ, M. (1995). 'Kinds of Third-Party Effects on Trust', *Rationality and Society*, 7/3: 255–92.

BURTON, M. D., SØRENSON, J. B., and BECKMAN, C. (1998). 'Coming from Good Stock: Career Histories and New Venture Formation', Harvard Business School.

BUTLER, J. S. and MOFFITT, R. (1982). 'A Computationally Efficient Quadrature Procedure for the One-Factor Multinomial Probit Model', *Econometrica*, 50/3: 761–4.

BYGRAVE, W. D. and TIMMONS, J. A. (1992). *Venture Capital at the Crossroads*. Boston, MA: Harvard Business School Press.

BYRNE, D., CLORE, G. L., and WORCHEL, P. (1966). 'The Effect of Economic Similarity-Dissimilarity as Determinants of Attraction', *Journal of Personality & Social Psychology*, 4: 220–4.

CANNELLA, A. A., JR. and LUBATKIN, M. (1993). 'Succession as a Sociopolitical Process: Internal Impediments to Outsider Selection', *Academy of Management Journal*, 36/4: 763–93.

CARTER, R. B. and DARK, F. H. (1992). 'An Empirical Examination of Investment Banking Reputation Measures', *The Financial Review*, 27/3: 355–74.

——and MANASTER, S. (1990). 'Initial Public Offerings and Underwriter Reputation', *Journal of Finance*, 45/4: 1045–67.

——DARK, F. H., and SINGH, A. K. (1998). 'Underwriter Reputation, Initial Returns and the Long-Run Performance of IPO Stocks', *Journal of Finance*, 53: 285–311.

CASCIARO, T. (2003). 'Determinants of Governance Structure in Alliances: The Role of Strategic, Task and Partner Uncertainties', *Industrial and Corporate Change*, 12/6: 1223–51.

CHAMBERLAIN, G. (1985). 'Heterogeneity, Omitted Variable Bias, and Duration Dependence', in J. J. Heckman and B. Singer (eds.), *Longitudinal Analysis of Labor Market Data*. New York: Cambridge University Press.

CHAN, S. H., et al. (1997). 'Do Strategic Alliances Create Value?' *Journal of Financial Economics*, 46/2: 199–221.

CHANDLER, A. D., JR. (1977). *The Visible Hand: The Managerial Revolution in American Business*. Cambridge, MA: Belknap Press of Harvard University Press.

CHI, T. (2000). 'Options to Acquire or Divest a Joint Venture', *Strategic Management Journal*, 21: 665–87.

CHINTAGUNTA, P. K., JAIN, D. C., and VILCASSIM, N. J. (1991). 'Investigating Heterogeneity in Brand Preferences in Logit Models for Panel Data', *Journal of Marketing Research*, 28/4: 417–28.

CHUNG, S., SINGH, H., and LEE, K. (2000). 'Complementarity, Status Similarity and Social Capital as Drivers of Alliance Formation', *Strategic Management Journal*, 21/1: 1–22.

COASE, R. H. ([1937] 1952). 'The Nature of the Firm', in G. J. Stigler and K. E Boulding (eds.), *A.E.A. Readings in Price Theory*. Homewood, IL: Irwin.

COHEN, W. M. and LEVINTHAL, D. A. (1990). 'Absorptive Capacity: A New Perspective on Learning and Innovation', *Administrative Science Quarterly*, 35/1: 128–52.

COLEMAN, J. S. (1988). 'Social Capital in the Creation of Human Capital', *American Journal of Sociology*, 94: S95–S120.

—— (1990). *Foundations of Social Theory*. Cambridge, MA: Harvard University Press.

COMMONS, J. R. (1970). *The Economics of Collective Action*. K. H. Parsons (ed.). Madison: University of Wisconsin Press.

CONNER, K. R. and PRAHALAD, C. K. (1996). 'A Resource-Based Theory of the Firm: Knowledge Versus Opportunism', *Organization Science*, 7/5: 477–501.

CONTRACTOR, F. J. and LORANGE, P. (1988). *Cooperative Strategies in International Business*. Lexington, MA: Lexington Books.

COOK, K. S. and EMERSON, R. M. (1978). 'Power, Equity and Commitment in Exchange Networks', *American Sociological Review*, 43/5: 721–39.

—— —— (1986). 'Corporate Odd Couples: Joint Ventures are the Rage, but the Matches Often Don't Work Out', *Business Week*, 100–5.

COX, B. A. (1970). 'What is Hopi Gossip About? Information Management and Hopi Factions', *Man*, 5/1: 88–98.

CREED, D. W. E. and MILES, R. E. (1996). 'Trust in Organizations: A Conceptual Framework Linking Organizational Forms, Managerial Philosophies, and the Opportunity Costs of Controls', in R. M. Kramer and T. R. Tyler (eds.), *Trust in Organizations: Frontiers of Theory and Research*. Thousand Oaks, CA: Sage Publications.

CYERT, R. M. and MARCH, J. G. (1963). *A Behavioral Theory of the Firm*. Englewood Cliffs, NJ: Prentice-Hall.

DACIN, M. T., HITT, M. A., and LEVITAS, E. (1997). 'Selecting Partners for Successful International Alliances: Examination of U.S. and Korean Firms', *Journal of World Business*, 32/1: 3–16.

DAILY, C. M. (1996). 'Governance Patterns in Bankruptcy Reorganizations', *Strategic Management Journal*, 17/5: 355–75.

DAS, T. K. and TENG, B.-S. (1998). 'Between Trust and Control: Developing Confidence in Partner Cooperation in Alliances', *Academy of Management Review*, 23/3: 491–512.

DATTA, D. K. and PUIA, G. (1995). 'Cross-Border Acquisitions: An Examination of the Influence of Relatedness and Cultural Fit on Shareholder Value Creation in US Acquiring Firms', *Management International Review*, 35: 337–59.

DAVID, P., KOCHHAR, R., and LEVITAS, E. (1998). 'The Effect of Institutional Investors on the Level and Mix of CEO Compensation', *Academy of Management Journal*, 41/2: 200–8.

DAVID, P. A. (1985). 'Clio and the Economics of QWERTY', *American Economic Review*, 75/2: 332–7.

DAVIS, G. F. (1991). 'Agents without Principles? The Spread of the Poison Pill through the Intercorporate Network', *Administrative Science Quarterly*, 36/4: 583–613.

—— and THOMPSON, T. A. (1994). 'A Social Movement Perspective on Corporate Control', *Administrative Science Quarterly*, 39/1: 141–73.

—— KAHN, R. L., and ZALD, M. N. (1990). 'Contracts, Treaties, and Joint Ventures', in R. L. Kahn and M. N. Zald (eds.), *Organizations and Nation-States: New Perspectives on Conflict and Cooperation*. 1st edn. San Francisco, CA: Jossey-Bass Publishers.

DAY, G. S. (1999). *The Market Driven Organizations: Understanding, Attracting and Keeping Valuable Customers*. New York: Free Press.

DECAROLIS, D. M. and DEEDS, D. L. (1999). 'The Impact of Stocks and Flows of Organizational Knowledge on Firm Performance: An Empirical Investigation of the Biotechnology Industry', *Strategic Management Journal*, 20: 953–68.

DEEDS, D. L., DECAROLIS, D., and COOMBS, J. E. (1997). 'The Impact of Firm-Specific Capabilities on the Amount of Capital Raised in an Initial Public Offering: Evidence from the Biotechnology Industry', *Journal of Business Venturing*, 12: 31–46.

DEMB, A. and NEUBAUER, F.-F. (1992). *The Corporate Board: Confronting the Paradoxes*. New York: Oxford University Press.

DIALDIN, D. A. (2004). 'Multi-Firm Alliance Formation and Governance Structure: Configural and Geometric Perspectives', Northwestern University.

DIBNER, M. D. (1988). *Biotechnology Guide, U.S.A.* New York: Stockton Press.

—— (1991). *Biotechnology Guide, U.S.A.* New York: Stockton Press.

—— (1995). *Biotechnology Guide, U.S.A.* New York: Stockton Press.

DIERICKX, I. and COOL, K. (1989). 'Asset Stock Accumulation and Sustainability of Competitive Advantage', *Management Science*, 35/12: 1504–11.

DIMAGGIO, P. J. and POWELL, W. W. (1983). 'The Iron Cage Revisited: Institutional Isomorphism and Collective Rationality in Organizational Fields', *American Sociological Review*, 48/2: 147–60.

DORE, R. (1983). 'Goodwill and the Spirit of Market Capitalism', *British Journal of Sociology*, 34/4: 459–82.

DOZ, Y. L. (1996). 'The Evolution of Cooperation in Strategic Alliances: Initial Conditions or Learning Processes?', *Strategic Management Journal*, 17/Summer: 55–83.

—— and HAMEL, G. (1998). *Alliance Advantage: The Art of Creating Value Through Partnering*. Boston, MA: Harvard Business School Press.

—— and PRAHALAD, C. K. (1991). 'Managing DMNCs: A Search for a New Paradigm', *Strategic Management Journal*, 12/Special Issue: Global Strategy: 145–64.

DUNCAN, J. L., JR. (1982). 'Impacts of New Entry and Horizontal Joint Ventures on Industrial Rates of Return', *Review of Economics and Statistics*, 64/2: 339–42.

DYER, J. H. (1997). 'Effective Interfirm Collaboration: How Firms Minimize Transaction Costs and Maximize Transaction Value', *Strategic Management Journal*, 18/7: 535–56.

——— (2000). *Collaborative Advantage: Winning Through Extended Enterprise Supplier Networks*. Oxford: Oxford University Press.

——— and CHU, W. (2000). 'The Determinants of Trust in Supplier–Automaker Relationships in the U.S., Japan, and Korea', *Journal of International Business Studies*, 31/2: 259–85.

——— and NOBEOKA, K. (2000). 'Creating and Managing a High-Performance Knowledge-Sharing Network: The Toyota Case', *Strategic Management Journal*, 21/3: 345–67.

——— and SINGH, H. (1998). 'The Relational View: Cooperative Strategy and Sources of Interorganizational Competitive Advantage', *Academy of Management Review*, 23/4: 660–79.

——— KALE, P., and SINGH, H. (2001). 'How to Make Strategic Alliances Work', *Sloan Management Review*, 42/4: 37–43.

ECCLES, R. G. (1981). 'The Quasifirm in the Construction Industry', *Journal of Economic Behavior & Organization*, 2: 335–57.

EISENHARDT, K. M. and SCHOONHOVEN, C. B. (1996). 'Resource-Based View of Strategic Alliance Formation: Strategic and Social Effects in Entrepreneurial Firms', *Organization Science*, 7/2: 136–50.

EMERY, F. E. and TRIST, E. L. (1965). 'The Causal Texture of Organizational Environments', *Human Relations*, 18: 21–32.

EMIRBAYER, M. and GOODWIN, J. (1994). 'Network Analysis, Culture, and the Problem of Agency', *American Journal of Sociology*, 99/6: 1411–54.

FAMA, E. F. and JENSEN, M. C. (1983). 'Separation of Ownership and Control', *Journal of Law and Economics*, 26/2: 301–25.

——— FISHER, L., JENSEN, M. C., and ROLL, R. (1969). 'The Adjustment of Stock Prices to New Information', *International Economic Review*, 10/1: 1–21.

FELDMAN, M. S. and MARCH, J. G. (1981). 'Information in Organizations as Signal and Symbol', *Administrative Science Quarterly*, 26: 171–86.

FENIGSTEIN, A. (1979). 'Self-Consciousness, Self-Attention, and Social Interaction', *Journal of Personality & Social Psychology*, 37/1: 75–86.

——— and VANABLE, P. A. (1992). 'Paranoia and Self-Consciousness', *Journal of Personality & Social Psychology*, 62/1: 129–38.

FERNANDEZ, R. M. (1991). 'Structural Bases of Leadership in Intraorganizational Networks', *Social Psychology Quarterly*, 54/1: 36–53.

——— and MCADAM, D. (1988). 'Social Networks and Social Movements: Multiorganizational Fields and Recruitment to Mississippi Freedom Summer', *Sociological Forum*, 3/3: 357–82.

FINKELSTEIN, S. (1992). 'Power in Top Management Teams: Dimensions, Measurement and Validation', *Academy of Management Journal*, 35: 505–38.

——— and HAMBRICK, D. C. (1988). 'Chief Executive Compensation: A Synthesis and Reconciliation', *Strategic Management Journal*, 9/6: 543–58.

FLIGSTEIN, N. (1985). 'The Spread of the Multidivisional Form Among Large Firms, 1919–1979', *American Sociological Review*, 50/3: 377–91.

FOOTE, N., et al. (2001). 'Making Solutions the Answer', *McKinsey Quarterly*, 3: 84–93.

FORSYTHE, J. B. (1977). 'Obtaining Cooperation in a Survey of Business Executives', *Journal of Marketing Research*, 14/3: 370–3.

FOWLER, F. J., JR. (1993). *Survey Research Methods*. Newbury Park, CA: Sage.

FRIED, V. H. and HISRICH, R. D. (1994). 'Toward a Model of Venture Capital Investment Decision Making', *Financial Management*, 23/3: 28–37.

FRIEDKIN, N. E. (1984). 'Structural Cohesion and Equivalence Explanations of Social Homogeneity', *Sociological Methods & Research*, 12: 235–61.

FUDENBERG, D. and TIROLE, J. (1983). 'Learning-by-Doing and Market Performance', *Bell Journal of Economics*, 14/2: 522–30.

GAERTNER, S. L., et al. (1989). 'Reducing Intergroup Bias: The Benefits of Recategorization', *Journal of Personality & Social Psychology*, 57/2: 239–49.

—— (1990). 'How Does Cooperation Reduce Intergroup Bias?' *Journal of Personality & Social Psychology*, 59/4: 692–704.

—— (1999). 'Reducing Intergroup Bias: Elements of Intergroup Cooperation', *Journal of Personality & Social Psychology*, 76/3: 388–402.

GALASKIEWICZ, J. (1985a). 'Interorganizational Relations', *Annual Review of Sociology*, 11: 281–304.

—— (1985b). *Social Organization of an Urban Grants Economy: A Study of Business Philanthropy and Nonprofit Organizations*. Orlando, FL: Academic Press.

—— and ZAHEER, A. (1999). 'Networks of Competitive Advantage', in S. Andrews and D. Knoke (eds.), *Research in the Sociology of Organizations*. Stamford, CT: JAI Press.

GALBRAITH, J. R. (1977). *Organization Design*. Reading, MA: Addison-Wesley.

GAMBETTA, D. (1988). 'Can We Trust Trust?' in D. Gambetta (ed.), *Trust: Making and Breaking Cooperative Relations*. Cambridge, MA: Basil Blackwell Ltd.

GELETKANYCZ, M. A. and HAMBRICK, D. C. (1997). 'The External Ties of Top Executives: Implications for Strategic Choice and Performance', *Administrative Science Quarterly*, 42/14: 654–81.

GERLACH, L. P. and PALMER, G. B. (1981). 'Adaptation Through Evolving Interdependence', in P. C. Nystrom and W. H. Starbuck (eds.), *Handbook of Organizational Design*. Oxford: Oxford University Press.

GERLACH, M. L. (1992). *Alliance Capitalism: The Social Organization of Japanese Business*. Berkeley, CA: University of California Press.

GHEMAWAT, P. and SPENCE, A. M. (1985). 'Learning Curve Spillovers and Market Performance', *Quarterly Journal of Economics*, 100/5: 839–52.

GIDDENS, A. (1984). *The Constitution of Society: Outline of the Theory of Structuration*. Berkeley, CA: University of California Press.

GNYAWALI, D. R. and MADHAVAN, R. (2001). 'Cooperative Networks and Competitive Dynamics: A Structural Embeddedness Perspective', *Academy of Management Review*, 26/3: 431–45.

GOMES-CASSERES, B. (1994). 'Group Versus Group: How Alliance Networks Compete', *Harvard Business Review*, 72/4: 62–74.

—— (1996). *The Alliance Revolution: The New Shape of Business Rivalry*. Cambridge, MA: Harvard University Press.

GOMPERS, P. A., et al. (1998). 'What Drives Venture Capital Fundraising?' *Brookings Papers on Economic Activity—Microeconomics*, 149–92.

GOOD, D. (1988). 'Individuals, Interpersonal Relations, and Trust', in D. Gambetta (ed.), *Trust: Making and Breaking Cooperative Relations*. Cambridge, MA: Basil Blackwell Ltd, 31–48.

GORMAN, M. and SAHLMAN, W. A. (1989). 'What Do Venture Capitalists Do?' *Journal of Business Venturing*, 4/4: 231–47.

GOURMAN, J. (1980). *The Gourman Report: A Rating of Graduate and Professional Programs in American and International Universities*. Los Angeles, CA: National Education Standards.

_____ (1983). *The Gourman Report: A Rating of Graduate and Professional Programs in American and International Universities*. Los Angeles, CA: National Education Standards.

_____ (1985). *The Gourman Report: A Rating of Graduate and Professional Programs in American and International Universities*. Los Angeles, CA: National Education Standards.

_____ (1987). *The Gourman Report: A Rating of Graduate and Professional Programs in American and International Universities*. Los Angeles, CA: National Education Standards.

_____ (1989). *The Gourman Report: A Rating of Graduate and Professional Programs in American and International Universities*. Los Angeles, CA: National Education Standards.

_____ (1993). *The Gourman Report: A Rating of Graduate and Professional Programs in American and International Universities*. Los Angeles, CA: National Education Standards.

_____ (1996). *The Gourman Report: A Rating of Graduate and Professional Programs in American and International Universities*. Los Angeles, CA: National Education Standards.

GRANOVETTER, M. S. (1973). 'The Strength of Weak Ties', *American Journal of Sociology*, 78/6: 1360–80.

_____ (1974). *Getting a Job*. Cambridge, MA: Harvard University Press.

_____ (1985). 'Economic Action and Social Structure: The Problem of Embeddedness', *American Journal of Sociology*, 91/3: 481–510.

_____ (1988). 'The Sociological and Economic Approaches to Labor Market Analysis', in G. Farkas and P. England (eds.), *Industries, Firms, and Jobs: Sociological and Economic Approaches*. New York: Plenum Press.

_____ (1992). 'Problems of Explanation in Economic Sociology', in N. Nohria and R. G. Eccles (eds.), *Networks and Organizations: Structure, Form, and Action*. Boston, MA: Harvard Business School Press.

GROSSMAN, S. J. and HART, O. D. (1986). 'The Costs and Benefits of Ownership: A Theory of Vertical and Lateral Integration', *Journal of Political Economy*, 94/4: 691–719.

GROVES, R. M., CIALDINI, R. B., and COUPER, M. P. (1992). 'Understanding the Decision to Participate in a Survey', *Public Opinion Quarterly*, 56/4: 475–95.

GULATI, R. (1993). 'The Dynamics of Alliance Formation', Harvard University, Doctoral Dissertation.

_____ (1995a). 'Does Familiarity Breed Trust? The Implications of Repeated Ties for Contractual Choice in Alliances', *Academy of Management Journal*, 38/1: 85–112.

_____ (1995b). 'Social Structure and Alliance Formation Patterns: A Longitudinal Analysis', *Administrative Science Quarterly*, 40/4: 619–52.

_____ (1998). 'Alliances and Networks', *Strategic Management Journal*, 19/4: 293–317.

_____ (1999). 'Network Location and Learning: The Influence of Network Resources and Firm Capabilities on Alliance Formation', *Strategic Management Journal*, 20/5: 397–420.

_____ (2006). 'Silo Busting: Transcending Barriers to Build High Growth Organizations', Harvard Business School Press, forthcoming.

——— and Gargiulo, M. (1999). 'Where Do Interorganizational Networks Come From?' *American Journal of Sociology*, 104/5: 1439–93.

——— and Higgins, M. C. (2003). 'Which Ties Matter When? The Contingent Effects of Interorganizational Partnerships on IPO Success', *Strategic Management Journal*, 24/2: 127–44.

——— and Kletter, D. (2005). 'Shrinking Core, Expanding Periphery: The Relational Architecture of High-Performing Organizations', *California Management Review*, 47/3: 77–104.

——— and Nickerson, J. (2006). 'Interorganizational Trust, Asset Specificity, and Their Effect on Organizational Choice and Performance for Component Sourcing in the U.S. Auto Industry', Northwestern University.

——— and Oldroyd, J. B. (2005). 'The Quest for Customer Focus', *Harvard Business Review*, 83/4: 92–101.

——— and Singh, H. (1998). 'The Architecture of Cooperation: Managing Coordination Costs and Appropriation Concerns in Strategic Alliances', *Administrative Science Quarterly*, 43/4: 781–814.

——— and Sytch, M. (2006a). 'Dependence Asymmetry and Joint Dependence in Interorganizational Relationships: Effects of Embeddedness on Manufacturer's Performance in Procurement Relationships', *Administrative Science Quarterly*, forthcoming.

——— and Sytch, M. (2006b). 'Does Familiarity Breed Trust? Revisiting the Antecedents of Trust', *Managerial and Decision Economics*, forthcoming.

——— and Wang, L. O. (2003). 'Size of the Pie and Share of the Pie: Implications of Network Embeddedness and Business Relatedness for Value Creation and Value Appropriation in Joint Ventures', in Vincent Buskens, Werner Raub, and Chris Snijders (eds.), *Research in the Sociology of Organizations.* Vol. 20. Oxford: JAI Press.

——— and Westphal, J. D. (1999). 'Cooperative or Controlling? The Effects of CEO–Board Relations and the Content of Interlocks on the Formation of Joint Ventures', *Administrative Science Quarterly*, 44/3: 473–506.

——— Huffman, S., and Neilson, G. (2002). 'The Barista Principle: Starbucks and the Rise of Relational Capital', *Strategy+Business*, Third Quarter: 1–12.

——— Khanna, T., and Nohria, N. (1994). 'Unilateral Commitments and the Importance of Process in Alliances', *Sloan Management Review*, 35/3: 61–9.

——— Lavie, D., and Madhavan, R. (2006). 'Unpacking the Performance Effects of Interorganizational Networks: Richness, Reach, and Receptivity', Northwestern University.

——— Lawrence, P. R., and Puranam, P. (2005). 'Adaptation in Vertical Relationships: Beyond Incentive Conflict', *Strategic Management Journal*, 26/5: 415–40.

——— Nohria, N., and Zaheer, A. (2000). 'Strategic Networks', *Strategic Management Journal*, 21/3: 203–15.

——— et al. (2004). 'How CEOs Manage Growth Agendas', *Harvard Business Review*, 82/7–8: 124–32.

Hackman, J. R. (1987). 'The Design of Work Teams', in J. W. Lorsch (ed.), *The Handbook of Organizational Behavior.* Englewood Cliffs, NJ: Prentice-Hall.

Hage, J. and Aiken, M. (1987). 'Program Change and Organizational Properties: A Comparative Analysis', *American Journal of Sociology*, 72: 503–19.

Hagedoorn, J. (1993). 'Understanding The Rationale of Strategic Technology Partnering: Interorganizational Modes of Cooperation and Sectoral Differences', *Strategic Management Journal*, 14/5: 371–85.

HAGEDOORN, J. and SCHAKENRAAD, J. (1994). 'The Effect of Strategic Technology Alliances on Company Performance', *Strategic Management Journal*, 15/4: 291–309.

HAMBRICK, D. C. and MASON, P. A. (1984). 'Upper Echelons: The Organization as a Reflection of its Top Managers', *Academy of Management Review*, 9/2: 193–206.

——CHO, T. S., and CHEN, M.-J. (1996). 'The Influence of Top Management Team Heterogeneity on Firms' Competitive Moves', *Administrative Science Quarterly*, 41/4: 659–84.

HAMEL, G. (1991). 'Competition for Competence and Inter-Partner Learning within International Strategic Alliances', *Strategic Management Journal*, 12: 83–103.

——DOZ, Y. L., and PRAHALAD, C. K. (1989). 'Collaborate with Your Competitors—and Win'. *Harvard Business Review*, 67/1: 133–9.

HAMILTON, G. G. and BIGGART, N. W. (1988). 'Market, Culture, and Authority: A Comparative Analysis of Management and Organization in the Far East', *American Journal of Sociology*, 94/Supplement: S52–S94.

HAMMER, M. (2001). *The Agenda: What Every Business Must Do to Dominate the Decade*, 1st edn. New York: Crown Business.

HANNAN, M. T. and CARROLL, C. R. (1992). *Dynamics of Organizational Populations: Density, Competition and Legitimation*. New York: Oxford University Press.

——and YOUNG, A. A. (1977). 'Estimation in Panel Models: Results on Pooling Cross-Sections and Time Series', in D. R. Heise (ed.), *Sociological Methodology*. San Francisco, CA: Jossey-Bass.

HANSEN, G. S. and HILL, C. W. L. (1991). 'Are Institutional Investors Myopic? A Time-Series Study of Four Technology-Driven Industries', *Strategic Management Journal*, 12/1: 1–16.

HANSEN, M. T. and NOHRIA, N. (2004). 'How to Build Collaborative Advantage', *Sloan Management Review*, 46/1: 22–30.

——and OETINGER, B. VON (2001). 'Introducing T-Shaped Managers: Knowledge Management's Next Generation', *Harvard Business Review*, 79/3: 106–16.

HARRIGAN, K. R. (1985). *Strategies for Joint Ventures*. Lexington, MA: Lexington Books.

——(1986). *Managing for Joint Venture Success*. Lexington, MA: Lexington Books.

——(1988). 'Strategic Alliances and Partner Asymmetries in International Business', in F. J. Contractor and P. Lorange (eds.), *Cooperative Strategies in International Business*. Lexington, MA: Lexington Books.

HAUNSCHILD, P. R. (1993). 'Interorganizational Imitation: The Impact of Interlocks on Corporate Acquisition Activity', *Administrative Science Quarterly*, 38/4: 564–92.

HAVILAND, J. B. (1977). 'Gossip as Competition in Zinacantan', *Journal of Communication*, 27/1: 186–91.

VON HAYEK, F. A. (1949). 'The Meaning of Competition', in F. A. von Hayek (ed.), *Individualism and Economic Order*. London: Routledge & Kegan Paul.

HAYES, S. L. (1971). 'Investment Banking: Power Structure in Flux', *Harvard Business Review*, 49/2: 136–52.

HECKMAN, J. J. (1979). 'Sample Selection Bias as a Specification Error', *Econometrica*, 45: 153–61.

——(1981*a*). 'Statistical Models for Discrete Panel Data', in C. F. Manski and D. L. McFadden (eds.), *Structural Analysis of Discrete Data with Econometric Applications*. Cambridge, MA: MIT Press.

——(1981*b*). 'Heterogeneity and State Dependence', in S. Rosen (ed.), *Studies in Labor Markets*. Chicago, IL: University of Chicago Press.

——— and BORJAS, G. J. (1980). 'Does Unemployment Cause Future Unemployment? Definitions, Questions and Answers from a Continuous Time Model of Heterogeneity and State Dependence', *Economica*, 47/187: 247–83.

HEIDE, J. B. and MINER, A. S. (1992). 'The Shadow of the Future: Effects of Anticipated Interaction and Frequency of Contact on Buyer–Seller Cooperation', *Academy of Management Journal*, 35/2: 265–91.

HELLMANN, T. (1998). 'The Allocation of Control Rights in Venture Capital Contracts', *Rand Journal of Economics*, 29/1: 57–76.

——— and PURI, M. (2000). 'The Interaction Between Product Market and Financing Strategy: The Role of Venture Capital', *Review of Financial Studies*, 13/4: 959–84.

HENNART, J.-F. (1988). 'A Transaction Costs Theory of Equity Joint Ventures', *Strategic Management Journal*, 9/4: 361–74.

HERMALIN, B. E. and WEISBACH, M. S. (1988). 'The Determinants of Board Composition', *Rand Journal of Economics*, 19/4: 589–606.

HERMAN, E. S. (1981). *Corporate Control, Corporate Power*. New York: Cambridge University Press.

HERRIOTT, S. R. (1996). 'Control of Strategic Alliances Through Partial Acquisitions', Department of Organization Behavior, Maharishi International University.

HIGGINS, M. C. and GULATI, R. (2003). 'Getting off to a Good Start: The Effects of Upper Echelon Affiliations on Underwriter Prestige', *Organization Science*, 14/3: 244–63.

——— ——— (2006). 'Stacking the Deck: The Effects of Top Management Backgrounds on Investor Decisions', *Strategic Management Journal*, 27/1: 1–25.

HILL, C. W. L. and SNELL, S. A. (1988). 'External Control, Corporate Strategy, and Firm Performance in Research-Intensive Industries', *Strategic Management Journal*, 9/6: 577–90.

HITT, M. A., et al. (2001). 'Guest Editors' Introduction to the Special Issue—Strategic Entrepreneurship: Entrepreneurial Strategies for Wealth Creation', *Strategic Management Journal*, 22/6/7: 479–91.

HOANG, H. and ROTHAERMEL, F. T. (2005). 'The Effect of General and Partner-Specific Alliance Experience on Joint R&D Project Performance', *Academy of Management Journal*, 48/2: 332–45.

HOEM, J. M. (1985). 'Weighting, Misclassification, and Other Issues in the Analysis of Survey Samples of Life Histories', in J. J. Heckman and B. Singer (eds.), *Longitudinal Analysis of Labor Market Data*. New York: Cambridge University Press.

HOETKER, G., SWAMINATHAN, A., and MITCHELL, W. (2006). 'Modularity and the Impact of Buyer–Supplier Relationships on the Survival of Suppliers', University of Illinois at Urbana-Champagne.

HOLLAND, P. W. and LEINHARDT, S. (1970). 'A Method for Detecting Structure in Sociometric Data', *American Journal of Sociology*, 76: 492–513.

HOSKISSON, R. E., JOHNSON, R. A., and MOESEL, D. D. (1994). 'Corporate Divestiture Intensity in restructuring Firms: Effects of Governance, Strategy, and Performance', *Academy of Management Journal*, 37/5: 1207–51.

HOSMER, D. W. and LEMESHOW, S. (1989). *Applied Logistic Regression*. New York: Wiley.

HSIAO, C. (1986). *Analysis of Panel Data*. New York: Cambridge University Press.

INKPEN, A. C. (1998). 'Learning and Knowledge Acquisition Through International Strategic Alliances', *Academy of Management Executive*, 12: 69–80.

JACCARD, J., TURRISI, R., and WAN, C. K. (1990). *Interaction Effects in Multiple Regression.* Newbury Park, CA: Sage.

JACKSON, J. E. (1991). *A User's Guide to Principal Components.* New York: Wiley.

JAIN, B. A. and KINI, O. (1994). 'The Post-Issue Operating Performance of IPO Firms', *Journal of Finance,* 49/5: 1699–726.

——— (1995). 'Venture Capitalist Participation and the Post-Issue Operating Performance of IPO Firms', *Managerial & Decision Economics,* 16/6: 593–606.

JENSEN, M. (2003). 'The Role of Network Resources in Market Entry: Commercial Banks' Entry into Investment Banking, 1991–1997', *Administrative Science Quarterly,* 48/3: 466–97.

—— and MURPHY, K. J. (1990). 'Performance Pay and Top-Management Incentives', *Journal of Political Economy,* 98/2: 225–64.

JOHNSON, R. A., HOSKISSON, R. E., and HITT, M. A. (1993). 'Board of Director Involvement in Restructuring: The Effects of Board Versus Managerial Controls and Characteristics', *Strategic Management Journal,* 14/Special Issue: Corporate Restructuring: 33–50.

JOHNSTON, R. and LAWRENCE, P. R. (1988). 'Beyond Vertical Integration—The Rise of the Value-Adding Partnership', *Harvard Business Review,* 66/4: 94–101.

JOSKOW, P. L. (1987). 'Contract Duration and Relationship-Specific Investments: Empirical Evidence from Coal Markets', *American Economic Review,* 77/1: 168–85.

KALE, P., DYER, J. H., and SINGH, H. (2002). 'Alliance Capability, Stock Market Response, and Long-Term Alliance Success: The Role of the Alliance Function', *Strategic Management Journal,* 23/8: 747–67.

—— SINGH, H., and PERLMUTTER, H. (2000). 'Learning and Protection of Proprietary Assets in Strategic Alliances: Building Relational Capital', *Strategic Management Journal,* 21/3: 217–37.

KAPLAN, M. R. and HARRISON, J. R. (1993). 'Defusing the Director Liability Crisis: The Strategic Management of Legal Threats', *Organization Science,* 4/3: 412–32.

KATZ, D. and KAHN, R. L. (1966). *The Social Psychology of Organizations.* New York: Wiley.

KATZ, M. L. and SHAPIRO, C. (1985). 'Network Externalities, Competition, and Compatibility', *American Economic Review,* 75/3: 424–40.

KECK, S. L. and TUSHMAN, M. L. (1993). 'Environmental and Organizational Context and Executive Team Structure', *Academy of Management Journal,* 36/6: 1314–44.

KESNER, I. F. and JOHNSON, R. B. (1990). 'An Investigation of the Relationship Between Board Composition and Stockholder Suits', *Strategic Management Journal,* 11/4: 327–36.

KHANNA, T., GULATI, R., and NOHRIA, N. (1998). 'The Dynamics of Learning Alliances: Competition, Cooperation, and Relative Scope', *Strategic Management Journal,* 19/3: 193–210.

—— GULATI, R., and NOHRIA, N. (2000). 'The Economic Modeling of Strategic Process: "Clean Models" and "Dirty Hands" ', *Strategic Management Journal,* 21: 781–90.

KHURSHED, A. (2000). '*Discussion of* Does the Presence of Venture Capitalists Improve the Survival Profile of IPO Firms?' *Journal of Business Finance & Accounting,* 27/9–10: 1177–83.

KILDUFF, M. and TSAI, W. (2003). *Social Networks and Organizations.* London: Sage.

KOGUT, B. (1988a). 'Joint Ventures: Theoretical and Empirical Perspectives', *Strategic Management Journal,* 9/4: 319–32.

—— (1988b). 'A Study of the Life Cycle of Joint Ventures', in F. J. Contractor and P. Lorange (eds.), *Cooperative Strategies in International Business.* Lexington, MA: Lexington Books.

_____(1989). 'The Stability of Joint Ventures: Reciprocity and Competitive Rivalry', *Journal of Industrial Economics*, 38/2: 183–98.

_____ and SINGH, H. (1988). 'The Effect of National Culture on the Choice of Entry Mode', *Journal of International Business Studies*, 19/3: 319–32.

_____ SHAN, W., and WALKER, G. (1992). 'The Make-or-Cooperate Decision in the Context of an Industry Network', in N. Nohria and R. G. Eccles (eds.), *Networks and Organizations: Structure, Form and Action*. Boston, MA: Harvard Business School Press.

KOH, J. and VENKATRAMAN, N. (1991). 'Joint Venture Formations and Stock Market Reactions: An Assessment in the Information Technology Sector', *Academy of Management Journal*, 34: 869–92.

KOZA, M. and LEWIN, A. (1998). 'The Co-Evolution of Strategic Alliances', *Organization Science*, 9: 255–64.

KRAATZ, M. S. and ZAJAC, E. J. (2001). 'How Organizational Resources Affect Strategic Change and Performance in Turbulent Environments: Theory and Evidence', *Organization Science*, 12/5: 632–57.

KRACKHARDT, D. (1987). 'QAP Partialling as a Test for Spuriousness', *Social Networks*, 9: 171–86.

_____(1988). 'Predicting with Networks: Nonparametric Multiple Regression Analysis of Dyadic Data', *Social Networks*, 10: 359–81.

_____(1992). 'The Strength of Strong Ties: The Importance of Philos in Organizations', in N. Nohria and R. G. Eccles (eds.), *Networks and Organizations: Structure, Form and Action*. Boston, MA: Harvard Business School Press.

KRAMER, R. M. (1994). 'The Sinister Attribution Error: Paranoid Cognition and Collective Distrust in Organizations', *Motivation and Emotion*, 18/2: 199–230.

_____(1996). 'Divergent Realities and Convergent Disappointments in the Hierarchic Relation: Trust and the Intuitive Auditor at Work', in R. M. Kramer and T. R. Tyler (eds.), *Trust in Organizations: Frontiers of Theory and Research*. Thousand Oaks, CA: Sage.

_____ and TYLER, T. R. (1996). *Trust in Organizations: Frontiers of Theory and Research*. Thousand Oaks, CA: Sage.

KREPS, D. M. (1990). 'Corporate Culture and Economic Theory', in J. E. Alt and K. A. Shepsle (eds.), *Perspectives on Positive Political Economy*. New York: Cambridge University Press.

KUMAR, N. (2003). *Marketing as Strategy*. Boston, MA: Harvard Business School Press.

_____ SCHEER, L. K., and STEENKAMP, J.-B. E. M. (1995). 'The Effects of Perceived Interdependence on Dealer Attitudes', *Journal of Marketing Research*, 32/3: 348–56.

LABIANCA, G., BRASS, D. J., and GRAY, B. (1998). 'Social Networks and Perceptions of Intergroup Conflict: The Role of Negative Relationships and Third Parties', *Academy of Management Journal*, 41/1: 55–67.

LARSON, A. (1992). 'Network Dyads in Entrepreneurial Settings: A Study of the Governance of Exchange Relationships', *Administrative Science Quarterly*, 37/1: 76–104.

LAUMANN, E. O., GALASKIEWICZ, J., and MARSDEN, P. V. (1978). 'Community Structure as Interorganizational Linkages', *Annual Review of Sociology*, 4: 455–84.

LAVIE, D. (2006). 'The Competitive Advantage of Interconnected Firms: An Extension of the Resource-Based View', *Academy of Management Review*, forthcoming.

LECHNER, C. and DOWLING, M. (2003). 'Firm Networks: External Relationships as Sources for the Growth and Competitiveness of Entrepreneurial Firms', *Entrepreneurship & Regional Development*, 15/1: 1–26.

LEE, C., LEE, K., and PENNINGS, J. M. (2001). 'Internal Capabilities, External Networks, and Performance: A Study on Technology-Based Ventures', *Strategic Management Journal*, 22/6–7: 615–40.

LEE, K. and BURRILL, G. S. (1995). *Biotech 96*. Palo Alto, CA: Ernst and Young.

LERNER, J. (1994). 'Venture Capitalists and the Decision to Go Public', *Journal of Financial Economics*, 35: 293–316.

——and MERGES, R. P. (1996). *The Control of Strategic Alliances: An Empirical Analysis of Biotechnology Collaborations*. Boston, MA: Harvard Business School Press.

LEVIN, R. C., et al. (1987). 'Appropriating the Returns from Industrial Research and Development', *Brookings Papers on Economic Activity*, 1987/3: 783–831.

LEVINE, S. and WHITE, P. E. (1961). 'Exchange as a Conceptual Framework for the Study of Interorganizational Relationships', *Administrative Science Quarterly*, 5/4: 583–601.

LEVINTHAL, D. A. and FICHMAN, M. (1988). 'Dynamics of Interorganizational Attachments: Auditor–Client Relationships', *Administrative Science Quarterly*, 33/3: 345–69.

——and MARCH, J. G. (1993). 'The Myopia of Learning', *Strategic Management Journal*, 14/Winter Special Issue: 95–112.

LEWICKI, R. J., McALLISTER, D. J., and BIES, R. J. (1998). 'Trust and Distrust: New Relationships and Realities', *Academy of Management Review*, 23/3: 438–58.

LEWIS, J. D. (1990). *Partnerships for Profit*. New York: Free Press.

——and WEIGERT, A. (1985). 'Trust as a Social Reality', *Social Forces*, 63/4: 967–85.

LI, S. X. and ROWLEY, T. J. (2002). 'Inertia and Evaluation Mechanisms in Interorganizational Partner Selection: Syndicate Formation Among U.S. Investment Banks', *Academy of Management Journal*, 45/6: 1104–19.

LIN, T. H. (1996). 'The Certification Role of Large Block Shareholders in Initial Public Offerings: The Case of Venture Capitalists', *Quarterly Journal of Business & Economics*, 35/2: 55–66.

LINCOLN, J. R. (1984). 'Analyzing Relations in Dyads', *Sociological Methods & Research*, 13/1: 45–76.

LIST, P., PLATT, G., and ROMBEL, A. (2000). 'World's Best Investment Banks 2000', *Global Finance*, 14/11: 52–60.

LITTLE, R. J. A. and RUBIN, D. B. (1987). *Statistical Analysis with Missing Data*. New York: Wiley.

LITWAK, E. and HYLTON, L. F. (1962). 'Interorganizational Analysis: A Hypothesis on Coordinating Agencies', *Administrative Science Quarterly*, 6: 395–420.

LLEWELLYN, K. N. (1931). 'What Price Contract? An Essay in Perspective', *Yale Law Journal*, 40/May: 704–51.

LORENZ, E. H. (1988). 'Neither Friends nor Strangers: Informal Networks of Subcontracting in French Industry', in D. Gambetta (ed.), *Trust: Making and Breaking Cooperative Relations*. Cambridge, MA: Basil Blackwell Ltd.

LORENZONI, G. and BADEN-FULLER, C. (1995). 'Creating a Strategic Center to Manage a Web of Partners', *California Management Review*, 37/3: 146–63.

LORSCH, J. W. and MacIVER, E. (1989). *Pawns or Potentates: The Reality of America's Corporate Boards*. Boston, MA: Harvard Business School Press.

LOURY, G. C. (1977). 'A Dynamic Theory of Racial Income Differences', in P. A. Wallace and A. M. LaMond (eds.), *Women, Minorities, and Employment Discrimination*. Lexington, MA: Lexington Books.

—— (1987). 'Why Should We Care About Group Inequality?' *Social Philosophy and Policy*, 5/1: 249–71.

LUHMANN, N. (1979). *Trust and Power.* New York: Wiley.

LYLES, M. A. (1988). 'Learning Among Joint Venture-Sophisticated Firms', in F. J. Contractor and P. Lorange (eds.), *Cooperative Strategies in International Business.* Lexington, MA: Lexington Books.

MACAULAY, S. (1963). 'Non-Contractual Relations in Business: A Preliminary Study', *American Sociological Review*, 28/1: 55–67.

McCANN, J. and GALBRAITH, J. R. (1981). 'Interdepartmental Relations', in P. C. Nystrom and W. H. Starbuck (eds.), *Handbook of Organizational Design*, 2nd edn. Oxford: Oxford University Press.

McCONNELL, J. and NANTELL, T. (1985). 'Corporate Combinations and Common Stock Returns: The Case of JVs', *Journal of Finance*, 50: 519–36.

McDONALD, M. L. and WESTPHAL, J. D. (2003). 'Getting by with the Advice of Their Friends: CEOs' Advice Networks and Firms' Strategic Responses to Poor Performance', *Administrative Science Quarterly*, 48/1: 1–32.

MACE, M. L. (1971). *Directors: Myth and Reality.* Boston, MA: Harvard Business School Press.

MACINTYRE, A. C. (1981). *After Virtue: A Study in Moral Theory.* Notre Dame, IN: University of Notre Dame Press.

MADHAVAN, R. and PRESCOTT, J. E. (1995). 'Market Value Impact of Joint Ventures: The Effect of Industry Information-Processing Load', *Academy of Management Journal*, 38: 900–15.

MAHONEY, J. T. and PANDIAN, J. R. (1992). 'The Resource-Based View within the Conversation of Strategic Management', *Strategic Management Journal*, 13/5: 363–80.

MAITLAND, I., BRYSON, J., and VAN DE VEN, A. H. (1985). 'Sociologists, Economists, and Opportunism', *Academy of Management Review*, 10/1: 59–65.

MANLEY, B. F. (1992). *The Design and Analysis of Research Studies.* New York: Cambridge University Press.

MANSFIELD, E. (1993). 'Unauthorized Use of Intellectual Property: Effects on Investment, Technology Transfer, and Innovation', in M. B. Wallerstein, M. E. Mogee, and R. A. Schoen (eds.), *Global Dimensions of Intellectual Property Rights in Science and Technology.* Washington, DC: National Academy Press.

MARCH, J. G. (1991). 'Exploration and Exploitation in Organizational Learning', *Organization Science*, 2: 71–87.

—— and OLSEN, J. P. (1976). *Ambiguity and Choice in Organizations.* Bergen, Norway: Universitetsforlaget.

—— and SIMON, H. A. (1958). *Organizations.* New York: Wiley.

MARITI, P. and SMILEY, R. H. (1983). 'Co-operative Agreements and the Organization of Industry', *Journal of Industrial Economics*, 31/4: 437–51.

MARSDEN, P. V. and FRIEDKIN, N. E. (1993). 'Network Studies of Social Influence', *Sociological Methods and Research*, 22: 127–51.

MASTEN, S. E. , MEEHAN, J. W., and SNYDER, E. A. (1991). 'The Costs of Organization', *Journal of Law, Economics, and Organization*, 7: 1–25.

MEGGINSON, W. L. and WEISS, K. A. (1991). 'Venture Capitalist Certification in Initial Public Offerings', *Journal of Finance*, 46/3: 879–903.

MERGES, R. and NELSON, R. (1990). 'On the Complex Economics of Patent Scope', *Columbia Law Review*, 90: 839–70.

MERTON, R. K. (1973). *The Sociology of Science*. Chicago, IL: University of Chicago Press.

MESSICK, D. M. and MACKIE, D. M. (1989). 'Intergroup Relations', *Annual Review of Psychology*, 40: 45–81.

MEYER, J. and ROWAN, B. (1977). 'Institutionalized Organizations: Formal Structure as Myth and Ceremony', *American Journal of Sociology*, 83/2: 340–63.

MILLER, D. and FRIESEN, P. H. (1980). 'Momentum and Revolution in Organizational Adaptation', *Academy of Management Journal*, 23/4: 591–614.

MILLIKEN, F. J. (1987). 'Three Types of Perceived Uncertainty About the Environment: State, Effect, and Response Uncertainty', *Academy of Management Review*, 12/1: 133–43.

MINTZBERG, H. (ed.) (1983). *Power in and Around Organizations*. Englewood Cliffs, NJ: Prentice-Hall.

MITCHELL, W. and SINGH, K. (1992). 'Incumbents' Use of Pre-Entry Alliances Before Expansion into New Technical Subfields of an Industry', *Journal of Economic Behavior & Organization*, 18/3: 347–72.

_____ (1996). 'Survival of Businesses Using Collaborative Relationships to Commercialize Complex Goods', *Strategic Management Journal*, 17/3: 169–95.

MIZRUCHI, M. S. (1992). *The Structure of Corporate Political Action: Interfirm Relations and Their Consequences*. Cambridge, MA: Harvard University Press.

_____ (1993). 'Cohesion, Equivalence, and Similarity of Behavior: A Theoretical and Empirical Assessment', *Social Networks*, 15: 275–308.

_____ (1996). 'What Do Interlocks Do? An Analysis, Critique, and Assessment of Research on Interlocking Directorates', *Annual Review of Sociology*, 22: 271–98.

_____ and SCHWARTZ, M. (1987). *Intercorporate Relations: The Structural Analysis of Business*. Structural Analysis in the Social Sciences. Cambridge: Cambridge University Press.

MONGE, P. R. and CONTRACTOR, N. S. (2003). *Theories of Communication Networks*. New York: Oxford University Press.

MONTGOMERY, C. (1982). 'The Measurement of Firm Diversification: Some New Empirical Evidence', *Academy of Management Journal*, 25: 299–307.

MOON, J. J. and KHANNA, T. (1995). 'Product Market Considerations in Private Equity Sales', Harvard Business School.

MOWERY, D. and ROSENBERG, D. (1989). *Technology and the Pursuit of Economic Growth*. New York: Cambridge University Press.

_____ OXLEY, J. E. and SILVERMAN, B. S. (1996). 'Strategic Alliances and Interfirm Knowledge Transfer', *Strategic Management Journal*, 17/Special Issue: Knowledge and the Firm: 77–91.

MURPHY, K. J. (1986). 'Incentives, Learning, and Compensation: A Theoretical and Empirical Investigation of Managerial Labor Contracts', *Rand Journal of Economics*, 17/1: 59–76.

NELSON, R. R. and WINTER, S. G. (1982). *An Evolutionary Theory of Economic Change*. Cambridge, MA: Belknap Press of Harvard University Press.

NOHRIA, N. (1992a). 'Information and Search in the Creation of New Business Ventures: The Case of the 128 Venture Group', in N. Nohria and R. G. Eccles (eds.), *Networks and Organizations: Structure, Form and Action*. Boston, MA: Harvard Business School Press.

_____ (1992*b*). 'Introduction', in N. Nohria and R. G. Eccles (eds.), *Networks and Organizations: Structure, Form, and Action*. Boston, MA: Harvard Business School Press.

_____ and GARCIA-PONT, C. (1991). 'Global Strategic Linkages and Industry Structure', *Strategic Management Journal*, 12/Special Issue: Global Strategy: 105–24.

NOOTEBOOM, B., BERGER, H., and NOORDERHAVEN, N. G. (1997). 'Effects of Trust and Governance on Relational Risk', *Academy of Management Journal*, 40/2: 308–38.

NYSTROM, P. C., and STARBUCK, W. H. (1981). *Handbook of Organizational Design*. Oxford, NY: Oxford University Press.

OCASIO, W. (1997). 'Towards an Attention-Based View of the Firm', *Strategic Management Journal*, 18/Special Issue: Organizational and Competitive Interactions: 187–206.

OLIVER, C. (1990). 'Determinants of Interorganizational Relations: Integration and Future Directions', *Academy of Management Review*, 15: 241–65.

O'REILLY, C. A., III, SNYDER, R. C., and BOOTHE, J. N. (1993). 'Effects of Executive Team Demography on Organizational Change', in G. P. Huber and W. H. Glick (eds.), *Organizational Change and Redesign: Ideas and Insights for Improving Performance*. New York: Oxford University Press.

OSBORN, R. N. and BAUGHN, C. C. (1990). 'Forms of Interorganizational Governance for Multinational Alliances', *Academy of Management Journal*, 33/3: 503–19.

OXLEY, J. E. (1997). 'Appropriability Hazards and Governance in Strategic Alliances: A Transaction Cost Approach', *Journal of Law, Economics, and Organization*, 13/2: 387–409.

PALAY, T. M. (1985). 'Avoiding Regulatory Constraints: Contracting Safeguards and the Role of Informal Agreements', *Journal of Law, Economics, and Organization*, 1/1: 155–75.

PALEPU, K. G. (1985). 'Diversification Strategy, Profit Performance and the Entropy Measure', *Strategic Management Journal*, 6/3: 239–55.

PALMER, D. A., JENNINGS, P. D., and ZHOU, X. (1993). 'Late Adoption of the Multidivisional Form by Large U.S. Corporations: Institutional, Political and Economic Accounts', *Administrative Science Quarterly*, 38/1: 100–31.

PARISE, S. and CASHER, A. (2003). 'Alliance Portfolios: Designing and Managing Your Network of Business-Partner Relationships', *Academy of Management Executive*, 17/4: 25–39.

PARKHE, A. (1993*a*). 'Strategic Alliance Structuring: A Game Theoretic and Transaction Cost Examination of Interfirm Cooperation', *Academy of Management Journal*, 36/4: 794–829.

_____ (1993*b*). 'Partner Nationality and the Structure–Performance Relationship in Strategic Alliances', *Organization Science*, 4: 301–24.

PAULSON, S. K. (1976). 'A Theory and Comparative Analysis of Interorganizational Dyads', *Rural Sociology*, 41: 311–29.

PENROSE, E. T. (1959). *The Theory of the Growth of the Firm*. New York: Oxford University Press.

PERROW, C. (1986). *Complex Organizations: A Critical Essay*, 3rd edn. New York: Random House.

PETERAF, M. A. (1993). 'The Cornerstones of Competitive Advantage: A Resource-Based View', *Strategic Management Journal*, 14/3: 179–91.

PETERSEN, T. (1985). 'A Comment on Presenting Results from Logit and Probit Models', *American Sociological Review*, 50/1: 130–1.

_____ and KOPUT, K. W. (1991). 'Density Dependence in Organizational Mortality: Legitimacy or Unobserved Heterogeneity', *American Sociological Review*, 56/3: 399–409.

PETERSON, R. J. (2001). *Inside IPOs: The Secrets to Investing in Today's Newest Companies*. New York: McGraw-Hill.

PETTIGREW, A. M. (1992). 'On Studying Managerial Elites', *Strategic Management Journal*, 13/Special Issue: Fundamental Themes in Strategy Process Research: 163–82.

PFEFFER, J. (1987). 'A Resource Dependence Perspective on Intercorporate Relations', in M. S. Mizruchi and M. Schwartz (eds.), *Intercorporate Relations: The Structural Analysis of Business*. New York: Cambridge University Press.

——— and NOWAK, P. (1976). 'Joint-Ventures and Interorganizational Interdependence', *Administrative Science Quarterly*, 21/3: 398–418.

——— and SALANCIK, G. R. (1978). *The External Control of Organizations: A Resource Dependence Perspective*. New York: Harper & Row.

PINAR, O. and EISENHARDT, K. M. (2005). 'Startups in an Emergent Market: Building a Strong Alliance Portfolio from a Low-Power Position', paper given at Danish Research Unit for Industrial Dynamics (DRUID) Summer Conference 2005, Copenhagen, June 27–29.

PIORE, M. J. and SABEL, C. F. (1984). *The Second Industrial Divide: Possibilities for Prosperity*. New York: Basic Books.

PISANO, G. P. (1987). *The Development Factory: Unlocking the Potential of Process Innovation*. Boston, MA: Harvard Business School Press.

——— (1989). 'Using Equity Participation to Support Exchange: Evidence from the Biotechnology Industry', *Journal of Law, Economics, and Organization*, 5/1: 109–26.

——— (1990). 'The R&D Boundaries of the Firm: An Empirical Analysis', *Administrative Science Quarterly*, 35: 153–76.

——— (1991). 'The Governance of Innovation: Vertical Integration and Collaborative Arrangements in the Biotechnology Industry', *Research Policy*, 20/3: 237–49.

——— (1993). 'Collaborative Product Development and the Market for Know-How: Strategies and Structures in the Biotechnology Industry', in R. Rosenbloom and R. Burgelman (eds.), *Research on Technological Innovation, Management and Policy*. Vol. 5. Greenwich, CT: JAI Press.

——— and MANG, P. (1993). 'Collaborative Product Development and the Market for Know-How: Strategies and Structures in the Biotechnology Industry', in R. Rosenbloom and R. Burgelman (eds.), *Research on Technological Innovation, Management, and Policy*. Vol 5. Greenwich, CT: JAI Press.

——— RUSSO, M. V., and TEECE, D. J. (1988). 'Joint Ventures and Collaborative Agreements in the Telecommunications Equipment Industry', in D. C. Mowery (ed.), *International Collaborative Ventures in U.S. Manufacturing*. Cambridge, MA: Ballinger Publishing Company.

PODOLNY, J. M. (1993). 'A Status-Based Model of Market Competition', *American Journal of Sociology*, 98/4: 829–72.

——— (1994). 'Market Uncertainty and the Social Character of Economic Exchange', *Administrative Science Quarterly*, 39/3: 458–83.

——— (2001). 'Networks as the Pipes and Prisms of the Market: A Look at Investment Decisions in the Venture Capital Industry', *American Journal of Sociology*, 107/1: 33–60.

——— STUART, T. E., and HANNAN, M. T. (1996). 'Networks, Knowledge, and Niches: Competition in the Worldwide Semiconductor Industry, 1984–1991', *American Journal of Sociology*, 102/3: 659–89.

POLLOCK, T. G. and RINDOVA, V. P. (2003). 'Media Legitimation Effects in the Market for Initial Public Offerings', *Academy of Management Journal*, 46/5: 631–42.

PONDY, L. R. (1970). 'Toward a Theory of Internal Resource Allocation', in M. N. Zald (ed.), *Power in Organizations*. Nashville, TN: Vanderbilt University Press.

—— (1977). 'The Other Hand Clapping: An Information-Processing Approach to Organizational Power', in T. H. Hammer and S. B. Bacharach (eds.), *Reward Systems and Power Distribution in Organizations*. Ithaca, NY: Cornell University Press.

POPPO, L. and ZENGER, T. (2002). 'Do Formal Contracts and Relational Governance Function as Substitutes or Complements?' *Strategic Management Journal*, 23/8: 707–25.

PORTER, M. E. (1980). *Competitive Strategy: Techniques for Analyzing Industries and Competitors*. New York: Free Press.

—— (1990). *The Competitive Advantage of Nations*. New York: Free Press.

—— and FULLER, M. B. (1986). 'Coalitions and Global Strategy', in M. E. Porter (ed.), *Competition in Global Industries*. Boston, MA: Harvard Business School Press.

PORTES, A. and SENSENBRENNER, J. (1993). 'Embeddedness and Immigration: Notes on the Social Determinants of Economic Action', *American Journal of Sociology*, 98/6: 1320–50.

POWELL, W. W. (1990). 'Neither Market nor Hierarchy: Network Forms of Organization', in L. L. Cummings and B. M. Staw (eds.), *Research in Organizational Behavior*. Vol. 12. Greenwich, CT: JAI Press.

—— and BRANTLEY, P. (1992). 'Competitive Cooperation in Biotechnology: Learning Through Networks', in N. Nohria and R. G. Eccles (eds.), *Networks and Organizations: Structure, Form, and Action*. Boston, MA: Harvard Business School Press.

—— KOPUT, K. W., and SMITH-DOERR, L. (1996). 'Interorganizational Collaboration and the Locus of Innovation: Networks of Learning in Biotechnology', *Administrative Science Quarterly*, 41/1: 116–45.

—— et al. (2005). 'Network Dynamics and Field Evolution: The Growth of Interorganizational Collaboration in the Life Sciences', *American Journal of Sociology*, 110/4: 1132–205.

PRAHALAD, C. K. and RAMASWAMY, V. (2004). *The Future of Competition: Co-Creating Unique Value with Customers*. Boston, MA: Harvard Business School Press.

PURI, M. (1999). 'Commercial Banks as Underwriters: Implications for the Going Public Process', *Journal of Financial Economics*, 54/2: 133–63.

PUTNAM, R. D. (1993). 'The Prosperous Community: Social Capital and Public Life', *American Prospect*, 4/13: 35–42.

RANGAN, S. (2000). 'The Problem of Search and Deliberation in Economic Action: When Social Networks Really Matter', *Academy of Management Review*, 25/4: 813–28.

RAO, H. (1994). 'The Social Construction of Reputation: Certification Contests, Legitimation, and the Survival of Organizations in the American Automobile Industry: 1895–1912', *Strategic Management Journal*, 15/Special Issue: Competitive Organizational Behavior: 29–44.

—— and DRAZIN, R. (2002). 'Overcoming Resource Constraints on Product Innovation by Recruiting Talent from Rivals: A Study of the Mutual Fund Industry, 1986–1994', *Academy of Management Journal*, 45/3: 491–507.

RAU, P. R. (2000). 'Investment Bank Market Share, Contingent Fee Payments, and the Performance of Acquiring Firms', *Journal of Financial Economics*, 56/2: 293–324.

RAUB, W. and WEESIE, J. (1990). 'Reputation and Efficiency in Social Interactions: An Example of Network Effects', *American Journal of Sociology*, 96/3: 626–54.

REICH, R. B. and MANKIN, E. D. (1986). 'Joint Ventures with Japan Give Away Our Future', *Harvard Business Review*, 64/2: 78–86.

REUER, J. J. and ARINO, A. (2006). 'Strategic Alliance Contracts: Dimensions and Determinants of Contractual Complexity', *Strategic Management Journal*, forthcoming.

____ and RAGOZZINO, R. (2006). 'Agency Hazards and Alliance Portfolios', *Strategic Management Journal*, 27/1: 27–43.

____ ZOLLO, M., and SINGH, H. (2002). 'Post-Formation Dynamics in Strategic Alliances', *Strategic Management Journal*, 23/2: 135.

RICHARDSON, G. B. (1972). 'The Organisation of Industry', *Economic Journal*, 82/327: 883–96.

RING, P. S. and VAN DE VEN, A. (1989). 'Formal and Informal Dimensions of Transactions', in A. H. Van de Ven, H. L. Angle, and M. S. Poole (eds.), *Research on the Management of Innovation: The Minnesota Studies*. New York: Ballinger Publishing Company.

_____ (1992). 'Structuring Cooperative Relationships Between Organizations', *Strategic Management Journal*, 13/7: 483–98.

_____ (1994). 'Developmental Processes of Cooperative Interorganizational Relationships', *Academy of Management Review*, 19/1: 90–118.

RITTER, J. R. (1984). 'The "Hot Issue" Market of 1980', *Journal of Business*, 57/2: 215–41.

ROSENKOPF, L., METIU, A., and GEORGE, V. P. (2001). 'From the Bottom Up? Technical Committee Activity and Alliance Formation', *Administrative Science Quarterly*, 46/4: 748–72.

ROSENTHAL, R. and ROSNOW, R. L. (1991). *Essentials of Behavioral Research: Methods and Data Analysis*. New York: McGraw-Hill.

ROTHAERMEL, F. T. (2001). 'Incumbent's Advantage Through Exploiting Complementary Assets via Interfirm Cooperation', *Strategic Management Journal*, 22/6–7: 687–99.

ROWLEY, T., BEHRENS, D., and KRACKHARDT, D. (2000). 'Redundant Governance Structures: An Analysis of Structural and Relational Embeddedness in the Steel and Semiconductor Industries', *Strategic Management Journal*, 21/3: 369–86.

RUMELT, R. P. (1974). *Strategy, Structure, and Economic Performance*. Cambridge, MA: Harvard University Press.

SABEL, C. F. (1993). 'Studied Trust: Building New Forms of Cooperation in a Volatile Economy', *Human Relations*, 46/9: 1133–70.

____ and ZEITLIN, J. (1985). 'Historical Alternatives to Mass Production: Politics, Markets and Technology in Nineteenth-Century Industrialization', *Past and Present*, 108: 133–76.

SAH, R. K. and STIGLITZ, J. E. (1986). 'The Architecture of Economic Systems: Hierarchies and Polyarchies', *American Economic Review*, 76/4: 716–27.

____ (1988). 'Committees, Hierarchies and Polyarchies', *Economic Journal*, 98/391: 451–70.

SAHLMAN, W. A. (1990). 'The Structure and Governance of Venture-Capital Organizations', *Journal of Financial Economics*, 27/2: 473–521.

SARKAR, M. B., ECHAMBADI, R., and HARRISON, J. S. (2001). 'Alliance Entrepreneurship and Firm Market Performance', *Strategic Management Journal*, 22/6–7: 701–11.

SAXENIAN, A. (1990). 'Regional Networks and the Resurgence of Silicon Valley', *California Management Review*, 33/1: 89–112.

SCHERMERHORN, J. R., JR. (1975). 'Determinants of Interorganizational Cooperation', *Academy of Management Journal*, 18: 846–56.

SCHMIDT, S. and KOCHAN, T. (1977). 'Interorganizational Relationships: Patterns and Motivations', *Administrative Science Quarterly*, 22: 220–34.

SETH, A. (1990). 'Value Creation in Acquisitions: A Reexamination of Performance Issues', *Strategic Management Journal*, 11: 99–115.

SHAN, W. and HAMILTON, W. (1991). 'Country-Specific Advantage and International Cooperation', *Strategic Management Journal*, 12/6: 419–32.

SHAPIRO, D. L., SHEPPARD, B. H., and CHERASKIN, L. (1992). 'In Theory: Business on a Handshake', *Negotiation Journal*, 8: 365–77.

SHARFMAN, M. P., GRAY, B., and YAN, A. (1991). 'The Context of Interorganizational Collaboration in the Garment Industry: An Institutional Perspective', *Journal of Applied Behavioral Science*, 27/2: 181–208.

SHARMA, D., LUCIER, C., and MOLLOY, R. (2002). 'From Solutions to Symbiosis: Blending with Your Customers', *Strategy+Business*, Second Quarter 2002.

SICHERMAN, N. W. and PETTWAY, R. C. (1987). 'Acquisition of Divested Assets and Shareholders Wealth', *Journal of Finance*, 42: 1261–73.

SIEGEL, S. and CASTELLAN, N. J. (1988). *Nonparametric Statistics for the Behavioral Sciences*, 2nd edn. New York: McGraw-Hill.

SILVER, M. (1984). *Enterprise and the Scope of the Firm*. Oxford: Martin Robertson Press.

SIMMEL, G. (1964). *Conflict and the Web of Group Affiliations*. New York: Free Press.

―― (1978). *The Philosophy of Money*. London: Routledge and Kegan Paul Ltd.

SIMON, H. A. ([1947] 1997). *Administrative Behavior: A Study of Decision-Making Processes in Administrative Organizations*. New York: Free Press.

SINGH, H. and KOGUT, B. (1989). 'Industry Effects on the Choice of Entry Mode', *Best Papers and Proceedings of the Academy of Management*, 116–21.

SITKIN, S. B. and STICKEL, D. (1996). 'The Road to Hell: The Dynamics of Distrust in an Era of Quality', in R. M. Kramer and T. R. Tyler (eds.), *Trust in Organizations: Frontiers of Theory and Research*. Thousand Oaks, CA: Sage.

SMITH, K. G., et al. (1994). 'Top Management Team Demography and Process: The Role of Social Integration and Communication', *Administrative Science Quarterly*, 39/3: 412–38.

SORENSON, O. and AUDIA, P. G. (2000). 'The Social Structure of Entrepreneurial Activity: Geographic Concentration of Footwear Production in the United States, 1940–1989', *American Journal of Sociology*, 106/2: 424–61.

STEINER, I. D. (1972). *Group Process and Productivity*. New York: Academic Press.

STINCHCOMBE, A. L. (1985). 'Contracts as Hierarchical Documents', in A. Stinchcombe and C. Heimer (eds.), *Organization Theory and Project Management*. Bergen, Norway: Norwegian University Press.

―― (1990). *Information and Organization*. Berkeley, CA: University of California Press.

STRAUSS, D. and IKEDA, M. (1990). 'Pseudolikelihood Estimation for Social Networks', *Journal of the American Statistical Association*, 85: 204–12.

STUART, T. E. (2000). 'Interorganizational Alliances and the Performance of Firms: A Study of Growth and Innovation Rates in a High-Technology Industry', *Strategic Management Journal*, 21/8: 791–811.

―― HOANG, H., and HYBELS, R. C. (1999). 'Interorganizational Endorsements and the Performance of Entrepreneurial Ventures', *Administrative Science Quarterly*, 44/2: 315–49.

SUCHMAN, M. C. (1995). 'Managing Legitimacy: Strategic and Institutional Approaches', *Academy of Management Review*, 20/3: 571–610.

SUTCLIFFE, K. M. and ZAHEER, A. (1998). 'Uncertainty in the Transaction Environment: An Empirical Test', *Strategic Management Journal*, 19/1: 1–23.

SYTCH, M. and GULATI, R. (2006). 'Dancing with Neophytes or Professionals: The Effects of Firms' Relational Capabilities on the Likelihood of Alliance Formation', Northwestern University.

TEECE, D. J. (1980). 'Economies of Scope and the Scope of the Enterprise', *Journal of Economic Behavior & Organization*, 1: 223–47.

——— (1986). 'Profiting from Technological Innovation: Implications for Integration, Collaboration, Licensing and Public Policy', *Research Policy*, 15/6: 285–305.

——— (1992). 'Competition, Cooperation, and Innovation', *Journal of Economic Behavior & Organization*, 18: 1–25.

THOMPSON, J. D. (1967). *Organizations in Action: Social Science Bases of Administrative Theory.* New York: McGraw-Hill.

THOMPSON, L. (1998). *The Mind and Heart of the Negotiator.* Upper Saddle River, NJ: Prentice Hall.

THORNTON, P. H. (1999). 'The Sociology of Entrepreneurship', *Annual Review of Sociology*, 25/1: 19–46.

——— (2001). 'Personal Versus Market Logics of Control: A Historically Contingent Theory of the Risk of Acquisition', *Organization Science*, 12/3: 294–311.

——— and OCASIO, W. (1999). 'Institutional Logics and the Historical Contingency of Power in Organizations: Executive Succession in the Higher Education Publishing Industry, 1958–1990', *American Journal of Sociology*, 105/3: 801–43.

TINIC, S. M. (1988). 'Anatomy of Initial Public Offerings of Common Stock', *Journal of Finance*, 43/4: 789–822.

TOMER, J. F. (1987). *Organizational Capital: The Path to Higher Productivity and Well-Being.* New York: Praeger.

TONG, T. W., REUER, J. J., and PENG, M. W. (2007). 'International Joint Ventures and the Value of Growth Options', *Academy of Management Journal*, forthcoming.

USEEM, M. (1982). 'Classwide Rationality in the Politics of Managers and Directors of Large Corporations in the United States and Great Britain', *Administrative Science Quarterly*, 27/2: 199–226.

——— (1984). *The Inner Circle: Large Corporations and the Rise of Business Political Activity in the U.S. and U.K.* New York: Oxford University Press.

——— (1993). *Executive Defense: Shareholder Power and Corporate Reorganization.* Cambridge, MA: Harvard University Press.

UZZI, B. (1996). 'The Sources and Consequences of Embeddedness for the Economic Performance of Organizations: The Network Effect', *American Sociological Review*, 61/4: 674–98.

——— (1997). 'Social Structure and Competition in Interfirm Networks: The Paradox of Embeddedness', *Administrative Science Quarterly*, 42/1: 35–67.

VAN DE VEN, A. H. (1976). 'On the Nature, Formation and Maintenance of Relations Among Organizations', *Academy of Management Review*, 1/4: 24–36.

——— (1993). 'The Institutional Theory of John R. Commons: A Review and Commentary', *Academy of Management Review*, 18/1: 139–52.

VAN DE VEN, W. P. M. M. and VAN PRAAG, B. M. S. (1981). 'The Demand for Deductibles in Private Health Insurance', *Journal of Econometrics*, 17/2: 229–52.

VENKATRAMAN, N. and LEE, C.-H. (2004). 'Preferential Linkage and Network Evolution: A Conceptual Model and Empirical Test in the U.S. Video Game Sector', *Academy of Management Journal*, 47/6: 876–92.

——— LOH, L., and KOH, J. (1994). 'The Adoption of Corporate Governance Mechanisms: A Test of Competing Diffusion Models', *Management Science*, 40/4: 496–507.

——— (1997). 'Venture Capitalists: A Really Big Adventure', *The Economist*, 342: 20–2.

WADE, J. B., O'REILLY, C. A., III, and CHANDRATAT, I. (1990). 'Golden Parachutes: CEOs and the Exercise of Social Influence', *Administrative Science Quarterly*, 35/4: 587–603.

WALKER, G., KOGUT, B., and SHAN, W. (1997). 'Social Capital, Structural Holes and the Formation of an Industry Network', *Organization Science*, 8/2: 109–25.

WASSERMAN, S. and PATTISON, P. (1996). 'Logit Models and Logistic Regressions for Univariate and Bivariate Social Networks: I. An Introduction to Markov Graphs and P*', *Psychometrika*, 61: 401–26.

WEISS, L. (1984). 'The Italian State and Small Business', *European Journal of Sociology*, 25/2: 214–41.

——— (1988). 'Giantism and Geopolitics', in L. Weiss (ed.), *Creating Capitalism: The State and Small Business Since 1945*. New York: Basil Blackwell.

WELCH, J. and BYRNE, J. A. (2001). *Jack: Straight from the Gut*. New York: Warner Books.

WERNERFELT, B. (1984). 'A Resource-Based View of the Firm', *Strategic Management Journal*, 5/2: 171–80.

WESTPHAL, J. D. (1999). 'Collaboration in the Boardroom: Behavioral and Performance Consequences of CEO–Board Social Ties', *Academy of Management Journal*, 42/1: 7–24.

——— and ZAJAC, E. J. (1997). 'Defections from the Inner Circle: Social Exchange, Reciprocity, and the Diffusion of Board Independence in U.S. Corporations', *Administrative Science Quarterly*, 42/1: 161–83.

——— GULATI, R., and SHORTELL, S. M. (1997). 'Customization or Conformity? An Institutional and Network Perspective on the Content and Consequences of TQM Adoption', *Administrative Science Quarterly*, 42/2: 366–94.

WHETTEN, D. A. (1977). 'Toward a Contingency Model for Designing Interorganizational Service Delivery Systems', *Organization and Administrative Sciences*, 4: 77–96.

WHISLER, T. J. (1984). *Rules of the Game: Inside the Corporate Boardroom*. Homewood, IL: Dow-Jones Irwin.

WHITE, H. C. (1981). 'Where Do Markets Come From?' *American Journal of Sociology*, 87/3: 517–47.

——— (1992). *Identity and Control: A Structural Theory of Social Action*. Princeton, NJ: Princeton University Press.

WHOLEY, D. R., CHRISTIANSON, J. B., and SANCHEZ, S. M. (1992). 'Organization Size and Failure Among Health Maintenance Organizations', *American Sociological Review*, 57/6: 829–42.

WILLIAMS, K. Y. and O'REILLY, C. A., III (1997). 'The Complexity of Diversity: A Review of Forty Years of Research', in D. Gruenfeld and M. Neale (eds.), *Research on Managing in Groups and Teams*. Thousand Oaks, CA: Sage.

WILLIAMSON, O. E. (1975). *Markets and Hierarchies: Analysis and Antitrust Implications*. New York: Free Press.

WILLIAMSON, O. E. (1983). 'Credible Commitments: Using Hostages to Support Exchange', *American Economic Review*, 73/4: 519–40.

____ (1985). *The Economic Institutions of Capitalism: Firms, Markets, Relational Contracting*. New York: Free Press.

____ (1991). 'Comparative Economic Organization: The Analysis of Discrete Structural Alternatives', *Administrative Science Quarterly*, 36/2: 269–96.

____ (1993). 'Calculativeness, Trust and Economic Organization', *Journal of Law and Economics*, 36/1: 453–86.

WINSHIP, C. W. and MARE, R. D. (1992). 'Models for Sample Selection Bias', *Annual Review of Sociology*, 18/1: 327–50.

WINTER, S. (1964). 'Economic "Natural Selection" and the Theory of the Firm', *Yale Economic Essays*, 4: 225–72.

WOLFE, G. A., COOPERMAN, E. S., and FERRIS, S. P. (1994). 'An Analysis of the Underwriter Selection Process for Initial Public Offerings', *Journal of Financial Research*, 17/1: 77–90.

Worldscope (1980–1990). Bethesda, MD: Disclosure, Inc.

ZACHARAKIS, A. L. and MEYER, G. D. (1988). 'A Lack of Insight: Do Venture Capitalists Really Understand Their Own Decision Process?' *Journal of Business Venturing*, 13/1: 57–76.

____ ____ (2000). 'The Potential of Actuarial Decision Models: Can They Improve the Venture Capital Investment Decision?' *Journal of Business Venturing*, 15/4: 323–46.

____ and SHEPHERD, D. A. (2001). 'The Nature of Information and Overconfidence on Venture Capitalists' Decision Making', *Journal of Business Venturing*, 16/4: 311–32.

ZAHEER, A. and BELL, G. G. (2005). 'Benefiting from Network Position: Firm Capabilities, Structural Holes, and Performance', *Strategic Management Journal*, 26/9: 809–25.

____ and VENKATRAMAN, N. (1995). 'Relational Governance as an Interorganizational Strategy: An Empirical Test of the Role of Trust in Economic Exchange', *Strategic Management Journal*, 16/5: 373–92.

____ McEVILY, B., and PERRONE, V. (1998). 'Does Trust Matter? Exploring the Effects of Interorganizational and Interpersonal Trust on Performance', *Organization Science*, 9/2: 141–59.

ZAJAC, E. J. (1988). 'Interlocking Directorates as an Interorganizational Strategy: A Test of Critical Assumptions', *Academy of Management Journal*, 31: 428–38.

____ and OLSEN, C. P. (1993). 'From Transaction Cost to Transactional Value Analysis: Implications for the Study of Interorganizational Strategies', *Journal of Management Studies*, 30/1: 131–45.

ZENGER, T. R. and LAWRENCE, B. S. (1989). 'Organizational Demography: The Differential Effects of Age and Tenure Distributions on Technical Communication', *Academy of Management Journal*, 32/2: 353–76.

ZOLLO, M., REUER, J. J., and SINGH, H. (2002). 'Interorganizational Routines and Performance in Strategic Alliances', *Organization Science*, 13/6: 701–13.

ZUCKER, L. G. (1986). 'Production of Trust: Institutional Sources of Economic Structure 1840–1920', in B. M. Staw and L. L. Cummings (eds.), *Research in Organizational Behavior*. Vol. 8. Greenwich, CT: JAI Press.

____ DARBY, M. R., and BREWER, M. B. (1994). *Intellectual Capital and the Birth of US Biotechnology Enterprises*. Cambridge, MA: National Bureau of Economic Research.

ZUCKERMAN, E. W. (1999). 'The Categorical Imperative: Securities Analysts and the Illegitimacy Discount', *American Journal of Sociology*, 104/5: 1398–438.

☐ INDEX

Baum, J.A.C (*Cont.*)
 reasons for alliances 2
 size-localized competition 71
Bayus, B.L. 114
Beatty, R.P. 76, 212, 213–14, 246,
 247
Beckman, C. 236
behavior of firms
 in alliance formation 6–7
 and embeddedness 31–2
 and network resources 23, 68–9
Behrens, D. 176, 270
Bell, G.G. 8, 260
Belliveau, M.A. 83, 277
Ben-Akiva, M.E. 115
Berg, S.V. 31, 152
Berger, H. 106
Berger, P.L. 220
Besnier, N. 81
Bies, R.J. 91, 92
Biggart, N.W. 146, 269
biotechnology firms 23, 24, 51, 104
 affiliations with research institutions 217,
  223
 appropriability regime 135, 142
 FDA approval 219, 248
 hierarchical controls research 141–4, 145,
  277
 investor concerns 247–8
 IPOs research 249–55
 product stage 229, 230, 231, 234, 236, 248,
  253, 254
 research 213–40, 280–1
Biotechnology Start-ups Database 249,
 280–1
Black, B.S. 279
Black, M. 66, 282, 285
Blau, P.M. 225
Bleeke, J. 49
Board and Alliance Database 82, 276–7
board interlocks 2, 6, 7, 12, 16–17, 33, 73–95,
 261
 and alliance formation 78, 82
 common appointments 85, 86, 88
 cooperation 79–80, 83–4, 88–9, 90–3
 costs 260
 effects on alliances 75, 88–9
 empirical research 82–92
  analysis 85
  control variables 84–6, 88, 89, 91
  descriptive statistics and correlation
   coefficients 86
  Heckman selection models 88, 90–1

 hypotheses 75, 78, 80, 82
 logit regression analysis 88
 measures 82–4
 results 87–92
 risk set 87
 survey response rate 276–7
 friendship ties 85–7, 88, 89, 90, 91
 functional background 84
 heterogeneity 94
 intergroup bias 78
 out-group bias 77–8
 and outcomes 270
 outside directors' home companies 78, 80,
  88, 90
 role of indirect ties 80–2
 sent interlock ties 85
 shaping behavior 262
 and strategic alliances 261
 and subsequent alliances 75, 82
 third-party ties 82, 84, 86, 88, 89–90, 91,
  93
 and timely information 75
 and trust 77–8, 79–80, 90–2, 93
 see also management-board relationships
Bochner, S.E. 244
Boeker, W. 36
Boothe, J.N. 83
Borgatti, S.P. 275
Borjas, G.J. 62, 85, 94, 282, 285
Borys, B. 132, 133, 162
boundarylessness of relationships 198–9
Bourdieu, P. 33
Bowyer, J.W. 222, 246, 251
Bradach, J.L. 101, 105, 106, 116
Bradley, M. 279
Brandenburger, A. 199
Brantley, P. 1, 215
Brass, D.J. 81, 93, 259
Brewer, M.B. 77, 78, 217, 225, 250
Bryson, J. 107
Burgers, W.P. 51
Burkhardt, M.E. 259
Burrill, G.S. 225
Burt, R.S. 94, 176, 221, 259, 260, 277
 deterrence for unreliability 53
 drivers for alliance formation 49
 employee relationships 2
 enforceable trust 59
 information flows 31, 34
 market constraint 84
 resource dependence 49
 social structure theory 54
 third-party ties 80, 81, 82, 93, 158